RED TAILS

An Oral History of the Tuskegee Airmen

JOHN B. HOLWAY

DOVER PUBLICATIONS, INC.
Mineola, New York

Bibliographical Note

This Dover edition, first published in 2012, is a revised and updated republication of *Red Tails, Black Wings: The Men of America's Black Air Force* by John Holway (Yucca Tree Press, 1997). This edition also includes a selection of sixteen new photographs and a new Introduction by the author.

Library of Congress Cataloging-in-Publication Data

Holway, John.
   Red tails : an oral history of the Tuskegee Airmen / John B. Holway. — Rev. ed.
      p. cm.
   Originally published: Red tails, black wings : the men of America's Black air force / by John B. Holway. 1997.
   Includes bibliographical references and index.
   ISBN-13: 978-0-486-48500-3
   ISBN-10: 0-486-48500-5
   1. World War, 1939–1945—Aerial operations, American.   2. United States. Army Air Forces—African American troops.   3. African American air pilots—History— 20th century.   4. World War, 1939–1945—Participation, African American.   I. Title. II. Title: Red tails, black wings.
   D790.H655 2011
   940.54'497308996073—dc23

                                                                  2011027669

Manufactured in the United States by Courier Corporation
48500503
www.doverpublications.com

To all the brave men, black and white,
who fought our battles
in the skies

Table of Contents

Introduction

In 1982 I was sent to cover a Smithsonian program on the Red Tails, a subject I—and most Americans—had never heard of. "Hey," I remember thinking, "this is interesting."

So I had lunch with George "Spanky" Roberts, a former commander of the group, and he filled my ears with stories. Then I called on Lou Purnell, who had put the program together, and he bubbled over with more tales. Several Red Tail conventions later, a book took shape.

Here was a great American adventure story, and almost nobody in America knew about it. Now, almost 30 years later, everyone knows of the Tuskegee Airmen, who will star in a major motion picture.

The stories they told were compelling and exciting to me, an old ground pounder, who couldn't fly a kite. I had already done two oral history books on baseball, and I decided that that was the only way to tell this story, too. Twelve years later I finished it.

The result is the most detailed personal story ever done on a fighter unit in World War II, or any other war. The adventure is told through the eyes of the men who lived it. Their unique experience has been captured for generations to come with a vividness and intimacy that only the men themselves could bring.

It was not the first book on the subject. Charles Francis' excellent *The Tuskegee Airmen*, has that distinction.

Like most laymen, and the authors who came later, I concentrated on the race prejudices of the times and the exciting aerial battles. I wanted to report on the experiences of these men through their own eyes, with all the detail and passion only they could bring.

The Red Tails weren't the best fighter Group in the U.S. Air Force, but they were one of them. They carried a burden of prejudice that no other Group did, more pervasive than today's blacks have to face. Pilot Roscoe Brown put it this way:

> This effort was unique and hopefully will never be repeated.
> The real meaning of the Tuskegee Airmen goes beyond what I call the "combat BS." The story on the ground is what it was all about. The stories

in the skies are exciting, sure, but they're not unlike those of a lot of white pilots. The thing that makes them important is that we did exactly what the white pilots did and sometimes did it better.

The first edition was primarily an oral history, a self-portrait in words of their experiences, capturing the chapter in history that they lived and helped write. It was the story of the underdog who triumphs over adversity. Writers and readers both love to pull for the underdog, and so did I.

Thanks to much new information that has come to light, through diligent research by Dr. Daniel Haulman, Craig Huntly, and others, this edition has more critical analysis, along with expanded narratives.

Some of the things we thought we knew 15 years ago are being questioned. I myself am revising my stories based on the new evidence. As a baseball historian, I've often taken new looks at icons such as Joe DiMaggio, Branch Rickey, Babe Ruth, Ted Williams, and Satchel Paige. I've even questioned the conventional histories' conclusions about the sainted Abraham Lincoln. They and many others had their portraits painted in romantic strokes that their own mothers wouldn't recognize. It's a painful and unpopular job to sketch clearer, more realistic, pictures.

As the late Colonel Harry Sheppard, a walking history book of the Red Tails, said, "Why embellish the story? The truth is good enough."

The second biggest myth, that the Red Tails "never lost a bomber to enemy fighters," has now been punctured, thanks to indefatigable historians such as Haulman of the Air Force history office in Montgomery Alabama, Huntly, Ron Brownstein, and William Holton of the Tuskegee Airmen.

The Red Tails did lose bombers. It would be impossible to fly dozens of missions for many thousands of miles into enemy air space infested with German fighters without losing any. The news was painful for many of the veterans to digest, but I think that, with time, they have come to accept it. However, not all writers do—books are still published making that claim.

The folklore could have been corrected before it got started. Colonel Davis was awarded a Distinguished Flying Cross for leading one of the Group's first missions in Italy on June 9, 1944, when "only a few" bombers were shot down. (Actually, it was two.) When historian Dr. Alan Gropman, asked Davis about the "no bombers lost" report, Davis replied that he couldn't confirm it, but he didn't deny it either.

Estimates of how many they lost vary from ten to 29—I think ten is the most accurate. Surely many Red Tails saw one or more of those bombers go down. However, no one corrected the error. Still, that's a lot less than most other fighter Groups in Italy, where the average was about 50 or more per Group. It's still an achievement to be proud of.

The new research shows that the Air Force has been focusing on the wrong objective: All the generals then and historians now have emphasized shooting down enemy fighters. The 15th Air Force meticulously counted every enemy that its pilots knocked down. The records show that they destroyed 483 German fighters while losing only 33 of their own fighters, a ratio of 14-1. This is so lopsided as to be useless in measuring effectiveness.

In the England-based 8th Air Force, fighters were used to wipe the skies clean of fighters in May in order to establish complete air superiority before the D-Day Normandy landing. At Anzio the purpose was to protect the invasion forces on the beach. Otherwise, the mission of the fighters was to protect bombers, who were attacking Germany's war industries. Shooting down enemy fighters that attacked the bombers was obviously a means to that end. But the end was to help bombers do their jobs of destroying targets on the ground.

So the real statistic—the only one that matters—is: How many bombers did each fighter Group save? The reverse side of the question is: How many bombers did each Group lose? Amazingly, the 15th Air Force didn't care even enough to count. They knew the total for all Groups, but had no idea—nor apparently any interest in knowing—which fighter Groups were best at it and which were worst. This information would have been of vital importance as a management tool to improve the efficiency of all commands.

The Theater air commander, General Ira Eaker, told Red Tails commander, Colonel B.O. Davis that he wanted his Group to protect the bombers at all costs and not to leave the bombers to "go hunting" for kills. Davis took him at his word and threatened to court martial any pilot who disobeyed. This caused a lot of grumbling among the Red Tails, who were just as thirsty for glory as the white flyers were.

The Red Tails had the worst record in the Theater for shooting down enemy fighters—but one of the best in protecting the bombers. It may not have been a coincidence.

I don't think it's racial profiling to say that blacks have a reputation for excelling in sports. Flying also requires fast reflexes and high hand-eye coordination. There is no reason to suppose they would not have been as excellent in aerial combat as they are on the basketball court.

Thanks to the patient scholarship of Dr. Daniel Haulman of the Air Force historical office in Maxwell Field Alabama, we also have exclusive new insights into the worst disaster in the history of the 15th Air Force— the battle of Memmingen, in which the Americans lost 14 bombers to enemy fighters. The operation was poorly planned and executed; half the bomber force disobeyed orders and failed to make the rendezvous. Those were the bombers who suffered all the losses. With odds of 4-1 against them, the under-manned Red Tails gallantly raced back to the late-arriving bombers to try to stem the rout.

Yet, after it was over, the generals quickly shifted the blame from themselves and the errant bombers and pinned it on the Red Tails instead, saying it was the Red Tails who didn't show up!

Another persistent myth is that of a Red Tail ace. However, again, a careful review of the records shows that no Tuskegee Airmen even claimed five victories. Thus it was not a case of a white officer in headquarters arbitrarily denying a claim.

A third folklore is that the Red Tails were the first to shoot down a jet. They were one of the first, but the England-based 8th Air Force and the Italy-based 31st Fighter Group had done it earlier.

In investigating that story, Huntly found a new truth: A Red Tail was the first in the Italy-based 15th Air Force to defeat the world's first rocket-powered Messerschmitt-163, which was almost twice as fast as America's best fighter, the P-51.

Above all, as Dr Haulman points out:

> The very first myth, which is now dead, was the misconception that black pilots were inferior and would not succeed in combat. The Tuskegee Airmen proved beyond the shadow of a doubt that they were the equal of the white fighter pilots with whom they served so heroically.

Foreword

How did a ground pounder come to write about flyers? My only military acquaintance with airplanes was jumping out of them during the Korean war.

In 1982, I attended the opening of the Smithsonian's exhibit on the Tuskegee Airmen, where I met Colonel George 'Spanky' Roberts, a former commander of the Red Tails, and Lou Purnell, another former Red Tail and curator of the exhibit. The subject was entirely new to me, and during an extended lunch Roberts gave me a long account of the outfit and his own experiences before, during, and after his great adventure in World War II.

My experience was in writing oral history, primarily baseball, and I was particularly attracted to stories that other writers had neglected. The Red Tails' story cried out to be written. Charles Francis has also written a fine history of the unit, but I couldn't resist learning more. I began attending Tuskegee Airmen conventions and button-holing veterans. It was like eating popcorn, I couldn't stop.

I want to salute Charles E. Francis, whose loving and painstaking pioneering work, *The Tuskegee Airmen* (Branders Publishers, Boston, 1988), inspired countless readers, including myself. It will be read a century or more from now, whenever future generations want to learn the exciting story of this chapter in history.

Twenty-seven years later I was still collecting stories and watching the men of that colorful era take shape and come to life on the computer screen. I hope the reader will enjoy getting to know them as much as I have.

Table of Organization

15th Air Force
Major General Nathan Twining

      306th Fighter Wing
      Brigadier General Dean Strother

            332nd Fighter Group
            Colonel Benjamin O. Davis

                  99th Fighter Squadron
                  100th Fighter Squadron
                  301st Fighter Squadron
                  302nd Fighter Squadron

Prologue

OUR history books and movies don't always report it, but blacks have fought in every American war since the French and Indian war, with the possible exception of the Mexican war. They have won Medals of Honor, though not as many as their numbers show they should have won. They were often promised freedom in return for their service, and often found that the promises were not kept.

The military has been a reflection of our society at large and the discrimination which has stained the nation's history. The full story has gradually become known and is documented in many new books that detail that heroic story. Today the military is a leader in giving equal opportunities to minorities. But that hasn't always been the case.

By the time of Pearl Harbor in 1941, anti-black virulence in the Armed Forces was perhaps the strongest it had ever been.

White sailors refused to eat or bunk with black shipmates, whose roles were restricted to mess stewards, and in 1919 the Navy cut off all new black enlistments.

That year bloody race riots erupted in several cities. In Chicago 38 persons were left dead and 500 injured. Lynchings spread across both North and South—77 were reported in all. Some blacks died merely for wearing their old uniforms. The hooded Ku Klux Klan paraded openly down Washington's Pennsylvania Avenue.

In this atmosphere General John Pershing, the Army Chief of Staff, in 1922 commissioned a study of how to utilize blacks in the future. The panel concluded that they should continue to be employed in combat so that whites would not make all the sacrifices, but it recommended continuing segregation.

In 1925 the Army War College released a study, which concluded that the cranial cavity of the Negro is smaller than a white man's and therefore he is inferior in intelligence, unless he happens to have "a heavy strain of white blood." It added that a black is superstitious, subservient, and "a rank coward in the dark." In addition, he is prone to "petty thievery, lying, promiscuity, and ... atrocities connected with white women."

Socially, the War College said, the Negro could not associate with "any

1

except the lowest class of whites," although it conceded that "Negro con-
cubines" did sometimes attract white men who were otherwise considered
"high class."

As for the Negro officer, the War College said, he shared "all the faults
and weaknesses of character inherent in the Negro race, exaggerated by
the fact that he wore an officer's uniform." Even Negroes didn't want to
serve under Negro officers, it said.

This remained Army policy for the next 15 years and was still quoted
approvingly well after Pearl Harbor. Army recruitment policies reflected
this attitude. In the 1930s African-Americans made up less than two percent of the men in the Army as scarce Depression openings went to whites.

1

Black Wings

As is true of the military, the contribution of blacks to the history of aviation is long—and long neglected.

Tom Steptoe of Chicago became one of the first airmail pilots in history in 1911, when he flew a four-mile leg of an experimental route in Long Island. Some Chicago veterans claim that he was actually a very light-skinned Negro. He later urged Congress to appropriate money for a permanent air mail service, though his idea was rejected as impractical.

Eugene Jacques Bullard

THE first American black pilot we can identify for sure was Eugene Jacques Bullard, who flew with the French in World War I.

The son of a Martiniquan father and Creek Indian mother, Gene was born in 1894 in Georgia, where he listened to his father spin stories of a paradise named France, where *egalite* and *fratemite* reigned. When masked Ku Klux Klansmen made a midnight ride around the family cabin, young Gene decided to run away to find that fabled land.

For the next two years he lived with gypsies, broke and rode race horses, hoboed on freight cars, and stowed away on a ship to Scotland. He supported himself as a "target" in carnivals and later by hefting heavy loads as a longshoreman. At 16 he became a boxer, fighting all over Europe as far away as Russia, until he finally reached his promised land, France.

When World War I broke out, Gene enlisted to defend his adopted country in the famous Foreign Legion, reputedly the toughest soldiers in the world, in their distinctive *kepi* headgear with white cloth hanging down behind. His Moroccan regiment was called "the Swallows;" the Germans called them "the Black Swallows of death." He carried a machine gun in the battle of Artois Ridge, where 175,000 men were killed or wounded. At Champagne, he attacked along with 500 men, of whom only 30 survived.

Bullard trudged under the greatest artillery barrage the world had yet seen and into the trenches of Verdun. There some 650,000 men on both sides would be killed, gassed, or wounded. "Men and beasts were hanging from the branches of trees."

A shell knocked out most of Gene's teeth. Almost every man "got one more hole in him than he was born with.... We were damn near wiped out dodging from shell hole to shell hole under fire."

When his machine gun grew too hot to fire, he threw it away and, diving into a crater, looked up to see a German dive in on top of him. "I pulled the trigger. Thanks be to God, I pulled it in time." Bullard leaped back out, his face whiter than the German's.

Bullard tried to join the U.S. Air Corps but was turned down for flat feet and bad tonsils. "I'm not going to march across France or sing grand opera," he protested. All the other American fliers were transferred to the U.S. Air Corps. But not Bullard.

So Sergeant Bullard joined the French Air Service. Another volunteer, James Norman Hall, co-author of *Mutiny on the Bounty,* described the new cadet:

> Suddenly the door opened to admit a vision of military splendor.... His jolly black face shone with a grin of greeting and justifiable vanity. He wore tan aviator's boots, which gleamed with mirror-like luster.

He also wore vivid scarlet breeches and a black tunic. On his chest was a *Croix de Guerre,* and the *fourragere* [shoulder cord] of the Foreign Legion, plus "an enormous pair of wings." While the other pilots gasped, Hall "repressed a strong instinct to stand at attention."

With his mascot, Jimmy the monkey—dressed in a tiny uniform and tucked inside Bullard's own jacket—Gene flew his bi-winged Spad fighter on patrol over Verdun at speeds up to 125 miles an hour. He called it a *cage au pule*—a chicken coop—held together with wire and glue. On the side he painted his motto, "All blood runs red." He described his first mission.

> In the distance we spotted four big German bomber planes with 16 German fighter planes to protect them.... As the *Boches* kept coming, we got the signal from the Commandant to divide into sevens and maneuver into fighting position. Then the attack was on.
>
> An air battle generally lasts from one to three minutes—very rarely as long as three. In this one everything happened so fast that I didn't have time to get frightened. All I could see were burning planes earthbound and a long trail of smoke coming from one of the German bombers which... exploded in the air....
>
> I started shooting at every damn enemy plane that I even thought might be heading in my direction. It was all very confusing with planes roaring by and the smoke-filled air resounding with the tat-tat-tat of machine guns.

On one patrol "I was sure I had my first *Boche* victim in the air." He had his adversary in his sights and pursued him until "I was being machine-gunned from the ground by the Germany infantry," and he made a forced landing just inside friendly lines. When his mechanic arrived by truck with a doctor, they found Gene and Jimmy walking around the plane counting the bullet holes. There were seven in all.

After the war, he returned to the prize ring, played drums with a Montmartre jazz band, married and divorced a French countess, and opened his own nightclub, where he played host to Charlie Chaplin, movie stars Gloria Swanson and Rudolph Valentino, writers F. Scott Fitzgerald and Ernest Hemingway, song writer Noel Coward, and others.

With the 1940 German invasion, Bullard, then 46, hiked to the front to join his old regiment but was warned to get away.

In New York, Gene once again supported himself by lifting heavy loads on the docks until a bus driver punched him, blinding him in one eye. He carried a protest sign and marched with Paul Robeson, and got his head bashed in again, this time by the police.

At the French embassy, he donned his old Legionnaire's uniform, and General Charles de Gaulle himself embraced him and presented him with the Legion of Honor, France's highest decoration.

Bessie Coleman

A NOTHER intrepid pilot had become the first confirmed African–American to fly in the United States. She was Bessie Coleman, "the black Amelia Earhart." Both women were photogenic and colorful and began their flying careers in the 1920s.

Like Bullard, Coleman had to go to France to win her wings. Also like Bullard, she was half-Indian, a pretty Texan, who was born in 1893. Her father decided that the only thing worse than being a Negro in Texas was being an Indian and left his family and escaped the state. Little (5'2") Bessie picked cotton, attended a one-room school, and helped her mother raise 12 children. Moving to Chicago, she manicured nails near the White Sox park on the fringe of the roaring Chicago underworld. She may have danced in Negro stage reviews. She opened a chili parlor and saved her tips for flying lessons.

At that time there were only a handful of women fliers in the world, black or white. (The first U.S. woman, Harriet Quimby, made her first flight in 1911 and died in a crash the following year.) Facing the double handicap as a woman and a black, Coleman found U.S. airports closed to her.

So she took French lessons and, in 1920, sailed to France. Strangely, there is no evidence that she met Bullard; she never mentioned him in her writings and probably had never heard of him. She enrolled under a French ace, and, according to Bessie, one of her fellow students crashed and died in the first week, "a terrible shock to my nerves."

For nine months she walked every day to the airport and back—Bessie claimed it was nine miles each way, possibly an exaggeration. At any rate, she finally came home with an international pilot's license.

But Coleman was still unable to break into the white male world of flying, so she sailed back to Paris to learn stunt flying. Bessie had a great sense of style, according to her biographer, Doris Rich, and designed dashing flying togs for herself. She looked equally stunning in a fringed and beaded evening dress on the dance floor.

She dreamed of opening a flying school for blacks, so "Brave Bessie" came home again to barnstorm in air shows across the country, doing loops and figure-eights and parachuting to the oohs of the crowds. However, Rich writes that Coleman faced prejudice, not only from the white world, but also from blacks, both men and women. The Negro press scolded her for scandalously breaking with tradition.

While Coleman couldn't enforce integrated seating at her shows, in her hometown in Texas she did succeed in eliminating separate entrances.

A crash and a broken leg grounded her for a year, but by 1926 Coleman had raised almost enough money for her flying school and planned one more show, in Jacksonville, Florida, to put her over the top. The day before, Bessie declared, "I'm on my way now" and went up with a white mechanic at the controls of a flying crate that, according to Rich, shouldn't have been allowed off the ground. Coleman wasn't wearing a 'chute and may have unbuckled her belt in order to stand and peer over the side of the cockpit. The plane suddenly flipped over and Bessie was thrown out, falling 1,000 feet to her death.

A monkey wrench was found lodged in the engine. Ever since, the suspicion of sabotage has hovered over Coleman's death. Rich, however, suggests a less sinister explanation: There was no firewall between the cockpit and the engine, and a loose wrench may have slid into the engine.

In 1995 Coleman was honored with an airmail stamp.

The anniversary of her death, April 30, is still marked with a fly-by of planes dropping roses on her grave in Chicago.

Hubert Fauntleroy Julian

THE most flamboyant of all early black fliers, "the black eagle of Harlem," was born in Trinidad in 1897. Moving to Canada, he took his first airplane ride with the World War I ace, Billy Bishop, in a Sopwith Camel.

In 1924, Julian decided he would be the first man to fly the Atlantic from New York to Africa, in his plane, "Ethiopia I."

Young Harry Sheppard, a future Red Tail, remembered him: "He was flamboyant, ebullient—a little floppish, I'd say—full of grand ideas, undaunted by anything."

"He was my inspiration when I was a kid," laughed future Red Tail Louis Purnell:

> He was the most elegant rogue in black aviation. Julian didn't want to be classed as a Negro, because he was from Trinidad. His attire was a derby, monocle, finely trimmed mustache, formal collar with the tips bent, a morning coat with tails, striped trousers, and spats. It befitted his character. He had that haughty air about him. When he was flying, he'd wear riding breeches and leather boots. I thought he was glamorous.
>
> When I was about six years old, he came through Wilmington, where I lived, going to the churches and speaking to collect funds for the flight [to Africa]. After he passed the plate at church, he pulled off this trick at a big air show:
>
> He was supposed to jump out and descend in a 'chute while playing a saxophone. He had a big open LaSalle touring car with the top pulled back, and he rode in front of the grandstand with his flying suit and disappeared over a hill at the far end of the airport.
>
> The plane took off and circled us, and out he jumped, but as far as I could see there was no evidence of a saxophone.
>
> The plane landed at the far end of the airport, over the same hill, and our attention was turned to the displays of different planes in the hangar. But I happened to see a truck go by—what attracted my attention was the billowing 'chute in the back. It was another guy, altogether different, in the truck, with a scuffed-up suit. Anyhow, a switch was made, and a moment later Hubert Julian once more rode in front of the grandstand with an open 'chute in the back.

Finally Julian got his plane to the Harlem River, took off, and managed to get as far as Flushing Bay, about five miles away. He crashed in the middle of the bay. That was the end of his flight.

> He'd pull all kinds of stunts. He was the only guy who ever made a parachute jump over New York City without a license—and landed on the skylight of a police precinct station!
>
> He was a pilot in Haile Selassie's air force in Ethiopia and wrecked the whole air force—it had about two planes. They fired him.

Another black aviation pioneer, Cornelius Coffey, recalled Julian: "He was a parachute jumper, but I question whether he was a pilot. Julian had the world in a jug and the stopper in his hand. But they told him not to fly the emperor's personal plane, and when he crashed it, they were going to expel him.

According to Purnell:

> Julian would sell or smuggle arms to both factions in any uprising.
>
> But he was the only Negro who could go into the White House unannounced and be received. This was during Franklin Roosevelt's time.
>
> Although he may have been a bit of a deceiver, he was quite a showman, quite a showman. He was the clown prince of aviation. You'll find his whole personality in the book, *The Black Eagle of Harlem* by P. Nugent. You're going to die laughing.

In the 1950s the Black Eagle smuggled weapons to Cuba's Fidel Castro. In 1964, he was arrested in the Congo for carrying concealed weapons to the rebel province of Katanga. He was thrown in prison, boasting to his guards that "I have a 14-room mansion overlooking the Harlem River." Scheduled for execution, Julian was rescued by the African-American Nobel Prize winner, Dr. Ralph Bunche. Finally, Julian was picked up in London for shoplifting.

Purnell once asked the famous African-American aviator and instructor, Alfred "Chief" Anderson: "Where did you get your inspiration from, Chief?"

Anderson broke out in a grin. "Don't tell me you were inspired by the same fool I was, Hubert Julian?"

"We both fell out of our chairs laughing."

In 1927, Charles A. Lindbergh captured the nation's imagination with his one-man flight across the Atlantic, and African-Americans dreamed of one day being 'the brown Lindy.' Lindbergh reflected the prevailing stereotype of blacks. In his autobiography, *We,* he told of an elderly African-American woman who asked if he could fly her "up to Heaben." He recounted giving a ride to another boastful black passenger, who promised to wave a red flag throughout the flight to signify to friends below that he was not afraid. Lindy said he put the plane into a loop, and the passenger cringed on the floor of the cockpit, hanging on for dear life.

Joel "Ace" Foreman and Artis Ward in 1927, the year of Lindbergh's flight, climbed into a small JN-4 "Jenny" to attempt a cross-country flight. They made it from Los Angeles to Chicago before they were arrested for flying an unlicensed plane.

Samuel Sozereseteo, apparently an African, reportedly flew from Moscow to Berlin and followed that with a flight from Belgium to the Congo. He was reported to have been black, but little else is known about him.

Bill Powell

A RMY veteran Bill Powell returned to Paris in 1927 for the Armistice Day parade. He visited Le Bourget airport, scene of Lindbergh's arrival, took his first airplane ride, and was hooked. (He too didn't look up Gene Bullard, suggesting that Americans still had not heard of the "Black Swallow.")

Back in the States Powell tried to take flying lessons. However, although he held an engineering degree from the University of Illinois, he was turned down by the Air Corps and several civilian schools. Finally, Powell was accepted at a flying school in Los Angeles and recruited seven more students to form a Bessie Coleman Club. One woman mortgaged her house, and Powell put down $6,000 of his own savings to purchase two biplanes.

Powell wrote a book, *Black Wings*, and a play, "Ethiopia Spreads Its Wings," to popularize flying among black youths.

The Flying Hoboes

J AMES Herman Banning was one of 18,000 licensed American pilots in 1932. Twelve, including himself, were black.

His ambition was to be the first African American to cross the country by air. But he had two big problems. One, in those Depression days, he couldn't afford gas. Two, he didn't have a plane to put it in.

Banning had been born 27 years earlier in the little town of El Reno Oklahoma. After studying engineering for two years at Iowa State College, he applied at flying schools in the Chicago area but was turned down by them all.

In 1926, he finally found an army lieutenant in Iowa to give him lessons. After three hours and 45 minutes of air time, Herman watched his mentor die in a cornfield in a ball of flame and smoke.

Herman poked through the wreckage, found the motor more or less intact, and bought it. From other spare parts, he nailed and glued together a fuselage of wood and canvas around the engine, then built and attached two pairs of wings to the body. When he climbed into the cockpit, the ignition coughed and sputtered, the propeller turned, and Banning at last had a plane he could solo in.

In 1928, Banning joined Powell's group in Los Angeles, and he and Powell climbed into one of the planes to attend an air show. Navigating by road map, they took a wrong turn in the desert, ran out of gas, and crashlanded on a strange beach, where the sun rose over the ocean and set over the land. For five days, with almost no food or water, they trekked across the sand until they reached a fishing village, where they learned they were in Baja California. They bought gas and hauled it back coolie-style on poles.

On Labor Day 1931, the Bessie Coleman Club achieved its greatest triumph—the first all-Negro air show, before 15,000 people in Los Angeles. It starred parachute jumper Lottie Theodore and other daredevils, such as Marie Dickerson Coker, Willie "Suicide" Jones, and Dorothy Darby, who barnstormed around the country.

Tom Allen, a cocky kid, was hanging around the airfield in Oklahoma City, working in trade for flying lessons. The only instrument on planes in those days, Tom recalled, was an oil gauge. When the other fellows at the field told him he was "too yellow" to solo, he jumped into a plane and took off and landed before anyone could stop him. By his fifth hour in the air, he said, he was doing loops and spins.

Tom thumbed his way to Los Angeles, arriving with empty pockets, to join Powell's club.

Meanwhile, a prize of $1,000 had been offered to the first black to fly across the country. (The feat had first been accomplished in 1911 by Cal Rogers in his biplane, "The Gin Fizz"—it advertised a soft drink. He took 49 days.)

Irvin Wells and Powell decided to try. They headed east over the desert, putting down frequently for gas and to catch a few hours sleep.

They were doing all right until they came to the mountains east of El Paso. Flying at night without an altimeter, Powell crashed into a peak, flipping the plane. The two airmen climbed out and scrambled over rocks, skirting cacti and howling coyotes, until they spotted the lights of a ranch house and arrived in time for breakfast.

Meanwhile, Banning and Allen decided to try to reach New York. Arthur Dennis, a character known as "Small Black," a leader of the "sporting class" [gamblers] in Los Angeles, bought them a plane, the "Eagle Rock." It was a surplus World War I plane with a 100-horsepower engine, though Allen said it looked like "some of the horses were dead." They still didn't have money for gas but decided to stay with friends on the ground and pass the hat to buy enough to get to the next stop. They laughingly called themselves "The Flying Hoboes." Wearing no 'chutes, to save weight, they buckled the chin straps of their leather helmets, pulled their goggles down, waved to four well-wishers, gunned the engine, and bumped down the runway.

As Allen later put it: "We angled down into Arizona and New Mexico, listening to the motor very close." Lodging, Allen would reminisce, was hard to find, and they often went to bed hungry. At Yuma they sold a suit of clothes and a wrist watch for ten dollars worth of gas.

In New Mexico, they were grateful they carried no parachutes—"the extra weight would have made us crash at the end of the runway."

Approaching the mountains where Powell had come to grief, they flew in fog so thick they couldn't see their wingtips. "We just lucked through." That night they slept in a one-room shack as hogs rooted in pens next to them.

In Carthage Missouri, the "Lindberghs of their race" were forced down with engine trouble, then sputtered into St Louis, where they picked up contributions ranging from nickels to a two-dollar bill—eight dollars in all. The gas pump thirstily drank it all. At Pittsburgh the presidential election was in full swing, Franklin D. Roosevelt against Herbert Hoover, and the local Democratic Party agreed to finance the rest of their flight if they would drop campaign leaflets from the plane.

And so they finally arrived over the tall buildings of Manhattan, landing, not in a shower of ticker tape, but in a shower of political leaflets. It had been two weeks since they had left. The Hoboes were hailed and treated to dinner. But they never did find the sponsor who had promised the $1,000.

Back in Los Angeles, Banning and Powell agreed to fly together in an upcoming air show, but Powell had to cancel. Banning went up with a Navy pilot who stalled and crashed back to earth, killing Banning immediately.

Chief Anderson

IN 1933 C. Alfred "Chief" Anderson and Dr. Albert Forsythe became the first African Americans to fly round trip coast-to coast.

Anderson, one of the most beloved of the early black pioneers, was the first to qualify for a transport pilot's license, the highest rating. Raised in the Blue Ridge Mountains of Virginia, he once told an interviewer how he started flying:

> It was impossible for blacks to fly then. They would just point-blank tell you, "We don't take colored people up." So I bought a second-hand plane. Naturally, I had to learn, but nobody would teach me, so I taught myself. I became familiar with the feel of it and watched what other people were doing, and when it came time to solo, I just did what they did.

Forsythe was raised in Jamaica. He earned a medical degree from McGill University in Canada and asked Anderson to teach him to fly.

After their cross-country flight, Forsythe proposed an ambitious 20-nation goodwill tour to the Caribbean and South America. They borrowed money and bought a Lambert Monocoupe, "The Spirit of Booker T. Washington."

They made the over-water hop to Jamaica, landing on a dirt road at dusk by the light of automobile lights. They continued to Havana, Jamaica, and Haiti, but engine failure forced them down in the mountains before they reached Santo Domingo, where they had to wait three weeks for new parts. Then they continued to Puerto Rico and the Virgin Islands and island-hopped the Lesser Antilles to Grenada and Trinidad, almost to the coast of British Guiana on the South American mainland. Heavy with fuel, they took off from a primitive field, clipped a bamboo tree and crashed, ending their trip.

Cornelius Coffey and Johnny Robinson

TWO auto mechanics, Coffey and Robinson, met in 1925 in Detroit, where Robinson was hiding out from Chicago gangsters. "Coffey was a brilliant man, but very quiet," one of his students, Chauncey Spencer, remembered. "He wouldn't say 20 words all day."

When Bessie Coleman was killed the following year, they decided to carry on her dream, "realizing," as Coffey put it, "that it was rough for African-Americans to get into aviation."

As told by Coffey, they traded a second-hand Hudson car plus $200 for a Hummingbird biplane and four hours of lessons. Next they mailed applications to the Curtis-Wright master mechanics course, but when they reported for class, they were stopped at the door. When they threatened to sue, they were grudgingly admitted with the warning that "we won't be responsible for what happens to you."

"We accepted the challenge," Coffey said. "It was plenty rough." At first the other students were hostile, but at graduation in 1931, the director declared:

> "These two young men have proven themselves beyond a doubt. This school will now be open to every African-American student. If they know any others, we'll enroll that class and make these two the assistant instructors. The doors will always be open."

Cornelius and Johnny recruited 30 more students, and the Challenger Pilots Association was born.

Janet Bragg was among their first students. A registered nurse, Bragg came from Georgia, the granddaughter of a Cherokee Indian. She saved her money and bought a plane, which she allowed the club to use.

Willa Brown, a preacher's daughter from Kentucky, was the glamor girl of black aviation. Enoch Waters, editor of the black Chicago *Defender*, recalled his first meeting with her—"a shapely young brown-skin woman, wearing white jodhpurs, a form-fitting white jacket and white boots." When she "strode into our newsroom...all the typewriters suddenly went silent."

She soon became Mrs. Coffey. "Many people wondered how those two got together," a later student, Felix Kirkpatrick, said with a smile and a shake of his head.

On the anniversary of Bessie Coleman's death in 1931, Coffey, Brown, and Bragg made a memorial flight to drop flowers over the grave, inaugurating a custom that continues to the present.

In 1934, Coffey and Robinson went on a barnstorming tour of the South in Bragg's plane. In Georgia, Robinson tried to take off over-loaded with fuel and clipped a chimney. Coffey:

> I felt a thud and turned to look. The stabilizer on the tail was practically gone; the only thing holding it was the top wire. There was a tree right in the line of our approach, and the left wheel caught the top limb and swung us around 90 degrees. We cart-wheeled to the left and completely washed the plane out.

Luckily, they walked away.

After Julian muffed his chance in Ethiopia, Robinson rushed to the embassy and applied for the job. While Coffey stayed home to recruit others and ship equipment, Robinson bought himself a uniform, named himself a colonel, and flew to Addis Ababa, the embattled capital bracing for an invasion by Mussolini's Italian army. The African-American press dubbed him "the brown condor," who would lick Mussolini as "the brown bomber," Joe Louis, had licked the Italian ex-world champ, Primo Carnero.

The first enemy Robinson licked was Julian in a knockdown fight in an Addis Ababa hotel room, and Julian finally left town. Johnny found that Ethiopia had only a handful of obsolete planes and a few European aviators. In 1936, the capital fell and Robinson escaped just ahead of the invaders.

The self-effacing Coffey sold his own plane to buy Johnny a ticket home, where 8,000 people gave him an ovation and tried to squeeze into the hero's banquet.

The two friends started a new ground school and borrowed $1,000 for a plane. Coffey invented a new carburetor that wouldn't freeze, permitting year-round operations. The system is still in use today, though Coffey never got a dime for it. But because they could fly 12 months of the year, they paid off the loan in six months. Coffey said:

> The rates we could charge the students were unbelievable—six dollars an hour dual and four dollars solo. If you sold empty bottles, you could get enough money to buy a 15-minute flight. And after the student soloed, we

could rent the airplane to him for four dollars an hour! It allowed many of our people to fly who wouldn't be able to otherwise.

And we made money too. Our actual expense was $1.98 an hour—gas, oil, and hangar. So it helped all the way around.

Robinson returned to Ethiopia in 1944. Ten years later he was flying blood plasma to a hospital when he collided on takeoff with a student, caught pneumonia, and died. He is buried in Addis Ababa.

Coffey continued teaching—and learning. He took a course in the 707 jet engine, taught in the public schools and remained actively working until his ninetieth year. He died in 1995.

James Peck

IN 1936, the Spanish civil war broke out, and hundreds of Americans volunteered to fight against General Francisco Franco and his patrons, Hitler and Mussolini. Among those was a handsome, soft-spoken Pittsburgher, James "Jimmy" Peck, reputedly the world's only African-American ace.

Peck caught the flying bug watching World War I fliers in a field near his Pittsburgh home, and after two years at the University of Pittsburgh, he won his pilot's license and applied for appointments to the Air Corps and the Navy. Neither service bothered to answer.

Jimmy worked as an elevator operator and as a trap drummer with the Victor Recording Orchestra. After war erupted in Spain, Peck and another black, Paul Williams, sailed to France, made a treacherous 14-hour trek across the Pyrenees mountains at night, and arrived in Valencia during the worst air bombardment of the war. He wrote that the civilian suffering he saw gave him a personal motive to fight.

Peck flew a snub-nosed bi-wing Russian Polikarpov against the best German fighters. His squadron mates were Spaniards, Dominicans, Brazilians, and Russians. He was credited with five victories over Italian and German planes, although the total is not confirmed. He wrote about his experiences in two books in a poetic style reminiscent of France's Antoine de Saint-Exupery. Jim described his first sight of enemy planes:

> At our approaching speeds, the dots—I make out nine of them—become larger and round.
>
> We open with a solid wall of fire. Grayish threads of smoke stream from the pointed noses of the enemy craft as they reply—tracers [bullets]. One of the planes veers crazily, turning cartwheels like a kid's kite gone mad, and their formation scatters. I line up on one of the enemy, who is pulling up slightly below and to my right.

A tiny streamer flies from the pilot's helmet. I had to choose the best pilot for an enemy! Only the squadron commander wears that ribbon. I'm not so frightened as I'm going to be in just a moment.

Suddenly it happens—my ship is hit. A long burst of slugs chews its way into my lower wing with a succession of thudding impacts.

I'm hitting him, too—I can tell by the path of my tracer bullets. As his biplane flashes by close beneath, I pull up into the tightest wing-over turn that I can execute.

But the commander has outwitted me by making a left turn. He executes an Immelmann—half a loop, the ship rolling right side up at the top—then, before I realize it, his guns are spewing more of those slugs into my tail. This guy is clever.

I whip into a tight vertical turn. He sticks behind me as if I were towing him on an invisible rope. Our ships wind up chasing each other around in a circle, nearly opposite each other. Perhaps if I take the initiative I may gain a momentary advantage. That is all that one gets in modern combat. But who-ever breaks the circle leaves himself wide open for an interval. This decision is the most momentous I have ever been called upon to make in my young life.

I roll over on my back—upside down. The pull-up slows down one's for-ward speed and the other plane gains during this interval.

I stop the biplane's roll, and the commander's plane is directly opposite, and he is just waking up. But he is too late. From my inverted position I clearly see the glass and metal frames of his goggles, the gray, set face, that streaming ribbon. I fire all four guns.

A crazy line of bullet holes stitch along the bottom of his cockpit and creep back along the fuselage. That ugly, black cross on the plane's rudder seems to disappear in a shower of flying tracers, metal and fabric. Then the ship is gone.

A cloud swallows him up, like some eerie thing devouring a victim. Vic-tory in my first combat.

Reviewers hailed the books—*Armies With Wings* and *So You Want to Fly*—and excerpts appeared in the *New York Times*, London *Chronicle*, *Harpers Magazine*, and *Reader's Digest*. Peck devoted only two chapters to his own exploits and in them did not claim to have bagged five planes. Still, the story grew. There is probably no way to confirm or disprove it.

In 1972, Peck was working on the B-1 bomber project at North Ameri-can. His last known address was San Diego in the mid-1980s. After that his trail petered out.

Chauncey Spencer

B Y 1939 war clouds were gathering, and the government was gearing up a Civilian Pilot Training (CPT) Program to prepare college men for the Air Corps if war broke out. The black press—the Pittsburgh *Courier* and Chicago *Defender*—and many other Negro voices were clamoring to include black colleges in the program. Chauncey Spencer found himself a catalyst in the campaign.

Spry and hearty in 1996 at the age of 89, he called himself "a sixth-generation American" with roots going back to 1705. As a 15-year-old in 1921, he took a train to Chicago to see Bessie Coleman put on an air show and met the famous aviatrix. He remembered her as tiny, enthusiastic, and determined.

Eleven years later, Oscar DePriest, the only African-American in Congress, visited Spencer's hometown of Lynchburg, Virginia, on a speaking tour and dined at the Spencer home. He suggested that the youth enroll in Coffey's new school. Soon Spencer was flying, stunting, and parachuting. "A friend dared me to go up and race another parachutist down. I crawled out on the wing and jumped," free-falling for 2,000 feet. Soon he was performing at shows with Bragg and the Coffeys, doing barrel rolls, wing-overs, and spirals. Bill Powell came all the way from Los Angeles to see them.

Chauncey and his friend, Dale White, were working on a black history project for the government's Works Progress Administration (WPA), when, he recalled:

> Enoch Waters of the *Defender* tried to interest other people outside of Chicago in aviation. Dale and I planned to fly to all the Negro colleges, but Waters said, "Why do that? Why not try to get into Congress and get support there?"
>
> My mother and father came out to one of the air shows, and they put up the first $500 to rent a Lincoln-Paige biplane with a radial engine and only two instruments, the flight instruments and the oil gauge. We called it "Old Faithful."
>
> George and Ed Jones ran the numbers racket in Chicago [similar to today's lottery but then illegal]. Enoch, Dale, Coffey, and I went to see them at their business "front," a five-and-ten-cent store on 47th Street, for money for fuel and supplies. George turned to his secretary and said, "Give Coffey a check for $1,000."
>
> So on the ninth of May 1939, Dale White and I jumped off from Harlem Airport, Chicago, at six o'clock.
>
> Then Fate stepped in. Flying over Ohio, the engine threw a crankshaft, and we made a forced landing in a field. We sent word back to Chicago, where Coffey got the parts and said, "Don't worry, I'll be there this afternoon." And he was. We rebuilt that plane in two days and one night.
>
> After Coffey tested it in flight, we took off and stopped overnight at West Virginia State College and met the student body. In Pittsburgh we met Jim Peck and spent six to eight hours with him—a very quiet man. Then we flew directly into Washington.

Edgar Brown, a friend of my family, was a top tennis player and head of the Federal Workers Union, which broke down segregation in restaurants in Washington. We took a little train under the Capitol building and when we came into the corridor of the Senate Building, someone said, "Good morning, Ed."

Edgar said, "Good morning, Senator, how are you?"

It was Harry Truman. He asked a few questions: "Are you citizens? Do you pay taxes? You mean to tell me, because of your color you can't get into the U.S. Air corps?"

"Yes, sir."

"Well, I'll see that that doesn't happen again." He said he'd like to meet us at the airport.

When we got there, I said, "Would you like for us to take to take you for a flight?"

He said, "No, but I see you've got guts to fly that plane all the way from Chicago."

We visited the Senate Committee on Military Appropriations. Next we went to New York for a parade on the birthday of Joe Louis. On the way back I got a telegram from Enoch Waters: The Committee had appropriated money for the CPT, including Negroes!

But it was all purely by accident. If we had flown straight into Washington, we would have missed Harry Truman. Fate designed that delay. There were two ways we got into aviation—Faith and Fate. I say I was "the right man at the wrong time."

How do you like *that* story?

2

Civilian Pilot Training

CIVILIAN Pilot Training (CPT) was a landmark in black aviation history. Coffey:

> It was the first time the government became involved in paying for flight training for African Americans. Until then, we were on our own. We got the training started early enough so when the Air Force finally decided to train black pilots, most of my students ended up in the 99th Fighter Squadron.

His protégés included future Red Tails Jack Rogers, Clarence "Lucky" Lester, Felix Kirkpatrick, and Hannibal Cox. Several got their first training in CPT.

Lou Purnell also signed up:

> I grew up in Cape May, New Jersey, so I've gone to school where I was the only speck of pepper in the salt shaker. My mother and father were both school teachers, and my father told me, "In order to appear equal, you've got to be twice as good." Mathematically that's wrong, but everyone in our race knows it's true.
>
> When I was in high school, I went to the airfield in Newcastle, Delaware and swept the hangar floor and cleaned greasy wrenches. On Saturdays and Sundays the instructor, Guy de Regaudier, would take me up. Soon he let me take over the controls, and from then on, it really bit me.
>
> About 1938 I went to Lincoln University, a black school between Philadelphia and Washington on old Route 1. Civilian Pilot Training was given at the college, and we'd drive to the field in an old Model-A Ford with isinglass windows all during the winter—and I mean it was cold as hell. But we had flying on our minds. I soloed in a Piper Cub. The instructor's pride and joy was a Taylorcraft, and if you were pretty good, he'd let you fly it, and then I really was bitten by the bug.

Another youth who joined was Spann Watson. He was ten years old when his father brought his family to New Jersey from South Carolina. The move followed a sensational 1925 triple lynching of a man, his wife, and son—a case that reached the New York papers.

My dad was a farmer, carpenter, millwright, and a station engineer, supplying power for big mills. That was an exceptional job for a black man in South Carolina at that time.

We left the cotton fields in 1927 when I was ten and moved to Lodi New Jersey, adjacent to Teterboro Airport. Back in the country we'd see or hear an airplane a couple of times a year, but after we moved, there were nothing but airplanes flying around. We were so fascinated, the whole family would visit Teterboro one or two times a week. They used to conduct flying circuses and triangular races with biplanes and high-wing planes—low-wings were ugly airplanes, and we'd laugh at them, but they'd win the races every time.

I never forgot anything I saw. My parents sent me to the post-office to buy a two-cent stamp, and it had a picture of the "Spirit of St. Louis," Lindbergh's plane. Shortly afterward, on July 4, 1927, we were visiting Teterboro. There must have been 12- to 15,000 people. An airplane came over the airport, and I yelled, "That's the 'Spirit of St. Louis!'"

The announcer looked at me, and before those thousands of people, he said, "Hey, look, this little colored boy said that's the "Spirit of St. Louis," and gave a big laugh.

The plane taxied up, and it *was* the "Spirit of St. Louis." That was a key point in my lifetime. That announcer embarrassed me before 15,000 people. He didn't say, "That little colored boy was right." I just stood there quivering. I never forgot that. I'm one of those guys, you laugh at me, I'll show you what I can do.

The people went completely wild. The crowd would have destroyed Lindbergh and his plane, so they grabbed a bunch of men, including my dad, to push the plane down to a cleared space while this howling mob followed. My dad made sure each of his three sons touched the Spirit of St. Louis. They opened a big hangar door and pushed it inside, and Lindbergh escaped out the back door.

All the big pilots of the era came into Teterboro, and I saw them all—Frank Hakes, Jimmy Waddell, Lee Goldbeach. Amelia Earhart with her tousled hair was quite an idol, everybody loved her. Wiley Post, the one-eyed part-Indian who had a black patch over one eye, was flying around the world, racing, and making a big name for himself; he flew a big old "barrel" airplane, the "Gee Bee," that looked like a bumble bee.

I built model airplanes with rubber bands and sold them to other kids for a nickel. In a wind they would take off like a balloon. Flying school was completely inaccessible to us, so I wanted to be an aeronautical engineer. I went to Howard University, which didn't offer a course in aeronautical engineering, but I majored in mechanical engineering—maybe I could be a mechanic at least. Then I studied more and more and said, "Why the hell don't you fly?"

In 1939, the CPT came along, and the Pittsburgh *Courier* campaigned until they finally established a program at four or five black schools, including Howard University. The school thought we were absolute fools to think white folks would let us fly airplanes, but Addison E. Richardson of the school of engineering pushed it, and Howard got it.

There were ten of us, and Chief Anderson came to train us. He was unaffected and friendly, and he'd do anything to make you learn to fly. The better you could fly, the better he liked you.

Now that they had learned to fly, they had to find a field that would let them.

Here we were, broke students, and not one Washington airport would let us fly from their field.

Finally, an airport at Hybla Valley, Virginia, which was going broke, agreed to let us fly. My younger brother had a '34 convertible and was kind of rowdy with it, so my dad told me to take the car to school, and that's how we all got to the airport.

Tuskegee had an advanced program with a Waco biplane, similar to a military trainer, and again Chief Anderson was there. Tuskegee had set a national record for scholastic achievement—this little black school beat all the white schools around there; *Time* magazine had a story about it.

The NAACP pushed for integrated training, but Watson wondered. In a big white university, with 20,000 students and only 20 CPT spaces, what chance would he have had of getting one of them?

If I'd gone to a white school, no way in hell I'd have had a chance. When they handed out the good things, they wouldn't have given me a thing. I only know four or five black people who had a chance to fly at a white university. So sometimes segregation is not so good, and sometimes it is.

The Air Corps commander, General HH "Hap" Arnold, called the question of Negro air units academic. It was unthinkable for black pilots to order white mechanics to service their planes, and it would take nine years to train black ground personnel; the approaching war would be over by then.

Ironically Arnold was very supportive of Jacqueline Cochrane's women, who flew military planes on non-combat missions. The women ran into prejudice from male pilots much like that encountered by the black pilots, and Arnold came to their rescue when others tried to scuttle them.

However, when Janet Bragg applied, she was turned down. She next applied to be an Army nurse and was told that quota was filled.

The Navy restricted blacks to cooks, mess stewards, and work crews. President Roosevelt's idea to integrate the Navy was to put a Negro band on each ship—"the colored race is very musical," one official pointed out.

Navy Secretary Frank Knox, the old Rough Rider, nixed it; he thought blacks should join the Army instead.

The Marine commandant, General Thomas Holcomb, declared that the Marines "are a club that doesn't want them."

Secretary of War Henry L Stimson upheld the Services. "Leadership," he insisted, "is not embedded in the Negro race." Meanwhile, the black Pittsburgh *Courier* dubbed the coming war, a war to "make the world safe for hypocrisy."

By mid-1940, when Hitler's army goose-stepped down the Champs Elysees, completing its conquest of most of Western Europe, the Army didn't know what to do with its only black colonel, Ben Davis, Sr. None of the major commanders wanted him. The NAACP asked Douglas MacArthur to give him a job befitting his rank of colonel; the general did not reply. When it urged a general's star, the Army answered that he was too old. Wearily, Davis went back to Wilberforce College for his fourth tour teaching ROTC, a captain's position.

But the presidential election was coming up, and the Republicans were making inroads into the Negro vote. Just before election day, orders arrived promoting Davis to brigadier general. He was assigned to the Inspector General's office to investigate race problems. However, despite the star on his collar, he was still not allowed to go to the post movie or eat with white officers. Rather than dine alone, he brought a brown bag or skipped lunch.

Roosevelt favored opening the Air Corps to blacks, though without "intermingling" the races. When Congress passed a law requiring all Services to enlist Negroes, the Air Force complied by forming all-black "Aviation Squadrons (Separate)." In fact, the men were used as laborers.

3

The Tuskegee Experiment

Mrs. Roosevelt's ride

In March 1941, Eleanor Roosevelt arrived at Tuskegee and watched the CPT pilots go through aerial acrobatics. Chief Anderson recalled:

> The first thing she said was, "I always heard the colored can't fly an airplane."
> I said, "Oh yes, they can, Mrs. Roosevelt."
> She said, "Everybody here is flying. You must be able to fly. As a matter of fact, I'm going to find out for sure. I'm going to take a flight with you."
> It caused a lot of consternation among her escorts: "Oh, Mrs. Roosevelt, you can't do that!" But she was a woman who, when she decided to do something, she was going to do it.

Someone called the White House and President Roosevelt reportedly laughed, "Well, if Eleanor wants to fly, she's going to fly."
She told Anderson, "Come on, let's go."
Anderson:

> She got in the plane with me, and we had a delightful flight. She enjoyed it very much. When we came back she said, "Well, you can fly all right." I'm positive that when she went home she said, "Franklin, I flew with those boys down there, and you're going to have to do something about it."

Meanwhile, Watson applied for the Eagle Squadron, the American volunteers in the Royal Air Force. "I thought they would integrate one black, but they just laughed at me, and that was that."
The NAACP agitated to integrate the Army Air Corps. Watson recalled sitting on the steps of the university library waiting to greet their lawyer:

> No less than Thurgood Marshall, the future Supreme Court justice, came to Howard University and wanted someone for a test case to sue the U.S. government. The man they selected was Yancey Williams, a senior, a year ahead of me, who was in the CPT class with me. I was Williams' backup.

23

Before the case could be brought to court, Watson recalled, "I remember as clear as yesterday, I heard the announcer over WOR radio say the Air Corps was going to form a Black Eagle Squadron."

To avoid "hobbling" the defense effort with integration, the Air Corps decided to train the black pilots on a separate field. (Meanwhile, the infantry was training white and black officers together at Fort Benning, Georgia.) Segregated schools for enlisted specialists would be too expensive, so they would be trained alongside whites at regular Air Corps schools.

Coffey hoped the school would be located in Chicago, but this was turned down because of the weather.

The Air Force had a choice of California, Texas or Alabama and made what many felt was the worst possible choice—the deepest part of the Deep South—Tuskegee, Alabama at the Institute founded by Booker T. Washington. Racial tension plagued the new school; nobody wanted it there. The people of the town appealed to their senators to keep it out of their bailiwick, while the NAACP opposed the whole idea of a segregated school.

In a blistering report, Judge William Hastie, a black civilian aide to Secretary of War Henry Stimson, blamed both the Institute and the Air Corps for the Jim Crow conditions at Tuskegee. He said the school had bid for the Air Force contract only as a source of revenue—"a mess of pottage."

The Institute replied defensively that "when Negroes are not segregated, they are subject to humiliation,"

Watson agreed:

> The NAACP, of which I was a great supporter, because everything I got had been spearheaded by it, wanted to integrate the training with white cadets, but we'd have been blown away! No one would ever have graduated, they'd have found a way to wash us out.

The announcement of a Negro flying unit sent black men across the country scurrying to the recruiting offices. What kind of men were they? Pilot Roscoe Brown called them the cream of black youth of their generation. "We had a group of high-achieving people who had their own egos and a disproportionate percentage of leaders. That was implicit in the way we were selected: They went out and recruited the brightest and the best."

Bill Campbell, one of the first candidates, disputed that notion. The Tuskegee Airmen were chosen with exactly the same criteria as all Air Force recruits, he said.

However, another pilot, Lee Archer, sided with Brown. "The cadets were uniformly arrogant and conceited, a different type of people from those I had left in New York. It was a group just like me. If there was a modest, shy man there, I didn't meet him."

* * *

Elmer Jones was the first black taken in the Air Corps. He was an engineering graduate of Washington's Howard University and one of the graduates of CPT. In May 1941 Jones was one of six called to begin cadet training as a maintenance officer. Jones was about to begin military pilot training when his unit was order overseas and spent the war as a maintenance officer.

The First Class

TWO months after the ground support training began, the first aviation cadets began training.

The announcement of a Negro flying unit sent black men across the country scurrying to recruiting offices. A later replacement pilot, Roscoe Brown, called them the cream of black youths of their generation.

> We had a group of high-achieving people, who had their own egos and a disproportionate percentage of leaders. That was implicit in the way we were selected: They went out and recruited the brightest and the best.

Campbell disputed that. The Tuskegee Airmen were chosen with exactly the same criteria as all Air Force recruits, he said.

However, Lee archer sided with Brown:

> The cadets were uniformly arrogant and conceited, a different type of people from those I left in New York. It was a group just like me. If there was a modest, shy man there, I didn't meet him.

Benjamin Davis, Jr.

LIEUTENANT B.O. Davis, a West Pointer and son of General Ben Davis, was the first student chosen and the commander-presumptive of the squadron to be formed.

Called B.O., he was born in 1912 while his father was serving on the Mexican border.

The elder Davis had been turned down by West Point, so he enlisted with a view to winning a commission through the ranks. Riding with the cavalry in the Utah desert, Davis passed the exam in 1901, finishing third among 23 candidates.

When his son was 12, he sat with his father, mother, and younger sister on the porch of their Tuskegee home one summer night with the porch light defiantly lit and grimly watched torch-waving Klu Klux Klansmen march past.

The next year:

> My father paid five dollars to a barnstormer to give me my first ride in an airplane. Two years later I was living in Cleveland, twisting the dials of the family Atwater-Kent radio, listening avidly to the daily reports of Lindbergh's solo flight.
>
> Newspaper accounts of air battles of World War I reached a crescendo with Lindbergh's flight. Lindbergh has remained one of my heroes throughout these sixty years. But I couldn't think of any course of action that would let me get into aviation.

The youth attended Western Reserve University and the University of Chicago before a West Point appointment appeared.

From 1870–89, 12 black cadets had entered West Point, but only three graduated.

Johnson Whitaker was found tied to his bunk and beaten unconscious, with his ear slit. An official inquiry concluded that he had done it to himself! He left soon after.

Henry O. Flipper was the first to graduate, in 1881. He was later court-martialed for embezzling funds, a case that remains a mystery. Flipper claimed he was railroaded because he had gone riding with a white lieutenant's fiancee. However, another study suggests that his Mexican mistress had stolen the money. We will probably never know.

In 1976 the Army reviewed Flipper's court martial and changed his dishonorable discharge to honorable.

John H. Alexander graduated in 1887 but died seven years later, leaving little record.

Charles Young

BORN in a Kentucky log cabin in 1864, he was the son of a free black soldier in the Union Army. He entered West Point in 1884, enduring what the *Washington Post* would call "a lonely cadet life" in "a silent environment." One classmate, later Major General Charles Rhodes wrote, "we esteem him highly for his patient perseverance."

A white cadet, from South Carolina came to Young's defense after a Yankee classmate made a remark "that reflected on the chastity of the Negro's female forebears." They met in a bare knuckles duel behind the barracks at four o'clock one morning.

Young wrote poems and composed songs, played the piano, harp, and cornet, and spoke French, German, and Spanish. But he was apparently no student, graduating last in his class. He would be the last black in West Point for 40 years.

Young served with the cavalry in Nebraska and Utah and, after Alexander's death in 1894, was the only black officer in the Army.

When the Spanish-American War broke out in 1898, Young hoped for a combat command. But that would have meant a promotion to colonel, a move the Army forestalled by giving him command of a volunteer regiment in the States.

Did Davis know of how earlier black cadets had been treated a half-century earlier, and did he know what was in store for him?

> No, as a matter of fact, I was naive, as I look back. I had excelled in high school, I was confident of my ability, and I thought there was nothing unusual about being a black cadet. The roof kind of caved in on the third night when I went to attend a meeting and was told I was not supposed to be there.

Davis soon discovered the reason: His fellow cadets were meeting to debate "the nigger problem."

> I learned later the purpose of the meeting was to instruct my classmates to make me withdraw from the Academy. For four years I was "silenced." I became an invisible man. My classmates treated Filipino, Nicaraguan, and Thai cadets better than they treated me.

Not another cadet spoke to him. Davis roomed alone, sat alone on the bus going to football games, and when he attended mandatory dance classes, he also danced alone. Although he was assigned a table at the mess hall, Sunday breakfast was "open seating," and he was forced to go from table to table, mess tray in hands: "Request permission to join your table."

"Permission denied."

This "silencing" was usually reserved for violations of the honor code, and Davis asked himself how it was reconciled with West Point's motto of "Duty, honor, country."

> West Point is supposed to train leaders, but there was no damn leadership at all. The superintendent, Lieutenant Colonel Richardson, an old cavalry officer, was a fine gentleman, but he wasn't about to interfere with what went on. The first captain of cadets was William Westmoreland [later commander

of U.S. forces in Vietnam]. If he'd been a true leader, he would have stopped that crap.

It was designed to make me buckle, but I refused to buckle. They didn't understand that I was going to stay there, and I was going to graduate.

I was not missing anything by not associating with them. They were missing a great deal by not knowing me.

Davis graduated in 1936, ranking 35th in a class of 276. General Pershing presented lieutenant's bars to the new cadets. When Davis stepped up to receive his, his classmates dropped their silent treatment and gave him a cheer.

Ordinarily, his marks would have given him his choice of arms, and he chose the Air Corps. It was denied on the grounds that there were no black flying units. He had only two choices, infantry or cavalry. One general advised him to drop out and study law. "The general did me a favor," Davis wrote. "He brought out my stubborn streak."

Assigned to the Infantry School in Fort Benning Georgia, Davis and his bride drove south. When they had to make stops along the way from calls of nature, they were careful to choose "a treed area, so we wouldn't be any more embarrassed than we were."

When they arrived, the Officers' Club refunded his check for dues with a note that he wouldn't be using the club. According to Army etiquette, Lieutenant and Mrs. Davis made an appointment through the adjutant to call on the post commander. They arrived to find the lights on at his home, but nobody answered his knock, so he slipped his card under the door. The next night the commander's card was found under his own door.

Davis was assigned to the black 24th Infantry regiment.

I was the training officer for young black recruits. What happened to them after they were trained? They were given duties as servants in officers' quarters. The 24th had no combat mission.

B.O. was also assigned to ROTC at Tuskegee Institute, "a useless existence" that consisted of giving one 45-minute lecture a day before egot the notice to report for a physical before flight training. However, the doctor apparently hadn't been briefed and reported that Davis had was suffering from a serious case of leprosy. The Air Force quickly found another doctor and explained the situation, and this time the leprosy symptoms were found to have magically vanished.

Davis and his wife hastened to their new assignment in Tuskegee, "aware of the high stakes game we were about to be involved in."

George "Spanky" Roberts from West Virginia was the second student selected. In 1982 Roberts, then a rotund man with a goatee, appeared at the opening of a Smithsonian exhibit on the Red Tails and told how he became a Tuskegee Airmen:

> I'm Indian, black, Caucasian, a little Jewish. Our son married an Armenian, so our grandchildren have that to add to their lineage.
>
> My father was a Kentuckian. He had been a jockey and done a little baseball pitching, and when World War I came around, he wrote asking to be in the combat engineers, the glamour service. They wrote back OK, but when they got a look at his face, they said uh-uh, they didn't want any niggers. He was later drafted and became a first sergeant in a port battalion. He had 11 "slaves" in his organization, people who had never heard that there had been a Civil War or an Emancipation Proclamation. A great many whites didn't know they were violating the law either.
>
> I grew up in Fairmont West Virginia. I remember seeing Josh Gibson, the great baseball batter, hit in a little coal mining town, Grant Town, near Fairmont. The ball went out of the park at least 20 feet above the fence and still climbing. It must have gone 700 feet, allowing for exaggeration over the years.
>
> I've loved flying all my life. When I was junior high school age, my parents dug up the money from some place to take a hop in a fourseater aircraft. The pilot asked me if I'd like to fly it. I had to stand up to reach the pedals, but I flew the airplane for probably 20 minutes.
>
> I went to West Virginia State College, which was a segregated institution at that time, taking psychology, sociology, and engineering. I was pretty young, and with hazing what it was, I said, "I'll spank you if you don't let me alone." I was small enough that the upperclassmen thought it was funny, so I became "Spanky," and it followed me all the years of my life.
>
> I was haunting the hell out of the Air Corps to let me enroll. Finally got a telegram from the War Department that the Air Corps was opened to blacks, and I was the first one accepted as a flying cadet. [Davis, who was already commissioned, was not a cadet.]

Two other cadets were CPT graduates:

Mac Ross from Dayton went to West Virginia State, Roberts' alma mater. "A real slick guy," said Spann Watson, "a real glossy officer in his dress and demeanor."

Charles DeBow, an Indiana school teacher, attended Hampton Institute in Virginia. Lou Purnell recalled him as "very loquacious, verbose, with a sarcastic sense of humor."

Lemuel Custis, the first black police officer in Connecticut. Custis "was a little older than most of us, very diplomatic, a real gentleman," future cadet C.C. Robinson said.

I came out of college right in the middle of the Depression—the Great One, I'm talking about. There weren't any jobs, particularly for young blacks who had some education. I didn't want to hang around the street corners and do nothing—my mother and father had raised me that you have to go out and work for anything you got. So I became a cop, walking a beat. When the Air Corps opened up, I jumped at the chance and never regretted it.

Honestly, I don't know why I was selected in the first group. There were a couple of us who didn't have the benefit of going to schools that had CPT, so I was a real greenie who had to start from scratch. I think Davis and I were the only ones. We had to climb a little higher mountain than the others did."

John Anderson of Toledo University was a Phi Beta Kappa and 16-letter athlete chosen on the All-American football team. He was Roberts' choice as the standout of the first class.

In all, 13 students were selected. According to Roberts, the base commander, Major James "Straight Arrow" Ellison, told them: "Take a good look at the man on your left and on your right, because on graduation day they won't be there."

"Of course we didn't believe it," Spanky said. "We promised each other that we'd hang in there no matter what"

Watson was upset at being passed over. "We were the ones who had been pushing the fight to get in, but when they made the call for the first class, most of them were strange names to us, not the people who had been out battling to get in. Where some of them came from, it beats me."

Some of the white instructors were pretty intimidating.

Captain Robert Lowenburg was basic instructor and commandant of cadets. Lou Purnell:

> He looked to be about seven feet tall, big as a barn door, with crew-cut hair, which made him look ferocious, and this big deep voice. When he'd come through the barracks, you could almost feel the quake of both his weight and his voice.

Another cadet, Charles Dryden, called him "raw-boned and humorless. I don't remember ever seeing him smile."

Major Scotty Magoon was from Buffalo, and "everyone was deathly afraid of this guy," Ed Gleed admitted. The cadets parodied the hit love song by trumpeter Harry James, "A Sleepy Lagoon, a tropical moon (and two on an island...") The Tuskegee version went: "Oh, Major Magoon will get him a coon by mid-afternoo-oon." ("We used language among ourselves that we'd fight about if anybody else used it," cadet Ed Gleed smiled.)

After basic, the cadets still faced the hurdle of advanced training.

Captain Gabe Hawkins was from Mississippi. If the students survived Lowenburg and Magoon in basic, they had to face "the Hawk" in advanced. His clerk, George Abercrombie, told the National Park Service oral history project:

> He was a large rugged southerner with a loud voice, and he didn't like niggers. He could chew you up and spit you out. In those days, if you were a black soldier and a white major ordered, "Shit," you started farting.

"If you draw the Hawk," one student said, "you can forget about getting your wings."

A story often repeated said the Hawk crashed and was almost killed. "They had to scrape him up with a shovel." He was rushed to the base hospital, where all the doctors were black, as his wife pleaded, "If the only blood you have is black, let him die."

He didn't die.

But for years fellow officers could get his goat by pointing to one of his kids and remarking, "He looks a little darker than you, Hawk."

Then they'd duck.

Major Robert "Mother" Long, from the Huey Long family in Louisiana, was head of advanced instruction. He wasn't prejudiced—nor was Huey—and got his nickname because he watched over his students like a mother hen. Said Archer: "He and Parrish were crackers and rednecks, but they were fair."

Campbell defended the white instructors from charges of racism, citing two basic instructors, both white:

> One was a young captain from Indiana. He'd been told I was a licensed pilot, and one of the things he said when he got me was, "You won't have any trouble here." The other was a young first lieutenant from Union Springs, Alabama, 16 miles from my home.
>
> They both treated me just like I'd want anyone to treat me, whether white or black. I didn't know of any racial incidents. All of them had volunteered. I firmly believe those people were there because they said, "I'd like to be."

James Wiley, who was both an instructor and a student, agreed:

> There were a bunch of fine white instructors, whom I kept up with after integration. You have to give the man a lot of credit. I don't know if I'd have done it—give up a chance for a career and a chance to make general, as some of them did, in order to train blacks.

Every Tuskegee Airmen interviewed enthusiastically agreed. The cadets faced plenty of racial and other problems, but flight instruction was not one of them. All gave the instructors thumbs up.

The black instructors were carefully hand-picked.

Archie Williams, who taught meterology, was the 1936 Olympic champ at 400 meters. That was the Games where Hitler refused to shake Jesse Owens' hand. "He didn't shake mine, either," Williams said. A CPT grad and licensed pilot, he graduated from the University of California with an engineering degree.

Most black flight instructors were CPT graduates.

Jim Wiley "was a natural-born pilot," cadet Clarence Jamison said, "and a brilliant student of physics. He knew the engineering, he loved the mechanics of it."

He was quiet, C.C. Robinson said, "but he was a brain."

One of his grandfathers was Jewish, the other had fought with General Sherman at Lookout Mountain, Tennessee. Wiley's mother, a teacher, had traveled widely in Europe; his father earned an engineering degree at the University of Pittsburgh, but the only job he could find was as a postman.

Jim grew up in Pittsburgh, "and all my friends were mostly white kids. I owned my own newspaper route—you bought a route in those days—and I made money."

With a scholarship to Pitt, Jim worked for the New Deal for $30 a month, enough to put some money in his pocket, buy a car, and woo "this beautiful, beautiful" coed. Driving to class through a park, he ran into a race riot where Italians tried to drive blacks out of the pool, "dragged them off buses, and beat them up." Wiley drove safely through, but clutched a butcher knife just in case.

In the summer he worked in a steel mill for five dollars a day, six days a week, "big money in those days." When he went back to school, he was "muscle-bound but rich."

Wiley graduated in 1940 and looked forward to a job like his white friends who "disappeared" into secret government work. Instead, he got a job as a chauffeur. He also enrolled at Carnegie Tech, where he joined the CPT. "They couldn't turn me down, because I was a good as, or better than, anyone else. And I knew it. It was the turning point of my life."

His physics professor and flying instructor wrote a glowing letter to the chief of Pan American Airlines in New York. "I submitted my letter to the receptionist and sat in the outer office all day. Finally, at 4:30 she brought the letter back. They weren't even going to interview me."

When Jim got an offer to teach flying at Tuskegee,

I saw an opportunity and I grabbed it. I arrived on campus with one and a half bucks in my pocket. I had never been in an all-colored outfit before. My eyes were opened to a new way of life.

Daniel "Chappie" James had starred playing football at Tuskegee. He was born in Pensacola, the last of 17 children. After his father died, his mother taught school in the backyard and instilled in her children the Eleventh Commandment: *Thou shalt not quit.* She helped pay his way into Tuskegee, where he starred in football and yearned to fly.

Future Airmen Charlie Bussey and Chappie were future cadets together:

Chappie was a giant of a man, must have weighed 260–280 pounds, six-foot-five. He was playful, liked to wrestle—I was always getting slammed against the wall.

And hyper-extroverted. He could sing, dance, tell jokes, and fly an airplane. At the club, if the floor show wasn't real sharp, he'd get up and take over from them.

Chappie loved fun a little too much. His pranks often got him in trouble, and when one of them went too far, he was thrown out in his senior year two weeks before graduation.

But he enrolled in CPT and won his wings. Too big to be a fighter pilot, he became an instructor at Tuskegee. He became a bomber pilot too late to serve in World War II, but he flew jets in Korea and Vietnam and went on to become America's first black four-star general.

Roger "Bill" Terry from Los Angeles, named after a baseball player, was also too big for a fighter:

Jackie Robinson and I were teammates. We were the first two blacks to play basketball in the Pacific Coast Conference—that was before they knew Negroes could play basketball. I had played against Jackie in junior college. Tuition at the university was $50 a semester—that was a lot of money—but only five dollars at the junior college level. He was a forward and the top scorer in the PCC. I played everything, center most of the time; that was back when they were still using a jump ball after every point, not taking it out of bounds like they do now.

I was a political science major, just finishing college, and they started the "Bruin Squadron" at UCLA. One thousand took the test, about 250–300 guys passed. They had it on the front page of the Los Angeles *Times* with a picture of us:

BRUIN ATHLETES
JOIN AIR CORPS

The colonel called me up at school: "Why didn't you tell us you were colored?"

"Why didn't you ask me?" In 1940 they didn't have race on the form.

I was already sworn in, but I got a letter saying I was too tall and weighed too much. I was six-foot two-and-a-half, 172 pounds, 19 years old, a graduate of UCLA, and in perfect condition. They said the restriction was five-feet nine inches, 160 pounds. They didn't have the same damn restrictions for Chinese or anybody else—B.O. Davis was six-feet. But they told me to go home and wait.

A month later Dr James O. Plinton, later vice-president of Eastern Air Lines, called me. He said if I paid my way to Tuskegee, they'd teach me to fly and make me an instructor.

Bill Campbell had been, of all things, a stenographer at the Institute—he had graduated in business administration and also won his pilot's license through CPT.

Bernard Knighten called him "mature and thoughtful...very thorough, never made any rash decisions.

Though soft-spoken, Bill was a natural leader.

Spann Watson:

> I thought he was one of the most capable blacks who ever came through the Air Force—a brilliant, fair-minded man, who looked at all sides. You couldn't come up with a one-sided story and get it through Bill Campbell, because he was going to digest it with all the information he needed. His family were all college graduates.
>
> And he was a hell of a flyer.
>
> He should have been a general.

A retired professor when he was questioned for this book more than 50 years later, Campbell was a difficult interview, answering questions slowly, and, after careful reflection, pausing to express his thoughts precisely. Of course, the author wanted more colorful quotes, but Campbell wouldn't cooperate.

Ernest Henderson invented a new maneuver, "the vertical 8." He also liked to quote Scripture. When one student on a solo flight came in for a landing straight toward Henderson:

> I thought of Proverbs 3:16: "Acknowledge Him and He will direct your path." The airplane was on a northwest path, so I headed northeast."
>
> I had to wash him out: "If you stop flying now, the life you save may be your own."

Henderson let his best students alternate as pilot with him.

I saw pine trees below my heels. In Ecclesiastes 1, it says, "There's a time to keep silent and a time to speak." I asked if he was flying the plane."

He said, "No, sir. I thought *you* were flying it."

Roscoe Draper had a tremendous amount of flying time, cadet Lee Archer said:

> But he was a very odd character. I thought he despised me. I could never do anything to please him. Never once did he say anything nice: "My God! You call that an *Immelman*? That's the worst Immelman I've ever seen in my life!" When he got a little peeved at you: he'd shake the dual-control stick so it hit you between the knees. You got so you sat with your knees together.
>
> You had to solo in ten hours. On my third flight with him, he racked me up. "Stop it! Stop it! What did I do to deserve this?" I landed. He got out of the back seat, said, "I'll never fly with you again; I'm not gonna let you kill me!"
>
> I stood up to climb out. He said, "What are you doing?"
>
> "What do you want me to do?"
>
> "Take it back up and see if you can solo it!"
>
> I think he was trying to prepare me to operate under pressure. He was telling me, "Things aren't going to be easy when you have a white instructor."

The First Enlisted Trainees

AT Chanute Field, Illinois 280 black enlisted men had already begun seven months of intensive training. They attended classes with whites but slept and ate at a separate barracks across the runway. As they graduated, they were sent to Tuskegee to service the training plane and also to teach technical subjects.

Harry Sheppard was the son of a West Indian fisherman. After grammar school in Barbados, he attended DeWitt Clinton high school (which produced two other Tuskegee Airmen, Lee Archer and Wilmeth Sidat-Singh) and the City College of New York—CCNY.

> I had very little interest in aviation. I was studying electrical engineering at CCNY, working in the day and going to college at night. Money was hard to come by. My cousin was a student at the Manhattan School of Aviation Trades and said, "Harry, they just opened the Air Corps to Negroes."
>
> I said, "That's fine, Walt, why don't you join?" This was for airplane mechanics and technicians, mind you, not for pilot training. He pestered me to the point where I began to think: The storm clouds in Europe were getting darker and darker, and we couldn't avoid getting embroiled in it. So I finally thought, "Boy, here's a chance to get into a branch of service that wasn't oriented to menial, heavy physical labor."

So bright and early one Monday morning around the 30th of March, my cousin and I went out. The test was history and current events, civics, economics, mechanical skills, and math. Well, Walter failed, and he was out; I passed, and I was in.

They inducted me as a private, $21 a month. My cousin got a job a week later as a machinist making $174 a week. My father almost died! He said, "I thought you knew something about arithmetic." I thought he was going to kill me.

About 275 entered the 99th Pursuit Squadron—fuel system specialists, hydraulic specialists communications technicians. There wasn't one guy who wasn't at least a high school graduate. We had college students and college graduates and people who were in the teaching profession. We were young and full of vinegar and the other thing.

Sheppard enrolled as an engine mechanic and earned a propeller specialist rating.

We went to class eight solid hours a day, from 6:30 to 2:30. After school we had our manual of arms, regular basic training. We were segregated as a group, of course, but we were going to an integrated Air Corps school. The instruction was excellent. We studied together late into the night. We were really a proud outfit.

Fred Archer enlisted with Sheppard.

I called him Stinky, and he called me Alfalfa. Remember in the "Our Gang" movies, the one with the cowlick back there? I used to have one like that.

Fred was an armorer and an ordnance man, took care of the guns and ammunition. He retired as a chief master sergeant. He would have made a very fine officer, but he never seemed to care about it.

Arthur Freeman was Bessie Coleman's nephew.

Sheppard:

At that time there was very low esteem for soldiers, black or white. A black soldier was even one layer lower.

The Air Force completely under-estimated the caliber of people whom they had so carefully screened. It thought we were black and ignorant and not capable of anything but the more menial assignments. I resented this.

They were competent and dedicated. It takes 10–12 people on the grand to keep one plane airborne—medical, operations, technicians, communications, administration, security.

We lost some of our NCOs overseas. They lost their lives, just like the pilots did.

One man was named Clayter. He bugged the captain to send him to
school to be a meteorologist. The captain said, "What! Do you realize you
have to have differential and integral calculus, you have to be able to create
skew curves and compute these things?"

He said, "Yes sir, I think I can make it."

So the captain said, "Well, let him go, the worst that can happen is he'll
fail and come right back here."

Clayter did so well that they retained him to be an instructor. Later they
found he was a PhD. from the University of Chicago in mathematics. We
rolled on the floor when we heard this.

We left for Tuskegee in November of 1941 with the highest grade point
average of any group that had ever passed through there, or would pass
through, in the future.

Tuskegee was still "pretty much of a mud hole," Jones recalled. He and
the cadets were quartered in tents there. The enlisted men were sent to
nearby Maxwell Air Base to wait for housing at Tuskegee. There was plenty
of aircraft maintenance to do there, but "they sat on their butts doing
menial tasks."

Sheppard:

We performed guard duty and swept the streets, although we were
mechanics and they needed mechanics on the line. They were teaching
British, French, and other cadets at Maxwell Field, but they wouldn't relax
and allow us to ply our trades.

Conditions were primitive as the Air Corps began building a school. The
men lived in tents. The mess hall consisted of four walls and a sand floor,
a tin stove was used to boil water, and November rain turned roads into
"rivers of mud."

Chauncey Spencer, at 35 too old for pilot training, was an undercover
agent for Judge William Hastie in the War Department. He reported that
200 students were forced to use a 20-by-20-foot dining room and ate sitting on empty soft- drink crates. The white personnel dined at tables with
linen cloths and were served by black waitresses in uniform. White officers
also slept, washed their hands, and went to the base theater and Officers'
Club separately. The PX cafeteria was divided in half; the relatively small
number of whites dined in one half, the blacks, who greatly outnumbered
them, lined up outside the other half.

Spencer spent the war as employee relations officer at Patterson Field
(later Wright-Patterson Air Force Base), Ohio, trying to enforce integration. In his book, *Who Is Chauncey Spencer?* (Broadside Press, 1975), he
described the experience as months of frustration. While white officials

told him to "drag his feet" on integration, black employees sought special favors. One side called him a Communist, the other, an Uncle Tom.

The town of Tuskegee was the domain of Sheriff Pat Evans, a "fat frog," in Purnell's words. Town police arrested a black enlisted man, and when a black officer asserted jurisdiction and tried to take the prisoner into military custody, the police arrested him too and beat up his driver!

Ellison succeeded in getting the MP released and returned to base, but this only enraged the townspeople, who were already in an uproar over armed Negroes in their midst.

Evans demanded that MPs carry no weapons. If they did, he disarmed them end locked them up. It almost caused a revolt on base when a black nurse was hit and thrown off a bus for refusing to move to the back.

The cadets were in a mood to march into town and fight. Luckily, Colonel Noel Parris, the director of instruction, scouted the town and saw the whites passing out weapons, and ordered the cadets to stand down.

Meanwhile, classes went on. Some 40 to 45 primary instructors gave the students their first lessons on the Stearman PT-17, an open cockpit biplane that cruised at 80 miles an hour. It had a narrow landing gear, which made it susceptible to ground loops, that is, a cross-wind could lift one wing, making the other wing hit the ground while the plane spun around.

As they soloed, each man was doused with green beer and went on to the next level, the BT-13 Vultee "Vibrator" with enclosed cockpit, radio, flaps, and wider landing gear. They learned Immelman turns, chandelles, snap rolls, vertical reverses, "falling leaves," spin recovery, and pylon-8s.

Advanced training in the AT-6 "Texan" introduced the students to formation flying. The Texan cruised at 160 miles an hour, requiring faster reflexes. It also had retractable landing gear, which gave the students something else to worry about.

The cadet considered most likely to succeed, Anderson, was the first to wash out. When white cadets flunked they were reassigned to another field. Black washouts had nowhere else to go. They reverted to buck privates in the ranks at Tuskegee, a humiliating situation.

Custis:

> Even having CPT didn't guarantee that they'd get their wings. There was more than simply your ability to fly; there was also ground school and overall conduct. I was consumed with making it, not washing out. Next to my wife, flying has been the greatest love of my life.

The cadets were worked so hard that "we didn't have radios or any contact with the outside world," Roberts said. He didn't even hear the news of Pearl Harbor until three days later!

* * *

Colonel Frederick von Kimble replaced Ellison as base commander. A West Pointer and veteran of 28 years as a flyer, he was "a dour, humorless officer," according to another future cadet, Charles Dryden. Although a northerner, from Oregon, he strictly enforced segregation.

Wiley:

> He was an aloof type of person, typical of commanders of colored troops at that time. They were in it for the rank. A colonel has to be a leader, especially with pilots, who are intelligent; you wreck their spirit by being very authoritarian. You're supposed to inspire them and come down and be friendly with them. I never saw Kimble.

Kimble believed that conflicting policies at bases in the North and South led to confusion among cadets from the North and encouraged "certain colored individuals" to clash with local customs and police. The result was "friction and strife." His proposed solution: that the armed forces adopt a single policy, essentially that of the South.

His prediction came true when town police arrested a black enlisted man for drunkenness and refused to release him to the military police. Then they arrested a black MP who was directing traffic in front of an army warehouse, to the anger of white drivers.

Finally, when MPs arrested a soldier for disturbing the peace, a crowd of armed whites demanded that he be turned over to them. They refused, and state troopers quickly arrived and beat the MPs Airmen tried to join the scene before Parrish stopped them, averting a possible race riot.

TUSKEGEE RIOTS.
MOB ATTACKS
NEGRO FLYING FIELD

the black press cried. It was answered by similar rhetoric by southern white papers.

When General Benjamin Davis Sr. came down to observe, he was closely guarded by Kimble. Tuskegee, his son wrote, was a prison camp, and his wife penned a long poem beginning:

"Dear Mom, This is a hell of a hole."

By New Years Kimble was promoted and kicked upstairs.

Colonel Parrish replaced him. It was one of the most critical events in the history of the Tuskegee Airmen.

Parrish, quickly acted to defuse the worst of the tension. Although many things were outside his control, he listened sympathetically to complaints, joined the black Officers' Club and regularly dined there, and, as Davis said, treated the students on an "equal man-to-man" basis.

He invited singer Lena Horne and other black entertainers to visit the base.

Parrish gave up his own hopes for a combat command and stayed in Tuskegee to make the experiment work. "Tuskegee wasn't supposed to succeed," said Roberts, "but Colonel Parrish decided that, instead of making it fail, he would make it succeed."

"We can't say enough for that guy," Purnell declared. "He had to be a buffer between the black cadets and the white citizens of the town. He was neither on their side nor our side, but he sure did protect his troops."

Cadet Herbert Carter, a Southerner himself, said:

> Parrish was a very wise man with vision beyond that day and time. He judged people by their performance and their potential and not by their color. The flight instruction was second to none. Parrish insured that it produced quality pilots.

A Tuskegee pilot, Lee Archer, flew Parrish to Washington a number of times.

> On the flight back you could almost see the depression as he got beaten up by the top brass. He ended up with only one star because he defied the system. But without him, I don't think the Tuskegee experiment would have gone anywhere. That man was an integral part of the Tuskegee Airmen. We look on him as one of us. I loved the guy.

For decades afterward, at reunion dinners, when Parrish's name was called, everyone applauded with a standing ovation.

Of the original 13 cadets, only five graduated—Davis, Roberts, Custis, DeBow, and Ross. On March 7, 1942 they received their wings before a statue of Booker T. Washington. Lou Purnell, who was three classes behind them, recalled: "There's no way to describe their elation, standing on the platforms with their uniforms rippling in the wind. They had done the impossible."

Nobody left after the ceremony as Second Lieutenant Roberts took his second oath of the afternoon. Joined by his fiancée, he took his marriage vow: "There were major generals, a lieutenant general, and our parents. It was on the *Pathe* news reel, in the magazines, and all the rest of it."

On the train back to Indiana, DeBow's father kept walking back to the water fountain, stopping to chat with passengers and ask if they had heard the news that black men had graduated from the Army's flying school. "In fact, we have one right here in this car," he would add casually. There he is, there. That's my son."

4

The 99th

MEANTIME more classes had been forming once a month and were moving through training. For many, the first shock was getting on the train to Tuskegee.

C.C. Robinson, who held a degree in chemistry, boarded a Pullman in South Carolina after the ticket agent dithered for 15 minutes whether to honor the government voucher. It was 2:30 pm.

As soon as I got on, the porter came by and wanted to put me to bed. Twenty minutes later the conductor came by with the same thing, to get me out of sight. I said, "No, no way. I went to bed with everyone else."

Class #2, April 29

ONE month behind the first class, ten more cadets enrolled. Clarence Jamison, a pre-med student from Cleveland, knew the Davis family from when the senior Davis had taught ROTC at Wilberforce. Jamison was one of six children, and their father worked two shifts to send them all to college. Clarence was in his third year at the University of Chicago when he and a buddy, Sherman White, signed up for CPT "just on a whim" for extra credit.

When war broke out, Clarence wrote to Eleanor Roosevelt to get into the Air Corps.

It seemed to work, because I got a letter from the War Department and soon after that I was accepted. I was the oldest in my class. I felt protective of the other guys. I felt more mature and had much more flying experience than they did.

C.C. Robinson would fly in Jamison's flight overseas. He remembered:

He was a little quiet fellow, very nice. You wouldn't know he was in the room if he didn't speak. Jamie would laugh at a joke, but that was about all. Smiled all the time.

Sidney Brooks was, Dryden recalled:

> Aggressive, athletic, and vigorous. He loved touch football and basket-
> ball. And a ladies' man. He was like a big brother to me. I was a kid, didn't
> know how immature I was. He helped me grow up.

Charles Dryden's father was a Jamaican, who was almost killed in World
War I. Charles learned to read on pulp magazines about the exploits of
World War I airmen. He loved the Coney Island roller coaster—"No roller
coaster was too fast. I was *flying!*"

Dryden was studying mechanical engineering at CCNY when he signed
up for CPT, one of two blacks in the program. He left home in the Bronx
at five a.m. to reach the field, but he didn't mind. "I was greedy for flying"
and received his civilian pilot's license. As soon as the Army announced it
would accept blacks in the Air Corps, he rushed to take his physical. Nine
blacks took it; only two were accepted.

On the trip south Dryden said:

> Even though I had a Pullman ticket, when I went up to the dining car,
> they'd pull the curtain around my table.
> I was scared as hell of the South. I had read of lynchings and the cruelty
> of whites to blacks if someone didn't say "yes sir" or didn't move off the side-
> walk when he was expected to. I had a healthy respect for the cruelty of the
> crackers down there.

Thanks to CPT, Dryden found ground school—theory of flight, navigation, meteorology, engines etc.—a "snap."

But aerial gunnery was almost his "Waterloo." So were snap rolls.

When Lowenberg called the mess dietician "Drew!" That did it! The
cadets stood up and walked toward him. Brooks said, "Captain Lowenberg,
the lady's name is *Mrs.* Drew." Lowenberg turned beet red, turned on his
heels, and stomped out.

Dryden's favorite class was formation flying.

> I loved it with a passion. Taking off singly and joining close up on a lead-
> er's wing by swiftly judging the necessary curve of pursuit got my adrena-
> line flowing. Sliding smoothly, safely, from one position in the formation to
> another with only inches of clearance between props and wings.

Still he was worried. "Lowenberg never gave me the impression that
he was pleased with my flying." Dryden could do everything except snap

rolls—rolling the plane sharply on its vertical axis and coming to a quick, steady stop at the end. "I sweated out Basic, fearing the 'washing machine' the entire ten weeks."

It was instructor Charlie Foxx, "Mr. Aerobatics," who showed Dryden how to do a snap roll, in a two-seater with dual controls: "Watch the pedals, the stick, and the throttle." Foxx made it look easy. In fact, it *was* easy. "And fun."

Hazing by upperclassmen was an Army tradition. Rookies had to "duck walk" with their hands on their hips for painful distances, or with arms out-stretched, slowly come down to a "sitting" position an inch at a time with no chair to support them and hold it for several minutes. Another was to sit against the wall, alternately kicking one foot then the other in front of them like a Russian dancer. Cadet Alexander Jefferson took it philosophically. He wrote in *Red Tail Captured, Red Tail Free*, that he knew they were toughening him for combat. It also gave him muscles in his legs, which he would need later when he flew the p-40.

A later cadet, Bert Wilson, found the black upperclassmen tougher than the white instructors:

> They were really bastards, but they didn't want you to screw up. You hated their guts. But you learned the hard way. Some said, "Hey, we're not going to take this crap." They were the ones that washed out.

Another future cadet, Walter Palmer, described it in his book, *Flying With Eagles:*

> All Pre-Flight cadets were called "Dodos," because that extinct breed of bird was incapable of flight....We had classes all day and after dinner we were subjected to hazing until bedtime. Our days were crammed with classes that included physics, math, Morse code, and weather....
>
> The man who spent the most time with us was a black officer who was director of physical training, Captain Bracken. He was extremely tough on us and issued gigs for the slightest infraction. We were required to walk them off on the quadrangle of Tuskegee Institute—one hour for each gig, usually on Sundays after church services. Sometimes it caused us to lose our weekend passes entirely.

After chapel the other cadets could drop in on the lab of the renowned George Washington Carver "to talk with a genius." Dryden found him to be "a gentle, brown-skinned man with a high-pitched voice and a friendly, sunny, manner."

Watson:

Two-thirds of the second class washed out. Some were good pilots, but they were victims of the quota.

Lang Caldwell had finished all the requirements, but the night before graduation he was told, "You're not going to graduate tomorrow." Obviously, they had counted the numbers and decided someone's got to go. The whole cadet corps was shocked. I understood he went to medical school and he's still quite bitter about it, and I can understand why.

Only three of the original 11 graduated—Jamison, Brooks, and Dryden. It may have been the smallest graduating class in the history of the Air Corp. Just one hour before graduation, they were ordered to report to the theater for the ceremony. No time for guests to attend. Mrs. Drew was the only witness.

Lowenberg wouldn't even shake hands.

Nevertheless, Dryden wrote, "the highlight of my entire life, even up to now, was receiving my wings. I've never had such euphoria before or since as I did that day."

He caught the train to New York with his shiny new wings and bars. At Pennsylvania Station, someone told him, "Boy, pick up my bags."

Class #3, May 20

Bernard Knighten was the son of a bricklayer from Tulsa and graduated from high school in St. Louis, the same school that produced two other Tuskegee Airmen, Jim McCullin and the flamboyant Wendell Pruitt. "Pruitt had two gorgeous sisters," Knighten said, "I used to go around with the older one."

Knighten graduated from Dillard University, majoring in "football and social science," but the only job he could find was as a Pullman car waiter on the Chicago-Los Angeles run.

He recalled having a drink in a Chicago bar when the radio announced that Negroes were going to be admitted to a new flying cadet program. "I had never been in an airplane," he said, "I had never touched one and had no real desire to fly." But he took the exam anyway. He also put in for law school and divinity school, to cover all bets. When he got home from his next road trip, there were three letters waiting, accepting him into law school, the seminary, and the aviation cadets. He picked the cadets.

"Somebody up there really hated me."

Most of us had never been inside an airplane before we got down to Tuskegee. My first ride was the first time I had been in an airplane.

We had a little feud going between the northern boys and the southern boys. We called them 'Bandanna Heads' because they wore headbands in the cotton fields. I don't know what they called us.

"Knighten was a funny fellow, a funny fellow," C.C. Robinson remembered. "Happy-go-lucky. Liked women."
Jamison smiled:

Another non-soldier like me. He'd take out the band that made his dress hat stiff, then crumple the hat. We'd have dress parade, and he'd look the sloppiest, even when he was trying to look like a soldier. Davis tried his best to make a soldier out of him, but he was wild, undisciplined. He was a brainy guy, though, and he did have good flying skills.

Even the fun-loving Knighten stayed on base and kept his nose in the books:

If you went downtown the police would throw you in jail. I didn't like jail.
One day flying the Stearman biplane I got lost, but I didn't panic. I looked for a big level field, set the airplane down before I ran out of gas, and got out to congratulate myself.
The schoolhouse nearby declared a recess and the teacher lined the students up and brought them to the field. Within minutes, the school kids were all over the airplane, standing on the fabric wings, pulling on the struts and kicking the tires. I certainly was not going to tell those white kids in Alabama that they couldn't do this. So when the sheriff arrived, I quietly told him that this was Uncle Sam's property, and he made them all move away.
After I removed my goggles and helmet, he asked me, "Boy, where you from?" I told him I was born in Tulsa, OK. He beamed, "I knowed it!" Then he turned to the crowd: "It's all right, folks, he's Indian. I could tell by his high cheek bones."

Dryden said, "The Eel" made himself into "one of the 99th's best pilots in everybody's opinion."
Lee Rayford of Washington, DC was tall for a fighter pilot and "the most handsome of all the original 99th," Dryden said. "The women were just wild about handsome flying boys with silver wings and glib talk." Jamison:

He was the lover-boy. You never would pick him for a soldier; he was strictly a civilian in uniform. The life of the party, loved to party, a lot of fun to be around. And a damn good pilot. In the evening at the bar, he'd get the stick in his hand and show what he'd do to this man or that man.

Knighten recalled him as a "happy-go-lucky poker-playing guy. We called him 'General,' because he was kind of chubby."

✦ ✦ ✦

Sherman White, Knighten's roommate, from Montgomery, Alabama, had been Jamison's best friend at the University of Chicago and married a fellow student. White and Jamison signed up for CPT together:

> The instructor wanted to check our coordination, so he had us drive a car. Sherman didn't know how! He bluffed his way through. He learned to fly before he could drive.

"A lot of guys didn't have a car in those days," his roommate, Knighten said. "I never had a car, and I had no prospects of getting a car."

One class behind, Spann Watson called White "an easy-going, nonchalant man. I used to get on edge, and Sherman would say, 'Hey, Spann, calm down, calm down, it'll be all right, calm down.'"

Dryden remembered "White's mischievous smile as he took money from someone at the pool table."

"White was the most uncoordinated man," Knighten chuckled. "He couldn't even march. In a parade one head would be bobbing up and down at the wrong time—it was always White."

Only four cadets—Knighten, Rayford, White, and George Knox—went on to graduate. Knighten recalled:

In the first three classes, only 12 students out of 30 finished. To the students, this was proof that the Air Force was not in a hurry to form a black squadron.

"It was such an expensive waste," said Jamison. "There were a lot of good pilots who didn't make it." Some may have been washed out because they were too big for fighter planes.

"The little runts like me went to fighters," Dryden smiled. White cadets could go to the Air Transport Command or to bombers. "We couldn't."

Class #4, July 3

B ECAUSE of all the washouts and the urgent need for pilots after Pearl Harbor, Colonel Noel Parrish, the director of training, insisted that the fourth class be made up mostly of CPT graduates. They skipped the pre-flight and primary flight phases and went directly into basic flight training.

Two were former civilian instructors at Tuskegee—Jim Wiley and Bill Campbell. His fellow cadet, Spann Watson, called Campbell "the top pilot in our class—in the whole 99th."

Watson himself acquired a reputation for being outspoken, but as a cadet, "he was the quietest man you'd want to see," Knighten said. "He'd just sit there and grin. He got to be outspoken later on."

Before long Spann became "a man of strict opinions about the right thing to be done," Dryden said. "He insisted on meeting the top standards and was critical of people who were goofing off." As Clarence Jamison added, "He just wouldn't take any crap."

Spann could not tolerate injustice and spent his life swimming upstream against it. "We could all look up to Spann as a model," Wiley said. "He was determined. But he didn't restrain himself at all times and became a bit obnoxious to the leaders. If you're going to get ahead, you have to play ball."

The previous graduates doubled as instructors. "Custis was a pain in the ass," Watson said with his customary bluntness. "Every little thing was wrong. But a great guy, and became a great leader."

Spann developed a personality conflict with Roberts, who almost washed him out—one more pink slip and Spann would have been gone.

> I was one of the top pilots, a professional from the word go. I thought we were doing a noble thing, and I went in thinking that everyone is going to do 1,000% to prove we can be first-class and can compete with any squadron in the world.
>
> But it didn't exactly work that way. Other people had personal ambitions and didn't mind trying to eliminate someone who was a threat to them. Blacks have intrigues and cliques just like whites do. The 99th was rife with cliques from the beginning.

Davis remained above such intrigues. "There were a lot of problems he was unaware of," Wiley said.

Charlie Hall

HALL hailed from Indiana.
Spanky Roberts:

> He was afflicted with a rare disease—he didn't know fear. A comparatively small individual, but an outstanding athlete. I've talked to people who went to high school with him, and they said he threw his body into 240-pounders without thought.

Hall had been one of Wiley's students in basic. "A very good student, caught on quickly," Wiley said proudly. "I soloed Charlie Hall."
Lemuel Custis:

> Hall was an outgoing fellow. Not like me—I'm an old stick in the mud. Hall was very ebullient. If you were around him for five minutes, you'd get to like him. Very jolly. Probably his only weakness was he'd bend the elbow a little too much.

"Charlie Hall was a great one," Jamison said, "got along with everybody. Get him at a party, get him high, he'd start singing dirty songs, and he knew all the verses. A life-of-the party guy, down to earth."

Willie Ashley was from Sumter, SC, a graduate of Hampton University. "He was a very comical fellow." his close friend and fellow South Carolinian, Robinson, recalled: "He knew everyone, and everyone liked him. He liked to have a good time, but was a very religious fellow. He was an only child, and he'd get attention—you know how only children are."

"A real down-home country boy," was Knighten's thumbnail sketch. "Old home-spun humor. Liked to run around, dance, always full of fun, knew a thousand stories."

Watson agreed:

> He was the funniest man I ever did see—a clown and a comic. Everyone loved him. What's he going to do next? And no woman got by him; he'd say, "Who's going to fix me up?" You had to lock him up. But when you got him in an airplane, he was a different guy; he'd fly like hell.

Erwin Lawrence, another Clevelander, was just the opposite. "Very quiet," said Purnell. "If he stood in the corner, you wouldn't know he was there. He didn't have the knack of being a hail-fellow. His mind was on flying."

"Very handsome," said Dryden, "squeaky clean, never swore, very reliable."

"Tall and good-looking, quiet and efficient," Robinson said.

Wiley liked Lawrence and was best man at his wedding. Jamison also thought highly of him: "Quiet, personable, loved the military. Determined and courageous, a typical 99th fighter pilot. Colonel Davis liked him quite a bit."

Graham "Peepsight" Smith "was a real country boy, laughed at all our jokes," Knighten said. He stood barely five feet tall and could hardly see over the gunsight in his plane, hence his nickname. (He also "looked like he was blinking all the time," Wiley said.) Smith carried a variety of cushions to increase his height in the cockpit.

Faythe McGinnis from Muskogee, Oklahoma was "very good-looking," Wiley said, "a fine type person, with a lot of personality and flying ability."

Percy Sutton, a New Yorker, was another CPT alumnus. He shared a barracks room with Wiley and Campbell—they gave him an upper bunk. "He was very jovial," Wiley said, but just an "OK" pilot.

Lou Purnell was anxious to get into more advanced flying.

> I heard there was a course in stunt flying—we called it aerobatics—with a heavier plane and hotter horsepower, a bi-plane called a Waco. But being black, the only damn place we could fly this plane was at Tuskegee. I left with nothing but my bus ticket in my pocket and didn't know how the hell I was going to survive, but luckily I got a job in the laundry at the Institute.

There was a big group of cadets on campus, and we'd look at those guys, going to and from their classes. I'd sneak around the building and sit under the window. I absorbed the whole course by sitting under the window and listening.

Training was rigid. The red clay of Alabama clung to our feet like Elmer's Glue. If we got our shoes muddy, we were told to fall out of formation and come back in ten minutes with those shoes cleaned and shiny.

Our washout ratio was 60%. At Maxwell Field up the road, where the white pilots trained, it was 15 to 30%. But it made us good pilots. It gave us the feeling that, hell, if we could get through, we must be damn good.

One annoyance the cadets faced was obtaining whiskey for their cadet club. Pat Evans barricaded the roads from the wet counties, "but we got around that," Purnell said. Every Saturday they made a training flight to Columbus Georgia, where they stocked up at the Fort Benning liquor store. "Pat Evans never knew the difference."

Purnell's biggest scare was not in the air but on the ground.

I have a knack for imitating, and it nearly got me in trouble. A week before graduation, we were off on gunnery practice in Florida. One morning, when things were quiet, I got outside the tents and in a big Lowenberg voice ordered all the men to get over here on the double. I got good response, because everyone thought I was Lowenberg.

When we returned to Tuskegee, one of the officers told him, "I've got a man who can really imitate you."

One day at lunch Lowenberg came to the cadet mess hall. Naturally we all jumped to attention. He said he wanted to see Aviation Cadet L.R. Purnell immediately after the meal in his office. You can imagine how I felt, just three days before graduation: I thought it meant washout. I choked through the rest of the meal.

When I got to his office, he made me come to a brace [attention] and kept me in it for about five minutes. It was a hot day in June, there was no air-conditioning at that time, and sweat was running down my face and the small of my back. Then he popped the question: "I heard you can imitate me. This is a command performance. Start your act."

I couldn't move a muscle.

At last he said, "At ease," and his voice changed, and he was really one of the nicest guys. We talked about where I was from, how I felt about the training, and whether I was ready for combat. Then he dismissed me. I went around to the side of his office to recuperate, because my legs had given out.

Parrish was right about selecting CPT grads. Of 28 who started, 14 graduated on May 30, 1942—Campbell, Hall, Lawrence, McGinnis, Purnell, Watson, Wiley, Ashley, George Bolling, Herbert Carter, Herbert Clark, Allen Lane, Graham Mitchell, and Peepsight Smith.

One who washed out was Sutton. He remained in the 99th as an intelligence officer and after the war bought Harlem's Apollo Theater, became a millionaire and the borough president of Manhattan.

McGinnis was on his bunk, waiting to get married that afternoon, when they needed one more flier to make up an eight-ship flight. He said he'd go. But, as tail-end in the flight, when the group went into a loop, he didn't come out. He was killed on his wedding day. McGinnis may have blacked out, Knighten believed, or he may have misjudged how much space he had left.

He was the first Tuskegee officer to die. His fiancee "was a sad picture for a long time," Watson said.

Although the white flying instructors were excellent, Carter said, "Those eyes were always upon you. It was very easy to become almost paranoid."

Roberts believed some of the students were nervous flying with whites:

> One cadet, from Louisiana or Alabama, had been taught all his life not to perform with whites. He just couldn't land with his white instructors. But he was able to relax with me. With me in the plane with him, he shot perfect landings all day long.

Wiley shrugged:

> Some students I had to wash out. That was the time to catch them before they faced worse consequences later. But it was not an easy decision to make. One guy was just about ready to be sent back. A nice guy, but not a good pilot, and Spanky was about to ground him.
>
> He came to me and said, "Save me. I don't want to go home in disgrace, I know I can do better."

"OK," Wiley said, "you fly with me for awhile." He flew Wiley's wing, "and finally I got him to the point where he could turn right with me." He went on to graduate and flew many combat missions with the 99th.

As each class graduated, the new pilots checked out in battle-weary, oil-leaking P-40s from the renowned "Flying Tigers" of the China Theater. They were sometimes called "Flying Coffins."

"There was no two-seater version," said Howard Baugh. "They just put you in the cockpit, the instructor knelt on the wing, you read the characteristics of the airplane and studied the cockpit, then he said, 'Go.'"

On his first flight, Custis said:

> I was a bundle of nerves. It was a heavier plane than our trainer, with much more power. It was a hot day, and the plane had an air-cooled engine, so until you got off the ground, it was like being enclosed in an oven.

Alexander Jefferson, one of the smallest pilots to go through Tuskegee, remembered:

> That old girl had a bad habit of pulling to the left as you were going down the runway for a takeoff. I would have to stand on the rudder pedal with all my 112 pounds to keep her from running off into the woods. The nerves in my leg would be quivering like crazy as we fought it out. I was determined to be a pilot, and this clumsy old plane was just as determined that I wouldn't.

With its narrow landing gear, the P-40 was susceptible to ground loops on landing. "You had to work on every landing; there was no relaxing," Sheppard said. "And chopping the throttle or advancing the engine produced all kinds of torque to keep you busy in the cockpit."

Mac Ross had a close call on his first flight in one. Smoke began streaming from his engine, and the others called to him to jump, which he finally did, and became the first black officer to join the so-called "Caterpillar Club." He sweated that "maybe they'll start saying Negroes can't fly after all;" however, he was cleared of pilot error.

Practicing a power stall, Howard Baugh pulled the nose up. But instead of stalling, the plane climbed to 13,000 feet, then suddenly stalled, went into a spin, and "threw me around the cockpit. It took me 6,000 feet to recover. It was a damn good thing I had a lot of altitude."

Jerome Edwards' engine quit on take-off. He plowed into some trees, banged his head against the gun-sight, and was killed instantly. His best friend, Baugh accompanied the body home to his wife and two children

Still, Sheppard insisted:

> The P-40 was a good aircraft. Tough. I was a prop specialist, and it had an electrically controlled prop. You could change the pitch on the blade with a control in the cockpit.

Said Custis: "I found out that if I followed the advice, 'Fly the airplane, don't let it fly you,' I mastered it. It was really like any other airplane, and I had no more trouble with it."

Tuskegee had now turned out almost enough pilots to form a squadron and needed only a few more. Class Five produced them.

Class #5, August 5

WILLIE Fuller was "a big, bearish fellow," said Roberts. "He was probably our tallest pilot, because fighter pilots were generally smaller."

On December 6, 1941, Fuller was in Florida playing in the Orange Blossom football classic against Florida A&M. On the way back home Sunday morning, December 7, he heard of Pearl Harbor. "The next day I made up my mind that I would see about getting into the Air Corps."

Meanwhile, he had his commercial and instructor's ratings. He was on the field in Tuskegee for a check-out ride to become a civilian instructor when a sergeant hailed him: "I just got authority to accept you into the Air Corps."

Said Fuller: "I dropped my flying suit and took off."

John "Jack" Rogers was what Watson called "Radical":

> We were the "radicals" in the squadron. When something was not as good as it should be, Jack and I would speak up—he'd say he'd kick your butt. He and I got the lowest appraisal ratings, although he got along a hell of a lot better than I did.

Like White and Jamison, Rogers had taken CPT at the University of Chicago. Jamison:

> He was my closest friend. I got married when I graduated from Tuskegee, didn't wait for payday, and borrowed a couple hundred dollars from John. He always had money—and he was just a cadet.

Leon Roberts, a dentist's son from Mobile, was the youngest pilot to join the 99th. His brother, Leon, was a mechanic with the same unit. "Leon was a ladies man—oh, a ladies man!" Robinson laughed. "That's what he lived for. He lived well, and he played a lot."

But, said Dryden:

> You could always count on him. Call on Leon, and he'd do it. One day on a training mission Roberts flew under some wires and cut off the top of his rudder. We shouted, "Bail out! Bail out!" But he flew back and landed. That took quite some airmanship.

Not all were so lucky.

Wilmeth Sidat-Singh was a football and basketball star at Syracuse University, the fore-runner of Jim Brown and O.J. Simpson, who followed him. A light-skinned Negro, Singh had been adopted by his step-father, an East-Indian doctor, hence his name. He went to Syracuse on a basketball scholarship, but when a coach saw him throw a football 60 yards, Singh suddenly became a two-sport man.

Most fans thought Singh was East-Indian until he arrived for a game at the University of Maryland, and the local black paper proudly revealed that he was actually a Negro. The hosts demanded that Syracuse drop him from the squad. A dark-skinned "Hindu" had been acceptable. Syracuse might have protested, or refused to play, but it didn't, and lost a close game. The next year the schools met in Syracuse, with Singh in the lineup and won by a lopsided score.

When Syracuse upset heavily-favored Cornell, Grantland Rice, the most famous sportswriter of his day, was moved to report it in verse:

> The shadows of night were falling fast,
> And the score was ten-to-zero,
> When Sidat-Singh, the wizard, passed
> Six times to become a hero.

More prosaically, Rice called Singh better than Sammy Baugh, who went on to become a legend in the new National Football League, but of course the NFL was closed to Singh. He was pounding a beat as a policeman in Washington DC when he reported to Tuskegee for cadet training.

In advance training at Like Huron in Michigan, Singh's P-40 suddenly lost power and plunged into the water. He bailed out but was entangled in his parachute and drowned.

Meantime the pilots waited and waited for orders—and flew and flew. There was a lake near Tuskegee with two bridges and a power line about 20 feet off the ground.

Knighten:

> Yes, I've been under that wire. That was part of the fun. We'd go under both bridges, under the power line, make a loop, and go under them again. The propeller would spray water on the fishing boats. We were dumb. We didn't know it was dangerous. We were young college men just having fun, just stupid. If we'd had any brains in our heads, we'd have quit. How we got through, I'll never know.

Walter Lawson was flying with Richard Dawson in an AT-6 advanced trainer when he tried to fly under a bridge and didn't make it. Dawson was killed; Lawson was found wandering, dazed, in the woods, the origin of his nickname, "Ghost."

Earl King rounded out the class, and the 99th had its full complement.

Davis takes command

AUGUST 24, 1942. Davis was promoted from captain to lieutenant colonel and appointed commander of the 99th Fighter Squadron, the first black squadron in U.S. history.

When secretary of War Henry Stimson visited Tuskegee, the Negro press thought it strange that he had not had his picture taken with Davis, so a photo was quickly pasted next to one of Stimson and released to the press.

Davis may not have been a natural seat-of-the-pants flier ("he made nice, slow easy turns," one of his officers would say), but all agree that as a commander he drove the unit to achieve.

Wiley:

> Davis just commanded attention. Whenever he came into the room, you knew B.O. was there; everyone became silent, no one said anything. He still has that bearing. He reminds me of what I think MacArthur was like.

Davis was rather aloof, said Jamison.

> A typical West Pointer, spit and polish. It was hard to get close to him. I knew Davis from Cleveland; my family lived down the street from his. But you wouldn't know it from our relationship in the 99th. Now he's a little warmer than he was then. But he was what we needed at the time.

"He went strictly by the book," nodded Fuller. "He also played a mean hand of poker."

"Davis was respected by most and hated by some," said Felix Kirkpatrick, another poker buddy, "but it was because of the discipline he exacted that we were able to make the record we did."

Charles Bussey, who would later serve under him, called Davis "the most positive commander I ever had. He stressed the awful price of failure. He brooked none, and he got none."

Behind his back, he was "the Whip," "the Thin Man," or, usually, the time-honored Army appellation, "the Old Man."

Hannibal Cox, another future pilot, said:

> You had a bunch of young and well-educated blacks to control and discipline, which was not easy to do. He did it. He was the epitome of an officer and a role model for us. He was the single greatest influence in my life, other than my father.

Roberts worshipped him:

> Davis was very bright, ambitious, and self-controlled, which in my opinion was a result of his Academy days. His intensity to achieve made many people think of him as a martinet. That made him, to the outside observer, cold, and he's not; he's a very warm person. Many people have tried to build a competition between B.O. Davis and me, but I loved him with all my heart.

Davis led every major raid while he was in Europe. Usually we alternated, but if there were two biggies in a row, he'd take both of them. He considered the place of a leader to be out front.

I don't name my heroes in order, but if I did, he would be number one.

Davis named Roberts his second in command. Purnell admired Roberts greatly: "the kind of guy you would go to hell with and for."

"A regular guy," nodded Fuller. "He knew his onions about flying."

Jamison agreed that Roberts was "a good leader," but added, "I wasn't cut out to be a military man at that time, and Spanky loved the rigid discipline."

He took up pipe smoking, Knighten said, to give himself an aura of maturity with the younger pilots.

Erwin Lawrence was named assistant operations officer. Herbert Carter doubled as a pilot and squadron maintenance officer.

The pilots were divided into four Flights of four planes each under Custis, Wiley, Jamison, and Hall.

Watson flew with Jamison. "He was a real decent individual and a good leader," though Spann criticized him for being "too soft on going to bat against some of the knuckle heads we had."

The pilots had dogfights among themselves, and rivalries were strong. Jamison:

> My Flight, C Flight, didn't have all the flair of some of the other guys, but we told 'em, "We'll kick your butts, A Flight or B Flight." Whenever we went up, I'd head for a P-40 and dogfight. I'd take on everyone—Bill Campbell, Charlie Hall. Hall was a tough fighter. In dogfights, we'd go right down to the ground together, I couldn't get on his tail, and he never got on mine.
>
> Just like Wiley—I couldn't get the best of him either. Wiley didn't get nearly the recognition some of the other guys got.

The 99th probably had the most training of any unit in the Air Force. They were ready to go, but the War Department wasn't ready for them. No overseas commander wanted them. Liberia on the west coast of Africa was most often mentioned as a posting—the Liberian Task Force was a labor-oriented black organization.

While white units were flying off to the wars, the 99th trained. And trained. And trained. They trained for a year, Jamison said, and went through three training cycles:

> Until we were bored. We had several hundred hours, which would have been unusual for white pilots before going into combat. We would try all kinds of maneuvers—snap rolls, whip stalls, spins, etc. We were pretty good.

Watson:

> White pilots were being rushed overseas soon after graduation. They didn't even get five weeks of training. After they graduated, they were gone.
>
> But they wanted to make a service unit out of the 99th. The black papers said, "We want our boys to get over there like everyone else. We're Americans, and we want to fight just like everybody else."

But the 99th had one problem the white units didn't: They didn't have experience. "We didn't have anyone to teach us combat," Dryden said. "We just did the best we could, based on what we thought we should do."

For Knighten, it wasn't all work and no play:

> Ashley and myself would sneak out of the barracks and run to Montgomery. As soon as that sun went down, we were out the back window. We were going somewhere!"
>
> "Are you out of your mind?" the others asked.
>
> "We might get killed tomorrow, but we're going to have fun tonight."

On weekends they headed for Atlanta and the coeds there.

Not everyone followed them, Knighten said. "Jamison was quiet and studious, one of the most studious guys I knew. You'd never catch him sneaking out like us."

The morning after a big Christmas party in '42, the men were ordered into the air for gunnery practice. They were flying again on new year's day. It was hard enough to find the camouflaged runway when you were cold sober, Dryden groused. "The sneaky bastards! Even in combat they wind down for Christmas and respect the Lord's birthday."

Meanwhile, the black squadron remained a white elephant.

The 92nd Division

WHILE the airmen waited, the Army ground forces were training two black infantry divisions, the 92nd and 93rd. The latter fought with the French in World War I and wore a French helmet as a shoulder patch. It included the old Indian-fighting 24th and 25th Infantry Regiments. The division was sent to the Pacific, but there was no intention to fight it; rather, the Division was broken up and assigned piecemeal to white units to be used as laborers, security, and truck drivers.

The 92nd, the "Black Buffaloes," trained in Fort Huachuca in the Arizona desert, possibly the worst hell-hole of all the Army's posts. Their commander, Major General Ned Almond, was not well-liked, and the unit developed severe morale problems, which General Ben Davis, Sr. was sent to try to solve. However, the problems were still acute when the division embarked for Italy in 1944.

A black cavalry unit was sent to North Africa and was also broken up for labor battalions. Other African-American GIs built the Burma Road to China and the Alcan Highway to Alaska and later drove the Red Ball Express trucks in Europe.

Negro nurses, one percent of the nurse corps, didn't have black casualties to attend to, so they were sent to care for German POWs. Some 4,000 African-American women joined the WACs; while white WACs typed, black WACs worked in the laundries and mess halls.

Things weren't any better on the civilian front. North American Aircraft Company, makers of the P-51 Mustang fighter, had a policy of not hiring blacks, except as janitors. (Ironically, the P-51 was the plane the Red Tails would fly to their greatest successes.)

When an ammunition ship exploded at Port Chicago, California, 300 dock workers were killed, most of them African-Americans. Survivors who refused to return to the job were court-martialed for mutiny and were defended by Thurgood Marshall, later a Justice of the Supreme Court.

Finally, in March 1943 the 99th received orders to North Africa. On March 25 the squadron went up for its final flight before going overseas. Earl King's plane hit a power line and crashed into a lake, killing him.

Jim McCullin of the sixth class replaced him. Although small, he had starred in football at Knighten's old high school in St. Louis. "He was quite an athlete," said Watson. "A short man, but he had tremendous strength in his hands and shoulders, the type of guy you'd want on your side in a fight."

Overseas

APRIL 1. The Airmen held one last dance before filing onto their train the next morning to begin their historic mission. The recently married Allen Lane arrived on crutches with his wife, having broken his leg on their wedding night, a source of much ribbing from his buddies.

Dryden:

> Some nurses had arrived by overnight train from New York that same day. One of them had graduated from Harlem School of Nursing and had volunteered as an Army nurse that same week. She was tired and going to retire, but the Chief Nurse told her, "Our boys are going overseas, and everyone on base is going to the dance at the Officers' Club," so she went with them.

A friend told us, "You two New Yorkers ought to meet each other."
It was love at first sight.

Jackie was "petite and cute with a figure that her uniform could not completely conceal." They danced dreamily, "slow-dragging" to Duke Ellington's music. "I flew without wings" until an announcement abruptly ordered all the men to return to barracks for their pre-dawn departure.

Just before they left, Colonel Parrish stressed, "You have the future of the race on your backs. If you don't succeed, there will be a catastrophic change in the country's attitude. So do well!"

Wives and girlfriends were at the railhead. Jackie was there of course. Dryden wrote:

> We left after a week of high emotion, because we were feeling the grim certainty that some of us weren't coming back...The train whistle split the cold night air, and a locomotive came round the bend in a cloud of steam.

One last kiss, and they were off.

Jamison's brother, an Army lieutenant colonel, was also boarding a train for the 92nd Division in Italy. They passed each other somewhere in North Carolina.

The 99th crossed the Atlantic on a converted luxury liner at the height of the German submarine war campaign. "Where's our escort?" Elmer Jones asked nervously. "Oh, we don't have an escort," a crewman replied. "This is a fast ship and we sail a zigzag course."

As Commanding Officer of the only combat unit on board, Davis was named troop commander, the first time an African-American officer ever commanded white troops. However, on their first morning at sea, the pilots walked on deck to find a rope separating them from the white troops. "But it didn't worry us," said Purnell. "We were on our way to defend our country. We were flying. We had done the impossible."

Davis eagerly looked forward to the test ahead.

> The coming war represented a golden opportunity for blacks, one that could not be missed...We owned a fighter squadron, it was something that would have been unthinkable only a short time earlier. It was all ours.

5

Combat

North Africa

APRIL 24. The 99th arrived in Casablanca, on the Atlantic coast of Morocco, marching off the ship in pink and green dress uniforms "like a proud squadron," Jamison said.

It was their first look at a foreign land, and Lou Purnell remarked on the "brown, chocolate soil" and "deep azure blue skies." They arrived in a city of refugees, many of them Jewish. Spann Watson called it the cleanest city he'd ever seen, with an Arab at every corner to keep the block clean.

The fliers had all seen the movie, *Casablanca*, so they wrote to their wives and girlfriends that they had been to "Rick's place." "I don't know how the censors let us get away with it," Watson smiled.

The Allies had only recently driven the Germans out of North Africa and were preparing to invade Sicily when Davis and Roberts reported to General John K. Cannon, commander of the Northwest (Africa) Training Command. The general gave them what Roberts called "a very cordial and warm" welcome.

Then they proceeded to their airfield at the religious city of Fez. The pilots shouldered full packs and began a ten-mile hike. "We should have been infantrymen," Purnell grumbled. Some were luckier; they rode in a "rickety old" 40-and-eight train—40 men or eight mules to a car—just as Roberts' father had done in France in World War I.

They arrived at Onediger, "the River of Snakes," near Fez where a former Nazi airfield was still littered with wrecked Messerschmitt fighters.

They were invited to the mayor's house for dinner, where they met Josephine Baker, the ex-patriate African-American singer who had made a career on the French musical stage and had fled France after the Nazis marched in.

Fuller was impressed that there were no racial inhibitions. Frenchmen and Moroccans walked into the room and kissed her on the cheek. She did the translating, and when she grew tired, Colonel Davis took over. Later, performing at a former sultan's palace before thousands of persons from all branches of the service, she threw a single flower into the audience while soldiers climbed over each other to get it. "It was quite a contrast to the

American South," Willie Fuller thought. "I began asking myself several questions."

The airmen were only the second black unit in the Army in North Africa. The 450th Anti-Aircraft battalion had fought with Eisenhower's ground troops. One GI, boxer Kid Chocolate, lost both legs.

The other white units were supposed to come over to conduct indoctrination and training. "But I only saw them one time," Bill Campbell said.

> We were strictly on our own, off by ourselves. Enlisted men drew rations and gasoline from fuel dumps without any problem; they got along with the white sergeants quite well. But most of us never saw anyone but black people, so we didn't come in contact with that [racial] sort of thing.

Davis remembered the stay there as pleasant. Some white officers from the ship stopped to say hello, and the pilots of the 99th and the neighboring white fighter outfit met in sports contests on the ground and in friendly "dogfights" in the air and strolled the streets of the town without incident.

Meanwhile, Purnell had found a treasure, a bottle of "America's favorite soft drink" and deposited it in the squadron safe awaiting a proper occasion to open it.

The men also received brand new P-40s. The plane could not out-climb the German Messerschmitt 109 nor the Focke-Wulf 190, and did not have their speed or altitude. But it could out-dive them and—very important—was superior on the turns. It could take a lot of punishment, which was important in ground support missions, and it had plenty of firepower—six .50-caliber machine guns, and a 1,000-pound bomb load. It wasn't a long-range plane, it was designed to come and go, like the 109.

Flip Cochran

WITH the new planes came a visit by a veteran P-40 pilot from the famous "Flying Tigers" in China, Lieutenant Colonel Philip Cochran, better known as "Flip Corkin" of the "Terry and the Pirates" comic strip about the war in China.

Purnell recalled Cochran pulling up in a jeep, without a proper uniform, and demanding, "Where's Davis?"—a breach of etiquette for a major visiting a lieutenant colonel. "Go in there and get Davis and tell him to get out here."

Roberts, however, had an entirely different impression:

> Philip Cochran was one of the finest things that happened to us. He was the prototype of what fighter pilots looked like—around my height,

five-foot-nine, sort of wiry but solidly built. Flip moved in with us, slept with us, ate with us, flew with us, talked with us, spent 24 hours a day with us for a week, and poured out information, lore, understanding, like a coffee pot that you turn to pour out coffee.

One of the top dive bomb experts of the war, Cochran called his new charges "you young birds" and put them through a rigid flight exam— maneuvers, formation flying, and aerobatics—and pronounced them a natural-born group of dive bombers.

Unfortunately, sighed Purnell, "that stayed with us. All our work after that was dive bombing. But we didn't care. We became very proficient at it."

Cochran taught them that if a pilot is caught in the sky alone, he should "clear his tail," that is, make a quick tight turn to be sure no one is back there. In the States the instructors had taught them to fly in V-formation, but because the enemy planes were much faster, Cochran told them to fly in a line abreast, so they could check each other's tails.

In case of attack from the rear, the leader called, "Break right (or left)," and each pilot "cranked his plane around 180 degrees in the tightest turn he could make" until the plane shuddered—but not too tight or it would stall or spin. Now they were all facing the enemy, each with six .50-caliber guns pointing toward them.

Watson:

> The Germans hated those .50s. The Messerschmitts had 20-mm can-nons, but they were too slow. In the heat of battle you could see the shell leaving the plane like a Roman candle, they didn't seem to be moving at all.

Cochran imparted another lesson:

> If you push your rudder, you look like you're flying straight, but you're actu-ally slipping to the side, not much, but just enough to fool the anti-aircraft guns on the ground. If they don't compensate, they miss you.

Cochran died in Pennsylvania about 1980. "No fanfare, no nothing," Fuller said. But to the pilots of the 99th, "he was one hell of a guy."

"He was like a nova," said Roberts. "He flashed on our horizon, affected us tremendously, and was gone. All I can say is, thank God for Flip Corkin— Colonel Philip P. Cochran."

Spike Momyer and the 33rd

MAY 31. The 99th boarded trains again and moved 1,000 miles east, across Algeria, to Cap Bon on the coast of Tunisia, barely 100 miles from the coast of Nazi-occupied Sicily. They were attached to the 33rd Fighter Group under Colonel William "Spike" Momyer.

An unsmiling, imposing man from Muskogee Oklahoma, Momyer had arrived six months earlier with 75 P-40s, of which 21 crashed while landing. When they went into combat in January, they quickly knocked down eight enemy planes. But, spurred by the triumph, Momyer sent them out too far from base, where the Germans were stronger. Losses were so heavy that in February the 33rd was taken out of the war to await fresh pilots and planes.

By the time the 99th arrived, Momyer had eight enemy planes to his personal credit, four in one day. When Davis and Roberts reported, he didn't return their salutes or stand up or say welcome, Roberts said. He merely looked at them and barked, "Well, I hope you've got replacements; I've been losing a lot of my squadron commanders."

Said Roberts: "His whole attitude spoke his distaste for us, the fact that he didn't want us."

Bernrd Knighten:

> When we first got to North Africa, one Sunday a chaplain came, playing an organ and preaching, and there were four or five people there. Leon Roberts was sitting there with his Bible, the rest of us all in town, running around. We teased him about it.

The party boys—Knighten, Lee Rayford, and Sherman White—"would jump in a jeep and go to Tunis, Knighten said."I didn't want to fly and get killed and not see the world."

MPs arrested them for impersonating officers.

June 2. Four pilots from the 99th—Campbell, Charlie Hall, Jim Wiley, and Clarence Jamison—climbed into their cockpits to fly into combat as wing men to the 33rd. Their assignment: to bomb the enemy island of Pantelleria. The first two, Hall and Campbell, paused at the head of the runway and gunned their engines to the cheers of the other pilots and crews. "I was scared," Campbell admitted later, "but I was determined to stay on my lead's wing if he carried me to the enemy's front door."

Wiley and Jamison were next. Wiley flew the wing for Momyer, who told him curtly: "You all boys, keep up."

"I stuck right with him," Wiley said. "He couldn't get rid of me, though I think he tried."

Jamison's counterpart also told him "get on my wing and stick with me."

"That's all he said. I'm sure I had more flying time than he had. I could handle the plane, no problem." Over the target the lead pilot signaled to follow him down. Jamison stuck so chose that when the other looked back, his eyes popped in surprise:

> When I saw those little black clouds of smoke, just a carpet 4,000 feet below us, it suddenly dawned on me: That was flak—they were *shooting* at me! That's when it really hit me. Until then it had just been an exciting game.

June 4. The first four led their own squadron mates on the identical mission. Each plane carrying 500-pound bombs dove on the targets while red tracer bullets streaked past their canopies "like a river of red sparkles," Dryden remembered his baptism in his book *A-Train*, after the Duke Ellington song: "I didn't have time to get scared." But after pulling up, he suddenly realized, "They were trying to *kill* me!"

When the enemy is on your tail, it is sheer terror, he said. "When you're on his, then it's sheer joy. That's a murderous thought, he admitted, "but war is horrible."

Still, Momyer ridiculed them and tried to embarrass them. He scheduled a briefing, then moved the time up one hour without informing the 99th, so that they walked in when the briefing was almost over.

The First Fight

JUNE 9. The 99th met its first enemy planes. Dryden was leading a patrol—Watson, Willie Ashley, Sidney Brooks, Lee Rayford, and Leon Roberts—in a line abreast when his radio crackled:

"Trooper Leader. Trooper 3 [Roberts] here. Bogies, five o'clock high [unknown planes, right rear]."

The sun blinded Dryden, so he replied: "Watch 'em."

Soon another message: "Several bandits, seven o'clock [enemy, left rear], diving." They were 12 German bombers and 22 fighter escorts.

"Trooper three, call the break!"

"Three here. Break right. NOW."

Six planes wheeled on a dime, flicked their gun switches and gun sights on, and faced the on-rushing enemy.

Dryden:

> When I saw the swastikas, I knew this wasn't play anymore, those Nazi pilots' mission was to kill me. My reaction was, "I'm going to get him first."
> The enemy scattered like quail. So did we, as we all took off after them.

I've been asked if I was ever scared in combat. Before I even saw a German, the thing I worried most about was being chicken, turning and running. I found out something about myself that day: I wasn't a hero, but I wasn't going to turn chicken and run from someone who was obviously trying to kill me. I knew then that, if I was going to run, I was going to run *after* him, not away from him.

Watson:

Willie Ashley lost control and spun out—stalled. When you lose speed, the airplane starts to spin, and he lost 3-4,000 feet. You've got to go down, gun the engine, and pick up speed again. I was his wingman. I could have gone on with the crowd, but I had to stay with him. He recovered, and we climbed back into the fight, but we lost a lot of time.

Back at base Ashley claimed a probable kill, which would have made him the first black to score a victory. However, Watson questioned it. "I personally don't think it was possible, because we were trying to pick up speed and get back to the formation. We were pointing up, we weren't in position to start firing."

Momyer charged that the 99th held their formation well—until the enemy appeared; then they became disorganized, scattered, and showed no discipline. "He lied." said Watson:

There was no white man there who could have told him that, so there was no way he could tell if we had broken up. We certainly went out together, and we certainly came home together. For years we've been refuting that story. Eight German planes attacked us, we turned around and shot them like tigers, and they took off.

Dryden: "Every one of us wanted to be the first to shoot down a German, that's why we took off."

In later days some in the 99th suspected that some white pilots dropped their bombs in the water so their planes would be light and ready in case of aerial attack.

Fuller:

Once or twice the white pilots made slurring remarks. For instance, one day it was pretty cloudy before we got to the target, so the 99th turned back. The next flight, all white fellows, flew through heavy clouds and two of their guys didn't come back. They said something about the fact that we turned around.

But we said it was better not to jeopardize the pilots and hit the targets another day. All our pilots returned; they lost two guys. Frankly, we thought it was unnecessary.

When the 99th flew with white squadrons, they often flew "ass-end Charlie." "That's the guy who gets the most flak," Fuller said. "The ground gunners had more time to zero in and the German planes had more time to get into the air.

June 11. Pantelleria capitulated, thus becoming a footnote to military history. It's a truism of war that artillery and air power can soften a target up, but only infantry can actually take the ground. Pantelleria, however, fell to air assault alone, a historic first.

Colonel J.R. Hawkins, gave the 99th their full credit. He sent "heartiest congratulations." They had met the enemy and borne up well.

Even Secretary of War Stimson called the performance "very creditable."

"We are ready for any assignment," Davis said, "and are anxious to get into the thick of it."

June 18. The bomber leader couldn't find his Initial Point (IP) for the final run over the target and went around again in a big circle.

The 99th pilots looked down and watched the German fighters scrambling to their planes and taking off from their dusty air strips. By the time the 99th got back to the IP, the German fighters were already in the air. The bombers dropped their loads and headed back to Africa.

Knighten:

> That's when all hell broke loose. Somewhere up there, thousands of feet above us, in the sun where we couldn't see them, the Jerries were waiting, and suddenly their cannon bursts and tracer bullets were all over the place. When we turned left after the bomb run, the Messerschmitts came down, and we all turned and shot at them. Each of us went in different directions, chasing the attacking fighters or being chased by them.
>
> I wish I'd been a German with a Focke-Wulf. We were flying airplanes at 280 miles per hour; the Germans were flying 380 miles an hour. We were the defenders:
>
> After the first week in combat, *everyone* was in chapel! When we crossed that bomb line [over enemy territory], we weren't heroes. I guarantee you, every guy was as scared as the next guy.

Sicily

The 324

JUNE 29. At last, to immense mutual relief, the 99th left the 33rd and reported to a new Group, the 324 under Colonel William McNown. Freed from Momyer's grip, the unit finally scored its first victory.

They also moved to Cap Bon on the North African coast in a position to hit Sicily.

Willie Fuller:

> The Italians on Pantelleria had sent up flak, but it wasn't too accurate. But when we started going into Sicily, the guns were manned by Germans, and they put it where they wanted to put it.
>
> They used to try to box us in. You looked at the ground and saw guns winking: two shots in front of you, two behind you, one to the left, one to the right. You're boxed, my friend—look out for the next one. You're flying through it and smell the powder from the first shells. That's close. That's close!

"You gotta be lucky," Knighten said. "You see all those flak bursts around you, one burst is all you need, and—*poof!*—your airplane is disintegrated."

Charlie Hall—the First Victory

JULY 2. Dryden was flying Campbell's wing, a wing-span away, when he saw two bandits coming head-on. "We had to stand and fight," he smiled, "we were too slow to run away."

"Break right!" he called.

Bill must not have heard.

"Break right NOW!" The enemies' undersides are yellow. That means they're the cream of the *Luftwaffe*—"Ooowee! It's balls to the wall." Hard right rudder, the stick in his gut. Steep right climbing turn. Squeeze the trigger. "Tracers show me that some are hitting home." The enemy break off the attack, and Dryden's finds himself alone in the sky.

Cochran's first rule was: clear your tail. Dryden's second rule was "Pray"—he didn't learn that from Cochran.

Rule three: Find a friend. Dryden saw a P-40 below, but it already had two 109s on its tail. "Here's a chance to save a Yank and get two victories." Charlie dove and started spraying bullets. He took aim at the first plane and hit the second ("I never was much good at aerial gunnery").

Then he realized that "I have a tail too" as tracers streamed past his own canopy. Looking over his shoulder, he saw an Italian Macchi fighter with a painted prop that looked like a corkscrew boring toward him.

> I immediately made a tight turn to my right. If he was fool enough to stay there, I would eventually end up on *his* tail. But as I kept looking over my shoulder, first I saw his cockpit canopy, then his nose cannon, then the belly of his aircraft, and I knew he was picking up the lead on me.

Sure enough, he started firing his machine guns, and I saw puffs of smoke coming out of the nose of his propeller. One round of 37-mm cannon hit my wing with a loud bang that shook my plane. I knew I was in trouble.

Dryden began "pinking"—making wild, erratic changes of direction: "If I don't get help, my party's over."

Looking around the sky for some kind of help, I saw that the bombers had already started home, and I could see the tails of the bombers disappearing, but there were still dogfights all over the sky. Then I saw another pilot in the distance. He must have caught sight of me, because he peeled off and in a diving right turn, settles in behind my tormentors, his six .50s blazing.

The unknown rescuer said:

I heard over the radio one of the planes calling for help. I looked out, and there, just below me, was one of our P-40s in a tight turn with German planes turning with him and shooting everything they had. Without thinking, I dove and started shooting. My tracer bullets must have scared them away, because they immediately turned right and climbed back up into the sun.

Dryden waved a thank you:

Then we got jumped in succession by two ME-109s coming up from low altitude. The Focke-Wulf also came back; he had played dead until he saw an opening, then he attacked. My buddy, whoever he was, and I turned into them and fought them off for ten minutes, though it seemed like three hours.

His paladin recalled:

Dryden dove down to the ocean to gain speed and headed home. I started to follow him, but then I realized those Germans were coming back out of the sun, and I was their target! So I was sitting there with four German fighters shooting at me. All I could do was go into a right turn, count the Germans as they dove past me, and then turn back toward Africa and safety.

But the Germans had other ideas. They climbed back up into the sun, and moments later they were coming down again, their machine guns blazing, cannons flashing. How they missed me, I'll never know. So for me it was another tight, tight turn, tracer bullets streaking past me, and counting those swastikas on their planes as they went under my wing and back up into the sun.

Dryden:

> We turn into them, then run for home again. They attack again, and we
> turn into them again. Two steps forward, one step back. An aerial *danse
> macabre.* My rescuer's guns are not firing. Out of ammunition. The Macchi
> rejoins the other two. But they must have been out of bullets or low on gas,
> because they leveled off and headed north, and I dove for Africa and headed
> south.

Should he take a victory roll? On the ground Dryden found a hole as big
as a grapefruit in his left wing. And 29 of his 32 aileron control cables had
been cut. A roll would have snapped the other three, "and I'd have bought
the farm."

The rescuer climbed down and took off his oxygen mask. It was Knighten.
"Any time, Hoss," he grinned. "Glad I was able to help." Their months of
training had paid off, but he admitted, "Lady Luck was riding in both
cockpits."

Amidst the celebration there was bitter news: Sherman White and
Knighten's wing man, Jim McCullin, never returned. "They were just gone.
We don't know what happened to them," Knighten said. All that was found
were two tails sticking up from the sea.

They were the first two combat fatalities suffered by the 99th.

Meanwhile, Charlie "Buster" Hall was making history. As the bombers
came off their run and turned to the left, two enemy fighters dove at them.

As quoted in Charles E. Francis' book, *Tuskegee Airmen:*

> It was my eighth mission and the first time I had seen the enemy close
> enough to shoot at him. I saw two Focke-Wulfs following the bombers just
> after the bombs were dropped, and I headed for the space between the
> fighters and bombers and managed to turn inside the Jerries. I fired a long
> burst and saw my tracers penetrate the second aircraft.
>
> He was turning to the left but suddenly fell off and headed straight into
> the ground. I followed him down and saw him crash in a big cloud of dust.

The 99th had scored its first victory. The fact that it came only four
days after the squadron had been liberated from Momyer is probably not
a coincidence.

But Hall's battle wasn't over yet. Suddenly he saw tracer bullets zooming
past his own nose. Now he was the prey. Two Messerschmitt's were on his
tail. He couldn't outrun them—they were faster than his P-40. So he did
the only thing he could: He turned and charged into them!

The three planes dueled across the sky, each pilot trying to line up a shot
on the other's tail, as Charlie's fuel gauge dropped lower and lower. At last

Hall saw two specks in the distance and headed toward them. Alas, they turned out to be more Germans. Now all four of them attacked in a string as Charlie dodged them. For 20 minutes the duel continued.

Then Hall sighted some American bombers and fighters and headed toward them. But the Americans assumed that he was a German and turned to attack him. He finally reached them by radio, and they flew back to their formation while Hall returned to base with the news of his kill.

U.S. Theater air commander, Carl "Tooey" Spaatz, and the World War I ace, General Jimmy Doolittle, offered congratulations and told him that he had won the Distinguished Flying Cross, the Air Force's top award.

Purnell had another, perhaps even sweeter, award. Lou retrieved the Coke from the safe and from a town 15 miles away got a block of equally precious ice. In the shade of a grove of olive trees the Coke, perhaps the only one in the Mediterranean Theater, "came to a well-deserved end."

It helped win the 99th a Distinguished Unit Citation. General Eisenhower drove over t offer congratulations. But it would be six months before they saw another enemy fighter plane.

July 3. The 99th was back in the sky the next day escorting British bombers of the South African air Force to Sicily. Sifting through the records six decades later, historian William Holton of Tuskegee Airmen Inc., came upon evidence that German fighters came up from below and hit two of the bombers, knocking them out of the sky.

They were the first bombers lost the enemy fighters. In the next 21 months, at least nine more would be documented.

Back to Momyer

July 19. After only three weeks with the 324, the squadron was sent back to Momyer's 33rd. It is not known why, but obviously it was not by mutual request.

Purnell:

> They gave us the dirtiest missions, dive bombing and strafing. Dive bombing, that was my specialty. At least four planes on the ground that I knew blew up as a result of strafing.
>
> We were flying two or three times a day. We'd sit in our aircraft waiting for a red flag to take off, then we'd go up, come down, refuel, and go back up. Some of the guys would make four missions a day.
>
> I've talked to other squadrons, and that was unheard of. But if we broke under the pressure, that would have been all they wanted. We were really under a magnifying glass. They reported the least little discrepancy.

The 99th was kept busy with close air support of the ground forces in Sicily, the moving artillery that went ahead of the troops to soften up the enemy. If they wanted a bomb placed on a target, said Roberts, "there was no question who they picked. We could throw bombs in the windows of a castle." They also strafed tanks on the ground. Roberts:

> The ground troops couldn't get to enemy tanks effectively, and we couldn't do much with our machine gun bullets unless we caught them on paved roads, when we could skip bullets at them.
>
> Bill Thompson, our armament officer, designed a way to put bazookas on the wings to give us a rocket firing capability. I doubt if Bill would bring it up himself, but with rockets we stood a much greater chance. Bill Thompson is the guy who did it. He finished just as we got word from the United States that they had done it back there. But Bill did it in the field.

But aerial victories remained the glamour statistic for fighter units, and white pilots were adding to their totals, while the 99th was not. Watson:

> We stayed in Sicily, hundreds of miles from the battle zone. Colonel Momyer knew it. He waited until all his squadrons had gained victories, then criticized us for not getting any.

"How could you get aerial victories flying ground support?" Purnell grumbled.

Ernie Pyle, America's most popular war correspondent, wrote about the 99th in his best-seller, *Brave Men*:

> Their job was to dive bomb and not get caught up in a fight. The 99th was very successful at this.... The dive bombers' job was to work on the infantry front lines, so they seldom got back to where the German fighters were.

Still, the brass was unhappy. Aerial victories remained the glamour statistic for fighter units, and white pilots were adding to their totals, while the 99th was not.

Hap Arnold dropped in on the 99th headquarters and tongue-lashed both Davis and Roberts. "I never felt so bad in all my life," Roberts said. "I felt like crying, and I could see that Colonel Davis was deeply hurt."

Meanwhile, in Washington a congressional committee released a report that the Curtis-Wright Company, which built the P-40s, had shipped obsolete and defective ones to the 99th.

July 20. Another Tuskegee Airman lost his life in an act of courage.

Master Sergeant Edsel Jett saw a man from another squadron in distress in the water. Though Jett couldn't swim, he jumped in to help and drowned. He was awarded the Soldier's Medal for heroism in a non-combat situation.

Wiley was the first pilot to fly 50 missions. The average white fighter pilot with 50 missions was sent home. But the only replacements for the 99th came out of Tuskegee, which was also sending its graduates to the new 332nd Group, so the 99th had to fly up to 70 missions before they were rotated home.

Replacements

JULY 23. The 99th received its first replacements. They arrived on board a Japanese luxury liner, "Empress of Japan."
Howard Baugh:

Of course we had to be segregated, so the Army gave us a complete barracks to ourselves. Everyone else was jammed in double bunks and lined up to go to the latrine.

On board ship they put us up on the promenade deck, and we had some of the best accommodations on the boat. All the others were sleeping in the hold and queuing up for the wash basin.

After we had been out to sea a couple days, we went on the deck, socializing innocently, and some white nurses joined in the conversation. The powers that be called the ladies in and told them they were not to be seen talking to us. Of course they came and told us right away.

At Casablanca we were on our own to try to find the outfit. No one had ever heard of the 99th. We found out they were up toward Tunis and got some rides on a C-47 [transport plane] and found out they'd moved to Sicily—we had to do this all on our own to get to combat. We joined finally joined them in Sicily in July, '43. I don't know how we happened to find them, but we did.

We were living in pup tents on the ground in an olive orchard and stayed there for most of the summer. Then we moved up on the northern shore of Sicily, near Mount Etna.

A later replacement, C.C. Robinson, said:

Baugh was a sweetheart. Soft-spoken. Would listen to everyone and would give his opinion if it wouldn't hurt anyone. The colonel liked him because he was quiet and efficient. You asked Howard Baugh to do something, it was done!"

Howard joined Wiley's A Flight, along with Peepsight Smith. "Howard

Baugh and I socialized quite a bit," Wiley said. "I bought a Bianchi motorcycle with him. We each paid ten dollars, and we'd go out together and look over the countryside."

Alfonza Davis had graduated first in his class in his Omaha high school and took two years of college before enrolling in Tuskegee, where he finished tops in his class again. He was "A *gung-ho* soldier," Woody Crockett said.

Ed Toppins was "very *gung-ho*," Baugh said. "Very aggressive, almost a daredevil."

Robinson:

> Ed was a brave and gutty guy. Loved to fly and loved to fight. He loved to play poker, and he'd bluff you in a minute with nothing. Money wasn't worth very much, because you couldn't spend it. If we were playing draw, he'd throw $15 in the pot and everyone would fold, and he'd come out with $50.

Once, when the pilots were sunning themselves on the beach, a P-40 buzzed them so low that the propellers kicked up sand in everyone's face as they dashed for their tents. "Everyone knew who it was—Topper."

Wilson "Swampy" Eagleson survived rheumatic fever as a child, and when his father, the football coach at Durham College, North Carolina, bought him a ride in a two-seater barnstorming plane, he was hooked. The next day his father was killed in an automobile crash.

Eagleson went to Spanky Roberts' college, West Virginia State, and took CPT. But when the war began, he ended up in the infantry for two years and was sent to OCS. Cadets feared the summons to the Commandant's office to be told they had washed out. When Wilson got the call, the colonel told him to pack his bags—he was going to Tuskegee.

Harry Sheppard smiled: "'Swampy' Eagleson—I never saw him with his hat on straight. He always had his jacket open and his galoshes open and flopping."

C.C. Robinson:

> We called him "Sloppy Mack," because his clothes were never neatly on him; they were usually a mess. He was what you would call "laid back—*very* "laid back." On the first Sunday of training at Selfridge, an announcer introduced each pilot and his wife at dinner. When he got to Eagleson, he said, "Presenting Sloppy and Mrs. Mack."

But Swampy could fly, as he was to prove before long.

Bob Deiz received his first flying lessons from a stunt pilot in Oregon.

I was so young, they had to wrap blankets around me to make me big enough for the seat belt. But I never had "a blind desire to fly."

My mother taught me to play the piano when I was six. I always tell this story: We had two peach trees in our backyard with no limbs below six feet high. My mother picked them off beating me, because I wouldn't practice. Later I went to the violin, but I couldn't stand it because I had a decent ear and knew when I was wrong. So I took up the trombone; however, we had six trombones in the high school band but no one to play bass horn. I took one home over Thanksgiving and by Christmas I was playing the bass horn.

In college Bob took up the cello and played in both the Portland Symphony and the Oregon University Band.

He also played football with his best friend, Bruce. Deiz was a running guard and he was also state champion in the 100- and 200-yard dashes. Another classmate, Jack Holsclaw, a hotshot third baseman, also went on to become a Tuskegee Airman.

In the summer of '38, Bob enrolled in Oregon's CPT Program. When the war began, the Navy recruited a special Torpedo Squadron from Oregon and Oregon State:

I signed up and was all set to go until someone looked at my application and saw "Negro," so they turned me down. Later the squadron lost every man except one. I said, "The hell with it, tore up my draft card, and went to California. That's where the FBI caught me.

The agent said, "You've got a good record, I'll give you two weeks to go back to Oregon and sign up for something." The head of the draft board, whose son and I had learned to fly together, said, "Bob, they're starting a Negro unit in a place called Tuskegee. If you'll sign up for that, I'll see that you're not called."

By that time I was thinking real slick. I figured, "Well, here are thousands of black guys all over the U.S. who want to fly. It'll be ten years before I'm called." So I went down and volunteered. Damn if they didn't pick me in three months time.

I didn't like going to a segregated unit because I didn't come from that environment. Some guys would sit around and say we had to do twice as much as the other guys to get half the recognition. But I didn't have any drive to prove myself.

I already knew how to fly—and I don't mean flying on Sunday and taking the girls for a ride in your porkpie boots. I had about 300 hours by then, so I didn't have any real trouble, except breaking normal rules and regulations going through the cadet corps. I didn't give a damn like some guys I've seen break down and cry like babies when they washed out.

I didn't particularly care for fighters, but that was the only thing for black pilots to fly in those days.

From the day he arrived, Deiz pestered Davis for a transfer, "because I was never interested in being a fighter pilot." He was continually writing letters to get into a twin-engine outfit. But of course there were none that would take blacks.

Sam Bruce was Deiz's best friend and fellow Oregonian. Sam wss happy as a fighter jock and an enthusiastic party-goer.

Knighten:

> Bruce was a super guy. Didn't have a care in the world, always smiling. He flew with a Bible in a pocket in his leg. And he was a food hound. We were flying, and he said he saw a patch of collard greens from the air and started toward the enemy lines looking for collard greens! We really loved him.

August 11. Bruce was getting into position for an attack when to his right Graham Mitchell developed engine trouble and veered into his path. Sam yanked his nose up, just missing a direct collision. "I thought we missed," Bruce said later, but his propeller chopped off Mitchell's tail. Mitchell "never had a chance." He was killed, but Bruce jumped, and his 'chute opened with seconds to spare. His only injury was a sprained ankle.

For months the 99th had almost no contact with German fighters.

Knighten:

> When we did see German planes, we were 100 miles per hour slower than they were, and they were always 10,000 feet higher than we were, unless they were stupid enough to come down.
>
> The first ones I saw were flying our wing. We said, "Look at that!" When they'd break it off, we'd wave. Later on it got a little dirtier.

Deiz:

> There were times we'd pass the Jerry going one direction while we were going the other. We wanted to drop our tanks and bombs and go after them and chase them all over hell. But we had this Colonel Davis, who wouldn't let us do anything but what we were supposed to do, and that was go over our target.
>
> So normally, while I was over there, we didn't have a chance to get at the German airplanes like the guys with the P-51s did later. Consequently, it didn't look good on our score sheets. However, the guys we flew protection for swore by us.

September 2. B.O. Davis returned to the States to take over the new 332nd Group. Roberts took over command of the 99th, with Lemuel Custis as operations Officer.

C.C. Robinson:

Roberts had a great ego, but he could back it up. He was very bull-headed. If he was wrong, he was wrong all the way. He wouldn't back down. You had to prove to him that he was wrong.

Italy

SEPTEMBER 2. The Allies invaded southern Italy at Salerno, and some 99th enlisted men crossed the strait to begin setting up an airfield. They came under fire immediately and had to fall back to join the British when the Germans counterattacked. They were handed rifles and rushed into the lines as infantrymen, Watson said.

When they finally found a suitable field at Foggia, they came under air attack and were pinned down for five days and nights.

For the men in the air, it was more of the same—strafing and dive bombing.

September 16. Dryden flew his last combat mission over Salerno beachhead on his birthday, then he was grounded pending transfer home. He recalled:

Sidney Brooks was assigned for a mission and got in his plane and cranked it up, but it didn't check out, so he jumped out of his plane and jumped into mine. The squadron had already taken off, and by the time 12 aircraft had gone down the runway, it had stirred up a lot of dust, the sun was getting low on the horizon, and visibility was pretty bad, just the worst conditions.

Jamison and I were sitting around, watching them go, when we heard his engine sputter—*hrrrup, hrrrup*. All eyes were on him.

Brooks apparently decided to abort and turned downwind. He had enough altitude, but apparently he couldn't see the ground. There was a brick fence at the end of the strip. When he saw he would over-shoot, he raised his landing gear and went in on his belly.

But his belly tank with gas was hanging below him. We were screaming at him, "Jettison your tank! Jettison your tank!" Of course he couldn't hear us. I'm not sure I would have done anything different if I'd been in the plane. It wouldn't have occurred to me to drop the tanks. I would have been concentrating on getting the aircraft down.

When his fuselage hit the ground, the tank sheared off and bounced around like a football and left a vapor trail of fumes. Fire raced along it until it reached the airplane, and all of a sudden the plane went up in flames.

He jumped out, and we ran up, caught him, and tackled him.

Knighten was also there.

Brooks pan-caked in, in a big burst of flames, and jumped out, his flying suit on fire. Someone patted the flames out and he laughed, "Ha-ha-ha, they almost got me that time, didn't they fellows?"

Dryden:

He was taken to a British hospital, and when we went to visit him, he was conscious. His hands were burned, but he dictated a letter to his wife, Lucille, and Jamie wrote it for him. He felt good and said, "Get me my clothes, I'm getting out of here." But they made him stay there that night.

Next day we went to see him, and he was dead! He had suffered secondary shock and smoke inhalation.

Dryden and Purnell flew home on a B-25 bomber, along with several white pilots. At each stop, said Lou, they went out together "carousing."

"One pilot in particular was on the same wave length I was—we thought the same things at the same time." When they landed in Florida, they waited for transportation to their quarters.

All of a sudden he acted strange, as if he didn't know me. He kept looking down, kicking at an imaginary stone. As the vehicle came up, he extended his hand to me but kept looking to the side, and when the headlights swept across his face, I could see his lower eyelids full of tears. The vehicle took him and the other bomber pilots to the BOQ [Bachelor Officers Quarters].

When a jeep came for us, it deposited us in a boarding house. There was a brass bed and something I hadn't seen since I was a kid—a wash stand, bowl, and pitcher—and a bare light bulb hanging down from the ceiling.

Next morning my friend told me, "You know, Lou, here we are in the good old USA, the country we've defended, and you can't even go to the same places I can. How do you feel?"

I was so astounded, I couldn't answer. I don't speak for the whole group, but if there's bitterness carried within a person any length of time, there's a good chance he could burn himself out within, while the object of that hate will be unscathed. I could pound this into the heads of young people nowadays, but their heads are much thicker than ours were.

Dryden immediately called Jackie before visiting his parents. "I'll go with you," she said. On their return, they were married in the chapel at Tuskegee. Purnell headed for the bright lights of New York for some action.

When I got to New York, I was in the Theresa Hotel and had a write-up in a couple of papers. There were three things I wanted—well, four, really—a good big pitcher of cold milk, because they didn't have any over there; a nice soft bed, and a good shower bath. I was upstairs enjoying those—I think I stayed in the shower until I was wrinkled.

I was all ready to go out on the town when I got a call from the girl at the desk downstairs to say I had a visitor. I put on my uniform, and the minute I stepped out of the elevator, there was Hubert Julian. I can still see him today. He looked just like he did when I was a kid.

He immediately went into his act. He strolled up and down, looking around at his audience. "Is this any way to treat a returning war hero?" he said in a loud voice. "He should be out on the town. Don't you know how to treat a celebrity? Give him the keys to the city!" He ran his hands in his pockets. "Here—here's the key to my car. Return it when you wish, tomorrow or whenever you're finished."

I felt like two cents. I could have shrunk down and hid in the pile rug. Julian just wanted to be seen, to make a big impression.

"My car is right outside," he said.

I just said, "Thank you very much." When I got outside, there was his car, a great big black Cadillac—"six rooms and a bath," I called it. It had a parking ticket on the windshield for parking near a fire hydrant. I guess he didn't think anyone would give him a ticket. I got in and turned the key. The gas tank registered empty.

What he was after, I thought, was gas. He knew I would like to go up and down Harlem with this car and pick up gals. I took it around the block and parked it back in the same place and gave him his keys.

He berated me for that right in front of the people in the lobby. He said I didn't know how to accept things graciously and his offer was like casting pearls before swine.

After he lost his audience, he extended an invitation to come up for breakfast in the morning. He was living in Morningside Heights, a brownstone house. When I arrived at his home, I could have cried. Not a damn thing in it. No furniture in the living room, the dining room had nothing but one big oak table, the kitchen was bare except for one table. And he was standing there in his satin smoking jacket and monocle. I couldn't smell any bacon and eggs anywhere, so I left.

I really pitied the guy. He was living in another world. He was playing the part of a king in an empty, cold house.

Meanwhile, a bombshell hit. *Time* Magazine reported rumors that the 99th's days were numbered. Momyer had forwarded a report calling the unit unsatisfactory. He said they hadn't learned to fight as a team, broke formation when attacked, chose undefended targets instead of defended ones, turned back from a target because of bad weather while white pilots went ahead, and asked for rest when other units didn't. In short, Momyer wrote, the 99th didn't show the "fighting caliber" or "aggressiveness" necessary to make good combat pilots.

Purnell:

Naturally your formation would scatter. They said we were scattered by
the enemy. Hell, you're not going to fly a pattern so they can fly in there and
shoot the hell out of you.

Wiley:

For anyone to put me in his gun sights and call me incompetent was just a
dirty lie, and I'd have told him that to his face. I was as good as anyone in the
field. I was as tenacious, I was proud of what I was doing, and I did it well.
And I resented that even the War Department considered us an "experiment." Here I was, fighting for my country, and I was just an "experiment!"

But you have to remember the time. The South controlled much of the
Air Force, and the commanding generals were mainly from the South.

Momyer's superior, Brigadier General Edwin House, concurred that
"the negro type has not the proper reflexes" for combat. House was head
of the Support Command; it's not clear why he was rating a combat unit.
But Major General Cannon, who had once welcomed them, endorsed it.
Lieutenant General Spaatz added his endorsement that he had found no
criticism of the 99th's discipline on the ground but suggested that it be
reassigned to rear area coastal patrol.

In Washington the Air Force chief of staff, Arnold, agreed.

Quoting "sources," *Time* magazine reported that despite seeing "little action," the 99th had done "fairly well." However, the top command
"was not altogether satisfied" with their performance. Time said the brass
wanted to take the 99th off combat duty and give it "combat patrols," where
it would be well away from any action.

The "Great Experiment" seemed to be over.

6

Triumph at Anzio

OCTOBER 16. Davis hastened to the Pentagon to save his unit. He told the brass that the 99th, himself included, had arrived in Africa with no combat experience at all. He agreed that there had been some lack of confidence and mistakes on the early missions but with experience, confidence had increased. He himself may have been conservative, he admitted, because he knew the crucial importance of the experience and did not want "to lose the whole ball game in a single operation." He concluded that he would put the stamina and aggressiveness of his fliers up against those of any comparable unit.

General George C Marshall, chairman of the Joint Chiefs, ordered a comparative study of all P-40 units, and agreed to take no action until the report was complete. Davis had saved his units, at least temporarily. But, he wrote, Momyer "had come within inches of destroying the future of black pilots forever."

79th Fighter Group and Earl Bates

THAT same day the 99th was transferred to the 79th Group under 29 year-old Colonel Earl Bates. Roberts recalled:

> Bates was the first commander who greeted us as I felt a fellow American should be greeted. No snide implications; he just expected us to do our job. We had a marvelous time in that organization.

"A super guy," Willie Fuller agreed. "Used to come over and get briefed with us and fly with us. A hell of a guy."
Wiley:

> You had bastards and you had princes. Bates was a prince. He came over to us and welcomed us aboard and made us part of his Group. We got promotions through Bates; he wrote recommendation letters for us. And he wrote letters that were read aloud to all his squadrons—that he was very happy and to keep up the good work.

Bates sent his other squadrons and the 99th on missions together in support of the British Eighth Army and named 99th pilots to lead some joint missions. Morale quickly improved, and the 99th won three Distinguished Unit Citations under Bates. Said Roberts: "General Davis, Colonel Parrish, General Cannon, Colonel Cochran, Colonel Bates—these are my heroes."

November 7. General Cannon visited the 99th and pinned medals on Charlie Hall and others. Wilson Eagleson:

> Not a single white reporter covered it. No papers in the states mentioned it, though the Army paper, *Stars & Stripes*, did. In fact, I don't recall any white press around during the time I was in service.

Swampy also recalled the local kids:

> From 20 to as many as 50 kids would gather outside our mess hall, holding buckets or plates. One beautiful child, about six or seven, Anna Maria, was out there every day. She never said a word, just stood there waiting.

November was a stormy month. Gale winds and rain whipped Italy, turning roads into black, sticky, slippery mud. General Clark's ground attack halted, defeated by an enemy he couldn't lick—"General Mud."

In the 99th almost all flights were grounded. Tents were blown away. While two men inside hugged the poles to hold them down, men outside braved the tempest to pound the stakes deeper into the ooze. Even so, the inside was soon as muddy as the outside.

When at last the sun came out, the 99th sent up 14 missions in two days. Eagleson told the North Carolina history project:

> We got word from the Resistance that high-ranking officers were being transported in Red Cross ambulances.
> That red cross made an easy target.
> One time we spotted a horse-drawn German convoy and made two passes over them. The horses went crazy and destroyed the whole convoy.

On a joint mission Bates and Roberts spotted a camouflaged train in the snow-covered Apennine Mountains:

> He and his wing man took one end of the train, I and my wing man took the other end to immobilize it. The rest of the squadron went in and did terrific damage while our elements stopped the enemy ground fire from doing any damage.

But there's no record of that train officially. If the mission is recorded, they may have recorded it under Bates, not the 99th. There were all these people who didn't want us to succeed.

The 99th also continued to strafe ground targets. Deiz was hit several times from ground fire—"holes in the wings, stuff like that," he shrugged.

More new pilots arrived.

C.C. "Curtis" Robinson was the grandson of a slave. His great-grandfather was a wealthy North Carolina plantation owner with thousands of acres, an "army" of tenants, three wives, and at least 46 children, biographer George Norfleet writes in *A Pilot's Journey*. But C.C. himself grew up in a two-bedroom house with a wood stove that was often cold because there was nothing to cook. At Christmas his father, a house painter, often had to fill his kids' stockings with an apple, an orange, some nuts, and some raisins.

The black school was over-crowded, with two bathrooms for 1400 kids. Teachers all carried big rulers or sticks "and would use them." There was no public high school for blacks, but Curtis went on to Claflin high school, founded by the Methodist church, "where I had to work to pay for my education."

He learned to play the bass fiddle and borrowed $2.90 train fare to play his first gig in Asheville and mountain resort areas. Ten musicians traveled in one station wagon. It was a good way to meet pretty girls, who followed the band around.

Robinson majored in chemistry to be a doctor. His teacher, Oscar Holmes, would become the first black Navy pilot, although the Navy refused to assign him to a squadron. He spent the war in Canada, ferrying planes.

After graduating in 1940 Curtis landed a job as a teacher at $75 a month. His school had no electricity or running water, but it did have a bus, the only black school in the state with one—city school buses picked up only white kids. C.C. boarded with an old man who hunted rabbits, squirrels "and whatever else the old gun-slinger could catch."

On a visit to an army camp, Robinson watched black GIs digging latrines under a lieutenant they called "Cap'n Boss" like a penitentiary road gang addressing their guard. "I can't do that," he decided. "I'm a teacher, I have a college degree."

Then he learned about the new aviation program for blacks, which paid $200 to cadets and $350 to officers. He rushed down to take his application to a notary, who told him, "This is where you put your X."

Robinson reported to Shaw Air Force Base, which didn't know what to do with him, so they kept giving him three-day passes home until he ran out of money. "Sir," he pleaded, "I can't afford another three-day pass."

At last he got orders to Tuskegee, but the railroad clerk kept walking back and forth, wondering what to do. At last he made a phone call and gave him a Pullman ticket.

Robinson boarded the train at one o'clock, and the conductor immediately tried to put him to bed. Then the porter tried. "No, I'm just going to sit here," he insisted. At five o'clock the dinner bell rang, but he had only 15 cents, so he skipped dinner. In Atlanta, 19 hours after boarding, he ate a free meal at the USO (servicemen's club).

In contrast to the earlier classes, this one had 52 cadets—but only three planes. The instructors took each man up. If he showed an "aptitude" for flying, he was in. If not, he was out. The instructors could be "brutal and merciless. But I guess almost all of us had that confidence that we could do whatever we tried, and you didn't have to tell us more than once."

Robinson was the first in the class to solo, gaining a nickname, "Hotshot."

- He was "the king of the snap-roll," which had almost wiped out Charlie Dryden. It should be done at 3,000 feet, but to impress his aunt, Robinson flew over her house and tried it at only 800 feet. Instead of snapping, the plane came straight down. His eyes bugged out, and "I thought I was a goner for sure." He leveled off right over his aunt's clothesline while she and her neighbor ran in terror.
- "Even in combat I've never been that frightened."
- Robinson was lucky. The P-40 killed two classmates, who couldn't pull out of a dive. Only 17 of the original 53 graduated.
- They took advanced gunnery at Selfridge Field, 19 miles from Detroit. "I was one of those guys heading into town without even waiting for dinner." He also dated a nurse, ending the evening with intensive last-minute "smooching" before he raced to catch the midnight bus back.
- Then he met the most beautiful woman he had ever seen, but just before their second date, Colonel Davis called him in and told him he was restricted to base prior to going overseas. It was top secret; married men couldn't even tell their wives. He never saw his dream girl again.

I went over on a Liberty Ship. About 110 ships were in the convoy—11 across and ten deep. We were in the first line, fourth row from the left. Every night we'd come under attack from U-boats. We could see fire and a ship going down ever night.

They knocked out the first two ships on our side, so we ended up in the second row.

A day and a half out of Gibraltar, the ship alongside of us lost a steering gear and rammed us at seven o'clock one morning and knocked a hole in the ship just below the water line. The water rushed in and, of course, we rushed out of our bunks. We had no place to sleep, so they put us in the officers' quarters upstairs and we used the officers' mess. That was of some concern to the white officers there.

We were disabled for a while and the convoy left a destroyer back with us. They were able to pump the oil from one side of the ship to the other to make us list less. The destroyer left us when he saw that we weren't going to sink. The last attack from a sub had been about three nights back, so I guess he thought we were safe. We crept along toward Gibraltar at about four knots and it took three days and two nights. That was scary.

- With everyone intently scanning the sea for subs, they finally limped into Gibraltar. But they still weren't out of danger as German frogmen swam from Spain every night to attach explosives to the allied ships.
- It took six weeks for Robinson to find the 99th. No one knew where it was. He hopped air corps rides from Gibraltar to Oran, to Algiers (pausing to check out the beautiful French girls), to Sicily, to Foggia in Italy, to Naples, where they ducked under a truck during an air raid, flirted with waitresses, and drew crowds of curious Italians, who were fascinated by their hair. Finally they found their outfit back to Foggia.

Robinson was given a plane which "I wish I didn't have"—a "rickety" battle-scarred veteran of the China theater. "You're the rookie," the others told him. "It's yours." He climbed in and joined in their strafing and dive bombing runs. There were no anti-aircraft guns, he wrote. "It was easy duty."

Later, however, we were very much out-numbered by the Germans, who sent up 16 or 30 planes to a flight; we sent up eight at a time. I usually flew in the mornings, and the Germans usually came in the mornings, so I saw quite a bit of action in that rickety old plane.

The P-40 could out-turn anything flying, but our top speed was 280, the Germans' was about 365, so we could never start a fight, we had to let them start it. We just sat and waited for them.

Leonard Jackson from Texas had taken CPT at Tuskegee before applying for the air force. He was called "Black Jackson" to distinguish him from Melvin "Red" Jackson, who came along later with the 332nd. He had taken CPT at Tuskegee.

Robinson:

My best buddy—my bunkmate—was Jackson. We were thick as soup and kept everyone else laughing. He was a great guy, and everybody liked him. We could go to any party and have a lot of fun. We were always invited somewhere.

Funny thing about him: Flying calls for a lot of coordination, and Leonard couldn't even throw a baseball or play ping pong—nothing. But he could fly the hell out of the plane.

Jackson and Robinson were a comedy team, who had kept the cadets laughing at Tuskegee. They kept it up in Italy as well.

Albert Manning "was more mature, more practical," though he was about the same age.

Elwood "Woody" Driver was 22, about three years younger than the other pilots. Robinson called him "The Brain."

He was top of his class in college in New Jersey, graduated when he was 19 or so and volunteered for the Naval Air Corps. They accepted him—until they saw who he was. He was a playboy and wanted everyone to like him and he never forgot a name.

Freddie Hutchins was "a jovial fellow," according to another cadet, Charles Bussey. Hutch was from Georgia, had learned to "roll with the punch," and didn't let discrimination bother him.

Hutch loved to spout folksy sayings, such as, "the blacker the berry, the sweeter the juice."

Clarence Allen of Mobile was sort of a playboy," Spann Watson remembered.

His old man seemed to be wealthy, at least from our point of view. He had had some seaplane training—it cost money to take lessons then. He attended most of the good schools and got kicked out of them. He was a rugged, hard liver.

1944

JANUARY 2. The 99th lost one of its new men.
Baugh reported:

John Morgan landed down wind, down hill and couldn't stop the airplane, and it ran off the end of the runway into a ditch and killed him. I made it a point to stay away from airplane accidents. It wouldn't help him, and it wouldn't help me.

Jim Wiley found an abandoned Italian Fiat fighter plane. After his mechanics put it in flying shape, he used it as a mail plane and for other errands for the squadron.

The 79th moved from the east coast and sent to Capodicino on the west coast near Anzio south of Rome. They didn't know it yet, but the Allies were planning a major invasion to cut off the Germans' retreat from General Mark Clark's Fifth Army, which was moving slowly up from Salerno.

January 22, 1944. Life became hot in a hurry as the invasion flotilla arrived.

Willie Fuller:

> We could look down at daybreak and see the ships unload and hit the beaches. There seemed to be no resistance, and they put all their vehicles and tanks in straight military lines. Beautiful. Made a graphic picture from the air.
>
> Later the Germans pulled out their big Bertha artillery piece and started shooting. All those vehicles disappeared in a hurry.

Wiley:

> The Germans were up in the hills peppering the beachhead and the transports out in the harbor. They peppered my plane, too—at one point there were nine holes in it. Our problems came from both flak and ground fire. We had to be very careful about flying without sufficient altitude, at least 5,000 feet.
>
> We had a lot of targets—hitting the German positions up there and flying almost continuous cover over the beachhead. The Germans were very tenacious; they wanted to push the Americans back into the water.
>
> The 109s came down from above Rome, and the invasion forces needed protection from them. Therefore, we were flying close support in the hills around Anzio and flying cover for the invasion. But many of the Germans were relatively new pilots, they weren't as good as the older ones we'd seen.

The Most Glorious Day

J ANUARY 27. This was the most crucial date in the entire war for the Tuskegee Airmen. As Roberts put it: "For the first time we were given the responsibility of knocking Jerry down to protect the beachhead."

Early in the morning about 8:30, under clear skies Jamison led three flights of 12 pilots, mostly rookies, who ran into 15 enemies and waded into the fight. Jamison described it:

> The radar ground controller said there were bogeys [unidentified planes] coming in very high, 20,000 feet or so. We were at 12,000. The British Spitfires were supposed to be up there, but I don't know where they were, and we couldn't climb that high to get to the Germans, so we held our altitude and dropped our belly tanks.
>
> I signaled our guys to arm, and we headed toward the Germans.

The enemy planes, Focke Wulf 190s, screamed through the American formation, about 100 mph faster than the P-40s.

"We really didn't need any aircraft identification," Deiz said. "The German planes were flying so fast, you knew they were German, they weren't ours." When the P-40s fired their six machine guns, the recoil knocked another ten miles off their speed. The P-40s had only one chance to catch the foe.

> We'd take a heading to intercept them, and for maybe ten seconds, as they leveled off, our air speeds were about the same. If you could get on the ass of one, you had a chance to do something.

Baugh:

> The only way we could get to them was to gain extra speed from a dive, so we dropped fuel tanks and dived down on them. Instead of zooming back to altitude, they stayed low to hedge-hop back to their friendly territory.

It was a fatal mistake. Jamison recalled:

> I did a 180—a split-S, we called it [The pilot rolls onto his back and pulls the stick toward him, so his plane dives down; then he rolls over again so he is going back the way he came]—and came out going in the same direction the enemy were going and above them. I had timed it just right luckily, and was right on the top of one of the German flight leaders. We were about 100 feet apart, 200 feet above the ground, and I looked right in his cockpit.
>
> Everything was happening so fast. Ashley and I were right on the tail of this guy, almost too good to be true. They were just determined to get back to Rome, they weren't about to stay around and dogfight. I gave him a blast with all six machine guns in my wings. ["Hits were registered on the right wing, and chunks flew off," the official report said.]
>
> Then my guns jammed. I know I hit him, he was smoking, but I don't know if he went down or not, so I got credit for a damage.

According to the official report, Willie Ashley "'jumped a 190 on the deck and chased him to within a few miles of Rome. The enemy craft first began to smoke and burst into flames."

Deiz spotted a 190 below and off to his side at about 750 feet. "I just pulled in behind him," he said laconically, "and let him have it. That's all." A portion of the enemy cowling flew off, and the plane went into a steep dive. It crashed and burned in a yard near a house.

Howard Baugh and his wing man, Clarence Allen, maneuvered behind a 190. Baugh recalled:

I just pulled the trigger, and he just flew into the ground, almost belly-landing in a cloud of dust. We flew right on over him, pulled a left turn, and we went out to sea. The whole thing was over in about a minute.

The two shared credit for the kill.

Baugh spotted another 190 and, the official report said, fired three-second bursts into him. "Tracers were seen going into the plane, and small fragments flew off from the wing and tail." A damage.

Leon Roberts also chased a 190 on the deck. "Roberts was a natural," Jamison said:

When he flew my wing, I felt secure with him out there. He got on this guy's tail. It must have been a young pilot, since he had a faster plane and could have outrun us, but when the bullets went by, he'd twist and turn instead of pouring on the speed and pulling away. Leon said he'd give him a blast, corrected a little bit, and finally hit him in the wing. He flipped over and went into the ground.

Toppins got a fifth plane. He fired a short burst into a 190 on the deck. The plane hit the ground and exploded.

The squadron report declared:

Jack Rogers and Elwood Driver caught another 190 heading in the general direction of Rome. As the plane was smoking excessively and diving into the ground at about 50 feet, it was probably destroyed as claimed.

George McCrumby spotted a 190 on the deck, picked a lead, and commenced firing at point-blank range. Sections of the horizontal stabilizer and rudder flew off. One 190 is claimed as damaged.

Henry Perry caught an FW 190 coming out of a dive and raked the enemy ship head-to-tail at about 300 yards. Pieces from the canopy flew off. The plane seemed to flutter...fell off on the wing and headed to the ground. A damage is claimed.

In all, 19 enemy planes were destroyed, plus one probable and four damaged. In five minutes the 99th had made up for five months of frustration.

That afternoon Custis led a second flight and ran into another large flight of Focke Wulfs and Messerschmitt 109s coming down from Rome:

We had a lot of experience by then, and most of the good German pilots had been sent to Russia, because they were desperate on that front. The German pilots at Anzio must have been young guys who didn't have experience; they didn't know how to veer or take evasive action. They were sitting ducks.

Custis himself wouldn't describe his action, but the official report did:

> Captain Custis spotted an FW-190 on the deck. Several bursts were fired at close range, and the plane crashed in a creek.
>
> Lieutenant Charles Bailey caught an FW-190 heading in the general direction of Rome with a 45-degree shot. The pilot was seen to bail out.
>
> Lieutenant Erwin Lawrence probably destroyed an FW-190 with a difficult shot almost from the side. Eagleson, flying in "Gerry," named for a student at Tuskegee, saw the FW roll over and dive for the ground, smoking excessively.

But Lawrence himself now had a German on his own tail. He swooped in front of Eagleson, who was flying on only his fifth mission. Swampy got in a split-second 90-degree shot, the most difficult of all. It tore the enemy's wing off and sent him spinning into the ground.

The results: three more destroyed and one probable. It brought the day's total to nine destroyed, one probable, and four damaged.

One plane did not return, however. Deiz's friend, Sam Bruce, was last seen pursuing two Focke-Wulfs. In the encounter, Bruce was hit and bailed out. What happened next is veiled in controversy. Spanky Roberts:

> While he was in his 'chute, he was deliberately shot and killed by a South African. The 99th was ready to declare war. The South Africans never contacted us, although they did contact the American headquarters and said it was a mistake.
>
> The Americans who knew about it began to have a changed attitude toward us, because even the worst ones didn't envision killing their own. They felt they too had been betrayed by an ally. There was no great outpouring of words or people hugging us, but there was less "Damn you, go to hell" and more "We're in this together."

Some veterans of the 99th said they knew nothing about such a report. Others heard it, though none can verify it and most can't believe it. Wiley said flatly, "I doubt it." There were a lot of tales out about Sam Bruce, he admitted, but there was so much anti-aircraft fire, and that was how he died. Knighten also couldn't believe a Spitfire would come down 30,000 feet to shoot at him. Knighten, himself, said he never encountered "personal problems" with any Allied pilots.

However, as Custis shrugs, "There will always be an element of doubt" about exactly how Bruce met his end.

January 28. The next day Hall led a second flight over Anzio. Robinson would be flying his wing:

Hall came to see me the night before. He said, "Look, when you take off, as soon as you see those mountains, you start to weave. If you fly straight, the German gunners will knock you out."

Robinson would fly 33 missions in all, and on every one, "just before I got in the plane, I had the jitters."

On this day Robinson learned that the formation tactics he had been taught at Tuskegee—wing-tip to wing-tip—were thrown out the window in Italy.

Our formation was a line abreast, 100 yards between each plane, because the Germans had many more planes than we did. Five minutes later I could see the mountains, so I started to go like this [his hands described a skate-boarder going up and down the walls of an inclined court].

We got over to Anzio and I could see a group of planes, about 30 of them, about 20 miles away. I started to call out, but said to myself, "These guys must see those planes because they've been here before," so I didn't say anything. And I was still weaving—up and down, around and around. My stomach was upset, and I threw up right in the cockpit.

Then it dawned on me—nobody else was doing it except me. When we got back, everyone laughed like that was the funniest thing in the world. That was a joke Charlie pulled on me.

Soon they were on us and we went into it. I dropped my belly tanks, but I forgot to switch to internal tanks and, with all that weaving, my engine cut off. Oh, my God, my first flight and someone is about to shoot me down! But I didn't panic. My hand automatically hit the switch. But by the time I switched tanks, everyone else had gone. The Germans turned and hit the deck [tree-top level], and I couldn't catch up.

The report recorded:

FW 190s at 4,000 feet approached from the north; our formation at 5,000 feet dove on them. As the enemy turned away, one of them was shot down by Captain Hall...closing in at 300 yards. The 109 was on the deck and burst into flames and crashed on the ground.

"He got one!" Robinson shouted.

But another 190 was on Charlie's tail, closing in at 200 yards and firing.

In an instant Robinson had his biggest scare of the war. He was diving on an enemy and had just opened fire when another plane flashed in front of him. It was Hall, who suddenly swung around and was blasting away at his foe. "I just knew I'd hit Charlie," Robinson said. "It looked as if I shot right through his wing." But miraculously he missed. Hall's prey spun and crashed into the ground—his second victory of the day and third of the war.

Meanwhile, Deiz, the reluctant warrior, suddenly also became a tiger and scored his second victory in two days. Whether the death of his friend, Bruce, was a factor, is not known. Deiz said laconically: "One of them got in my way."

> We were at about 4,000 feet, mixing it up in a dogfight, and my leader made a turn when a Focke-Wulf saw him and pulled in behind him. I don't know whether he saw me, but all I had to do was level my wings and there he was. Just a short burst, and that was it.

Graham "Peepsight" Smith also scored one. According to the report, he chased a Focke-Wulf and caught it with a difficult 50-degree shot from the left-rear, like a quarterback leading his receiver. "The aircraft veered out of control about 20 feet from the ground and burst into flame."

The total for the day: four more enemy ships destroyed.

In their first six months, the 99th had scored only one victory; it now had 14 in two days, plus two probables. "We poured the hell into them," Spanky Roberts exclaimed. "We laid to rest forever the word that blacks couldn't fly."

Charlie Hall was suddenly a star. Knighten:

> Hall was a very quiet guy until he got those three victories. Then he suddenly became a know-it-all about everything. Sudden stardom did it to him; he actually started strutting. Before that, he was just our buddy, running around with the rest of us.

Robinson:

> He was a "tutor" on the banquet circuit. He was quite good at it. Different units would invite him over to the mess hall and he'd take me with him. He'd speak, and we'd have a great meal.

The 99th was given another job: to find and destroy the "Anzio Express," the monster artillery piece that was pounding the American ships and troops on the beach from a tunnel in the hills several miles away. A 17 year-old infantryman, Joe Norwood, recalled hugging the sand so close that "even the buttons got in the way."

The fliers divided the area into grids and patiently looked for every likely spot where the gun could be hiding and laid their bombs into every opening they could find.

The gun was silenced. The invasion proceeded.

February 5. Elwood Driver spotted ten FWs diving on the beach, made a diving left turn and fired:

Even though my target was pulling away, my tracers straddled his cockpit and flames burst from his right side. I last saw him burning and heading for Rome at 50 feet.

On the same mission, the flight leader, Jamison, and George McCrumby tangled with six FWs until Mac was hit by *ack-ack* and went into a dive.

"The plane was spinning," Jamison said, "and his body was flying around inside." McCrumby tried to bail out but was blown back inside by the prop blast. Then he tried from the other side of the cockpit but got only half-way out, where he dangled until, only 1,000 feet from the ground, he finally fell free.

He grabbed for his rip cord and gave a yank. Nothing happened. He yanked five more times before the 'chute finally opened in the nick of time, depositing him in a cow pasture.

When he got back to the base, Jamison said, "his eyes were completely bloodshot from his face being beaten against the inside of the fuselage."

Meantime Jamison was having his own trouble.

It was low-level stuff, right above the ground. We were badly outnumbered. I had six guns but they jammed.

A Focke-Wulf got on my tail and I couldn't shake him—he must have sensed that my guns were gone. He was so close I could see the tracer bullets going by my plane and could see his 20-mm cannon shells exploding on the ground in front of me. He'd line you up with machine gun tracers, then let the cannon go.

I had no idea where I was; I just knew I was heading back to friendly territory. I burned up the engine and it quit right above the ground. It was too low to bail out, so I made a crash landing, sliding across a farmer's field, wheels up.

Some army Rangers came and got me and told me I was in no-man's land. They showed me a farmhouse and said the Germans were using it as an outpost and they thought the Germans were going to come out and get me. I had to spend the night on the ground.

Flying in the air was nothing, but being on the ground and hearing the artillery and feeling the ground rock was a different war for me. I wasn't cut out to be a ground soldier.

Roberts:

Heber Houston was shot down two or three times over Anzio. The other pilots laughed that every time they saw him he was either making a crash landing or coming back to base in a truck.

He just climbed in another plane and took off again.

February 7. Leonard Jackson, Wilson Eagleson, and Clifton Mills scored victories, bringing the squadron's total to 17 in the Anzio campaign, the best record of the four squadrons in the 79th:

99th	17
85th	15
87th	15
86th	2

The 99th lost only one man, Bruce, despite the superiority of the German planes. This suggests that the best German pilots had been lost over Russia or had been pulled back to defend the Fatherland.

This record would not have been possible if the 99th had still been under Spike Momyer, thus an equal share of the credit belongs to Colonel Bates. He has never been given his due as the catalyst who saved black military aviation and, in so doing, also played a key role in helping secure the Allied beach head at Anzio.

General Cannon sent congratulations. Even Hap Arnold admitted the unit had done a "very commendable job," adding, "my best wishes for their continued success."

After Anzio, Davis wrote, all criticism of the 99th was "silenced once and for all."

"If we had failed," said Custis, "the whole history of Air Force integration would have changed.

"But we didn't go into it to fail."

Time magazine reported:

Any outfit would have been proud of the 99th's record. Its victories stamped the final seal of excellence on one of the most controversial outfits of the Army.... The Air Force regards its experiment proven [and] is taking all qualified Negro cadets it can get.

7

The 332nd

100th Squadron

As soon as the 99th was filled, Tuskegee had begun sending graduates to the new 100th squadron while still supplying replacements to the 99th. The leader-presumptive was a West Pointer, the first black since B.O. Davis.

Bob Tresville was an Army brat, son of an old Buffalo Soldier band leader in the 24th Infantry Regiment. He was tall and handsome, "strictly military but a real smart guy and real *gung-ho*," one classmate remembered. "A fantastic guy—smart, bright, strong."

"A very fine man, a beautiful man, a gentleman," agreed Melvin Jackson. Chris Newman: "An eager beaver. Very aggressive and outgoing."

But, said Gleed:

> He was a mechanical pilot and he had a hard time soloing. The average expected time was six hours; I don't think he soloed until 12 hours. Anyone else would have washed out.

Tresville was put in command of the 100th Fighter Squadron, the first one formed after the 99th. "He was my idol," said Walter Palmer, who joined the squadron a month later. "He knew how to mingle with us but was still able to command our respect."

Some of the other leading members, in the order that they were assigned:

Andrew "Jug" Turner, the son of a Washington minister, was a student at Howard University when he volunteered for Tuskegee. Even for a fighter pilot, Turner was small.

"He could turn that airplane tighter than anyone, future cadet Woody Crockett said. "I attributed that to his short stature. He was very businesslike, and loved to play bridge and poker."

Melvin "Red" Jackson

A future Red Tail, Charlie Bussey, called him one of the most outstanding men in the 332nd. "Red was a tremendous man. He had very red hair and wild blue eyes. An exceptionally good flier, a real fine boxer, and a brilliant man academically."

Jackson was very light-skinned—almost white—hence his nickname. He was the son of a gardener from Warrenton, Virginia and remembered:

> The segregated school system didn't offer very much, so my father paid teachers to teach us at home. I was nine when the Depression hit, and we could no longer afford the teacher. A cousin came down from New Jersey so she could get some food—we're talking about rough times—and she taught us.
>
> As times got tough my mother's sister moved to California and wrote my father, "Why don't you come out here and live as a white man?" He just laughed; his community was his home, and his home was his life.
>
> I had no interest in passing either; it never once occurred to me to do it. I had too many friends and was enjoying my life.

A year later Jackson's father had a stroke. The boy quit school to go to work at the age of ten and then went back to a one-room school for a year. In high school a teacher encouraged him to go to college, and Melvin worked summers in one of President Roosevelt's New Deal CCC (Civilian Construction Corps) camps and winters in the WPA (Works Progress Administration) for $30 a month.

Eventually Jackson saved enough to enroll in the black Virginia State College to study agriculture, working on the school farm and as a part-time janitor. He also boxed on the college team. ("He was tough as nails," said Harry Sheppard.) "College was everything I ever wanted," Jackson said.

But when the Air Corps opened its doors to Negroes, he decided, "This is exciting, you can fly—and it's free! I'll join." He had to wait a year until he got orders to report to Tuskegee in March 1942. He was 24.

In all, 20 cadets reported. "They washed out as many as they could and graduated as few as they could, but I didn't worry about it." In the end only four graduated, including his college friends, Howard Baugh and Terry Charlton. "They washed out a lot of good pilots."

Woodrow Wilson "Woody" Crockett was the product of a two-room school in Arkansas. His mother taught grades one to four, his father, five to eight. Their own educational levels were unknown, but they somehow got teaching certificates. (His mother eventually received her college degree at the age of 60. "She was determined to get it," Woody said.)

But Crockett decided that "an eighth grade education wouldn't make it in this world." When a colored high school was opened in Little Rock, one of the many Paul Laurence Dunbar High Schools in the country, "black kids from all over the state descended on it." One of them was Woody.

Crockett went to junior college and dreamed of becoming a PhD in math. But he dropped out of school because he didn't have the six dollars a month tuition. "Those were tough times. About 1940 things were tight!"

Woody enlisted in the Army's black 349th artillery battalion, which was set up despite fears that the artillery was too technical for blacks. It had all white officers and was the fifth black unit in the Army after the two cavalry and two infantry divisions.

My first sergeant thought I should go to West Point, but they said I was too old. Then they said I should go to Officer Candidate School (OCS), but only the infantry was open to black officers. Instead, I would have been the first black to attend Artillery OCS, except that this announcement showed up on the orderly room wall: "Be a pilot and earn $245 a month." A lieutenant's regular pay was $125 a month.

So in August 1942, I arrived in Tuskegee. We were the first class to expand from the normal 20 per class. There were 35 in our class, including 15 who had previous Army experience. After nine weeks we were left with only 15. I read a book by Hap Arnold and Ira Eaker that said they washed out 75% of the cadets they took in—this was white boys. The "washing machine" was going, and after bivouacking two years at Fort Sill, I was properly motivated to be in the upper 25%.

The others criticized me for not going to town. I told them, "I didn't come here to go to town;" I was looking at that $245 a month.

C. Robinson:
"In the cadet corps we had some terrible math problems. Most of us had to study like the devil, but Crockett had no problems. I think he tutored some of the other guys."

Woody was already married when he reported, although cadets were not allowed to have wives. "I didn't say a word," he smiled. "That's how I escaped the bullet."

Johnny Briggs was from St. Louis.

When I got off the train at Montgomery to change for Tuskegee, having a first-class ticket, I was going to the back of the train. The conductor stopped me: "Where you going, boy?" he put me I behind the engine where the blacks sat, with the smoke and fight right in front of us.

"He had the shiniest shoes," Harry Sheppard remembered. "I don't care what the weather was, his shoes looked like finish on a cabinet. Used to wear jodhpur boots, and the gleam would put your eyes out."

At a reunion of Tuskegee Airmen, Briggs strode through the hotel lobby in cowboy boots and Stetson hat. Sheppard smiled: "I wonder if he takes that hat off to take a shower."

Walter Palmer, one class behind Briggs, was a New Yorker and Charles Dryden's cousin. As he wrote in his book, *Flying With Eagles* (1993), his parents had come to Harlem from Jamaica. His father, an elevator operator, also played trumpet in the Salvation Army band, which Walter followed proudly through the streets.

Moving to the Bronx, he grew up in "a virtual League of Nations." Most of his friends were Orthodox Jews, and he earned a few pennies on Friday nights lighting their candles, which they were forbidden to do. Walter played stickball in the streets and hiked several miles to the Polo Grounds to see the Giants. He entered New York's only aviation-oriented high school and worked as a delivery boy in the lower East Side garment district.

Palmer was training to be a police officer when Pearl Harbor hit. He rushed to volunteer for cadet training, then waited nine months for the call.

His fiancée traveled from New York for his graduation and their wedding, and the sun "came out in all its glory." Palmer and Al Lewis wore their new lieutenants bars for the double wedding at the chapel. Palmer then took his bride up for a spin, showing her a loop, a snap roll, and an Immelmann. It knocked her glasses off. "That was an expensive flight for me," he sighed.

The 301st

CHARLES DeBow, one of the original five Tuskegee grads, was given command of the next unit to be formed.

The 301st would go on the compare with the other three in aerial victories, which is the Air Force's only criterion, but less is known about its flyers than the other three squadrons. Many of the interviews were obtained at the national conventions, and, either from ignorance or by chance, only one 301st flyer was included, although some of the replacement pilots later were.

Moe Downs was a high school teacher from Tahoma Mississippi. He remembered a flight with one instructor who was demonstrating crash landing techniques and added so much realism to the lesson that they actually did crash. They ended up upside down, hanging from their safety belts, in an Alabama swamp.

Two of the most illustrious flyers in the 301st were Joe Elsberry and Frederic Funderberg, yet almost nothing is known about either one. This is a great loss to history.

The 302nd

Ed Gleed

GLEED graduated in Class #9, December 13, 1943—one of the most illustrious classes in Tuskegee, because it also included Tresville and Wendell Pruitt.

Gleed may have been the most colorful cadet to report to Tuskegee. "He was super-cocky," said Harry Sheppard.

Gleed:

My grandfather was a slave. He came out of West Virginia as soon as the Civil War was over and came west to Lawrence Kansas. The guy never had an education, he could hardly write his own name, but he became a produce dealer, buying chickens, cattle, eggs, and hogs, and died at the age of 99.

I was born in Lawrence November 3, 1916. My old man hit the skids when the stock market broke down, and when I was in the fifth grade, he and my mother divorced. My mother took my brother and me to Tuskegee, where she was going to teach home economics. That was my first experience with out-and-out segregation. We were in a Jim Crow car and saw white deputies bringing black prisoners on the train with their hands shackled.

My mother sent us back to an aunt in Lawrence to finish high school, and that's where I got my next taste of segregation. There was one movie in town we just couldn't go to: in the others we had to go upstairs in the "chicken roost." We even had a separate colored basketball team in high school.

After high school I went to Kansas University. I hesitate to say I was self-made, but my mother gave me a total of $15 during my college career. The only thing my dad gave me was his old Peerless roadster when he bought a new Phaeton to go out to the 1932 Olympics in Los Angeles. Plus the little gas I could drain from his gas pump and a small sum for working for him on weekends and in the summer. I put myself through college waiting tables. Most of the waiters at the sorority and fraternity houses were black.

I got thrown out of university swimming pools twice, along with another fellow who was a physical education major. Swimming was a required subject for him to graduate, but they ended up giving him credit for it rather than allowing him into the pool.

The famous Phogg Allen was basketball coach. His favorite saying to us was, "You can come out for the team, but you ain't gonna play." Yet later he was the one who sought out Wilt Chamberlain and brought him back from Pennsylvania. Ironic.

I graduated in 1937 and got a work-scholarship to Howard University Law School. I worked in the library in the afternoon, then worked to 12 o'clock at night waiting tables out in Chevy Chase.

Then I took off and went hoboing to New Orleans, riding on top of coal cars. I got on the wrong train up in the hills out of Bristol Tennessee and damn near froze to death.

In Chattanooga I got picked up by a railroad cop and got put in the county jail. At three o'clock in the morning a Negro deputy sheriff awakened me and asked me where was my family. I said I didn't have any folks, so he gave me a good meal, took me to the bus station, and bought me a ticket. I cashed the ticket in and hoboed the rest of the way.

In New Orleans I unloaded bananas, then I got a job as messman on a United Fruit boat and made two trips through the Panama Canal and back, making $45 dollars a month. I was working as a [non-union] scab when they had a strike, and I got my head busted open twice.

I ended up in a San Francisco drydock. Where to go? I had a cousin in Los Angeles but didn't know her address. So I hoboed down the road in three days, couldn't find my cousin in the phone book, and lived in a flea-bag hotel near Union Station for about two weeks, hustling, and rolling drunks at night.

The hotel room was occupied in the daytime by two other guys, and a friend and I occupied it at night. These other guys were up to really serious trouble; finally they got picked up, and they took our clothes to jail with them. If I'd gone on like them, I'd probably be in jail, too, or dead, by now.

I said, "We've got to get out of here," and we started walking across town. We'd walked four or five miles when one of those believe-it-or-not things happened. At a drugstore I saw an attractive young woman reading a letter. She was holding the letter down so that I could see the hand-writing, a very distinctive hand-writing. I said, "Aren't you Lolita? Isn't that a letter from Aunt Ellender?"

She stared at me! My middle name is Creston, which I detest. She said, "Yes! . . . Creston?!"

I got a job with Bing Crosby working a big circus party. He put up big tents over his tennis court and had an all-night bash for a day and a half. Shortly after that, his first wife, Dixie Lee, had an operation, and they were looking for a temporary chauffeur for four weeks. I was bumming, not doing too much, and it sounded like a good move, so I took it.

Then I went to work for Bob Hope as a butler in his house in North Hollywood, a house that Clark Gable had once owned. I did that for eight weeks until I got ticked off at his mother-in-law. For several days straight she'd say, "I left something out on the back porch." I'd go out there and couldn't see anything but dirty clothes in a washtub—she meant she wanted me to wash her laundry. So I said, "You didn't hire me. Go upstairs and get Mr. Hope and tell him I want my money." He begged me not to quit, said, "Come out to the studio, be my valet."

Instead, I hit the road again, to Tuskegee to see my mother. Damn near froze to death again in Texas in the Panhandle. I stayed in Tuskegee three months and met Captain Ben Davis and his father, later General B.O. Davis, Sr.

Then I went to North Carolina with two other guys in the photography business. It was one day pork and beans, the next day steak. So in 1940 I went back to Kansas University Law School.

I registered for the draft, and that's the first time I had ever been called black. For some reason, that was a blow. I said, "What's this 'black?' Do I look black?"

This was 1941. War clouds were rumbling. A letter from my mother said, "They are getting ready to start an experiment here to train Negro flyers, and Captain Davis is going to be the first one. I thought you'd be interested."

The only contact I'd had with airplanes, my dad had a ten-acre plot behind his store, and barnstormers would use it to land in. I'd been up twice, open cockpit, and I kind of liked it. I figured I would much rather fly to war than fight in the trenches. Then I got a brainstorm, this great big light bulb—I can get into aviation easier if I'm on the inside rather than the outside. So I enlisted in the Army.

I was sent to Fort Riley KS to the Ninth Cavalry, a black unit with all white officers. The famous Ninth and Tenth Cavalry were two of the major Negro units retained between World War I and World War II. I immediately put in my application for aviation cadet training.

There were only four black sergeants there to teach us to ride, and I was immediately made an acting corporal. I'd been there less than three weeks and had barely learned to ride myself. We started getting raw draftee recruits, who had never been over ten miles away from home in their lives. Seventy-eight percent were absolutely illiterate; only half of the rest could sign their names. Three days later they sent us 100 wild-ass horses from Arizona, supposedly broken. They weren't. Trying to teach these recruits how to ride wild horses! We killed a few horses. Some we never broke.

I was drawing $21 a month, was made acting sergeant, and put in for NCO school—I was putting in for everything.

In the meantime I was contacted by guys in civilian clothes asking a whole lot of questions. They were from military intelligence, and they were interviewing me for the counter-intelligence police, which was just being built up.

Meantime the Ninth was called out for maneuvers in Louisiana and Texas, and during a three-day lull, the troop clerk said, "Hey, you get that letter?"

"What letter?"

"You're supposed to be going to Washington, D.C."

I stormed up to troops headquarters, and reluctantly the first sergeant found the letter. The rascal made me walk over to the main highway to catch a bus to Shreveport. I had about four dollars in my pocket.

In Washington I was reassigned to military intelligence and was trained to go to Liberia under cover as a road construction engineer and check out clandestine German radios. We worked with FBI guys dressed in covert top coats—I spent all my clothing money and then some.

I went back to Fort Riley on furlough, just to say "hee-hee" to the old cavalry troops, when the troop clerk said, "Oh, I've got a letter I've been meaning to send you." This was the letter calling me to aviation cadet training.

I was sent to Tuskegee in April 1942. They had hazing of the new dummies, but they were afraid to touch me, because I walked in there in my covert topcoat. Word had gotten to somebody that there's something strange about this guy.

We had a class of 20 people. In fact, only eight graduated. But I didn't have any question in my mind I could fly—I soloed in four and a half hours.

The two white officers in charge of primary flying school would give check-rides to see what you could do. If you couldn't hack it, they would catch you.

I didn't even take the 20-hour check-ride, didn't take the 40-hour check-ride. Magoon gave me the 60-hour check. Didn't have any problems.

The last check-flight was a night cross-country flight to Chattanooga and back by way of Atlanta. The only night navigational aids they had back then were light lines. At intervals of 15 taught 20 miles, there would be beacons turning around, giving coded flashes. There were about five light lines going into Atlanta and several going out the other side.

There was a dance that night, and in my eagerness to get back, I cut the corner of Atlanta to pick up the light-line going back to Tuskegee. But I missed the damn line and hit the one going to Birmingham instead. I didn't know where I was, so I cut back and really got into trouble. I picked up another light-line, but it wasn't going where I thought either.

I was looking at the big E on the gas gauge. The low-settling fog that hangs over swamps had started building, and I had just made up my mind that "you've had it, pull up and bail out of this damn thing," when I spotted a small field, so I started down through the fog.

I pulled back on the throttle, pulled back on the stick, jumped on the brakes, and stopped three feet from this little weather shack. I got a farmer to let me call the base, and two instructors came and got me.

I didn't damage the plane, but needless to say, I missed the dance.

"Mother" Long was in charge of advanced training and chewed my ass out. I knew I was through. I had to write 150 times "Lessons for How Not to Get Lost." The next Monday at the start of advanced training, Mother Long told the class, "Several of you will probably not be here when we complete training." And he looked straight at me.

We had just finished the fourth week when I got called out of class. A lieutenant said, "Cadet Gleed, you're supposed to read up on the P-400."

"P-400! I never heard of it!"

It turned out to be a P-39 Aircobra

"They're going to bring three here, and you've been elected to fly one."

"What?!"

"Yeah, they're going to have a cadet and an instructor fly them."

My mind started spinning a thousand ways. The plane was brand new to me: You let the gear down with an electric switch; it had two .50-caliber machine guns and a 37-mm cannon that fired through the nose cone and dripped oil all over your pants. The engine was behind you, and there was always something going wrong with the doggone thing. While all this was going through my mind, he said, "You better get on up to the mess hall, get something to eat, and come back."

But I couldn't eat. Overhead I heard these strange-sounding planes coming in. There were masses of people around the flight line to observe this exhibition—they probably all figured I'd wash out.

When I reported to Mother Long, the crew chief took the plane's door off, and I squeezed in with my parachute. I was frightened enough, so I went to get another 'chute to try to get the butterflies out. I finally got the monster cranked up and got it onto the taxi strip. It was bedlam from then on.

The nose-wheel locked, and the damn thing spun around twice. But I got a takeoff, and everything went just as if I'd planned it. I went up and had a whole lot of fun in it. I did a couple rolls, then got nerve enough to do a snap roll, then decided to land.

But when I dropped my gear, for some reason the darn plane was sinking and sinking. The trees were coming up looking at me. I poured more coal, more coal, pulled my gear up, and climbed back up. The tower was screaming, but I couldn't hear half of it. Mother Long was out of his mind.

I made a 360-degree turn, and it was almost the same thing. It wasn't until the third pass, after I'd settled my nerves, that I realized I was stalling that thing, holding the nose too high. This time I came round and made a smooth landing of it.

Next the white instructor went up. He held the nose way back when he landed, dragged his tail and damaged it. The guys said, "No way you're going to wash out after this." But *I* damn near washed me out!

The 99th had by now been completely trained and sent overseas, and we were still putting out pilots. What the hell do you do with them? They established our squadron, to take the overflow. Then they formed the 332nd Group with three squadrons. At first we were flying P-40s, then they decided to give us P-39s.

I'm the only guy who had flown one, so one day in June 1943 I found myself being told that I was now the squadron commander of the 302nd as a second lieutenant.

Charles Bussey:

I like to tell young men that our squadron commander, a lieutenant colonel's job, was only 26 years old. Ed Gleed was a natural pilot. In a foot race or a fistfight, Gleed was your man.

Felix Kirkpatrick:

"If we wanted to give someone an accolade, we'd say, 'He's the greatest thing since Gleed.'"

Wendell Pruitt

GLEED'S classmate, Pruitt was a dashing figure. A St. Louis native, he was the youngest in a family of ten children, sang in the glee club, built radios, repaired automobiles, and learned to fly in CPT.

"He was easy-going, never cared about anything," a fellow student and future Red Tail, Arthur Pullam, said. Pruitt played guard on the basketball team. "You had to be ready for the ball any time, because you didn't know when he'd throw it."

Another cadet, Chris Newman, said:

> He was an eager beaver, always ramrod straight while the rest of us were lazy and sitting around.
> But later, as a pilot, Pruitt's attitude was sort of carefree.
> He was daring, and he had a little bit of the rogue in him. He didn't mind breaking regulations with his flying and did things the higher authorities didn't approve. He was the best we had in the skies at that time. On the ground Pruitt was a quiet, unassuming man. He just flew loud.

"He didn't mind taking a few chances," said Ed Gleed, "doing things the average guy wouldn't do."

Sheppard:

> Pruitt was a hell of a nice guy, a fun guy to be with. Always imaginative, especially in the air. I just loved to fly behind him in a string of six planes. When we were up doing our training thing, we'd engage in mock combat and 'rat races'—that's follow-the-leader. He'd peel off, heading straight for the ground, then pull up. We'd fly under the bridges at Port Huron.
> Everyone loved to fly with Pruitt and admired him.

Pruitt had the glamour and flamboyance of a typical fighter pilot. "A very good-looking guy," Bernard Knighten said. "The girls were crazy about him,"

"He was a flashy guy," future pilot Jimmy Walker, said—"a hot rod, a ladies' man, and a hell of a pilot. And he knew it."

Charles Bussey agreed that he was a leader—athletic and good-looking, but Bussey felt he was shy with women:

> They were looking for glamorous boyfriends, and maybe they just overwhelmed him.
> Pruitt flew all the time. Sunday morning, when all the guys were trying to

get over their hangovers, he was out flying. He had a distinctive, flashy style. You could see an aircraft flying by, and you knew it was Pruitt in it.

Jimmy Walker was a very religious man, Sheppard recalled. He was born in South Carolina but moved to Baltimore to attend high school, because there were no black high schools in his home state. He went on to Hampton Institute in Virginia, where he studied the building trade and attended CPT. He would graduate number-two in his class.

Class #14

A NOTHER vintage class, it produced several top pilots of the 302nd. Charles Bussey was "a big-chested, *gung-ho guy*," in Woody Crockett's words.

Bussey was born in 1921 in Bakersfield California.

> It was a disgustingly prejudiced place at the time. Even in kindergarten I became aware that there was something wrong, that I wasn't treated like the white kids, the oriental kids, or even the Mexican kids. I resented it bitterly.

Bussey's father had served in France, and his grandfather, an ex-slave, had fought in the Wilderness with Grant, on the western plains, and in Cuba. He carried three arrowheads in a pouch and one more around his neck. The old man, in his eighties, in a tattered army coat, drove a rickety buckboard wagon and six year-old Charlie used to climb up beside him to listen to tales of the old days.

> My other granddad had been a Methodist minister and had graduated from college back in 1887. He built churches in Bakersfield, Riverside, Pasadena, and Santa Monica. A very close relative of my father founded Voorhees College in South Carolina before the turn of the century, and I had an uncle who became the first black Supreme Court judge in California.
>
> Prior to the Depression, my dad was a railroad mail clerk; he carried a pistol and rode with sacks of mail. But the Civil Service was different then, so when the Depression hit in '29, this became a white boy's job, and Dad had none.
>
> Times were hard from then on. I'm not one of those people who talk about the good old days. The hell with them. I'd hate to go through them again. I worked in the fields from the time I was nine or ten, picking cotton, corn, all kinds of fruits. I got paid damn little, cotton went for one and a quarter cents a pound then.
>
> When I was 17 a friend and I rode freight trains all the way to Detroit. In Ogden Utah there was a wheat harvest on, and we bucked 100-pound

bales of wheat. We were there about ten days and made $30—that was big bucks.

In Nebraska we worked shucking corn for three dollars a day, room and board. So when we got to Detroit, I had 57 bucks, a king's ransom, it seemed at the time.

Then we went up the St. Lawrence river and out to sea on a "rust bucket." I'd never seen the ocean before. I shoveled coal eight hours a day, the toughest way to make a living. About 400 miles west of the Azores, the ship threw a bearing, and we were towed in by another ship, so we laid around the Azores about ten days, did some drinking, and the little money I had earned was soon spent.

We stowed away on another ship heading back to Norfolk, hopped freight trains, and hoboed our way home.

Stoking boilers by hand is a hard way to make a living, so I finished high school and went to Los Angeles City College for two years. College cost five dollars a semester, and I had a hell of a hard time raising that five bucks.

I applied to the U.S. Army in the middle of '41. Of course I was treated with the utmost discourtesy. I was disgusted and wrote to Eleanor Roosevelt, who responded within three days and apologized for the segregated nature of things and told me there was a program for black fliers in Tuskegee. As a result, in September 1942, I had an opportunity to go to Tuskegee for flight training.

Flying was exciting—tremendously rewarding, and there were new people, very fine, high-type people, some with masters' degrees. I was one of the few who didn't have a college degree, which was consistent with my age, but it made me sort of a pariah.

However, the town of Tuskegee itself was not a good place to be in. They had a sadistic sheriff named Pat Evans, who loved hassling black soldiers, and we got hassled at every opportunity.

Sheppard recalled Bussey as aggressive and straight-forward:

There was no hesitation about anything. And he was outspoken; he gave you his views on whatever the subject was, without hesitation. A lot of people didn't like him because of that. But he and I "bought" each other, warts and all.

Felix Kirkpatrick had followed B.O. Davis to West Point in 1935.

I didn't plan to go to West Point; it just happened by chance. I had finished my first year in the Armour Institute of Chicago, now the Illinois Institute of Chicago; at that time we thought it was second only to MIT. There were three of us blacks in the institute, although it was almost unheard of then for blacks to choose engineering, because they had to go to South America to get a job.

My credits in math were very good, and one of the students suggested, "Why don't you go to West Point?" Congressman Oscar De Priest [then the only black member of Congress] got me an appointment, and before I knew it, I was in West Point under a "dog ticket," that is, they waived my entrance exam because of my credits at Armour Institute.

You have to know something about the West Point tradition: They're very clannish in the Army. As commandant of cadets they had a lieutenant colonel whose father had been governor of Virginia. The southern boys at that time were bitterly against blacks, and they were in a position to put us under the silent treatment. If one of your classmates was too friendly, they made it so difficult for him he wished he'd never seen you.

I had a room built for four, but I lived in it by myself. Going to church was a formation, something you had to make; but I was in a pew by myself.

I was given demerits on a systematic basis. They'd tell someone, "Go over there and gig Mr. K."…."Mr. K., straighten your hat." I'd put my hand up, and my hat was already straight, but when you saw the gig sheet, it said, "Hat on head crooked."

I was always walking the yard on punishment tours until my classmates called me 'the iron man.' The main idea was to keep you away from your studies, but I was in the upper third of my class.

B.O. Davis was a first classman when I was a plebe [freshman]. He came by my room and said, "Don't worry, they can't afford to dismiss you because of demerits." But DePriest was no longer in Congress, so I no longer had a sponsor and no one to turn to.

In six months I was on my way home.

When you're young, you're very resilient, you bounce back. The only effect it really had was that it interrupted my school, and I never did go back to full-time formal schooling. I went to work for the Pullman Company in Chicago as an electrician in the yard.

Kirkpatrick visited the Chicago *Defender* office to see editor Enoch Waters just as Willa Brown was telling Waters of her difficulties in recruiting students for CPT. "Well," said Waters, "what about Felix here?"

"That," Felix said, "is how I started." At 27 he was the old man of his class and in fact had to get a special age waiver.

"Kirkpatrick was one of the funniest guys I ever met," Sheppard chuckled. Even hearing Felix say grace in the dining room sent Shep into uncontrolled laughter until the cadet captain made Harry eat his meal under the table.

Luther Smith came from Des Moines Iowa, one of eight kids. His boyhood heroes were the pilots who delivered the mail in open-cockpit planes, and when he was 13 he found five dollars in a field and spent it on his first plane ride. After that he walked five miles to the airport to hang around, do odd jobs, and hope for a chance to fly.

He studied engineering at the University of Iowa, enrolled in CPT, and grabbed his chance to join the Air Corps.

Harry Sheppard, the former mechanic, applied for flight training.

Harry was also a pianist. As often as he could, he got together with Lawrence Dixon, a jazz guitarist, in the playroom of the club.

He didn't have any interest going off base. For one thing, his pay had dropped from $96 a month as a staff sergeant to $75 dollars as a cadet. After deducting his allotment home, there wasn't much left.

For another, "you were looking for an encounter with the law enforcement people who were always baiting you, hoping you'd make a mistake." On a trip to Atlanta he and fellow cadet Melvin Brooks bought bus tickets to return to Tuskegee.

> The MPs would stalk through the stations, looking for excuses to break your head. An MP spotted me and put me under arrest.
>
> "Come with me."
>
> "What's the deal?"
>
> "Don't ask any questions." The guy took me to Camp McClellan and booked me.
>
> "What are the charges?"
>
> "Impersonating an officer." They locked me up! I guess he felt real proud of himself.
>
> The next morning they released me.
>
> I had been the class captain, and I lost that. I had to meet a board. Brooks was about to pass out laughing; I could see his shoulders shaking as they asked the questions. I sweated being thrown out but was restricted to base pending graduation.

Sheppard's kid brother, Herb, was an army sergeant, who wanted to be a pilot. "He came up from Camp Rucker, Alabama to see me graduate. He rode on top of the bus with all the duffel bags, and I flew him back to his base."

Charles McGee came along in the next class. He was soft-spoken and much admired by the others. "I wouldn't call him reticent," Sheppard said, "but he wasn't one of those voluble, effusive fountains of knowledge you couldn't shut up."

His mother died in childbirth when he was one, and his father, an army chaplain in Europe in World War I, raised the two kids. "We didn't have a lot," Charles said, "but whatever it was, it was enough. I never remember being hungry or not being clean." But he did remember stuffing paper in his shoes in winter for insulation. His father, a minister, took the family to Florida for a year. He didn't remember prejudice, but the schools were so poor, he had to repeat the third grade when they moved to Keokuk Iowa. In the summer he "cooled off" in the Mississippi river, and even in Iowa he had to sit in the balcony at the movies.

McGee graduated ninth in his high school class of 400. "My family didn't have enough money to send me to college, so I spent a year with the CCC" [Roosevelt's Civilian Conservation Corps, which gave Depression youths work in forestry projects.] He saved his money to enroll at the University of Illinois as an engineering student, working his way through school in a steel mill in Gary, Indiana and learing to fly with white students in CPT. He got married on a Saturday in October 1942, "and Monday that letter I knew was going to come," arrived, ordering him to Tuskegee, and he and his bride set out for Alabama.

> In the South, if you were a black man from the North, you had to be especially careful what you said and did. I learned to be extremely careful when you stopped to fill up your car and even avoid some filling stations.

Because of his college studies, McGee skipped pre-flight. But he flunked his first check-out flight and had to re-take it two times.

Charlie was also a physical fitness bug and led the calisthenics for his class and later for the 332nd Group.

Class #16

ANOTHER memorable class, it included Daniel "Chappie" James, the former flight instructor who went on to become a bomber pilot because of his size. Thus he missed World War II, but became the Air Force's first black four-star general.

But, Charlie Bussey remembered, "James wasn't the outstanding person in that group, not by a hell of a shot. We had many more people who were much more accomplished than he was. But he got the breaks."

Ernie Davis, another West Pointer, who was also in the class, was half the size of James.

Bussey said:

> He was very mild, very learned, very sharp. You'd never think of him as a fighter. For some reason Ernie and Chappie got into a little fisticuffs, and Chappie came out quite the worse.

Lee "Buddy" Archer

CAME out of Manhattan's DeWitt Clinton high school, along with Sidat-Singh and Sheppard and said Singh was his inspiration for joining the Air Corp. Archer was a typical New Yorker, Red Jackson smiled— "aggressive in speech, but a popular mixer socially, and he played a deadly hand of poker or blackjack."

Archer told the Veterans' History Project:

I was one of ten children. My mother died when I was 12, and my father raised us. He was quite a man—I still retain the Jr. He was very strict, into politics in Tammany Hall [the city's Democratic party organization].

I was a fan of World War II aviation; they were like knights in armor. In those days teachers could rap your knuckles. I skipped two grades in public school.

We lived at 119th Street in Harlem. On Morningside Ave the houses were grand. At that time Harlem had a lot of Irish and Italians. The neighborhoods didn't become polarized until the whites moved out and the area gradually became black. Woolworth department store never had black employees.

As a youngster with three sisters, I got to go to the Renaissance and the Harlem Opera House and the Savoy Ballroom. Every time someone wanted to go and couldn't get a date, especially the Savoy, where you needed a date, the cry was, "Dad, can't Buddy take me?" As soon as we got in, she'd ignore me from then on, and I danced with other girls and learned dancing quite well. I was a member of the Savoy 400 Club, who thought they were great dancers.

My sister Harriet became a professional dancer in shows in Switzerland and Sweden.

My brother was a horse trainer.

I spent one summer on boats, like the Eastern Steamship Line. A cook convinced me that I shouldn't stay too long, because I'd get stuck there, so I left to go back to school.

In 1941 it was obvious war was coming, and I wanted get into the Army before we got into the war. I have a family history of fighting for the country when it was in trouble. So a bunch of guys, most of them white, talked about doing what we should do for the country.

I didn't know about the discrimination in the Service at that time, it wasn't something I paid much attention to. I went down to join the Army Air Corps and did very well on the test. I waited, but I didn't get called. After I hassled them a bit, I was informed that I would never be called for the Army Air Corps, because there were no openings, and there never would be.

In November 1941 I got called by the Army. I said, "I volunteered for the Army Air Corps."

"No, you volunteered for the *Army*."

So I was put in the infantry and sent to Camp Wheeler, near Macon Georgia.

My first real shock was on the train to Atlanta. When we got to Washington DC, they got all of the colored military men and moved them to the first car behind the coal engine. In Washington, the capital of my country that I was going to fight for, they gave our seats to white people.

It was my first real blow. Back home I could get in a fight with a white kid and not worry about being lynched the next day.

Macon had a terrible reputation.

At Macon I got beautiful marks in telegraphy. Two hundred of us were taking the test. Two cadre, sergeants with swagger sticks, started standing over me to see if I was cheating. I got the second highest score, and they made me an instructor.

I remember sitting with a white friend in the military bus to go to town. We got out the gate on it. But later that evening we met at the bus station and sat together: the driver said, "You can go to the back or you can stay here."

I said, "We're buddies."

He got a civilian policeman, who came with blood in his eye and told me to get off the bus and wait for the next bus.

Recreation was separate, even on the base. Our PX was a little room. In Macon they had a big fancy one for whites, a little small section for colored. The white fellows went to the white one and had a great time. Some of us went in the wrong one and were promptly put out by the police. That was probably the biggest slap in the face I had.

For recreation we could go to the hard core bars, or we could go to the social club at Georgia Baptist College Friday and Saturday evenings. It was a little "nothing" college, but that was our salvation.

I met my future wife there, doing nice things for soldiers at the college. I had been a pretty gallant young guy. But she was only 16, I was 20. I asked her father for her hand, and he said, "No, wait. She's 17, it can't happen. You go overseas. If you make it back, then we'll talk."

I didn't want to marry her father. Why should I talk to *him*?

I finally got orders to report to Tuskegee. I arrived at Chehaw, a little shed alongside a railroad track, on Christmas Eve. No one met me, so I picked up my bags and walked to the base. I found a converted bath house they had turned into a barracks. It was empty; everyone was home for Christmas leave.

One thing struck me about the cadets: their egos. These guys knew that they were special in their own minds. If the Air Corps wanted Tuskegee to fail, why did they pick the best people to be cadets? There was an *esprit de corps* among us. Sixty years later we're still the best of friends.

I was Cadet First Captain at every level, the first to solo.

Pre-flight was taught by black instructors. Everyone in class was smart enough to use a slide rule [a math calculator, sort of an early computer].

In Primary we started to get our first problems. The instructors were black, but all the check pilots were white southern officers. They handed out pink slips. Three and you were out of the program. It had a lot to do with personality—of the instructor as well as the student. If you were rather arrogant and wouldn't take crap from anyone, you didn't make it. I don't remember ever having a second check ride.

William "Chubby" Green was "one of the finest pilots I ever knew," Lee said. The two became close friends and part of the famous trio of Pruitt, Archer, and Green.

Archer:

If there was any way we could fly together, we did. I flew 169 missions over there, and Pruitt and I flew close to 100 together. We were the two "Hip Cats," because we were both from big cities. We each had a little guy painted under our horizontal stabilizers, a guy with a zoot suit [wide lapels, long jacket, and baggy trousers] and a funny-looking hat.

Chubby was from the Blue Ridge Mountains of Virginia, near Red Jackson's home. "He was one of the youngest pilots, but an excellent pilot," Jackson said. When Jackson asked what Green's ambition was, he replied, "to be the best damn pilot in the world."

In Italy Jackson always picked Chubby for his wingman—unless B.O. Davis was flying, in which case Green flew the Old Man's wing.

Bill Melton was, in his own words:

an army brat from the old, old segregated army. My father was in the medical corps. They had one medical company assigned to each of the four black regiments scattered around the country and the Philippines. I was born in New Mexico and entered school in New York when my father was assigned to West Point. I grew up around Tucson—Fort Huachuca—and my father is buried there.

I got pretty good training as a child; I was in church every time the church door opened.

I lived very near the airport and used to ride my bike out there when they had these barnstorming air shows and wore my Boy Scout uniform so they'd let me in free. That's when I met Ernst Udet, a World War I ace, who could do unbelievable things. I became instantly fascinated with aviation.

Elmer "Chubby" Taylor was Melton's best friend:

He was bald, gregarious, full of humor. I called him Mussolini—he looked like him. He was from Pittsburgh, educated, sophisticated, but he had a weight problem, and the physical training instructor had him sucking a lemon all day long to lose a few pounds, just like boxers do.

The class graduated in July 1943. They all bought new pink and green dress uniforms, and while their families waited proudly in the auditorium, the cadets marched to the theater. Archer:

> I was leading the formation when I was stopped by an officer, who told me, "Have Cadet White fall out."
> I said, "Yes sir!"
> "Continue to the theater."
> At the theater I kept looking back out through the door to see where White was. Going back to the barracks, I met him. He said, "They gave me a 'ride.'"
> "What do you mean?"
> "'I got a pink slip.' I'm out!" It said, "Passed but not graduated for the good of the Service."
> We all were on the same orders, and his name was on it: Kenneth White. I never figured that out. OK, we had one over the quota. But why him? He was pushy, self-confident; he might have rubbed someone the wrong way. And he's down near the end of the alphabet. But he shouldn't have been pulled out marching to graduation.

Walter Westmoreland, a Georgian, was light enough to pass for white. He was a nephew of Walter White, head of the NAACP, and a cousin of Fredrick Funderberg of the 301st.

The 332nd now had a full complement of three squadrons and moved to Selfridge Field outside Detroit for advanced combat training and checked out in the P-40s.

Sheppard was practicing loops when the instructor told him, "You're going up to 8,000 feet and stick the nose straight down. Then point it straight up and take your hands off the throttle. If you touch the controls, the airplane will stall."

"Well," Sheppard gulped, "that was kind of hard to do!" He did loop after loop, hoping each time to be allowed to pull out. "No, not this time," the instructor ordered. "Finally I started to run low on fuel. My hair was standing straight up."

Oscar Kenney's plane plummeted into the ground. No one ever knew why. After the funeral Shep and each of his classmates received a letter from Kenney's parents, "urging us to perform our patriotic duty so that Negro people could share fully in the freedom for which we were fighting."

Two P-47 Thunderbolts were sent to tow targets. "No one was qualified to fly them," Gleed said. "So who gets selected? Me, although I'm the commanding officer."

The students doing the shooting were in P-40s that were even older and more un-airworthy than the ones the 99th had trained in. They still had the sharks' teeth of the "Flying Tigers" painted on their noses.

Wilmeth Sidat-Singh crashed into Lake Huron, and though he bailed out, he was never found; some speculate that he got tangled in his parachute and drowned "The entire Group was struck with grief," said Sheppard, "because he was one of our first losses. He was a hell of a nice guy."

Detroit, "the Big D," with its nightclubs and pretty girls, beckoned to the single guys, who headed for the Adams Bar and the St. Antoine nightclub. Clem Givings exhorted them:

> "Hair conked, shoes shined,
> and running to St. Antwine."

Palmer took his wife to town and passed Sergeant Joe Louis, the heavyweight champ, coming toward them. The champ threw him "a snappy salute."

The airmen found that Jim Crow was as alive in Michigan as in Alabama. When Detroit was wracked by a bloody race riot, the black officers' weapons were confiscated and they were confined to base, surrounded by a guard of white troops. The citizens of Iosco County made it plain that they didn't want the black fliers any more than the people of Tuskegee had.

"The town fathers wanted the U.S. government to close Selfridge," Sheppard said. "The government and some senators came to our rescue and really gave the town hell."

The base was just as bad as Tuskegee," Bussey nodded, "maybe worse." A scandal broke out when the commander, Colonel William T Colman, shot his Negro jeep driver. Some reports say Colman was drunk. There were also whispers that it stemmed from a triangle involving the colonel's wife.

Coleman was replaced by Lieutenant Colonel Robert Selway, a Kentuckian and a West Pointer, who ran the base much as Colonel von Kimble had run Tuskegee. Said Bussey: "His job was not to give us training but to see that we didn't use the Officers' Club or swimming pool; that was his biggest concern."

Selway was backed up by the commanding general of the First Air Force, a World War I ace and two-star general, Frank O'Driscoll "Monk" Hunter of Savannah Georgia, who had "a filthy mouth and a hatred for blacks."

Johnny Briggs:

> It was separate, but it was far from equal. We had our own barber shop. Our PX was a make-shift PX in the barracks, where you could get cigarettes, chewing gum, beer, that sort of thing. The Officers' Club was off-limits. That was up in Michigan! You wouldn't think that would be, but back in those days, that's how it was.

Meantime, as with the 99th before them, the 332nd found that no one overseas wanted them, so they trained endlessly. Keen rivalries developed.

"The 302nd 'Hellions' were the cockiest," Gleed maintained 40 years later. "We built up an *esprit*. We thought we had the best pilots. I still consider it that way."

Sheppard agreed.

> We had a dynamic bunch of guys. I think we were the most closely-knit bunch. We studied together, we fought together, we suffered together. There was a camaraderie you often didn't find in white units.

Gleed, Pruitt, Archer, and Green soon became a fearsome foursome. Archer remembered:

> We'd fly together every time we had a chance, even if we weren't scheduled to. We considered ourselves a natural group. At one time Ben Davis was going to court martial all four of us because of the way we flew together. We were trying to fly acrobatics in formation, and that was not done. He thought it was a risk we should not be taking. If something happened, it would reflect badly on the Group.

Sheppard and Palmer brought their brides and lived in the same motel. Whatever one tried in the air, the other tried to do better. "We were happy-go-lucky kids and just loved flying," Palmer said. "I was only 22, mind you, and I just thought flying was the greatest thing in the world."

Flying under bridges was great sport, even though Richard Dawson had been killed trying it at Tuskegee. "They were kind of high," said Sheppard, "30-40 feet above the surface; we had plenty of room—you just didn't want to arrive there at the same time someone was coming the other way."

The next step was to try it at night, Palmer said. "It would really test your instrument skills. Better know your altitude and hope your instruments were correct!"

"I'm not going to lie," admitted Alexander Jefferson, "I think all of us were scared when we did it. But you just didn't show the white feather."

Soon they were not only trained to a fine edge, they were over-trained and bored. It led to some dangerous antics. "Moe" Downs said that one day they dreamed up a game of 'peek-aboo' with a train. "We'd fly straight at the engine and then pull up. To enliven things, we did all kinds of loops just in front of the engine." Of course they got a stiff chewing out.

Palmer pulled another escapade.

> We heard that the Tuskegee football team was going to be playing in Detroit against West Virginia, another all-black school. I was assistant Flight

Leader, and I said to the group, "We'll fly down to Detroit and buzz the game," because we knew some of the members on the team. We made a cursory pass at the field at about 500 feet, and the other three members of the Flight said, "OK, we're heading back home."

I said, "That's ridiculous. We made this whole trip down here for one cursory pass? No way! I'm going to go down and let them know we're here." They went on back, and I came down to about 100 feet or so and checked to see if there were any telephone wires or anything. There was nothing in the area, so I came over a third time below the level of the stands, and as I was pulling up, I did a slow roll. When executed properly it is a beautiful maneuver, and this one was executed to perfection.

Who happened to be at this all-black football game? Colonel Selway, who didn't like blacks flying in the first place! I don't think I finished my slow roll before he got on the phone and said, "Have the pilot of plane B-5 grounded, and let him know he's going to be court martialed!"

By the time I got back to the field, they brought a military vehicle to take me back down to Detroit to be court martialed. I got rumors from my friends, who said Selway planned to have me expelled from the Service as an example.

Of course I was sick, because here I had just graduated two or three months before, and now I was going to be thrown out of the Service. I had made my wife and parents so proud, and this would bring disgrace on all of them.

While awaiting trial, Palmer was confined to the bachelor officers' quarters, and nights without his wife, Nita, were lonely. One weekend she snuck into his room, which was separated from the others by temporary dividers. She hid in a clothes locker until the coast was clear, then they tiptoed into bed.

Unexpectedly the officer across the divider, Virgil Richardson, had not gone home that weekend. While the couple snuggled, Virgil called out that he had a good book Walter would enjoy and tossed it over the divider. Wrote Palmer: "I don't know whether he suspected anything or not."

At the court martial, my commanding officer, Captain Tresville, testified in my behalf, and so did my Flight Commander and my Operations Officer. The question was put to them: "Would you take him in the squadron if he gets out of this court martial?" They said, yes, they would.

As a result, I'm sure, I was just given a fine of $75 a month for three months. I was also relieved of my job as assistant Flight Commander. But shortly thereafter I got it back because my commanding officer liked the way I flew.

Meanwhile, the War Department was still trying to decide what to do with the unit. General MacArthur's air chief didn't want them in the

Pacific; the British didn't want them in the British Isles, nor even in British islands in the Caribbean. The Danes vetoed Greenland.

"We went through three training cycles. The troops were growing restive," Sheppard said:

> Hitler is kicking their butts, and here's a force of trained combat pilots, and they're fooling around with this racial trivia. We really looked forward to getting into combat. We were on a keen edge, like tempered steel. But we lolled around. You can over-train and become dull.
>
> I'd been reading about the German 190s and 109s, like a boxer sizing up his opponent, and we wanted to get overseas and see what the *Luftwaffe* had for us.

At last orders came down: They were going to Italy.

Most white cadets went overseas after 40 hours. "I had 145 flying hours in the P-40 and 125 in the P-39," Crockett said. "So I felt I was red-hot when I hit Naples."

Just before they were to move out, three more replacements arrived for the 302nd—Roger Romine, Hubron Blackwell, and George Haley. They had to catch up fast. "We had those poor rascals strapped to the P-39 from the time they arrived," laughed Sheppard. "Their day was just jammed from dawn to dusk. Oh, they pissed and moaned."

Haley memorialized it in a poem:

> The 302nd worked like bees
> To get their outfit overseas,
> But none worked as long and hard as these—
> Romine, Blackwell, Haley.
>
> With frigid feet and fingertips,
> Horseshoe spine and aching hips,
> Commanding colonels still plan trips
> For Romine, Blackwell, Haley.
>
> When "each and every" off to town
> To some sweet pad to lay him down,
> Up in the sky still duty-bound
> Are Romine, Blackwell, Haley.
>
> If one dared take that evening date,
> By dawn he'd be in awful shape.
> But still they'd strap him to that crate—
> Romine, Blackwell, Haley.

"Operations thinks it's best
Because of weather take a rest,
But you three take a ground school test"—
Romine, Blackwell, Haley.

Flight leaders change throughout the day,
Let missions vary as they may,
From dark to dark in their ships stay
Romine, Blackwell, Haley.

Blessed peace, oh praise the will
That brings release from plans to kill.
Dear God! Tonight there's "dinghy drill"
For Romine, Blackwell, Haley.

Sheppard took pity on them. "I'll take one," he volunteered. "I'll take Haley." And Haley became Shep's wing man for his entire combat tour.

At last, in December 1943 the 332nd was on its way to Hampton Roads Virginia, its embarkation point.

Lou Purnell decided to go back with them.

At Tuskegee I was given a group of cadets to train, two of whom froze on controls while I was teaching spins and recoveries. After you stall, you make precisely two complete 360-degrees and kick out. I was counting three and four turns, and the ground was coming up right fast. You don't know when you're coming out until you break the strangle hold of that kid in the back seat.

Right then I decided to go back to combat, where it was safer.

At Camp Patrick Henry, Bussey found the whole camp "just riddled" with signs saying "Whites Only."

Directly across the street from our area was a movie that said "White Troops Only," and the PX said. "White Troops Only." The nearest PX for Negroes was two and a half or three miles away. I got a belly full of it. I just said, "The hell with this crap. I'll raise some troops, and we'll all go to the movie." I pulled the sign off the building, and we all bought tickets.

When we left the movie, a few fist fights broke out between the black and white soldiers. Later on it got more serious. They had issued us guns and ammunition that day, and the guys started firing at random up in the air and caused quite a bit of consternation.

The MPs arrived, but when they saw the situation, they chose not to act, so my squadron commander, Gleed, sent me down to put a stop to it. I went with a couple of enlisted men, and it was kind of scary, believe me. But finally we got the thing put down.

Purnell:

Some of those bullets must have come pretty close to headquarters, because we could hear them whistling overhead.

The next day soldiers went through the area and took all the signs down. Beginning that morning we could go to any damn theater we wanted to. That's one good thing we did before we left. The rules of segregation at Camp Patrick Henry were changed. Changed forever.

That's when Charlie got his nickname, "Bad Boy Bussey."
They had one last job to do, Kirkpatrick said.

On the ferry going to their ship were two more large signs, saying, "Whites Only" on one side of the boat and "Colored Only" on the other side. "Bussey was on one side and pulled down one sign, and I was on the other and pulled down the other one.

8

Naples

The P-39

THE 332nd was on the high seas when news of the 99th's triumph at Anzio reached them. "All we heard was about those black pilots who shot down eight planes in one day," Crockett said.

They spent a month on the Atlantic in a convoy of 80 Liberty ships, using speed to outrun enemy U-boats. Thirty officers were crammed into a 20 × 30-foot space. "We were sleeping on the floor," Charlie Bussey said. For amusement, musical instruments were brought out. They also played a cutthroat game called "dirty hearts"—the loser had to drink a pint of water. "When you had a long losing streak," said Bussey, "you were in deep trouble."

January 29, 1944. The 332nd stepped off their ship at Taranto on the toe of Italy. They saw a town almost flattened by both German and U.S. planes; where people in tatters poked through garbage, looking for food.

The airmen were trucked to their airfield at Capodicino outside Naples. Charles McGee:

> They told everyone to be prepared, we were in the war zone, and to dig fox holes. One night a German Heinkel bomber flew over Naples, and we were all out there watching the show with the searchlights on—until one of the planes made a run down our own airstrip, dropping frag [fragmentation] bombs, and damaged 27 aircraft.
> Of course everyone hit the fox holes.

"No one realized how dangerous anti-aircraft fire was," Walter Palmer said. "We'd shoot up little chunks of metal about the size of a poker chip or larger. One came down through our tent."

The next day, McGee said, "folks were out there digging those fox holes three times deeper!"

Meantime the Group began un-crating their new planes, the P-39s. Almost nobody liked them. Clarence "Lucky" Lester:

They were dogs, rickety old things, just lousy airplanes. It had the engine behind the pilot and a shaft with the cannon ran between your legs and shot out through the propeller spinner. It was good-looking, it had doors like an automobile, but it had very poor flying characteristics, because the center of gravity was off because of the engine placement.

It was lousy for air-to-air combat but pretty good for ground support because of its heavy shielding underneath. I didn't mind the airplane too much, because I could fly it. But there were a lot of pilots who were scared to death of it.

Woody Crockett:

It was a little faster than the P-40, but it couldn't turn. You could change you heading, but you couldn't change your direction, it just mushed. And I didn't like running interference for a big engine behind me. If you were tall, you had to put the seat down all the way to the bottom. I'm 5'11", almost the limit, so I had to press my head down to get inside the door.

There is no P-39 Pilots' Association today; apparently no one thought very much of it.

Harry Sheppard:

We got the P-39s back from Russia and England, some of the old Lend-Lease planes we had sent them. They very gleefully gave them back to us when we got to Italy. [Actually, several Russian aces flew the P-39.]

I never did trust it. It had very poor aerodynamic characteristics in combat; it didn't like sudden changes in altitude or direction. In a real tight turn where you're pulling streamers off your wing, it had a nasty habit of snapping into a spin, which was quite exhilarating.

It was known for killing people. The cannon sat between your legs; if you ran into something, that was the first thing you hit. The engine was behind you, so it would come forward, the guns would come back, and if your ordnance man wasn't too sharp about the head space, the aft part of the gun could change your whole social life forever.

They designed the cockpit last: "Oh, we gotta put a *guy* in there?" The P-39 was not a great airplane to get out of. It had a door on the right-hand side, like a car. If you had to bail out, you had to pull a lever which pulled the pins out of the door, and the air stream would take the door off. Then you had to dive for the wing to keep from being hit by the tail.

Chris Newman of the 100th had several near-death experiences in the P-39. He wanted to have a look inside Vesuvius and flew over the smoking cone. Suddenly his engine started sputtering—the sulfurous air had little oxygen—and he immediately headed out. "If I'd gone down a little deeper, I might not have made it."

On his second flight, Newman made a night landing without seeing the ground.

The ground controllers sent us out to sea to try to find a May Day [a downed flyer]. We flew a search pattern and didn't see anything, but they said, "Well, can you look a little longer? We hate to lose a pilot."

When we finally got back, it was dark and when it's a blackout, you don't realize how little you can see. The airfield put a light straight up in the air like a beacon. I didn't know what it meant or where it was in relation to the field, but I started looking for the ground and pulling back on the stick. I got it all the way back to the stop, but if you're too high, one of the wings may stall before the other one. I knew I should be touching the ground,

It seemed like an eternity before I hit. The landing broke the nose gear, and I slid down the field. Thankfully there was no fire.

The third time, Newman forgot to put his wheels down on landing. "I set down on an external tank and, BOOM! All I saw was fire. The door was supposed to fall off, but it didn't." He finally kicked it off and fell onto the wing. "I had first-degree burns on my face and third degree burns—where you're kind of 'cooked'—on my leg. I was in the hospital about two and a half months."

Only one man had kind words for the P-39. Another replacement, Alexander Jefferson:

It was a sweet ship to fly, because it flew straight and level. The tricycle landing gear was a relief after the tail-dragging P-40.

But there was one problem: You had to avoid violent turns or stalls, which might whip the plane over into a snap roll or up-side-down spin, which was usually fatal.

The next shock was their assignment: the insulting task of coastal patrol. Lester said, "A fighter pilot flying coastal was like a brain surgeon being a physician at a Boy Scout camp: it was just about the most boring mission you could perform.

"It was a slap in the face," Davis wrote. But he bit his lip and dutifully hunched his six-foot body into the small cockpit.

Presumably, the decision was made by the out-going Theater Commander, Carl Spaatz.

As the 302nd maintenance officer, Sheppard had no plane of his own. "I had to fly them all, test hop them. If something was wrong as reported by a pilot, I test-flew it the same day or flew it on the next mission." He grew bored with the constant patrols.

Haley and I buzzed the Isle of Capri. We came down and flew right over it, skinning the island. Crazy fighter pilots—they called us "bubble heads." We didn't know it was a British rest camp for war-weary guys back from the battle line.

We got a hiding. Gleed says, "Look, you two guys are always into some kind of mess. Well, I'm going to keep you busy."

He gave us dawn, lunch, and dusk patrols. That meant we took off before the rest of the guys were finished breakfast. Some of the barrage balloons were still up, which gave it a kind of hairy aspect.

Landing after sundown wasn't good either, because the anti-aircraft people are on edge, and they challenged us several evenings with lights— it's a good thing we knew the code of the day. You had a little telegraph key, and the lights on the side of your fuselage or wingtips would flash, and they used that for recognition.

Those British gunners could shoot, and we were at low altitude anyway. I couldn't remember whether I was giving the right code or not, I was so damn nervous.

Palmer, who had almost been cashiered for buzzing the football field, apparently hadn't learned his lesson. He was Johnny Briggs' wing man.

We always did a lot of buzzing around—well, that's the nature of fighter pilots to buzz. Johnny had an outgoing personality. We didn't mingle socially, but he flew with such smooth motions, I figured I could improve my flying by flying his wing; we flew as many as six hours a day together.

Johnny and I always flew a tight formation. We flew so close they used to call us "the P-38 boys." The P-38 was a twin-boom fighter with one wing and two fuselages, and when you saw our two P-39's together, it looked like one P-38; we flew that tightly.

Briggs:

Palmer was really sharp, he was doing all the work. I'd pull up, and he'd stay right in there with me. When we came back from a mission, the crew chiefs and ground crewmen would want us to buzz the field, and stuff would blow over the damn tents and everything. We'd circle around and come back and buzz it again, then we'd drop wheels together and touch down together. No, there was no one else like Briggs and Palmer.

The commander, Robert Tresville, told me, "Briggs, the next time you do that, you're going to be grounded." The very next day we did the same damn thing. Sure enough, he said, "You're grounded! Go to your tent."

I went to my tent and lay down on my bunk. An hour later the Operations Officer, Jug Turner [squadron commander], came up and said, "Briggs, we're short-handed, we need you on a mission in the morning." So that didn't last too long.

The fliers formed tent groups within their squadron rows. Sheppard gave a rundown on some in the 302nd:

"Poker Flats"—there was always a poker game going on, and they were the roughest poker players you would ever find. Before each game Weldon [Baldy] Groves would close his eyes in prayer, which would invoke Bussey's anger; he thought Groves was praying for celestial help.

The "Chargin'" Misters—Dudley Watson, Milton Brooks, Edwin "Evil" N. Smith, and Roger Romine. A very caustic bunch. They challenged everybody about every subject on earth.

Our tent was "the Damned Handicrafters." We used crates to insulate the tent. Jimmy Walker, a product of Hampton Institute, was adept at tools, and we were always hammering and sawing at night, and you could hear us throughout the area, much to the disgust of our neighboring tents, who used to complain vociferously.

There was always something going on. We'd give short sheets, and if you were lucky enough to get a metal cot, we'd very delicately balance it so when a guy sat down it would collapse.

We had nicknames for everybody. We had four Smiths. One stayed up all night carousing, so we called him "Dissipatin'" Smith. Another Smith told fantastic tales about everything; we called him "Fantastic" Smith. Edwin N. Smith had kind of a mean demeanor, although he was a good man; we called him "Evil" N. Smith. Lewis C. Smith always had a half-smile on his face so he was known as "Smirkin'" Smith. Luther Smith spoke too rapidly, and he was called "Quibblin'" Smith.

One day Gwynne Peirson popped his head in our tent while George Haley was eating an apple and said, "You guys got anything to eat in here?" That's why we called him "Hungry" Peirson.

Roger Romine negotiated with Italian workmen, and they made tiles out of pressed wood shavings and concrete, almost like concrete blocks. He built this damn hut all by himself. The other guys were teed off because they were all in the tents, and Roger had built himself this unauthorized hut, his palace, and he was quite happy.

Except, the tiles were flammable. He was in there reading on the bunk, and the stove exploded and set the hut on fire, and he ran out. All he had on was a pair of shoes and carrying his book and his .45.

After that he moved in with the Chargin' Misters.

February 2–7. The 99th was still seeing action in their P-40s.

On the 2nd they dive-bombed a key bridge north of Anzio, an escape for retreating Germans.

They also knocked down three more enemy planes by Elwood Driver, Clinton Mills, Swampy Eagleson, and Leonard Jackson.

Meanwhile, social mixing was problematic. Not, however, for the fun-loving Bernard Knighten. While the others stayed home and played poker:

> I'd go to town and hound the bars. No racial things happened to me, but I didn't look for those things, and the bars were open to everybody. I ran into a bunch of Australians, and believe me, they were real gems.
>
> Capri had an R&R camp and a big hotel, but we weren't allowed to stay there. The Negro pilots stayed right across the park in the home of King Victor Emanuel.
>
> They had a dance at the white hotel, and a captain stopped us at the door, said, "There are white nurses here." We just walked off. We weren't torn up about it, we assumed that was the way it was; we weren't the aggressive type at that time. There were 400 pilots there, and we couldn't get a dance anyway, so it didn't bother us one bit.

Purnell:

> We were well accepted by the Italians after they found out the stories that had been spread about us [white GIs told the girls that blacks had tails] weren't true.
>
> Our rest camp was a glorified mansion—ballroom, pool table, several nice bedrooms. One night we really pitched a good party with a band and girls from the University of Naples—good quality girls, really hand-picked, no whores; our Special Services officer made sure of that.
>
> We were really swinging when we heard gunfire outside. We looked out, and the whole place was surrounded by infantrymen just returning from the front.
>
> Immediately we called the MPs, but it looked like they were on the side of the infantrymen. So we called the British MPs, and they cleared the whole bunch of them out, infantrymen and American MPs alike.

February 15. The 332nd encountered enemy planes for the first time. Melton of the 302nd recalled:

> I was the first guy in the Group to encounter the enemy, a severely damaged Junker 88 bomber, while on patrol at the mouth of Naples harbor. They used to come over at a very low altitude and take pictures; they'd be low enough to throw wakes in the water with their props. They were always there a certain time of day, and we used to sit out there and wait for them.
>
> I thought I'd get one, but that old 37-mm gun jammed on me. The P-39 was a notoriously underpowered airplane, especially at sea level, so the Junker got away.
>
> Going over as we did, we didn't have combat returnees to lead us, and I learned more in the first three or four hours in combat than in all the prior months.

One white pilot recommended hanging our dog tags over our gun sights to tell our position with reference to the ground in case our instruments got shot out—whether we were skidding, whether our wings were level. That became a ceremony. My crew chief would take my tags off and hang them over the gun sight.

(I also had a good luck charm, some Pompeian jewelry I'd bought as a souvenir, some of that porno stuff.)

Every inch of that Anzio beachhead was bracketed by that damn German 88 gun up on higher elevation. It was one of the damnedest weapons ever invented. They used it for anti-aircraft, and it was murder.

Once I got hit by AA [anti-aircraft] fire, and my engine coolant temperature shot up. They had told me what to do in case I got hit in my radiator: Reduce all my power settings, drop my flaps, slow the airplane down to 170 mph and just wait until the gauge dropped.

I couldn't have learned this from any black, because none of them had had this type of experience. This was taught to me by a white fellow I don't even know.

Woody Crockett's wing man was Earle Sherrod from Columbus Ohio.

Sherard was a hotrod, always needed excitement. I had to do something outstanding every day just to keep him awake. Around Anzio we were flying, two guys low and two high. We made the Italians jump out of their sailboats, we were that low.

And he almost ran into a big rock out there. He complained when he got back: "You like to killed me!"

February 23. The 332nd suffered its first fatality when Harry Daniels was lost in bad weather.

Meanwhile, Woody Crockett found a jeep driver to see the sights of Naples. That night the Germans bombed it. The Army had smoked it to obscure it from the German planes, and the driver couldn't find his way down the street. "Then Vesuvius erupted, so the Germans had no trouble locating the city. I don't think they could have had a better beacon." For weeks afterward, the pilots had to fly out to sea to avoid the huge cloud of ash before beginning their patrols.

Walter Palmer had a taste for opera, which he apparently shared with the Germans, who had not bombed the Naples Opera House, so Walter spent his days off there listening to arias.

C.C. Robinson of the 99th also took in the sights.

The opera changed every week like a movie; we'd go every Sunday; I got to be quite an opera buff. There were a lot of museums, and I must have visited the Vatican five or six times" to see the Pope. Plus a lot of girl-chasing, what guys in their twenties would do."

March 30. Davis received the official report on the Army investigation of
Spike Momyer's charges. It rejected them completely.

But still "they were wasting three squadrons," complained Melvin "Red"
Jackson. "We had seen one German Junkers 88 bomber the whole time we
were over there."

Ed Gleed, commander of the 302nd, was impatient for more action. He
and Tresville, the CO of the 100th, tried to stir things up a little without
telling Davis:

> Bob Tresville and I dreamed up a "Cook's tour" a 16-ship formation of
> P-39s. We plotted to go out to sea, get up above Anzio and maybe stir up
> some enemy aircraft and get some kills. We'd done about three of these mis-
> sions but never ran into any airplanes.
>
> The Old Man, Colonel Davis, found out about it and chewed Tresville
> out: "Bob Tresville! You, above all!"

April 14. Gleed continued:

> Bob sent another mission up.
>
> Then I sent another one up, and it turned out to be a disaster. I did one
> of the dumb things I never should have done—took my operations officer,
> Pruitt, with me on the same flight—you shouldn't both be on the same
> flight. My plane acted up, and I had to turn back, so he took over and went
> on as planned.
>
> He wound up around Rome when they were running low on fuel.

The official report said they went 30 miles north of Rome, a 270-mile
round trip, instead of the planned 180. Three pilots ran out of gas, including Walter Westmoreland. When he had used up his last drop, he had to
jump. The plane was destroyed. He broke his leg, was treated at a hospital
and put on orders back to the States.

A three-man board blamed Pruitt and recommended a slap on the wrist.
Not Davis, however.

Gleed:

> That did it. The Old Man said, "You prepare court martial papers against
> Pruitt."
>
> I said, "I don't see how I can do it, sir. I was the one who scheduled the
> mission and flew on part of it myself."
>
> "I want those papers prepared, and have them to me by noon!"
>
> I said, "I just flat can't do it."
>
> Ben had a way of being very impressive. When he was a student flying
> with an instructor, Ben had had an accident and banged his forehead on a
> gunsight, and it left a scar. Whenever he'd get really worked up, that scar
> seemed as if it pulsated. He barked at me: "*Lieutenant!*"

I said, "Sir, I can't help but say again, I should be the one to be court martialed."

He said, "I want you off this field by 12 o'clock tomorrow! You're no longer commander of the 302nd Fighter Squadron."

Sure enough, I got orders to go to North Africa. I didn't know what it was all about, but when I got there, a lieutenant colonel said, "Oh, you're the new test pilot."

"What!"

"Yeah, we're badly in need of test pilots."

"Uh-uh"

"Well, you'll learn pretty fast."

They'd bring new aircraft to Europe disassembled, then re-assemble them. We took them up and tested them.

Pruitt never did get a command or another staff job. It's probably just as well; he was much more valuable as a pilot and turned out to be perhaps the hottest pilot in the 332nd.

Gleed was replaced by Red Jackson of the 100th:

Col Davis didn't inform me; he had a big tent, and I never saw him. The 100th was the senior squadron, had a West Point man in charge, and had more of the older people, so it would be natural for Davis to go to that squadron, and Tresville said, "I recommend Jackson."

The squadron areas were 100 feet apart, and I just walked on over to the 302nd. I knew everyone there, and everyone knew me. We had all trained together, we all ate in the same dining hall.

Jackson was a natural choice in point of seniority as well as in command ability. He had graduated at least two classes ahead of any pilot in the 302nd. Sheppard:

Gleed was a kind of happy-go-lucky guy, but in my estimation, he could be guilty of some rash decisions. A quick mind, but he had a typical fighter pilot's mentality: "Let's do it" without any thoughts of consequences. Gleed was a go-getter: "Hey, let's go! let's do the job," He was a good leader, but he was kind of brash—bordered on foolhardy, I thought. Pruitt was somewhat that way too.

Jackson's style was unhesitating, but the result of having put a little fore-thought into it. He would never give up, he had dogged determination. If the assignment was to attack the entire Reich on our own, he'd go ahead and do it. But first he'd think about ways to do it and what would happen after. There was nothing rash about Melvin T.

"A very even-handed, calm, judicious, capable man," Melton agreed.

Westmoreland, meanwhile, was treated at a hospital and put on orders back to the States, but he asked to return to the 302nd instead.

April 19. Roberts finally was given relief and sent home, along with Lemuel Custis, Herbert Carter, Charlie Hall, Jim Wiley, Willie Ashley, and Willie Fuller.

Wiley was welcomed home to Pittsburgh as a hero. He rode with the mayor at the head of a parade through the city he had left almost penniless.

> Now suddenly I was a hero. I was waltzed down to the mill where I had worked to talk to the laborers and tell them what a good job they were doing and was invited to downtown clubs I had never been in.

Roberts was replaced by Erwin Lawrence. According to Robinson:

> He almost got everybody killed. A British officer had given the briefing and said, half jokingly, "On your way back, why don't you stop by Monte Cassino and take a look?" There were a lot of anti-aircraft guns scattered around, and no one really wanted to go down there, because you were almost bound to be hit. But we went down and, hell, everybody got shot up.

Meanwhile, Harry Sheppard's kid brother, Herb, was awaiting assignment to Tuskegee:

> Harry is six and a half years older; he was my role model. I went to vocational school: I wanted to be a plumber in the worst way. I didn't want to be a doctor or a lawyer. I said, "Plumbers are making more than doctors are."
>
> We had a teacher who preached to us every day: "You guys ought to get that vinegar out of your blood and do something for your country." Every minute. He talked us all into joining up, but he stayed back—he was too old.
>
> But I couldn't wait to go in. Really. I enlisted in the Army as soon as I graduated in June 1942, with the intention of going into the Air Corps.
>
> I had a good infantry basic—map reading, weapons—and I had been to Ft. Sill, the Artillery School.
>
> I was in ordinance, at Aberdeen Proving Grounds, when they opened the quota for cadet training. I didn't have a college degree, but they were doing it on an exam basis, and they called me to go to Keesler Field in Mississippi, the pool they were drawing from for Tuskegee. I figured I was going to wind up in Harry's outfit.
>
> In April 1944 we were just set to go to primary training, and Hap Arnold sent out a telegram that the Air Corps had not lost as many men as they anticipated and thanked everyone. They wiped us out and sent us back to the ground forces.
>
> We were all crying.

I got orders to go to Italy as replacement in the 370th Infantry, 92nd Division.

The war in Italy went on.
Baugh:

I had one wing man, Smirkin' Smith, shot down. Smith saw a truck on the road, and I said, "You go down, and I'll follow you." He put a 500-pound bomb in the bed of the truck, right behind the cab.

Then we saw a convoy on the road. You should strafe across the road, but we strafed down the road to get more shots in, and they hit his airplane. He flew up a couple of thousand feet or so and bailed out and spent the rest of the war as a prisoner of war.

On another occasion:

I was dive bombing some gun positions in the Po Valley, and the anti-aircraft fire was thick. I remember seeing tracers going by my airplane. I'm going almost straight down as fast as I could get the airplane to go, 550 mph—in that airplane, that was fast. I remember very distinctly wondering, "Why did I ever take up flying?"

The Theater Army Commander, General Mark Clark, thanked the 99th for its support of his troops. General Cannon, the 12th Air Force Commander, called it one of the best ground support outfits in the theater. Tooey Spaatz requested more black units be sent to his command, and Air Force Chief Hap Arnold himself sent congratulations.

Eaker's Problem

APRIL 20. General Ira Eaker, the Mediterranean air commander, visited the 332nd and the 99th. The son of a Texas share cropper, he spoke in a Texas twang and told them the 99th had made a "magnificent showing." "They fight better against Germans in the air than they do on the ground support missions," he wrote.

Eaker had big things in mind.

He was facing a crisis. In London he had been engaged in a long debate with the British over strategic bombing. British night bombing had proved inaccurate, missing military targets and hitting civilians.

American daytime bombers used the new Norden bombsight, which could "put a bomb in a pickle barrel." But they suffered horrendous losses from enemy fighters. In February 114 bombers and 1,000 crewmen had gone down. More than 300 men were lost in a single raid over Ploesti oil fields in Romania. Sixty bombers with 600 men perished in another raid over Germany, the worst air disaster of the war and the inspiration for the Gregory Peck movie, *Twelve O'clock High*.

British Spitfires had a short range and could barely deliver the bombers across the Channel before leaving them to the Messerschmitts. The P-47s had somewhat better range, but still couldn't escort far into Germany. The promised P-51, with a range of over 1200 miles, could be the answer.

But that led to another debate, over deployment. The chief of the U.S. fighter Groups, Major General Frank O'D. Hunter, a World War I hero, argued that the fighters should fly ahead of the bombers, sweeping enemy planes from the skies, a tactic that would give the fighter pilots more opportunities for glory.

But Eaker protested that it would also leave the bombers to face the enemy alone; he insisted that the fighters stay with the bombers at all costs. Eaker won, and Hunter was sent home. There he would provoke a major crisis that led to a "mutiny" by black officers in training and would virtually destroy an entire black fighter-bomber Group before it even fired a shot at the enemy.

When Eaker was given command of the Mediterranean air forces, he formed a new strategic Air Force, the 15th, to hit targets in southern Germany, southern France, and eastern Europe. He needed fighter pilots. The 332nd could help solve the problem. But could Negroes stand the intense cold of high altitude escort missions?

With his own career on the line, Eaker paid a visit to the 332nd. He told Davis he needed them to join six other fighter Groups in the 15th Air Force. They must stay with the bombers at all costs, he emphasized— protect them with your own lives.

"Needless to say," wrote Davis, "I jumped at the chance."

Along with Anzio, this was the other most important development in the history of the "black air force."

Ironically, Eaker was replaced in England by Jimmy Doolittle, who soon dropped Eaker's stay-with-the bombers policy and adopted Hunter's fighter-sweep philosophy. He wanted to clear the Luftwaffe out of the skies to give the Allies complete air superiority for the Normandy invasion. Without telling the bombers, of course, Doolittle sent them up as bait to draw the fighters into the air, where they could be destroyed. As a result, the 8th Air Force fighters produced dozens of aces. Thursday the Red Tails were virtually the only fighter group in Europe that was put on a time leash and restrained from running up high victory scores.

In in northern Europe there may have been a rationale to aim at the German fighters in preparation for the invasion. But in Italy the emphasis was properly put on giving the bombers the chance to wipe out the German war industries.

May 12–14. Meanwhile, the 99th under Bates was busy, strafing and escorting bombers over Monte Cassino. This fortified medieval monastery atop rugged mountains was holding up Allied attempts to advance. They were awarded a Distinguished Unit Citation.

May 22. The 332nd left the 12th Tactical Air Force and joined the 15th Strategic Air Force under General Nathan Twining, where they would conduct long-range missions into Germany and east Europe in the P-47.

"Morale," Davis wrote, "was soaring."

Briggs and Palmer celebrated with one last burst of hubris. Palmer described it:

> On our last mission before transferring, I said, "Johnny, don't forget to give them a good closing when we come in."
>
> We were going to "cut the grass" on the field—we got down about two or three feet off the ground and flew the length of the field. I was almost scratching his fuselage with my wingtip.
>
> At the end of the field there was a fence about eight feet tall. All of a sudden Johnny looks over to verify that I'm in real tight, gives the old signal, and jerks his plane up. That's rough on the guy that's flying his wing. But I hung with him. When he pulled it up, I pulled it up. Back down on the ground, I said, "Johnny, why'd you jerk it like that?"
>
> He said, "You know how close we came to hitting that wall?"

Davis, who had been watching the exhibition, just shook his head.

"No question about it," Palmer declared, "the 100th was the best squadron in the Group; we had real close camaraderie." As for himself, "I knew I was as good or better than any fighter pilot in the skies with me."

Eaker wrote to Arnold: "These colored pilots have very high morale and are eager to get started."

9

Mutiny at Walterboro

MEANWHILE the returning veterans of the 99th and the new pilots of the 332nd had been engaged in another war, a war at home. It was actually a civil war between two armies of American soldiers, each of which had sworn to die for the ideal of America as it saw that ideal. Neither army was prepared to give quarter.

Said Spann Watson, "in the military, we started integration right up there in Selfridge Field, Michigan."

The base continued to give advanced training under Lieutenant Colonel Charles Gayle, a white officer. Instructors included Clarence Jamison, Charles Dryden, Bill Campbell, James Wiley, and Spann Watson.

Tuskegee was adding a cadre for a proposed new unit, the all-black 477th Bomber Group. It would include a future four-star general, Daniel "Chappie" James; a future Secretary of Transportation under Gerald Ford, William 'Bump' Coleman; a future mayor of Detroit, Coleman Young; and a future mayor of Los Angeles, Tom Bradley.

The 332nd's old nemesis, Colonel Selway, commanded the 477th. Wiley remembered him as "a pompous person, always surrounded by his white commanders. All of us black guys were just 'crew members.'" The base commander, Colonel William Boyd, was also white. General Frank O'D. Hunter, who had lost a policy struggle to Ira Eaker in Europe, commanded the First Air Force, the next echelon above Boyd.

There were several irritants at Selfridge. For instance, black officers were not allowed to occupy officer's housing on base. But the main battle was the same one the 332nd had fought—the Officers' Club.

Although Army regulations said all Officers' Clubs must open their doors to any officer on base, Selway ruled that his Club was for whites only and told the blacks to wait until a separate club was built for them. Wiley:

> The white Officers' Club, Lufbery Hall, was the usual plush Officers' Club. But we were told to stay out. Our so-called club was a room at the end of our barracks with a pool table and a bar. Most of the guys were putting their lives on the line, or had already put our lives on the line, and we said, to hell with this.

Foreshadowing the civil rights sit-ins of the 1960s, the black officers decided to go to the white club anyway.

Dryden:

> I was on leave in Detroit with my wife when a group of three pilots went to the main Club—they thought there would be more guys, but a lot of them chickened out. The three were ordered not to come back. It would be unwise for the same ones to go back and disobey a direct order in time of war. That would be tantamount to treason.
>
> So the next night some others of us decided to try again.
>
> That morning on the flight line when I was suiting up to fly, Lieutenant Colonel Gayle told me, "I hope you understand that, as the ranking first lieutenant, I expect you to keep these guys in line and make them understand Army policy."
>
> I said, "Yes, sir."
>
> That night we decided we would go to a movie, and then amble over to the Club and go for a drink or two so it wouldn't look like a conspiracy. But when I looked round, only two other guys were going in the door with me. Colonel Gayle and Colonel Boyd were the first two persons I saw inside the door. Colonel Gayle's face turned as red as a beet, and he said, "Goddam it, I thought you understood."
>
> I said, "I understood, but I don't agree. It's the Officers' Club, and we're officers." We were "guard-house lawyers," and we knew Army Regulation 210-10, paragraph 19-C, which obligated us to support the Officer's Club. That was pretty clear.
>
> Colonel Gayle almost had a fit. "You leave this club right now!" It was a direct order, so we left.

The next night a different group did the same thing. Jamison:

> I had flown 67 missions in combat, I was a captain, and I think I was the senior black officer on the base. I went over to the Club with the others, and a white captain said, "You can't come in." He was embarrassed because I'd been overseas getting my butt shot at. But we went on in anyway, stood around a while, and then left. At least we'd made the point. We did that for two or three nights.

The Air Force brass, nervous about race riots in nearby Detroit, charged that the whole thing was communist-inspired.

Campbell denied it: "Nothing could be further from the truth. The problems we had were strictly racial."

When the Pentagon got wind of the crisis, Dryden said,

> The Inspector General from Washington arrived to interrogate us. General B.O. Davis, Sr. spent 20 to 30 minutes with me. I was thrilled to get

a chance to spill my guts. About a week or two later, both Colonel Boyd and Colonel Gayle were relieved from command. We thought we'd won a victory.

May 8. However, Hunter called the officers to an assembly. An aide called "Attention!" and down the aisle strode Hunter, in a black mustache and trailed by his entourage. "Gentlemen," he snapped:

This is *my* airfield. As long as I am commander of First Air Force, there will be no racial mixing at any post under my command. There is no racial problem at this base, and there will be none.

You're not ready; colored officers are not qualified to lead anyone. The policy of the Army is the same as the rest of the country, and that policy will be enforced to the letter. Are there any questions? If there are any questions, I will deal with the man personally!

"We were thunderstruck," said Alexander Jefferson, who was preparing to join the 332nd. "He stood there and looked at us, and we looked at each other." His aide called "Attention!" again, all snapped to their feet, and Hunter strode out of the hall with his aides in tow.

"We black officers were immediately restricted to the base. They locked the gates, cut off the radios, phones, and all communications."

May 10. Dryden:

Two days later the fighter pilots were exiled by train at night. The black press and our relatives didn't know where we were going. We didn't know either. We crossed into Canada, then headed down the Mohawk Valley, through New Jersey and Washington, D.C., and raced through Virginia, North Carolina, and South Carolina. The next day we looked out the train windows and saw Carolina pines and GIs with carbines standing every hundred feet on both sides of the train.

We didn't know what the hell was going to happen. The Japanese Nisei had been interned in California; we thought we might be interned too. As it turned out, it was an air base far from public scrutiny or attention.

They were in Walterboro South Carolina.
Meanwhile, the 477th was exiled to Godman Field Kentucky. Campbell:

Some people thought, "We'll get them down there where they keep blacks in their place." That was one of the conjectures. You can draw your own conclusion.

Dryden:

In later years, I found out General Arnold wanted to deploy the outfit to the island of Antigua in the Caribbean so we would be far from the black press, although that fell through.

All our planes had been flown down from Selfridge—none of us was allowed to ferry the planes. We lived in beat-up World War I barracks.

We immediately tried to integrate the theater. There was a rope down the middle, and the guys cut the rope and 'checker-boarded' the theater, some sitting here, some there. The theater manager, a tech sergeant, refused to start the film until the officer of the day ordered us all out, and we went back to the barracks.

The base commander told us in no uncertain terms that he was going to enforce the segregation laws. I guess we acquiesced with the letter of the law, but the spirit of the law got me in trouble.

Campbell:

By that time the Army had come out with a regulation that you couldn't segregate government facilities by race, so the white officers went down town and formed clubs. They built a nice club for us about a mile from the base, where there wasn't much chance for us to come in contact with whites.

I stayed there about two and a half months and volunteered to go back overseas.

Dryden:

To me, the low point was seeing German prisoners of war who could use the white side of the PX cafeteria while we couldn't. I was so furious, I lost my self-control; I was going to show these crackers I could fly.

The next day I demonstrated how to attack a machine gun tower. There was a water tower in town about ten stories high, and our flight path took us right across the home of the mayor of the city. You can imagine a quiet sleepy Sunday morning with four P-39s at full power roaring across town.

Alexander Jefferson was among those on the "bombing" run.

Jefferson's grandfathers were both ministers. His father worked in a Detroit iron foundry, and died with lungs that "looked like branches of a black tree," and Alex vowed he'd never do that kind of work. He grew up in a Polish neighborhood in the Depression and said he didn't own a store-bought shirt until he joined the Army. In his book, *Red Tail Captured, Red Tail Free,* he said he worked on a junk wagon at 13.

He couldn't join the Boy Scouts, which were segregated, so he joined the neighborhood 28th Street gang. He was one of the smallest, and the only black kid, and they fought other gangs "with rocks, fists, and Coke bottles." They shot craps on the street corner, and "if the cops came, we grabbed the money and ran like hell."

Still, he must have been studying hard, because he skipped two grades and graduated from high school at the get of 15.

Jeff enrolled in Atlanta's Clark College to study chemistry, driving a 1932 "tin lizzie" day and night to get there, because no hotels along the highway would take him.

"Light, bright, and almost white," he joined a fraternity, sang bass in a quartet, took girls to lovers' lane in his "lizzie," or loaded it with cheerleaders to football games, drinking Southern Comfort whiskey out of Coke bottles.

Jeff wanted to join the Air Corporals. "I wanted wings, and, with any luck, even more lovely ladies."

"Hell, no!" his father exploded. "Finish college first." ("It was the first time I heard the old man swear.")

So he graduated and moved to Washington, enjoying good jazz at the old Howard Theater, and finally took his test for flying school.

> I was a "big" 117 pounds. You had to be 118 to be accepted. The guys at the recruiting center told me to go downstairs, buy some bananas, eat all I could, drink some water, and come back. I did. I weighed in at a little over 118.

Alex rode south in a Jim Crow railroad car—"soot and hard seats" and smelling of urine, because there were no black lavatories.

> I think there were 90 fellows originally in the class. I don't remember much about primary training except getting up, running, and, oh, those pushups!
>
> I remember soloing [he was first in his class to do it], but I bounced about five or six times as I landed, scared to death. Anybody who says he isn't scared on that first solo is a damn liar.
>
> I can say that I successfully ground-looped everything I flew up to the P-40. Anybody who ground-looped in primary was out; but by some miracle, I stayed in. Man, they check-rode me regularly. I even had the infamous Magoon check-ride me. It was well known that a check-ride by Magoon was the end of your flying career. It was one hell of a check-ride, but I miraculously survived.

Jefferson went to Selfridge in February 1944 and loved it. Watson and Dryden were instructors. He remembered Dryden as "an absolutely fantastic guy, very out-going with a dynamic personality, and a great instructor."

The students made navigation flights across Michigan at tree-top level.

We blew farmers off their tractors and blew chickens into the air. We had clothes-lines wrapped around our props and grass stains on the tips. We played follow the leader…and were so low over the river that the 11-foot prop threw up spray like a rooster tail.

Best of all, Selfridge was near Detroit—Paradise Valley, Black Bottom, the Flame Show Bar and the Horseshoe Bar—with their great bands— Duke Ellington, Louis Armstrong, Cab Calloway. Best of all, were the beautiful girls, "who found cocky young fighter pilots full of vim and vigor to be quite attractive."

With four or five other P-39s, he flew tight circles around the downtown Maccabees Building—at night—with throttles wide open, then screamed at tree-top level over the neighborhoods where the girls lived.

After the officers' club "mutiny," Jeff and the rest of the class were shipped to Walterboro.

I was on the flight that buzzed the water tower. The whole class was in on it. Dryden got court-martialed. Why I didn't, I'll never know. One class-mate, MacIvers, was given a dishonorable discharge—why he was selected to be an example was never made clear.

Dryden:

I was given a general court martial and dismissed from the Service. But I was granted a second trial because my rights had been violated when one member of the court was heard to say they were going to throw the book at me, which is a prejudicial statement.

He was acquitted in the second trial but was forced to pay a fine and restricted to base for three mouths.

After the court martial, Bill Campbell, one of my buddies, was seeking volunteers to join the 477th to be sent to the Pacific. I was so fed up with the South and Jim Crow, I said, "Take me! Please!"

Spann Watson remained an instructor with three or four other blacks and 24 whites.

The best training the fighter pilots ever got, they got at Walterboro. We put aside the race battles and put out good pilots. We had some of the most sincere people. I didn't see any sloughing off in training black people for combat. Lieutenant Colonel Joe R. Williams, director of flight training, turned out to be a great guy. The only thing, they asked us not to "brace" the white cadets [that is, to hold them at attention].

Hugh White, Carl Ellis, Yenworth Whitney, and "Doctor Death"—John Whitehead—were the best in my flight. You could do anything with them. Let me pick four or five pilots, give them 100 hours in a P-47, I'll lead 'em, and I'll compete with you in everything—dogfight, formation flying, anything!

Whitney looked like a little mouse, looked like he was about 17. But no matter what I did to confuse him and throw him off, he would end up sitting on my wing like a mouse, looking right at me.

White had one of the most spectacular women. This is something that's never been written about: The great Tuskegee experiment brought the most sensational black women from everywhere in the country, looking for husbands. We had jumped in pay from $21 to $250 a month, with esteem, respect, and beautiful uniforms. The most beautiful, most educated women anywhere flooded Walterboro. No matter where you'd go, you'd see one of these outstanding women, most of them college girls. From New York, Chicago, Los Angeles, you name it, they found out about Tuskegee.

It turned the social structure around. Before that, doctors and lawyers had had a monopoly on the best-looking women in black society.

Meantime, a black P-47 student with a white instructor collided with a B-24. It wasn't the student's fault, Watson said:

> But it brought up the whole racial thing about blacks flying. The next day the whole Group of B-24s flew over Walterboro with their flaps and wheels down, they knew their man had made a big mistake. The next day our squadron passed over their Group in a return salute.

Student Dick Macon from Montgomery Alabama was chatting at a bus stop with a white sergeant from Brooklyn. When the bus pulled up, they sat down together, still talking. A white man behind them asked the sergeant what he was doing sitting with a colored. In reply, the sergeant, a boxer, smashed the man's face, knocking him into the aisle. While women screamed, the man quietly picked himself up, resumed his seat, and the bus drove off without a word from the driver.

Another incident did not turn out so fortunate, Watson said:

> A white bus driver slapped a black female, and a black guy jumped up with a knife and put it to the driver's throat. They arrested the man and tried him that night and sent him to prison for a year and a day, and the goddam post commander let him go.

Another man refused to go to the back of the bus, the white police hit him on the head and blinded him. There was almost a sit-down strike the next couple of days. All the black folks said, "This can't go on, this kind of justice."

Watson himself was in the middle of another racial fight that could have been tragic.

I went to a Chevrolet dealership and asked to have a flat fixed. The black flunky said, "Sure, leave it, come back tomorrow."

I went back every day for about four days, but it was never ready. Finally, I said, "To hell with the damn thing, all you're doing is lying. Give me my damn tire back."

Some little short stumpy dude was standing by, said, "Who are those remarks directed to?"

"I was talking to him, but it could just as easily be you."

He hit me right in the mouth. The President himself isn't going to hit me in the mouth, so I floored him. He got up, and I floored him again—I beat the hell out of him. Then everyone in the shop jumped over the counter and rushed me, swinging at me with a long hose. I knocked one of them backward.

I found some MPs and told them I was having some trouble.

Two of them jumped down from their jeep and sent the driver to the base for help. The MPs said, "Here they come now. Lieutenant, you just can't talk back to them. No matter what they say to you, don't answer."

I said, "Look, this is not going to be a situation where one black man, usually in shackles, is shot dead and they said he was trying to escape. You leave your holsters open; when the time comes, I'll get 'em, you won't have to."

The city cops came, and the state cops, and the little guy who had the battered face, and a mob developed. They were calling me all kinds of names. The greatest hatred I ever saw was on the faces of these little scrawny state police. They'd snap their heads back and forth like goddam rattlesnakes.

By this time more MPs from the base had arrived. The MP officer was a redneck with a long-barreled gun, a private weapon, that stuck out of his holster half-way down to his knee. He went to the white folks and asked them what happened. They said this nigger had beaten up the mayor of the town for no reason. Then he came over to me, and I told him what happened. He said, "That ain't what they say."

I said, "You're a mobster like the rest of them. I don't want to talk to you at all."

The deputy base commander, Colpnel Lockwood, arrived. He told the MP officer, "I'm in command now. You follow my orders. Watson, let's go see if we can reason with these people. I'll do the talking."

We started over to the dealership with the mob behind us. Everyone started screaming, "Don't let that nigger in here!"

Lockwood said, "OK, Watson, stand here." He came back, said, "We can't deal with them. I'm going to give you six or eight police. Get your car and go straight to the base and don't go off until I tell you."

He said, "Of course you're going to be transferred. Where do you want to go? Do you want to go back overseas with the fighter Group?"

"Not particularly."

So I went to the 477th.

In May Jefferson and 14 classmates left Walterboro for overseas. The stationmaster at Walterboro ordered them around to the back of the tiny station, but they refused. The lieutenants unlimbered their weapons as a group of angry whites showed up with shotguns, yelling that they were going to burn some niggers. After 45 minutes the standoff ended when the train conductor said simply, "Get on board, fellas."

On board ship white troops and their officers occupied the lower decks. The 15 black officers were segregated alone on the top deck, along with 20 white nurses right across the corridor. They sunbathed and had a jolly time.

At Naples the guys were given barracks in a whorehouse and spent several days seeing the city and Pompei. "We hated to leave, but we had no choice."

As their truck pulled into Ramitelli, the last of a flight of P-47s was just returning to base. It crashed in a huge fireball.

Jefferson was assigned to the 301st in a tent with the squadron's hottest pilot, Joseph Elsberry.

10

The 15th Air Force

The P-47

JUNE 4. The day Rome fell the 332nd eagerly moved north and east to a new base at Ramitelli, on the east coast, closer to the bombers' targets. While awaiting the P-51s, it received another plane, the bigger, heavier Republic P-47 Thunderjet, nicknamed "the Jug." "It was like switching from a VW Bug [the P-39] to a Buick Roadmaster," Palmer said.

The snub-nosed P-47 didn't look as sleek as the P-39, but Davis welcomed it with its eight .50-caliber machine guns, 500-pound bomb load, and heavy armor protection. It could out-fight, out-climb, or outdistance any other plane in the sky, he declared. And "it took a lot of beating."

Briggs agreed. The P-39 had been water-cooled, and a hit in the coolant system would knock it out. But the P-47 was air cooled. "If you got shot in the engine with small arms, no problem, it would bring you back home."

The Jug was a workhorse at the gritty jobs of dive-bombing and strafing and was used to soften up southern France for the coming Allied invasion. There were fliers in English who loved the Jug and preferred it even to the vaunted P-51.

Crockett:

> Everyone who had to strafe thinks the Big Jug was best. It could take a beating, you could knock off a cylinder. It had 18 feet between landing gears [eliminating ground loops]. It had more room in the cockpit than any other airplane. The P-47 Club claims more victories than any other aircraft. It was a beautiful plane.

Sheppard also insisted that "it was a fine, hard-hitting airplane." He named his own ship "Thor," the god of thunder, and roared off.

All the other Groups in the 15th Air Force had P-51s. The 47s were "hand-me-downs" from the 325th Group, which had graduated to P-51s.

Most of the pilots didn't particularly like the plane. Lou Purnell: "You needed a step ladder to get into it and a map to find the instruments. It was like trying to fly your bathtub."

"It was a big heavy thing," Felix Kirkpatrick agreed. "We could barely get it off the ground loaded with belly tanks and ammunition."

According to Alexander Jefferson, the P-47's wing tanks "were guaranteed to incinerate at the slightest mishap." On the first day he joined the 332nd, Jefferson watched a P-47 take off. "He got 30 or 40 feet and nose-dived in. The result was just one massive ball of fire."

One of the replacements with the 302nd was Frank Pollard, who played saxophone with Jimmy Lunceford's dance band. He was with the squadron only three weeks when he was killed in a 47.

Four other men died in crashes.

Virgil Richardson had a close call. He hit a flock of sheep on the runway, crashed, and his gas tank caught fire as he leaped out. "Nothing can make you move faster than a fire on your ass!" he said.

Clarence "Lucky" Lester

A NEW arrival in the 100th, Lester was the son of a chef and grew up on Chicago's South Side, where his mother was a nurse and close friend of Janet Bragg, the aviation pioneer. He played football for West Virginia State, a black college. "I thought I was a hotshot football and basketball player in those days." After Pearl Harbor he applied for cadet training along with three other blacks and 12 whites. "I was the only one fortunate enough to pass."

In face and physique, Lester bore a resemblance to baseball star Willie Mays. The other pilots remembered him as a "cool" pilot, happy-go-lucky, who was always joking and kidding around. They called him "the Chicago Kid" or "Lucky."

One thing everybody asks me is, "How did I get the name "Lucky?"

I had the name before I even sat down in a P-47. I was younger than the others in the 332nd. I was 21 when I got overseas in April 1944. Most of the other fliers were three or four years older, and they all treated me like a kid. They called me Lucky because I was lucky playing poker.

I flew a total of 95 missions, and I never got a bullet the whole time I was in combat and never had an accident. I did have a couple of close calls, however. I was just plain lucky.

Those days weren't like it is today, where you go up in a two-seater and learn to fly with the instructor in back with dual controls. In those days you sat down and read what they called a TO, or Tech Order, which told you how the airplane flew. You memorized where all the instruments were, and the instructor gave you a written test: "What would you do if this happened? What would you do if that happened?" Then they put you in the cockpit, blindfolded you, and said, "Touch the air speed indicator," or "Touch the oil gauge." That was your orientation. Then they put you in a parachute and off you would go—it was sort of survival of the fittest. I'd never been in the P-47 before, had no idea of what it was like, but away I went.

You didn't have a lot of power in those planes, but I was doing pretty well until I tried to do ten loops in a row. I executed about eight or nine loops, but when I tried to fly through the next one, I knew I wasn't going to make it. The airplane began to shudder going straight up and did a hammerhead stall. It slid back down tail-first, then flipped over like a hammer striking a nail and started spinning upside down. In the normal spin, you apply the rudder opposite to the direction of the spin, but that doesn't work when the plane is upside down. In fact, they really don't teach you how to get out of an upside-down spin.

The standard operating procedure is, if you get below 5,000 feet and you don't have the plane under control, you are supposed to bail out. So here I was in this horrible maneuver—I had never seen anything like it in my life! The instruments were going crazy, some of them had actually broken. I said, "Well, I'm past my 5,000 feet, it's time to get out."

I reached up to pull the T-handle, which was supposed to release the canopy. I pulled, and nothing happened—the T came out in my hand. So I unbuttoned my seat belt, braced myself against the instrument panel, and tried to open it by hand. I was upside down, with everything spinning wildly, and I couldn't get the canopy open more than a couple inches.

All of a sudden it dawned on me that I wasn't bouncing off my head any more, I wasn't pulling any more negative G's. I said to myself, "Centrifugal force must be taking over."

[Negative Gs is the feeling of weightlessness when a roller coaster goes over the top; centrifugal force is the feeling of being pushed against the side of the car when it roars around a bend.]

The plane was in a tight spiral, but it was a controlled maneuver. It could be that just changing my position changed the flight characteristics enough to flip it over; we just don't know.

Anyway, I sat back down and started pulling the plane out of the spiral. I pulled out at about 500 feet off the ground, directly over the field, and came roaring across the runway at about 300 miles per hour. I pulled up, came around, and made a routine landing. They all said, "That was some kind of maneuver we were watching! What was that?"

I said, "Oh, that? That was just your normal hammerhead stall."

Later on I told my tent-mate what had happened. He said, "Boy, you're just as lucky as ever, aren't you?"

One P-47 was donated by students of Chicago's St. Alphonsus Catholic school, who raised $75,000 to buy it. Lester:

Since I was from Chicago, the obvious thing was to give that airplane to me. I wrote my mother and told her, and she called the school and told them her son was flying it. They ended up giving out souvenir postcards with my picture and the airplane they had bought. I still have a postcard in my scrapbook.

Crockett recalled:

Earle Sherrod challenged Lester to a dogfight, and Lester ran him all over the skies. Sherrod came down pulling his jacket over his head, because everyone was watching them. Lester licked him real good.

Like "the Red Baron," Manfred Von Richthofen of World War I, the 332nd painted their tails bright red. "Rather than camouflaging the planes," Herbert Carter explained, "we wanted the American bombers to know we were escorting them. The red tails would also let the German interceptors know."

The Red Tails also inspired a nickname. Because some whites derided them as "night fighters," they began to call themselves "spooks" and their outfit, the *Spookwaffe* or "Spook Air Force."

June 4. Rome fell to the Allies, and the 99th moved north of the capital and continued escort and dive-bombing.

Two days later, Leonard Jackson crash-landed in no-man's land between enemy and Allied lines. American GIs ran up to help him. So did two Germans carrying a white flag. He took the Germans' weapons and handed them over to the GIs.

June 7. One day after the Normandy invasion and three after the fall of Rome, the 332nd flew its first mission with the 15th—a fighter sweep, a good way to break a rookie outfit in. They didn't find any enemy, but Carroll Langston had engine trouble and was lost after bailing out.

In the following days the 99th flew four strafing missions, damaging or destroying over 70 vehicles and one large artillery piece.

The 15th Air Force was formed specifically to conduct daylight bomber raids. Its seven fighter Groups had one overriding mission, to protect the bombers, and Davis called his pilots to an assembly to make sure they all understood it.

He said he had been told by General Eaker, "We don't want aces. I don't care if you never shoot down another airplane.... Don't chase them, don't pursue them." (No "happy hunting," as Charlie McGee put it.) There would be opportunities to go hunting on other missions, Davis said. But when they were escorting bombers, they were to *stay with the bombers*, no matter what. "Protect them with your life." Any man found leaving the bombers in order to chase enemy fighters would be grounded and court-martialed.

This caused a lot of bitching.

The boys of the Depression had learned to read on pulp magazines of the exploits of Eddie Rickenbacker, Canada's Billy Bishop, France's Charles Nungesser, and the most celebrated of all, Germany's "Red Baron," the coolly handsome Manfred von Richthofen. Spellbound boys memorized their victory totals as they did Babe Ruth's homerun totals. Shooting down the enemy—that was what aerial war was all about.

Every fighter pilot in America, and probably the rest of the world, had seen the 1939 World War I movie, "Dawn Patrol." The debonair, insouciant Errol Flynn flew to meet his foe with a white scarf streaming from his helmet like a medieval knight on a white steed. He was the idol of every man and the heartthrob of every woman, facing danger and death with a wave and a grin.

Bussey, the tiger of Hampton Roads:

> We were damn unhappy, because the name of the game was shoot down airplanes. This took some of the glamour out of being a fighter pilot, because the movies create this glamour with the white scarves and all that.

But nobody dared disobey The Old Man.
As Lee Archer said:

> The enemy would hit and run, but we wouldn't chase them. I never thought about wandering off, and I'm considered a very independent person. We did not take on Colonel Davis. He could be as nice as possible and then turn around and tear your head off if you did something wrong. It kept a lot of people from becoming "heroes."
>
> But Colonel Davis had a longer range view than any of us.

Davis' orders "were brought home very vividly," Crockett said, when a white Group shot down eight or nine enemy fighters but lost 17 bombers on the same mission. Each B-17 cost a half million dollars and carried a crew of ten men or about 170 to 180 men in all. "So that wasn't a very good tradeoff."

However, there is some question about how diligently the white fighter Groups followed the policy. We are left with the impression that the old rules, passed down from von Richthofen and Rickenbacker, were still the rules goal: Kill the Enemy. Those who killed the most won the greatest fame and the swiftest promotions. Indeed, like every other air force in the world, the 15th Air Force kept scrupulous records of how many enemy planes each pilot and each squadron shot down. But it didn't even bother to count how many bombers each Group or squadron lost. No one in higher headquarters even asked.

June 8. The 332nd flew its first bomber escort mission, taking B-17 Flying Fortresses on the first leg of their flight. They ran into no enemy.

The Jug had a major drawback. It didn't have the altitude or the fuel capacity for long-range escort.

Lester:

> We'd meet the B-17s at 20,000 feet, but they would invariably want to keep right on going to 30- or 32,000, because the higher they got, the more protection they would have from ground defenses. Our P-47's struggled to get to 28,000; we could go to 30,000, but the plane became sluggish and started wallowing around in the sky.
>
> And the Jug used too much fuel. It would only let us go out at the most for three hours: then we'd have to turn around and come back. Other groups had P-38s or P-51s with longer range, and the action didn't start until after we had to turn back. We would hear the other pilots on the radio, talking about the dogfights.

"We had trouble getting much past the Po Valley," Red Jackson remembered. So they turned the handicap to an advantage. "The Germans had found out very early that the P-51s and P-38s were escorting the bombers deep into Germany, but we had neglected the short hops." The *Luftwaffe* expected that, close to home, the bombers would have no fighter cover. Jackson decided to surprise them.

June 9. Davis approved the plan and led the Group. As Jackson told it:

> We were lucky. I saw about 30 109s coming down from my right. They weren't looking for us, they were looking for nice pickings on the bombers, and we had 40 American P-47s just sitting there waiting for them. They started attacking the bombers the very moment we saw them. Skipper [Davis] called, "Go get 'em," and the 332nd waded into the fight.

"The Germans didn't know who we were, because we wore goggles," Harry Sheppard smiled. "If they had, we might have given them the cultural shock of their lives."

Jackson was flying with his wing man, Chubby Green.

> As soon as I heard "Go get 'em," I peeled off with Green following and fell in behind the second enemy aircraft, which was coming down in string

formation. Having a faster plane, I overshot him, but Green and Bussey, who were behind me, shot him down.

Actually, Bussey said, "I shot down the airplane that was on Green's tail," but instead of both getting a victory, Bussey and Green shared one. It was the first plane shot down by a Red Tail.

Bussey described the feeling:

Destroying another plane in combat is probably the most exhilarating experience a man can have. You're trained so you don't have to do a lot of thinking, everything is pretty automatic. But your heart's as big as your head. You don't breathe throughout the encounter, and when it's all over, you realize you haven't taken a breath.

Wendell Pruitt of the 302nd also downed his first enemy plane. Gwynne Peirson, a new replacement, described it later in a Tuskegee Airmen *Newsletter*. He found himself isolated without a wingman and spotted Pruitt, also alone, jockeying for position on the tail of a 109. Peirson "pulled up in line abreast off his right wingtip. I motioned him to move on the German fighter and indicated that I would cover his tail."

Pruitt:

A flock of ME 109s were attacking a flight of B-24s from five o'clock. Each enemy made a pass at the bombers and fell into a left rolling turn. I rolled over, shoved everything forward and closed in on a 109 at 475 mph. I waited as he shallowed out of a turn, gave him a couple of two second bursts, and watched his left wing erupt in flame, and he exploded.

The pilot quickly bailed out.

Frederick Funderberg of the 301st also got two victories. He spotted two ME 109s 400 feet below and dove, guns blazing, as pieces flew off one enemy craft. Pulling up sharply, he found two more 109s heading toward him. He pointed his nose straight into them and fired a burst at one plane, which exploded.

Jackson, meanwhile, pulled out of his dive and started to climb.

I noticed a 109 headed straight down at me, blazing away with all his guns. My plane seemed to be dragging on the climb, and I realized I hadn't dropped my wing tanks. Probably, in the busyness of combat I hadn't pulled both release pulls. A full tank weighed me down and gave me trouble in the first encounter.

When he finally remembered the tanks, they still refused to come off, so

Red applied a water booster for extra speed and pulled away. Below him were the Alps with a layer of clouds on their peaks, so he headed for the safety of the clouds and finally shook off his tanks.

> As I broke through the clouds, I found my pursuer waiting to shoot me down. He made a pass at me, but somehow he missed, and I fell in behind him. He began weaving from side to side, but every time he turned, I gave him a short burst of fire. On the fourth burst, he started to smoke, his canopy came off in two pieces, and he jumped.

Jackson circled him until he suddenly realized he was directly over an enemy airfield. "Flak was everywhere. I dove down on the deck and headed for the Adriatic Sea." Once over water, he cruised home "happy over my victory."

That made five victories in their first fight. "The Group's personnel are now in high spirits," the Baltimore *Afro-American* correspondent wrote. "Every pilot is eager for a chance at 'Herman.'"

However, there was unhappy news as swell.

First, the Red Tails lost one man, Cornelius Rogers.

Second, Air Force historian Daniel Haulman writes: "While the Tuskegee Airmen were shooting down enemy fighters, some of those fighters were shooting down two American bombers."

Davis was awarded the Distinguished Flying Cross, the air corps' highest honor, which seems a little hasty after only one major engagement. Perhaps it was bestowed as a sign of encouragement to welcome him and his Group. It read that he so skillfully disposed his unit that in spite of the large number of enemy fighters, the bomber formation suffered *only a few losses."* This alone invalidates the later claim that they never lost a bomber to enemy fighters.

However, the other fighter Groups, which completed the escort mission, lost 15 bombers to enemy planes.

Robert Pitts, the Group intelligence officer:

> Pruitt was the maverick of the 332nd. He was the only pilot that B.O. Davis never seemed able to severely reprimand. The men on the ground and particularly his crew chief really loved the guy.
>
> He knew the guys that kept him flying would like to see a little show now and then. After the other pilots had landed, Pruitt would circle the base, tip his wings, go into a chandelle [a steep, climbing turn] and a couple of rolls. After about ten or 15 minutes of beautiful flying, he would come in for a perfect three-point landing.
>
> Any other pilot would have been chewed out by the Boss. To my knowledge Davis never said one word to Pruitt. He was probably—no positively— the most popular pilot in the 332nd. Next would be Lee Archer.

As the 332nd pilots roared over the field, a technical representative from Republic Aircraft was briefing the Air Force brass on the P-47. Pruitt's crew chief, Staff Sergeant Samuel Jacobs, recalled:

> I remember the major standing atop a munitions carrier telling us "boys" all about the "flying bathtub" and how it should never be slow rolled below 1,000 feet due to its excessive weight.
>
> No sooner had he finished than down on the deck, props cutting grass, came Lieutenant Pruitt and his wingman, Lee Archer, nearly touching their wings. Lieutenant Pruitt pulled up into the prettiest victory roll you'd ever see, with Archer right in his pocket, as the major screamed, "You can't do that!"

June 13. Perhaps fitted with new wing tanks that extended their range, the 332nd shepherded B-24 Liberator to Munich. Over Italy one bomber slowed and fell out of formation and was jumped by enemy fighters. The pilot put in an emergency call to "Pixey-One," the Red Tails' radio call sign, but he was shot down before help could arrive.

It was the fourth bomber they had lost. It was perhaps understandable, historian Daniel Haulmann writes, because the number of bombers far exceeded the number of fighter escorts to cover them.

In the following days the 332nd escorted bombers to Munich, Slovakia, and Bucharest.

June 24. The 332nd suffered its first big tragedy when it lost three men on a strafing raid to Genoa on the Italian northwest coast. A fourth, Gwynne Pierson, crashed on take-off. Bob Tresville of the 100th led the flight. His assistant flight leader, Woody Crockett, recalled:

> We had three squadrons, 12 airplanes each—36 in all. We hit the deck [just above the water] after leaving Rome and were supposed to fly 50 feet or lower, with the radios off.
>
> That wasn't very smart. The water was glassy in the early morning, and, smart as the Germans were, and with their radar, you could hardly sneak up on those guys at that range anyway.

They flew in a whiteout with no horizon visible, skimming the waves, their wingtips almost touching. Each plane flew just below the man to his left until the last man was almost touching the water, which he could barely see in the fog.

Bill Melton recalled: "We were all about to switch to internal tanks when the two lead planes went into the water, one right after the other." Sam Jefferson crashed into the waves and exploded.

Earle Sherrod, in Crockett's third flight, was next to hit the water. He scrambled onto his wing, ripped off his 'chute, and began inflating his life raft.

His buddy, C.B. Johnson, peeled off to check on Sherrod, and he too hit the waves; he couldn't open his canopy in time and was quickly swallowed by the sea.

Unaware of these tragedies, the flight droned on toward the northern Italian coast and their objective.

Crockett:

> There was a mountain range by the coast and a lot of clouds below the peaks, and we couldn't get over the mountain tops. Three or four other units tried it and never made it to the target.
>
> I looked at Tresville, and he had maps all over the cockpit. He may have been a little cocky. West Point instills in you that you must succeed, and sometimes fellows try to do that at all costs. But at some point you have to back off when the odds become too great.
>
> It should have been a target for bombers anyway rather than fighters down at sea level. Or we should have hit the coast way down southwest of Genoa. Instead, we went into the harbor and never got to the target.
>
> I turned around and headed for Corsica to refuel, because we couldn't make it all the way home in the Jug. I started climbing up and pulled out my maps. My wingman said, "Why are you looking at your maps over water?" I'm a former field artilleryman and a good math student, and I held my heading 142 degrees back to Corsica for 30 minutes, and we were two of only four or six airplanes that landed at the air strip.
>
> I said, "There's nothing wrong with my navigation, kid."

On the flight back Tresville himself went into the water and was killed. Some believe he might have become disoriented in the white-out.

His operations officer, Andrew "Jug" Turner, took over as commander of the 100th with William Mattison as operations officer. Crockett moved up as Mattison's assistant.

Chris Newman thought Turner was more conservative than Tresville. "Maybe that's why Tresville didn't live and Turner did."

Sinking a Ship

JUNE 25. The 332nd was returning from a strafing run to Yugoslavia, when they scored a dramatic victory.

Gwynne Peirson was again flying Pruitt's wing. From the Berkeley area, he had attended college, had played a lot of semipro baseball. "He had a cryptic sense of humor," Shep said "He was a hell of a good pilot, smooth, dependable."

Pierson was surprised that Pruitt had chosen him. Perhaps Pruitt remembered the last dogfight, when they had teamed up, but Peirson thought there may a have been a second factor: "Three days earlier I had crashed on takeoff and completely destroyed my plane. It may be that Pruitt wanted me to get back into the air before I lost my nerve."

Peirson described the mission in the Tuskegee Airmen *Newsletter.*

> We were at low altitude, 50 feet, radio silence. Intelligence said there was a large contingent of enemy troops expected in a section of Yugoslavia; we were to strafe the troops with four planes.
>
> We became targets of heavy ground fire. Freddie Hutchins' right wing tank dropped, but his left tank wouldn't fully release. It was set on fire, with flame streaming behind him, and it caused him to lose speed, so Larry Wilkins stayed with him. Pruitt and I moved ahead at tree-top level, but we were forced off course and never made contact with the ground troops.
>
> Pruitt was on my left, and we made a low left turn to return. Flying over Trieste we crossed over houses on the waterfront and dropped even lower to just above the water, when we spotted a German destroyer a few miles ahead, crossing directly in front of us, left to right. We were already in range of the guns and would be exposing our undersides to gunfire if we turned left or right. We would also be unable to use our own guns, and it would slow us down.

Pruitt's flight path took him just to the stern of the ship. Peirson was flying directly toward mid-ship and opened fire:

> Tracers showed my first burst was failing far short, kicking up nothing but water. The next burst struck at the ship's waterline and started to walk up the side. All I could see was black smoke and flame, I pulled back on my control stick and climbed just enough to clear the smoke.

His gun-camera film "looked like Hollywood," Sheppard whistled. "The ship blew apart just aft of the bridge as if it had been staged in Hollywood."

The ship rolled over and sank.

Back in Italy Peirson found jagged holes on the underside of his wings and theorized that they were caused by fragments of the exploding destroyer.

Post-war divers would later identify it as an Italian torpedo ship from the Nazi submarine pens in Yugoslavia. Peirson had evidently set off one of the torpedoes.

The feat was unprecedented in the European theater. In the Pacific the Japanese had sunk U.S. battleships at Pearl Harbor, and in 1942 the Battle of Midway had been a victory of U.S. planes over Japanese carrier-borne planes. But in the Mediterranean, "the Navy took a little while to confirm that an aircraft had the nerve to sink a vessel," Sheppard smiled.

Meanwhile, a scandal hit the Group. The sergeant in charge of parachute rigging, a former cadet who had washed out, was caught selling the silk on the black market to support his Italian girlfriend. He was convicted and sentenced to federal prison.

June 30. The 332nd covered the first leg of an escort mission and turned the bombers over to the P-51s, which lost five of the big planes to German fighters. It was the last mission in the Jug. The most brilliant chapter in their history was about to open with a new and better plane, perhaps the best fighter ever they built until the age of jets.

11

Red Tails

The P-51

THE 332nd pilots happily got acquainted with their new plane, the P-51 Mustang, often called "the plane that won the war." The Germans agreed.

"If the P-39 was a VW and the P-47 a Buick," Walter Palmer wrote, "the P-51 was the Cadillac of fighters with a Rolls Royce engine."

Woody Crockett called it "a dream airplane. It could climb, turn, and fight at low level and at high altitude." The Mustang carried six 50-calibre machine guns, three in each wing. "It was great for strafing. It was fearsome." It was also big enough for a six-foot, 190-pounder to fit in.

Lou Purnell:

If that plane had been a girl, I'd have married it right on the spot. Damn right! It was like dancing with a good partner. You could almost think left turn, and the damn plane was right with you. Good response on controls, good stability. It was a miracle to get in and fly with all that horsepower at your fingertips. Speed, maneuverability, climb rate, reliability? We had it in the P-51. The cockpit was designed beautifully. Where you'd expect to find something, you'd find it.

Anyone who has flown a P-51 will agree with me. And those who haven't, wish they had.

The marriage of the Red Tails and the P-51 was the luckiest break the black fliers had in the entire war. Without it, the mystique and the history of the 332nd would have been quite different.

The 15th Air Force had six fighter Groups—three twin-boom P-38s and three of the new P-51s. The latter were far superior. In the old days on the western plains, black troopers were given the worst, most sway-back nags the Army had. Now, thanks to some nameless angel in the Pentagon, they had been handed the best fighter plane in the world. Data for the three months, June, July, and August, show that a pilot was in twice as much danger of beng killed in a P-38 as in the P-51. That general saved a lot of black lives and helped make the Red Tails immortal.

Crewman Buddy Huntley:

> At first the P-51 had an American Allison V-12 engine and performed like a P-40. Then they changed to a British Rolls Royce, like the Spitfire, changed the prop from three blades to four, and moved the scoop back a few inches, which gave it more air pick-up. After that the plane changed all around: more altitude and more speed—from 300-plus mph to 400-plus.

But the Mustang did have one important drawback. Like the old P-39, it was water-cooled and thus vulnerable to a hit in the engine. Once the plane lost its coolant, as Johnny Briggs said, "you gotta come down."

Roscoe Brown, who arrived a month later, had another complaint:

> The '51 had tremendous torque. The propeller spun in a counter-clockwise direction, and you countered with a little right rudder and a little right stick and trimmed it—trim tabs are little air foils within the wing that help you keep the plane straight. But if you were all tensed up, the torque could get away from you.

June 30. As the Red Tails began transitioning to the '51, Ed Laird crashed on take-off and was killed.

Alex Jefferson:

> My tentmate, Othel Dickson [considered one of the best pilots of his class at Tuskegee], spun in, doing acrobatics upside down in a Mustang. One of the hard and fast rules was, don't do any upside-down flying with over a half-tank of gasoline; it upsets the equilibrium. When they found him he was dead, burned, decapitated, footless and handless, but still sitting in the cockpit as if he were flying.

Jefferson's comment: "Read the tech order!"

As a rookie, Jeff got last choice of the new planes. He named it "Margo" after his sweetheart at home.

Once more the 332nd re-painted their tails red. Each squadron had its own color stripes on the wing.

Archer named his ship "The Macon Belle," raising speculation on who the mystery girl was:

> The intelligence officer, who read all our mail, said, "Lieutenant Archer is writing to some girl named Ina." So they went out and painted "Ina" in front of it. That's why it was in two different colors. I didn't notice it for two days. Shows how good an airplane inspector I am.

"We had four days to switch over to the '51," Woody Crockett said. "The fifth day we went out 54-strong with the Mustangs. Some guys flew without reading the pilot's handbook."

Chris Newman, still badly scarred from his injures, checked out his P-51: "I took the darned thing up, came down, and took it up a second time, a total of about two hours. The next day I was on a mission."

July 3. General Nathan Twining and Brigadier General Dean Strother, head of the 306th fighter Wing, dropped in to wish the Red Tails good luck on their first mission in their new planes the next day. An extra ration of beer was issued to everyone in the unit.

July 4. The 332nd celebrated Independence Day with a roar in their new Mustangs, heading for rendezvous hundreds of miles away at a precise time. Davis gave his pilots a margin of error of 90 seconds. But the rendezvous with the bombers never took place, because the Red Tails arrived 26 minutes late!

How could such a fiasco have happened? Dr. Daniel Haulman of the Air Force historical office carefully studied the events of that day. He uncovered a major boondoggle.

Under air corps doctrine, Twining did not issue an Order, as ground commanders do. Rather, he issued two or more "Plans" which were sent to each bomb and fighter Group by teletype. Plan A was the preferred target, but if it was covered by clouds, the force could switch to Plan B.

The system carried the seeds of confusion and loss of life. But there was no other way. Each Group operations officer—in this case, Mac Ross of the 332nd—had to calculate the route and distance to rendezvous and the take-off time that would get his planes there at precisely the right minute, and he had to do it for each Plan. Some times there were as many as three plans.

At some point Twining decided to go with Plan A, and a teletype message was sent to all Groups: "Execute Plan A." We don't know what Plan B was; no record remains. But the presumption is that Ross, for whatever reason, went with it. This was the first time apparently that he made such an error. In the month of May, when the 332nd was flying P-47s for the 15th, no such mistake was reported. But Twining and Brigadier General Dean Strother (306th fighter Wing), who was in charge of all fighter Groups, must have exploded and given Davis hell.

July 5. There was no hitch as the Red Tails shepherded bombers to the vital oil refineries at Ploesti, Romania, perhaps the most heavily defended target in all Europe. Although German fighters came up to challenge them, no American planes, bombers or fighters, were lost.

July 7. Again, two Plans were issued. Plan A called for rendezvous at 0902, Plan B at 0916. The Red Tails were rousted out of bed and received their briefing. Then they jumped into their cockpits and at 0755 roared off behind Melvin "Red" Jackson to join a massive raid to Vienna, involving almost every plane, both fighters and bombers, in the 15th Air Force. In the next few hours the entire force would lose 20 bombers.

And once again the 332nd missed it completely. It was the second time in their first three long-range missions.

At precisely 0916, they arrived at the rendezvous point "as briefed." But there were no bombers! That's because all the bombers and all the other fighters were following Plan A. The bombers had arrived at 0902 and, finding no escorts, flew on without fighter protection. Eight minutes later, at 0910, German fighters pounced on the undefended formation and knocked one bomber out of the sky.

The remaining bombers lumbered on and at 0945 hooked up with the 325th Fighter Group, again exactly on schedule under Plan A. Within three minutes, more enemy fighters hit the formation and sent two more B-24s spiraling to earth. Though it was technically on the 325th's watch, if the Red Tails had been nearby, they might have helped drive off the attackers without any losses.

Thus, of the 20 bombers lost that day, at least one, and maybe three, can be blamed on the *snafu* over which plan to follow. It was a huge black eye for the 332nd, to completely miss rendezvous on two of its first three big missions. One can imagine the choleric phone calls from Twining and Strother. The incident has never before been publicized. But it might have achieved what Momyer, Arnold, Hunter, Selway, and so many others had tried and failed to do—to scuttle "the black air force."

Two monumental foul ups right at the start of their career in the P-51 could have been fatal to the future of the 332nd. Twining and Strother must have been livid, and with good reason. They must have burned the phone lines up, chewing Davis' tail. And Davis, who had a trigger temper himself, must have turned around and given Ross hell.

The Red Tails had two quick strikes against them. One more and they were out. B.O. had to act fast. He relieved Ross on the spot.

Who should he put in the hot seat? Lou Purnell was the assistant operations officer. It would have made sense to let Lou plan the mission for the next morning, then name a permanent replacement as soon as possible.

July 8. The Red Tails roared off to escort B-24s to Munchendorf Airdrome. Rendezvous was on the dot.

As a permanent solution B.O. turned to Alfonza Davis of the 301st. It's not clear exactly when he stepped into the job, but it may have been for the July 9 mission to Ploesti, which also was flawless.

In fact, there is no record has been found that the 332nd missed another rendezvous for the rest of the war.

When link-ups were missed, it was the bombers that were late, almost always as a result of bad weather. In fact, it's a miracle of precision planning and execution that hundreds of planes can fly up to 500 miles across empty, trackless skies, sometimes through blinding clouds, and a couple of hours later meet at precisely the right moment and place. It's like a quarterback leading a receiver and putting the ball exactly in his hands—on a 500-mile playing field—and some times without being able to see the receiver!

Twining also showed a great deal of support for the 332nd. If Momyer or Hunter or Arnold had been in his position, they could have shot the 332nd down right after that second screw-up. He was risking his own career in giving the Red Tails a third chance. Along with Noel Parrish, Phil Cochran, Earl Bates, Eaker, and others, Twining deserves some special *niche* in the Red Tails Hall of Fame.

July 10. Ross took his P-51 up on a routine transition flight, and put it into a slow, steady glide straight into a mountain side, killing himself instantly. Lou Purnell's accident report called it suicide. However, Lou said, Davis refused to accept it, fearing the Pentagon would seize on it as a sign of poor morale. He told Purnell: "You'll be confined to the base for two months, when you'll have plenty of time to think it over."

Lou would later say that he refused to change it. However, the report as it exists in Air Force records today, above his signature, does not contain the word "suicide." Did Lou change it? If not, it must have been edited without his knowledge.

B.O. Davis also relieved a second of the five graduates of the original Tuskegee class, Charles DeBow, commander of the 301st. There was a strong personality conflict between the two men. DeBow was a school teacher and "was kind of laid back," Charles Dryden said. "He and Davis didn't quite fit in harness."

James Wiley:

> Davis was a very strict disciplinarian. DeBow was defiant. I didn't care for DeBow too much either. He wasn't a good pilot—I don't know how he was selected and got through the training. I like people with guts. He didn't have it. B.O. Davis just threw up his hands.

DeBow's replacement was Lee Rayford, back for a second tour after flying with the 99th over Anzio.

Clarence Jamison observed that Ross also "never clicked very well with Colonel Davis. Maybe Davis had higher expectations for the first class."

Bill Campbell:

> When the units were formed, we all had the same amount of experience. You didn't know who was going to exhibit leadership traits. Davis had to pick someone, and some didn't do as well as others. It wouldn't have happened if we had had more experience.

Both Ross and DeBow must have been good pilots; they survived the brutal 60% washout rate and graduated alongside Davis, Roberts, and Custis.

(B.O. himself might not have graduated, based on flying skill alone. But who else would command the new unit? Spanky Roberts was unknown. He would have done an excellent job, as Davis did. But would he have had the clout to save the unit in Washington, when almost every general in Africa, plus the Air Force Chief of Staff, was taking aim to shoot it down?)

Davis, a spit-and-polish regular army man, went strictly by rank, or date of rank, in making assignments. But DeBow and Ross apparently lacked executive talent for the jobs they were given. Both men and their families had been justly proud of their historic feats of graduating in the very first class. One can feel sympathy with them for the humiliation they must have suffered.

The 99th Joins Up

THE 99th had joined the 332nd at the end of June, creating an unorthodox Group of four squadrons. (As a separate squadron, the 99th was always the fourth, or "orphan," squadron, attached to a normal three-squadron Group, whatever it served.) At last this was their chance to give up the old P-40 and the thankless job of ground support in exchange for glory in an exciting new plane. They should have been overjoyed.

Instead, they grumbled about the change. The "old hands" of the 99th, many of whom had 50 missions or more, had enjoyed flying with their white Group and resented returning to a segregated Group of "newcomers." As Lee Archer put it, "They felt they had broken the grip of segregation." They also feared that the best assignments and promotions would go to the newcomers.

In contrast, the 332nd worried that the plums would go to the 99th veterans. Both Davis and Roberts worked hard to address the concerns on both sides. As a concession, the 99th was allowed to keep its blue-and-white checker pattern on the noses of their planes.

Rookie Dick Macon:

Spanky Roberts was my idea of an outstanding pilot. In my estimation, he was fearless. There must have been many things that scared the hell out of him, but he always chose the most dangerous missions to lead. I enjoyed flying with him, and he enjoyed flying with me. When he took one of the dangerous missions, he'd say, "Come on, Dick, let's get 'em," and I'd fly on his wing.

There were inevitable problems in coordination. Harry Sheppard recalls that "Swampy" Eagleson of the 99th joined Shep's plane in flight, easing in from the left. "I thought I saw a lot of flames coming from his wings," Sheppard said, so back on the ground Shep asked, "Did you fire your guns?"

"Yes," Swampy said. "Ever since I ended up over Anzio beach and my guns jammed, I decided I'd never let that happen again. That's why I always fire my guns."

"On joining up?!" Sheppard exclaimed.

A Typical Mission

THE mechanics woke up about three a.m. to begin getting the planes ready to fly. They gassed them up and taxied them to the flight line in the correct order they would be for take-off.

Harry Sheppard would be the first pilot awake, ready to fly any problem planes repaired the night before, "and if possible I flew it again on the mission that day." It also gave him a chance to make a weather-check and report on where the holes in the clouds were. "I was the first guy off the ground in the morning and the last one in at night."

Before dawn, two or three hours before the mission, the Operations Officer came by and woke the pilots, although, said Bussey:

He didn't need to—you were already awake. Chances are you didn't have any sleep the night before, because this was hair raising stuff. You listened to see if he went past your tent; if he did, you went back to sleep.

William Mattison was Operations Officer in the 100th. Crockett:

He was a pretty big guy, and he might turn a young pilot over in his bed if he didn't respond immediately. The guys said, "I'm going out to be shot at, I don't want you to come in and wake me like that." They said to me, "We want you to do the job." So Major Mattison got out of that work.

In the 302nd Dudley Watson "would stick his head in the tent and roar the names of the guys who were going on the mission. As usual, Sheppard hung a nickname on him: "Fearless Fosdick," "because he was a hammerin' son of a gun."

Grumbling, the pilots climbed out of their sacks and took a sponge bath with a helmet full of cold water—water was a scarce commodity. "Then we rushed into the mess tent," Sheppard said, where "the fiendish cooks could ruin the best food in the world." Bussey recalled the menu as "powdered eggs and oatmeal." Jefferson said it tasted like 100-octane gas.

Then they went back and put on their flying gear and piled into a truck or walked down to the flight line for the briefing in a huge converted barn. They took their seats on bomb casings, then a sheet was pulled away from the wall, revealing a tremendous map with a green string to the target, deep in the heart of Germany or elsewhere. If it ended at the vital oil refineries at Ploesti, Romania, the most ferociously defended target on the map, a loud groan of "Oh, shit!" went around the tent.

"Next "we were briefed by the weather officers—a bunch of liars," Sheppard said, and then by the intelligence officers (S-2), "another bunch of liars." The flyers had a poem, Jefferson wrote:

> S-2 is so effective,
> It seems it's their renown
> To get you quickly right to where
> You get yourself shot down.

Last was the briefing by the Operations officer.

Then the fliers picked up their parachutes and drove to their planes, which were already waiting for them. C.C. Robinson told biographer George Norfleet: 'I'd get out of the truck and start walking toward the plane on wobbly knees and think I could hardly make it."

Each man carefully inspected his plane, though the mechanics had already done it once.

Sheppard:

> We'd check the gas tanks personally to make sure they were topped off. The armorers and ordnance people checked the gun belts. At first the P-51 had some trouble: In tight turns the gravity forces exerted resistance on the movement of the ammunition belt, although later models corrected the problem.
> Then we'd wait for the signal to start our engines.

Everyone on base turned out to wave them good luck. The fuel trucks drove slowly by and topped off the tanks again, because the planes had already used up some gas getting into position. "The pilots' eyes would be right on them to be sure they put the gas cap on tightly," Sheppard said, otherwise gas would vaporize and stream out in flight while the gas gauge needle went down.

Sometimes the pilots sat under their wings or on them, watching the slower bombers pass overhead, wave after wave.

Red Jackson:

> I had some very vivid impressions. My strongest was the feeling of participating in a gigantic effort. I'd say to myself: "Here I am with 72 planes going to join with a whole armada of planes—big bombers, P-38s, P-51s—a gigantic effort coordinated to the second. We are to appear over the B-17s' wings at a certain minute over one little town in Germany. And a similar gigantic effort is taking off out of England.
>
> I said, "Gee, I'm a part of something big! I'm a real key part of the effort."

When the bombers had passed, it was time to start engines and catch up with them.

Ed Gleed (who would soon be rehabilitated from exile):

> Three or four minutes before we cranked up engines, I'd always get a rumble in my stomach. Anybody who said he didn't is pulling your leg—I'd say even Pruitt did.
>
> The only way to get rid of it was to get out and stretch flat on my stomach on the wing until we got the one-minute notice to crank up, climb in, and buckle on the 'chute. You hope all your calculations are correct and you haven't forgotten anything.
>
> Then I never thought about it again

Robinson:

> I'd climb in the cockpit. Most times I'd be so nervous I'd have to get out and regroup. There were 21 switches I had to hit before I could turn the engine on—it was a complicated engine.... But the minute I turned it on, all the tension went away.
>
> I was never afraid during engagements.

In his book, Jefferson described it:

> Waiting take-off, pulses race, canopies open, noise is deafening. You hope the bastard behind you doesn't chop your tail off and the guy beside you has his gun switch off so he doesn't blow you to smithereens. Sit at the end of the runway and wait, your plane throbbing and threatening to bolt, foot clamped on brakes, leg muscles knotted. Fumes and dust penetrate your oxygen mask.

Felix Kirkpatrick:

We had four squadrons, two side-by-side at one end of the runway and two at the other end. The first plane is waved off. No sooner than he takes off, the second airplane lines up and waits for the signal until we get all 18 off the ground for that squadron. Then the next squadron lines up and does the same thing.

Jefferson:

The planes on the other end take off directly toward you. Each one lifts off 50 feet in front of you, wobbling back and forth, and sails over your head with ten or 15 feet to spare.

When they all clear the runway, someone shoots a flare, a signal for the planes to take off from the other end. You're off! Tremendous acceleration pushes you back in your seat."

One by one, 72 planes—16 plus two spares from each squadron—take off and join up in slow climbing turns. "We circled the field in two 360s until we were all in position," Kirkpatrick said, "then we'd head off to rendezvous."

The Group leader navigates for the Group. They fly a "four-finger pattern" pioneered by the Germans—wingman, flight leader, second element leader, and his wingman—four ships to each flight, four flights per squadron, four squadrons in the Group. The spares fly as far as the "bomb line," that is, enemy territory. If no aircraft had dropped out with problems, the spares return to base.

The bombers go out from different bases, and the fighters meet them at the appointed place and time.

Each pilot can see a ten-to-15-mile string of 1,000-plus planes. The contrails of the P-51s are zig-zagging above the slower bombers. Because the fighters have to fly slower than their maximum performance, they use more fuel. Thus they prefer to escort the B-24s, which are faster than the heavier B-17s.

The Fortresses are at 24,000 feet. The 99th might be at 25,000, the 100th at 26,000, the 301st at 27,000, and the 302nd at 28,000. If the bombers fly higher to get above the flak, the fighters may be forced up to 32,000, where controls become mushy and planes might spin out, so "no sharp maneuvers."

In heavy clouds with no visibility, they flew by "dead reckoning," taking a compass heading for a calculated number of minutes. "We got pretty good at it," Sheppard said. Everyone else guides on the leader, almost wingtip to wingtip. "Those cats could fly formation!"

Lucky Lester:

Navigation was one of the big problems. I guess the biggest problems were, one, mechanical, two, weather, three, navigation, and four, the enemy. Only after you overcame the first three did you have to worry about the fourth.

Let's say it's overcast, which is not unusual, with the top of the clouds at 20,000 feet. Each flight takes off at a certain time on a climb-out heading, designed to get you above the clouds and to the Rendezvous Point to meet the bombers. The climbs out of Italy were over mountains most of the time, so you don't have a lot of latitude for error.

And you didn't have any navigational aids. Now they have all this fancy automatic equipment. Airplanes now can fly themselves; I flew jets later on, so I know it's nothing like flying a propeller airplane. On one jet recently, the crew was knocked out from loss of oxygen, and the airplane just flew on auto pilot until it ran out of gas and fell into the sea.

Lee Archer said today's planes have a computer and a vicious dog. What's the dog for? "To bite the pilot if he even touches the controls."

Lester continued:

Back then ground radar had a very limited range to reach out and see, and, anyway, you didn't have any radar on board the airplane. You had to maintain radio silence. You couldn't talk to anyone in your flight or on the ground, because that would give away where you were and what direction you were heading.

They used to marshal hundreds of airplanes out of Italy, all going basically the same place. Italy is not a very big place for hundreds of airplanes.

You started out on a correct heading as you entered the clouds, but if the wind was blowing, and you didn't know it, you might be drifting. You might be flying a heading due north but actually be going north-northwest. In the clouds you had no way to check visually.

You had to fly formation, guiding on your leader only, wingtips almost touching, and he in turn maintained position on his leader. It really took a strong heart to sit there, and you had no idea whether you were right-side up, in a turn, or upside down.

If the flight started feeling turbulence in the clouds and the plane started bouncing around, you began to wonder: What is it? Is it rough weather? Is the enemy shooting flak at me and I'm feeling the concussions from the exploding shells? Or is it the prop wash from another 16 planes crossing through your flight? More than one time there were mid-air collisions. A voice would yell on the radio, "I'm hit, I'm hit!"

That's where discipline was required. You just had to sit there and sweat it out. Boy, it took a strong heart sitting there and saying, "I'll just keep going...keep going...keep going, and hope I'll break out." It added years to your life. Those are the kinds of things you don't hear about in the movies.

Bobby Williams:

We lost more people in weather than to enemy aircraft. The P-51 is perhaps the best prop-driven plane you could have—as long as you're over land
and level terrain. Then it sounds like a Singer sewing machine. But out at
sea, or over the mountains, every little pop scares the pee out of you.

At last they break through the clouds. "One of the most beautiful things
I can recall is seeing 50 or 60 sleek P-51s climbing up from an overcast,"
Sheppard said.

But where are the bombers? The fighters aren't only worried about being
lost but also about being late. "We had a 90-second window of rendezvous—that wasn't very much. After that we were considered late."

And Davis will not tolerate being late.

Felix Kirkpatrick:

Navigation was usually by checkpoints on the map. But one time I was
leading my squadron, and when we got to the Yugoslav coast, there were
mountains and a wall of weather there. I couldn't see the ground, so I took
my squadron and kept climbing over the top of the clouds. The Group leader
was also trying to poke some holes where those clouds were, but he went
ahead and aborted his mission and went back.

I did some dead reckoning until I thought we must be where the objective was, and I put my planes in echelon [staggered] formation, and we came
down through the clouds, and there was the target, a railroad marshalling
yard, right below us.

Fuel management was critical, Lester said:

The P-51 had five tanks of fuel. The two main tanks were in the wings.
Then there were two external tanks on the wings, but you had to get rid of
those before you could maneuver in combat. Finally there was a tank right
behind the pilot, but if you kept that tank full, it threw your center of gravity
off and you lost a lot of maneuverability; you stalled at much higher speeds.
Our instructions were to take off on that tank, fly it 45 minutes or so, down
to 25 or 30 gallons, then switch to your external tanks.

Your point of no return was the point where, if you burned off your excess
fuel in the tank behind the pilot and dropped your external tanks, you still
had enough fuel to get home straight-line, plus about a 15-minute reserve—
if you were lucky.

Some pilots didn't want to burn off the fuel in the main tank. They figured, "Heck, that's 45 minutes worth of fuel I might need on my way home."
But this could cause trouble later on with your center of gravity. I religiously
believed in getting rid of that gas first.

There was another enemy not mentioned in the movies. At 25,000 feet or higher, about the height of Mount Everest, the cold is numbing.
Kirkpatrick:

> We knew we were going to freeze our behinds off. We didn't have any heat in our airplanes; the bomber crews had heat in theirs. The cold was something we had never considered. Summer or winter, it didn't make any difference, it was the altitude that made the cold.

"And aluminum was cold as hell," Sheppard shivered.
Crockett admitted that the old P-39 may have had the poorest performance, but it had the best heater. "The Mustang had no pressurized cockpits, even though we flew at 25,000 feet. Even in the summer months you ran into temperatures below freezing."
They were issued fleece flying gear, which worked well in the bombers but was too cumbersome in the tiny cockpits of the fighters. At first the fighter pilots were issued electric suits like those the bomber crews wore, that could be plugged in like blankets.
Crockett:

> But it overloaded the electrical systems, and we had a lot of communication failures. Rather than that, we didn't plug them in. The bomber crews had more room than we had, and they might have time to change if they got hit. We couldn't do that—if you bailed out, you had to wear what you could walk home in. So you just bundled up. You wore thermals outside and dress uniform underneath. You had heavy gloves and fur-lined boots that you put your GI shoes in. When we got down to lower altitudes, we were sweating through our leather jackets.

Then there was was the strain of long hours.
Charlie McGee:

> Several missions lasted six hours. That cockpit really gets small. To look back now, I find it hard to believe I sat in that little cockpit that long. The Ploesti oil fields in Romania were particularly rough missions, because it was a very heavily defended area, so it kept you on your toes for a long time.

Kirkpatrick:

> On a long mission we were on the ground for a full half-hour before we took off. In a fighter aircraft you're very confined. We had some pretty big guys—I'm five-foot nine. You can't stretch your legs. Your butt get really tired, but you have no choice. If we want to sit down, we can't. The minute we take off, we're over water, and coming back we're over water. We're either over enemy territory or over water.

Each man sat on a bag containing his parachute and life raft. "It didn't help any," Bussey grouched. "When you came back, your ass was raw!" (McGee used a British 'chute—it was softer.)

Sheppard:

> It was torture, because the last thing an aircraft designer puts on an airplane is the cockpit. He has room for the engine, he designs the size of the prop, the ammunition has space allocated for it. The last thing is the cockpit, and that's usually the most uncomfortable place.
>
> You're sitting on the floor with the comfort level of a brick, and most of us had bony behinds. A lot of fellows developed hemorrhoids.
>
> The B-17 had inner tubes in the tail wheel, about ten to 12 inches in diameter. We'd blow them up and sit on them. But as you went higher, the outside temperature and air pressure went down, which meant pressure in the tube was more, and it expanded, which pushed you up against the safety belt even tighter, which didn't do your piles any good. We had to stab the inner tubes to keep them from inflating under us.

Finally, there was one more hidden agony that the movies don't mention. The men had now been in the air two or three hours and were over-due for urination.

"We relieved ourselves the last thing we did before we left," Kirkpatrick said. "We also had 'relief tubes' leading out of the plane, but you can't use them when you're tied down in heavy clothing."

Sheppard:

> You had to unbuckle the parachute straps between your legs, then you had to unzip your flying suit and fish around. By that time, whatever you had down there was frozen up.
>
> The relief facilities were a funnel on the left-hand side under the seat. It vented outside to a tube, which was supposed to suck the fluid violently through the line. But it also froze up at altitudes and caused a lot of mental anxiety.
>
> Plus, if your wingman saw you holding this funnel up, trying to get it to empty, he'd fly ahead of you and put you in his prop-wash, which meant you got a flying bath. And sometimes I suspected some of our friends on the ground had reversed it so you got pressure blowing it back from the funnel.
>
> We roll on the floor sometimes when we get together and recall those days. We'll never forget them.

Kirkpatrick smiled.

> Now I tell people 15 minutes is my limit. But we were young and *gung-ho* and in A-1 physical condition. We had a mission to do, and we did it, that's all. We didn't expect to be in a soft plush easy chair to do it.

The P-51 was fitted with an oxygen tube that automatically increased the oxygen as altitude increased. But, said Sheppard, sometimes the tube could become blocked, and the pilot didn't realize he wasn't getting enough. Purnell:

> All of a sudden, I felt like this was the best day I had ever lived. Everything turned beautiful, I could hear music coming out of nowhere, I wanted to roll back the canopy and climb out on the nose of the plane and direct all 64 pieces of the orchestra. I didn't know it, but I had hypoxia, not enough oxygen. At first it feels as if you've had three martinis, the best feeling in the world.
>
> Then, about five minutes later, it felt as if someone had lowered a great mosquito netting right in front of my eyes. All of a sudden I began to get really sick to my stomach. It was an effort to do the things that should have been second nature. For instance, I saw the squadron leaving, climbing and making a turn. Usually my reaction would have been automatic, but now I had to think: "If I want to catch up with them, I'll have to advance my throttle, a little left rudder, yeah, that gets it."
>
> Then I got to the point where I said, "I don't give a damn." I had a feeling as if I was going to sleep. I remember the plane veering off to the right. I was following the plane, it wasn't following me. It was taking me where it wanted to go.

Luckily Lou landed safely. Some others didn't.

Meantime, the German defenses are waiting. Eyes are sharp, breathing is rapid, heads are turning right and left. "You've heard the term, "Swivel head?" McGee asks. "That was a fighter pilot."

After crossing the Aegean Sea, the first land they sighted was Yugoslavia—they dubbed it "Flak alley." "Those goddam German 88s [anti-aircraft guns] were waiting," Jefferson said, "and they were deadly."

Sometimes fighters linked up with the bombers just before the target, at the Romanian border, for example, relieving another fighter Group. Sheppard:

> At last we'd spot the bombers pulling streamers, and we'd head over there and see if it was our bomber Group. We were careful not to get between the sun and the bombers, because their gunners were keen-sighted people and could tear us up with their .50s. We'd fly a big circle so they could get a good look at us, zigzag across them and give them a good silhouette so they could see our red tails.

The fighters flew S-patterns over the slower bombers, which used up much of the P-51's fuel. For that reason they preferred the B-24s, which were slightly faster than the B-17s.

Roberts:

The fighter outfits met the bombers before the enemy line. "A" Group would pick them up first. "B" Group takes off 45 minutes after "A" Group, picks the bombers up and relieves "A" Group. "C" Group takes off maybe an hour later and picks them up at target and takes them around the target.

Since we had four squadrons instead of the usual three, they seemed always to put us where they felt the highest concentration of enemy fighters would be. Quite often it would be in one of two locations: The German fighters would try to hit us just before the target, to protect the target, or just as we were coming off the target, when we were likely to be disrupted.

Kirkpatrick:

The enemy aircraft also knew we were coming two or three hours before we got there [their intelligence was amazingly detailed, as future POWs were to learn], so they were positioned well above us when we arrived.

I suspected sometimes the white boys were using the bombers as bait to get some kills—you wondered if their bombers had any cover or not. But we were there where the enemy aircraft could see us. When the other fighters saw that the bombers had good cover, they'd say, "Hell, let's get some stragglers instead."

Lester:

Very seldom did the Germans try to attack the bomber formations we were escorting. Three squadrons had the mission of providing close support for the bombers. The fourth flew what we called a fighter sweep. They were free to do anything they wanted to as long as they kept the bombers in sight. That's when you had a chance to get at the enemy aircraft.

But if they ran into enemy fighters on the way to the target, the Group commander would order one or two pilots to "Go get 'em," while the rest continued on with the bombers.

Gleed:

We'd break off as they approached their Initial Point. The flak from the German 88-mm anti-aircraft guns was so black you could walk on it.

Kirkpatrick:

When you see the flak, it's too late. There were big puffs of smoke all around. When they shot at us, we assumed they'd tracked us, so we changed altitude, speed, and direction.

"That shrapnel is ragged," Bill Melton shuddered. "You could damn near shave with it."

The 17s might have been slower, but they had one big advantage over the B-17s, from the fighters' point of view—they could reach higher altitude. German anti-aircraft fire was very effective below 20,000 feet. Although the B-24's ceiling was about 20,000, the B-17s climbed to 25,000. The fighters liked to keep a protective position about 5,000 feet above the bombers, which meant that they were pushed up to 30,000 feet or more.

Sheppard:

> I was pretty glad to be up that high, because the bombers would soak up the flak. Every once in a while, a round would get through and cause a lot of excitement among the single-engine guys.
>
> Also, the extra 5,000 feet gave us an edge if we had to ward off attack. If you have speed, you can get altitude, and if you have altitude, you can get speed. That P-51 really accelerated when you put its nose down. Man, altitude just disappeared like smoke in the wind.

McGee:

> In many cases we went in with the bombers over the target. The ack-ack fire from the German guns was like a black blanket. Our fighters usually flew above the bombers, and we had the ability to do a little "jinking" around—dodging.
>
> But, boy, once the bombers got on the IP to go into the target, regardless of how heavy the flak was, they'd ride right on through to be sure their bombs were on target. You couldn't help but admire the guys who were flying them.

Over Ploesti, Romania, Jefferson said, the *ack-ack* fire looked "like a huge black doughnut or hockey puck suspended in air so thick you could damn near walk on it."

Gleed:

> We didn't want any part of that flak. The bombers had to go in. They flew straight into the hockey pucks and disappeared into the smoke. It was a horrendous sight to see six B-24 Liberators with all that flak starting to come up and *bang!*—there's only five airplanes left and one big ball of smoke.
>
> Or see one plane start lagging back and try to make it on into the target anyway.
>
> We'd pick them up coming out, some with three engines out, or half a tail shot off.

Sometimes a bomber fell out of the donut, "spinning down lazily, trailing smoke and flames." The fighters counted the 'chutes:...two...three...

hollering, "Jump! Jump!" Sometimes there were no 'chutes, only an explosion—"a big red ball"—and "ten men ceased to exist."

To Sheppard his most vivid memory of the war was not aerial combat:

> It was the sight of bombers being hit by an 88 and the bombs going off—a big red eruption with black smoke going by you. With one detonation we had just lost ten crewmen. Ten families had been left bereft—mothers, wives, children, brothers, and sisters. All bereft.

Jefferson:

> Planes fell in flames, planes fell not in flames, an occasional one pulled out and crash-landed, sometimes successfully, sometimes they blew up. Men fell in flames, men fell in parachutes, some candle-sticked [when their 'chutes didn't open]. Pieces of men dropped through the hole, pieces of planes.
>
> Have you any idea what it's like to vomit in an oxygen mask?

The airmen had a grim song to the tune of "As Time Goes By," from the Humphrey Bogart movie, *Casablanca*. They changed the words to:

> You must remember this,
> Those guns won't always miss.
> On that you can rely...
>
> It's still the same old story,
> The fighters get the glory,
> And bomber pilots die—
> The fundamental things of life
> As time goes by.

"After the *ack-ack* fire," said Melton, "the Germans fired a pink flare as a signal for their fighters to go in, and we'd take the bombers back."

Jefferson:

> We didn't worry about the *Luftwaffe*. These bomber guys had seen the inside of hell, and if they could stay airborne, we damned sure were going to take them back. Hell, the holes were so big in those damn planes, sometimes we could see the interior. They would jettison everything aboard but the men. Many had wounded aboard and couldn't effectively man their guns.

One bomber radioman recalled hearing his P-38 escort leader say that his planes, which had a relatively short range, were running low on fuel and had to head back to base. Then another voice came over the air: "Don't worry. We won't leave you." It was the Red Tails.

If the German planes attacked, each squadron leader gave the order, "Drop tanks!" and 36 silver tanks—two under every wing—"fell like giant raindrops," in Jefferson's phrase, and the battle was on.

Wilson Eagleson:

Combat is hours of complete boredom and 30–40 seconds of sheer bedlam. You either miss him or you get him. At 500 mph you don't have time to look around and go back and shoot again, so basically there's one pass at the most.

After their "babies" were safely out of danger, the Red Tails could head for home themselves. But their danger wasn't over yet.

Often the planes had been separated in dogfights and had to find their way as best they could. The pilots often had to contend with oil-smeared windshields or heavy cloud cover. Bob Williams:

You've gotta get back home, you're over the top of the clouds, and you don't know where the hell you are. You've got to get back down to find your base, and you're over the Alps. It was very, very hairy.

Lester:

I can remember several occasions where we navigated to the point we thought we were over the Adriatic Sea and we started letting down. Sometimes we would let down from, say, 20,000 feet to 500 feet before we saw the water. The mountains around Yugoslavia and Italy were ten to 12,000 feet, so once you got down to 12,000, you better hope your dead reckoning navigation was correct, your altimeter was set correctly, or you were over water.

They used their compasses and watches—fly on a heading for so many minutes—and tried to pick out landmarks when possible—a mountain, river, or coastline. Or they could switch to an emergency radar homing service, "Big Fence," and get a heading back to base. "Big Fence was good!" Sheppard said. "It had been helpful to us a number of times."

Jefferson: "Many times we flew with the bombers beyond our Point of Departure, where we were supposed to leave them, and sometimes it made us run low on fuel."

If they were lucky, they could follow a radio beacon to the Yugoslav island of Vis, which soon became a "boneyard of wrecked planes."

Other pilots headed over the Adriatic Sea, praying they could make landfall in Italy.

Jefferson:

> Once, Henry Peoples ran out of fuel as he was coming in and was ordered to bail out. He said they were out of their minds, he wasn't about to take to the air—he was allergic to heights. That fool cut off his radio and rode his plane down to a perfect landing.

Bussey:

> Most of our flying was great distances over water, and three-fourths of our men couldn't swim. We lost more men in the water than any other way.
>
> Sometimes, if you can't swim, you panic. Clemenceau Givings, the captain of our class, bellied into the water. He was fumbling, trying to get that dinghy to inflate, and the airplane sank under him. A damn good man; he should never have died in such a miserable way. It was sinful. No man should have to die because no one took time to put him through swimming lessons.
>
> The survival equipment we had in the old days was crude; it did very little to help people survive. Survival is just as important as accomplishing the mission itself—if you survive, you can fly again and accomplish other missions.
>
> An accomplished swimmer at least had a fighting chance. We lost a lot of guys, and we shouldn't have. There was a big Olympic-size swimming pool at Selfridge. Forty white officers and their wives could use it; we weren't allowed to swim in it. At least they could have given us swimming lessons in Detroit.
>
> It's the biggest hurt I've brought with me from the Service.

If a pilot did manage to reach his home field and the gas gauge was empty, he joined the "caterpillar club" [bailed out].

Kirkpatrick:

> As planes arrived, everybody on base would be there for the landing. If there was a victory to celebrate, the pilot went into his victory roll to the cheers of his crewmen, one roll for each enemy shot down.

The pilots, their leather flight jackets streaked with oil, dumped their yellow "Mae Wests"—life vests, oxygen masks, 'chutes—in an operations shack and piled into jeeps, laughing, jostling, and rough-housing, to ride to the interrogation room and debrief the S-2 on the target and enemy they had found.

Kirkpatrick:

> Then the Red Cross girls would serve coffee, and we'd have a critique, whatever the intelligence officer wanted to know—where and what kind of enemy fighters and *ack-ack* we ran into.

"Finally" McGee said, "you'd get a shot of liquor, and you're free." They climbed into the trucks to ride back to their tents. For most pilots the first objective was a good shower and scrubdown, a luxury because water was rationed and uniforms even had to be laundered in 100-octane gasoline. Then they made a rush for the mess hall.

Shep:

> By mid-afternoon we were ravenous. Our flight surgeon firmly believed there was tremendous benefit to our eyesight from eating carrots, so carrot sticks were the first thing on the table. I didn't find out until I was 50 that I had to eat 50 tons of carrots to get any benefit.

"The food was piss poor," Bussey grumbled. "Very little meat. Dehydrated food—I'd never even heard of it. On the whole, between missions we lived a very bleak and miserable life."

Meanwhile, out on the flight line, one or two ground crews might still be keeping a vigil, searching the skies for a warrior who hadn't returned. Charles Hill:

> You'd see them hanging around his stand, every now and then sneaking a look at the horizon as if to will him back. Sometimes they stayed there for hours, looking in the sky.

At night, Shep said:

> I'd have to go back to the line to check out the mechanics again. I worked many nights late at night at fuel dumps, pumping gas by hand from 55-gallon drums into 1200-gallon tankers to refuel the airplanes.

When possible he joined his tent-mates, who unwound with by playing cards:

> We played "dirty hearts" with about seven guys, two decks of cards, and we played endlessly, night after night after night. The penalty was 26 points per hand—13 for the queen of spades and one for each heart.
> The first one who lost 104 points had to drink a whole canteen of water. Some people who got nailed would come back for revenge and have to drink a second canteen. We played this thing until after midnight, knowing that we had to go over 25,000 feet early in the morning with all that pressure on the kidneys.
> Fighter pilots are known for doing dumb things.

"You can always tell a fighter pilot," Kirkpatrick nodded, "but you can't tell him much."

In the morning they did it all over again.

Shep:

White pilots were rotated home after 50 missions. I flew 123. [Lee Archer flew 169.] That was largely because Tuskegee was now forming a bomber Group and siphoning off a large percentage of pilots to put into twin engines, which meant that our replacements were at low ebb.

So we shook the dice and went up on the next mission, hoping the dice wouldn't turn craps on us.

The Crews

THE bond between the fliers and crewmen was strong.

Bill Melton:

It was just like being on a football team, we depended on each other. We had some shitty airplanes at first, but we had some superb, well-trained, bright ground people that kept us flying. No one ever gives enough recognition to those eight or nine people who are immediately behind the pilot. The early enlisted men who went to Tuskegee had to have two years of college. They were the high-tech boys of 50 years ago.

My crew chief came into my tent before he went on leave. He could borrow my money, my gabardines [dress uniform], anything else I had. We got two ounces of Old Hickory whiskey on each mission; when it was his turn to go into the rest camp, I'd give him my whiskey. All rank ceased when he walked through the tent door, because these were our backbone. My life depended on him. We were in fact like brothers.

Archer:

We had a group of enlisted men younger than the pilots—17 or 18—who did a remarkable job keeping us in the air. We flew four different planes in combat, and I don't remember one time these kids went back to school again when a new plane came in. They'd sit in a tent and learn how to take care of it.

If you ask my crew chief, "How's my bird?" he'd say, "Look, Lieutenant, let's get this straight: This is not your airplane—it's *my* airplane. You *fly* it."

One time I had been beaten up, had a hole the size of an ashcan in my wing. I was worried whether the wing would fall off. He was running along next to the aircraft, waving his hands. I thought he was happy to see me back. As I opened the canopy:

"My God, Lieutenant! Look what you've done to my *airplane!*"

Sheppard:

They were proud of their work and didn't like aircraft down for any non-sense. They were quite peeved if pilots brought the aircraft back early for insufficient reason. [Shep suspected that some pilots aborted as an excuse to avoid a tough mission. He hinted that he knew who they were.]

The crews worked outside—no indoor facilities. They swung engines on an A-frame, changed the props, changed the engines.

Sergeant William Surcey and his section toiled for over a month in wintry outdoor conditions with a skeleton crew and inadequate tools. They patched up seven downed fighters and sent them back into the air. Surcey received a Bronze Star.

Sergeant Clarence "Buddy" Huntley

To me one of the most impressive things that happened: They changed an engine in ten hours! That's amazing. Under combat conditions! A complete engine in ten hours—took it out, put another in, hooked it up, and back in the sky. I never heard of any other squadron doing such a thing as that.

Sergeant William Pitts was the guy who did it. His chief of engineers was Master Sergeant Wade.

As for Huntley himself:

I graduated from Los Angeles high school in '42 and went to work in Douglas Aircraft.

In October I went into the Service. Five of us volunteered—there were no draftees at Tuskegee, we were all volunteers. I was 19.

They didn't send me to school. I got "on the job" training, because I'd had previous experience.

We had a hard time for a long time, because they wouldn't let us do the job we had volunteered for: aircraft mechanics. I was a driver for Captain Tresville. Then I drove for Captain Turner. He was also a nice person, very nice.

Finally they let me be a mechanic, and we all started gelling together. Everybody fought the fight with no friction whatsoever. We were all young and together, just like one big happy family

We worked on them all: the P-39, P-40, P-47, and the 51—the one that won the war.

My ship never did miss a day! Every time she was scheduled to fly, she flew.

Several crewmen lost their lives.

Master Sergeant Edsel Jett leaped into the sea to help a drowning man, even though Jett himself couldn't swim. He was awarded the Soldiers' Medal for heroism in a non-combat situation.

Master Sergeant Bill Harris was crossing the flight line in a weapons carrier and drove into the path of a plane taking off. The pilot never saw him, and Harris was decapitated.

Sergeant Eugene Pickett, one of Sheppard's classmates at Chanute Field, was found dead around Naples.

Sheppard:

> I think he was murdered. There didn't seem to be a good investigation. The Military Police at that time were not black-indoctrinated; whether a black got killed or not was irrelevant to them.

The deaths hit Shep hard. Harris had been his line chief.

"There were some damn good men," Sheppard said, and I considered myself part of them. We had A-1 maintenance."

He was right. Fifteenth Air Force records provided by Ron Bronstein for June-July-August show that, among the four P-51 Groups, the four squadrons of the 332nd had the lowest number of early returns because of mechanical problems:

Group	Early Returns	Per Squadron
52nd	298	99
31st	296	72*
325th	261	84
332nd	300	75*

On one long-range flight deep over Germany, Charles Hill took off with a bad stomach ache and returned with acute appendicitis. The pain was so intense that he slipped in and out of consciousness. The tower screamed at him, "Drop your wheels! Drop your wheels!" Then, "Drop your flaps, man! Drop your flaps! OK, cut back on the throttle. . . ."

Then, apparently on the ground, he heard a hysterical, "Your brakes, baby! Cut your motor! Cut it off!" His crew chief was on the wing holding on for dear life as the plane spun on the runway toward a row of parked planes.

Hill blacked out, and when he came to, the chief had pulled him out onto the wing. Four hours later, he was on the operating table. In three weeks, he was flying missions again.

"If it hadn't been for the tower and the crew chief, I wouldn't be here."

1. Cadets reporting to Captain Benjamin O. Davis, Jr., at Tuskegee, September 1941.

2. Brigadier General Benjamin O. Davis Sr., Lt. Colonel Noel Parrish, and Lt. Colonel Benjamin O. Davis, Jr.

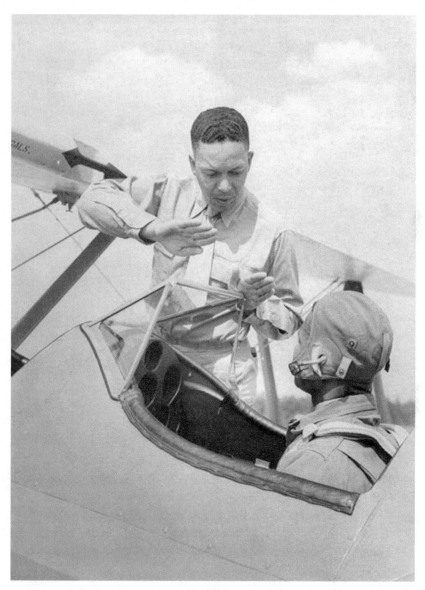

3. C. Alfred "Chief" Anderson, Chief Flight Instructor of the Tuskegee Airmen.

4. Members of the first class of graduates from the Tuskegee Army Flying School with Robert Long. From left to right: George "Spanky" Roberts, Benjamin O. Davis, Jr., Charles H. DeBow, Long, Mac Ross, and Lemuel Custis.

5. Pilots of the 477th flying B-25s in formation.

6. Base Commander Major James Ellison returns a salute as he inspects cadets at Tuskegee Army Airfield.

7. An aviation cadet practices instrument flying at Tuskegee Army Airfield, June 1942.

8. Officers of the 99th Fighter Group near Fez, Morocco, on May 12, 1943. From left to right: Lt. Colonel Benjamin O. Davis, Jr., Captain Hayden Johnson, Captain E. Jones, and Lieutenants William Thompson, Herbert Carter, Erwin Lawrence, and George Currie.

9. Captains Lemuel Custis and Charles Hall while on leave in New York City, June 1944.

10. First Lieutenant Lee Rayford of the 99th Fighter Group.

11. P-51 pilots in Italy in August of 1944. From left to right: Lieutenants Dempsey Morgan, Carroll Woods, and Robert Nelson, and Captain Andrew "Jug" Turner and Lieutenant Clarence "Lucky" Lester.

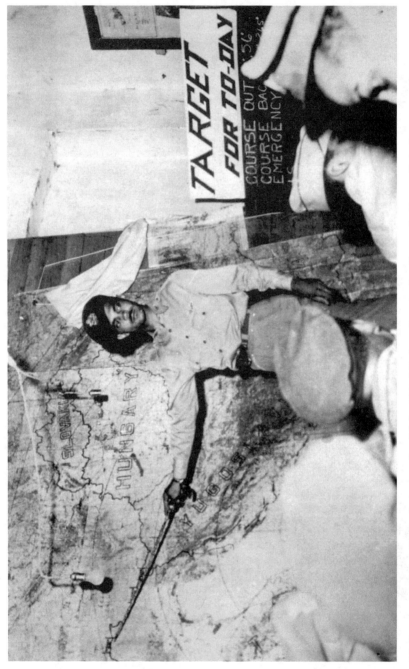

12. Lieutenant Edward Gleed giving pilots of the 332nd Fighter Group a briefing at the Ramitelli Airbase in Italy, September 1944.

13. Colonel Benjamin O. Davis, Jr., and Lieutenant Edward Gleed at the airfield in Ramitelli, Italy, 1944.

14. Pilots of the 332nd Fighter Group attend a mission briefing in Ramitelli, Italy, March 1945.

15. Captain Woodrow W. Crockett and Lieutenant Edward Gleed discuss the day's mission at the Ramitelli Airbase in Italy, March 1945.

16. Tuskegee Airman Daniel "Chappie" James, shown here as a fighter pilot in Vietnam. James would go on to become the first black American four-star general.

July 11. The 99th flew its first mission in the P-51.

Leon Roberts, the last of the original 99th, had volunteered to stay in Italy when the others were rotated home, and had 116 missions to his credit. When the Group hit German shipyards in southern France, Roberts plunged to his death from 30,000 feet. Friends speculated that he may have blacked out from lack of oxygen.

July 12. Seventeen planes of the 301st escorted B-24s hitting railroad yards in Nimes, Southern France, in weather so bad that they were the only fighters to get through. Fifteenth Air Force G-2 must have underestimated the German force awaiting them, as they were jumped by 28 Focke Wulf, which attacked the last flight of six bombers. In the ensuing dogfights the Red Tails scored their first victories in the P-51.

Harold Sawyer and Bernie Jefferson, an ex-football player at Northwestern, followed one down, and Sawyer peppered it until it dove to the ground and crashed. It was the Group's first victory in the P-51. Almost immediately he caught another coming in at ten o'clock, his second victory of the day.

Three enemy flew across the bow of Joseph Elsberry's plane, "Joe da Belle." As one was turning away, he fired a 30-degree deflection shot, and the plane fell off to the left with heavy black smoke pouring out. He claimed a probable.

Then another crossed in front of him. Elsberry dove and they fired. He told author Robert Rose in *Lonely Eagles*:

> I turned inside him, and he began to smoke and fell into a dive towards the ground. I followed him through a series of split-S maneuvers as he tried to avoid me and, *then he rolls out and is going back the other way*. We started at 11,000 feet, ending at about 2,000 before I broke off my attack . . . Just before reaching the ground, he tried to pull up but ran out of sky.

One minute later another enemy pulled across his path and turned, as if trying to get away. Elsberry gave him two bursts, and he crashed into the ground and exploded.

Finally Joe saw a fourth FW diving at a 45-degree angle. Only half of Joe's guns on his left wing were firing, so he kicked right rudder and hit the ship on the left wing near the fuselage. The pilot tried to pull out of his dive but too late. He crashed.

For some reason, it took the Air Force several years to give Elsberry credit. But when they did, it made him the second Tuskegee Airmen to claim three victories—Charlie Hall was first. As it turned out, Elsberry would earn one more victory. The probable may have cost him the chance to be an ace.

However, three bombers also fell out of the sky, hit by German bullets. As Air Force historian Daniel Haulman observed, "There were more bombers than fighters to cover them."

Walter Palmer of the 100th recalled one flight over France around that time:

> We had an overcast sky over our field, and we were the last flight. I took off, leading the flight, and got to 8,000 feet, above the clouds, and circled around, waiting for my flight to come up. None of them came, and I assumed they couldn't make it through the clouds. But when I took off on a mission, I never came back without completing it, so I flew off and tried to catch the rest of them.
>
> By the time I hit the coast of southern France, I saw a plane coming the opposite way. He waggled his wings, which was always a friendly sign among the Allied aircraft. I waggled my wings back at him, and he started to turn toward me as if he was going to join me, because it's terrible to be out by yourself in enemy territory. He came on in behind me.
>
> I figured there might be something wrong, because usually he'd join me from the side. The idea was never to show your guns to the plane in front of you, and sure enough, after a little while I noticed fire coming from his guns.
>
> I whipped around tight and recognized that he was an ME 109, which was similar to the P-51 we were flying. I knew my Mustang could outmaneuver him, so I kept it in a tight turn. When he noticed I was getting position on him, he decided to split-S and head on out. He was going all the way to the ground. I said, "No point going down there and endangering myself with small arms fire. I'll forget about it," so I turned around and headed on back.
>
> It was my first encounter with an enemy plane.

July 15. The 99th flew its first mission in the P-51. When the pilots arrived for their morning briefing, the older veterans let out a collective groan. The big situation map showed a green string from Ramitelli to the Ploesti oil refinery, the most heavily defended target in station Europe. This day both bombers and fighters got through the target safely; on the way home, some German fighters appeared to challenge the formation, but the Red Tails chased them away.

July 17. The *Luftwaffe* had been severely wounded at Stalingrad. Lost planes could be replaced, but veteran pilots could not.

The Group downed three more over southern France, by Lawrence Wilkins, Robert "Dissipatin'" Smith, and Luther "Quibbling" Smith, all of the 302nd. When a German ME 109 penetrated the flight of bombers, Luther Smith said:

I was parallel with one of the German airplanes. The pilot didn't have an oxygen mask on, so I could see his face, and he appeared to be about 16 or 17. But I had my job to do. I shot, and it went down.

Coming home, Maceo Harris picked up a wounded bomber and flew with it to a safe landing on the island of Corsica, where the bomber crew thanked him with kisses "in the French manner."

Meantime a "ghost" walked into the 99th headquarters at Ramitelli— Clarence Allen, the erstwhile playboy, who had been shot down more than a month earlier, June 4.

Allen said he saw two German sentries on a hill, and they saw him at the same time. He scrambled and slid down the hill and ran into a woods, where he hid in the bushes. The sentries poked around for awhile before giving up, and he ducked into a cave. But before long German soldiers arrived and set up a machine gun at the entrance, and Allen remained hidden until they left that night.

He crept out at sun-up and discovered that he had crawled into an enemy bivouac area with German troops moving about, eating breakfast, and shaving. Once more Allen laid low until the Germans moved out. He was finally rescued by tankers from the Japanese Nisei "Go for Broke" battalion.

12

Disaster at Memmingen

July 18

THE Red Tails' most controversial mission of the war was also one of their most glorious—they shot down 11 planes. But it was also a disastrous day for the 15th Air Force, which lost 15 bombers.

The 332nd had received their P-51s only two weeks before. This was their tenth long-range mission with the rest of the Fighter Wing. It was also the first time the 99th would join the others. The Red Tails, the rookies of the 15th Air Force, were given primary responsibility—in fact, as it turned out, the sole responsibility—for one of the largest and most complicated missions of the 15th Air Force.

Under a heavy overcast Lee Rayford of the 100th led 66 Red Tails on a flight to Memmingen Airdrome, Germany. Their mission: to cover 112 B-17s, strung out over more than 20 miles of sky. Ahead, intelligence warned, 240 or more German fighters were lying in wait—40 at Udine on the way, and perhaps 200 more at Memmingen.

Eight Red Tails turned back early with mechanical problems, leaving it with 58 planes against 240 on a playing field 20 miles long. Even if the operation went like clockwork, it was a prescription for disaster.

And everything did not go like clockwork.

Diligent detective work by Air Force historian Daniel Haulman reveals a badly bungled job of planning at headquarters. It was compounded by what appears to be an indefensible order early in the mission, plus an almost total breakdown of radio communications between headquarters and planes, as well as between planes in the sky. This is not Haulman's official conclusion but one drawn from the facts uncovered.

Yet the outcome of the entire mission fell on their shoulders, and the blame for the ultimate disaster would be hung around their necks.

It was the first mission that all four squadrons of the 332nd flew together. Why B.O. Davis was not leading has never been explained. Would the outcome have been different if he had? There is no way to know.

Exactly what happened in the next few hours? The records of the various units that took part are either vague, silent, or in dispute. And no man who was there is left alive to tell.

The plan was for three fighter Groups—the 332nd, 325th, and 52nd—about 188 planes—would protect the B-17 wing. However, as we shall see, only a fraction of that number actually met the Germans over Memmingen. In fact, the 52nd and 325th would play little or no role in the coming drama.

Meantime, two other fighter Groups—the 31st and 1st—also had responsibility for Memmingen, but their main mission would be to rendezvous with B-24s over another target, Friedrichshafen, about 30 miles away. The operation was similar to the notorious Schweinfurt raid by the 8th Air Force a year earlier, when two different targets were hit simultaneously. The hope in both cases was to confuse the defenders. Instead, it was the Americans who were confused—they lost 60 bombers at Schweinfurt and 15 at Memmingen.

According to the plan, the Red Tails, the 325th, and the 52nd were to rendezvous with the B-17s north of the Alps and escort them to the Initial Point (IP), where the bombers would begin their bomb runs. For some unfathomable reason, the 325th received orders to turn around and conduct a fighter sweep back in Italy! The 332nd and the 52nd droned on toward disaster. Under the plan, the 52nd was also ordered to leave the bombers just before the target and conduct another "fighter sweep," looking for enemy fighters miles away from the target. The 332nd alone was left with the job of protecting the Fortresses at their point of maximum danger.

While the bombers lumbered northward toward the Alps, the 332nd, leaving from a different airfield, was on a different vector. The 52nd was also heading for the target from its own field. The 332nd flight path led almost directly over Venice and the nearby German fighter base of Udine, the same one where the 332nd had scored its first major victory with five kills in their P-47s on June 9.

Because of heavy clouds, two of the four bomb Groups, 56 Flying Fortresses, had left their designated flight path. Led by Colonel Paul Barton of the 483rd Group, they chose to fly to the east, over the Adriatic, where visibility was better. It might have been a good idea, but it was a longer route, and Barton apparently did not inform anyone else, especially the fighter escorts. This would turn out to be fatal.

It has never been explained why he didn't tell the fighters. Perhaps he was maintaining radio silence to keep the Germans in the dark. If so, he failed.

First, as POWs learned later, the Nazis had a spy in headquarters, who was feeding them the most detailed secrets, even the password and counter-sign for the day.

Second, German ground radar all along the way would have alerted all

Luftwaffe bases in southern Germany that the Americans were heading their way. Thus, while no one was fooling the Germans, the Red Tails were fooled completely about the true situation.

At any rate, the fighter Order—the Air Force called it "plans"—gave every Group a radio call sign. Why give them a call sign if they weren't allowed to use it? Indeed, headquarters did use the radio to order the 325th to come home. So why didn't the "lost bombers" use their radios to inform the fighters that they were running late?

Headquarters A-2 (Intelligence) had predicted that 30–40 enemy fighters could be expected at Udine, and it was right. Like hornets, the German fighters swarmed up to protect their home field.

Rayford's 301st was leading, followed by the 99th low, the 302nd middle, and the 100th high. One was designated the "attack" squadron that day; we don't know which one it was; the records are silent. It was probably not the 99th, which was making its first flight with the Group. And it was probably not the 301st under Rayford, the Group flight leader, who had to stay with the main body. And it was probably not the 302nd, which would lose one of its pilots over Memmingen.

Therefore, it was probably the 100th, which dropped external tanks and peeled off while the other three squadrons flew on to shepherd the bombers.

Oscar Hutton of the 100th was the first pilot to die that day, killed in a freak once-in-a-million accident, when his plane was hit by a falling wing tank.

Walter Palmer:

We were 3–4,000 feet above the bombers, and we noticed about 25 or 30 planes above us. Not knowing what they were, we called them "bogeys." They usually didn't make aggressive moves toward the bombers while we were nearby. On this day they did! They dived at the bombers, and we, of course, followed in hot pursuit.

I got on the tail of one ME-109, and on the second or third burst, all of a sudden he burst into flame and heavy thick smoke and headed straight into the ground. I broke it off, because there were others to shoot down so the bombers could safely make their run.

When I pulled back up, I was under another 109, and this time he didn't notice me, because I came up underneath him, which is unusual. As I got close to him, I tested my guns, but only one of my four guns fired, and then it jammed, but those few rounds were enough to alert the pilot that I was on his tail. I figured, I'll just go chop his tail off, not thinking that I'm going to have to hit the ground too, because my propeller will be bent.

Anyhow, I was closing in and sensing my second victory when he turned sharply and headed into the clouds. We were near the Alps, and I said, "Well, he knows his way through the mountains, I don't. I'll let him alone."

Meanwhile, Jack Holsclaw shot down two enemy planes.

Palmer's tent-mate, Lucky Lester, flying "Miss Pelt," was also busy, the first time he had even seen an enemy fighter.

The fourth man in our Flight of four planes drifted off 6–700 feet, and suddenly he was attacked by ME-109s. As they came down from above us, they saw him out there by himself, and he probably looked like a straggler to them, so they jumped him. Either he couldn't get his external fuel tanks off in time, or, some people theorize, he might not have burned off the fuel behind the pilot's seat, so he wasn't as maneuverable. At any rate, they shot him down. The other three of us made a turn around to head into them.

I dove in behind one plane as he flew level. He started maneuvering a little bit, I started shooting, and the airplane started coming apart on him, smoke poured out of him, and he exploded. I was going so fast, I was sure I would hit some of the debris.

As I dodged pieces of aircraft, I saw this other plane all alone to my right on a heading 90 degrees to mine. I turned onto his tail and came up behind him, going like a bat out of heck. I closed to about 200 feet and started over-running him and began firing. The engine on the ME-109 was liquid-cooled like the P-51. If you hit the coolant, the airplane was through. His aircraft started to smoke and almost stopped. I was going so fast I skidded my airplane to the side, because I thought I was going to run right up his tail. I saw him climb out on the wing and bail out. I can still see him today with his blond hair, standing on the wing, just as plain as then. It was an amazing sight.

Then I saw a third airplane down below me, and I took off after him. I picked him up going pretty fast, because I had a 2,000-foot start on him before he saw me. He started to dive, trying to out-dive my P-51. Well, there's no way he'd be able to do that. When he got to about 1,000 feet, he leveled but wasn't having any luck, and I was still peppering him. He was desperate by then, because I'd scored so many hits, so he decided on a Split-S maneuver, that is, roll over and pull the airplane down so he was going back the other way. It's a very basic maneuver—but not at 1,000 feet. I wasn't about to follow him through on that. He never made it and went straight into the ground.

All this took place in four or five minutes—six at the outside. On the return flight, it took a little while to realize what had happened. Only then did the danger hit me.

These were the first planes shot down by the 100th. But, their fuel now low, 21 more planes had to turn back.

When Palmer got home, he did a slow victory roll, landed, and learned that Holsclaw and Lester had been victorious too. "There was some celebrating in our tent that night!" They were still unaware of the disaster over Memmingen.

Rayford's Group was down to 37 planes, when it plunged ahead to face a predicted 200 waiting German fighters When they reached the rendezvous point, they found no bombers. They circled over the area, waiting and using up precious fuel. If they waited too long, they would not be able to complete the mission. But if they left, the bombers would be abandoned without any cover. Lee decided to wait.

After ten minutes 56 bombers finally appeared out of the clouds. But, unbeknownst to Rayford, they were only half the B-17s. It was impossible to count them, and no one had informed Rayford that the other half—another 56—had taken a different and longer route. Rayford later reported that the bombers were in a good tight formation and easy to cover. That was because the other half was still about 15 minutes behind, in the clouds.

This fatal misunderstanding might have been avoided if "lost" bombers had radioed their estimated arrival time. It also might not have happened if the 332nd and the B-17 Wing had been assigned as a team that always worked together, whose commanders often met personally and had established a close working rapport. The concept is familiar in Army ground operations, but it was apparently not applied in the 15th Air Force. So it didn't occur to Rayford to ask, "Hey, where are Paul and Al?" (If Davis had been leading the mission, would he have asked? Perhaps not.)

Then, to compound the chain of blunders, as soon as the force reached the Initial Point to begin the bomb run, the 52nd flew away and left them to conduct their fighter sweep. They didn't find any German fighters. That's because they were all where one could have predicted they would be—back at the target area, attacking the bombers and the 332nd.

Swarms of German fighters had scrambled into the air to give battle to the 37 remaining Red Tails and the 56 bombers. Exactly what happened next we don't know in detail. But it must have been a furious dogfight, because the pilots of the 31st and 1st on the secondary mission, observed it from miles away.

How long the Red Tails had been fighting alone, no one knows. How much longer they could have held out against the overwhelming odds, we also don't know. Had most of the Fortresses dropped their bombs and emerged on the other side? Again, no one alive today can answer that. What we do know is that the Red Tails shot down six attackers and had not lost even one of the 56 bombers, with their 560 crewmen.

At this point occurred a stroke of luck (either good luck or bad staff coordination) that may have prevented an even greater disaster. Some 30 miles away the 31st and 1st (the latter a P-38 squadron) were circling, wondering where their own B-24s were. They also hadn't been told yet that the Liberators had either been called back or had decided to turn back, probably because of the weather. While their two first Groups waited, they spotted the B-17s and the Red Tails, fighting for their lives over Memmingen, which was part of the area of responsibility. Like John Wayne and the 7th Cavalry, the two Groups galloped full speed to help.

Once again the records don't tell us when the 31st and 1st saw the dogfight, how long it took them to decide to get into it, and at what time they actually arrived.

But with the arrival of up to 108 fresh fighters, the odds quickly changed. The three squadrons finished the job of getting all the first 56 Fortresses safely over the target.

The P-38s claimed 14 kills. The 31st, the hottest pilots in the 15th Air Force, with more victories than any other squadron, bagged 12 (though three were more properly strafing victories over fighters trying to land). The 332nd claimed 12 for the day, including the six over Udine.

These numbers could mean that the danger to the bombers was over, and the two new Groups could go hunting. Nine of the 31st flyers even left the bombers to dive to the deck and spray three damaged German planes attempting to land. Those were technically not "aerial" victories, although they were claimed as such. A more accurate count would be nine aerial kills and three destroyed on a strafing run.

In their mission reports, the 332nd, the 1st, and 31st all mentioned only their own activities. None gave the other two credit. This might have been because each Group was single-mindedly absorbed in its own battle. Or it might have been posturing to make the best showing. (The 31st said only that the bombers and 332nd had not followed the prescribed flight path—how did it know what the prescribed path was or whether they'd followed it?)

Then, the danger having apparently passed, the 31st and 1st gallantly shepherded the Fortresses home, leaving the 332nd once again alone over the target.

Finally, at 11:30—about 20 minutes late—to the amazement of the weary Red Tails, out of the clouds lumbered 56 more bombers!

About 60 fresh Messerschmitts and Focke Wulfe's had already risen to the attack, screaming up from below to pour cannon fire on them from the rear, where only the rear gunners could get shots at them.

Later the leader of the "lost bombers" complained that the escorts were not waiting to protect them and didn't arrive until eight minutes later. However, the bombers were wrong. They arrived at the IP at 11:30. At the same moment Wellington Irving of the 301st and Gene Browne of the 302nd were seen in combat with about 30 Messerschmitts.

Irving sacrificed his life.

Browne, one of the shortest men in the Group, who "looked like a high school kid," told Charles Francis:

> I was chasing an ME-109 and had him lined up in my sights when another one stole up behind me and began to fire. Joseph Gomer tried to warn me, but I was so eager to make the kill that it didn't register on my excited brain.

Browne took three 20-mm slugs in his left leg; and a bullet grazed his head as it came through the canopy. "My plane was so badly damaged I had to crashland." He spent the rest of the war as a prisoner.

The bomber leader, Lieutenant Colonel Paul Barton, reported, "They were very effective...despite the fact that they were heavily outnumbered."

Nevertheless, Fortresses were spiraling out of the sky, a plane a minute.

Meantime the 52nd had returned empty-handed from its "sweep" and took a position on the sideline to watch the end of the drama with rapt fascination while bombers continued to plummet to earth. Finally, its commander, Colonel Robert Levine, woke up. He sent two of his squadrons to help while he and his third squadron remained on the sideline, out of the fight. There is no explanation.

In all, 14 bombers—half of Barton's entire 483rd Group—were shot down by German fighters. A 15th was last seen, flying undamaged toward the Swiss border.

Of the Red Tails' victories, Ed and Charles Bailey of the 99th each got his second. Howard Baugh:

> Toppins was very aggressive, almost a daredevil. He was chasing a German fighter and got the airplane well above the designed speed limit in a dive. He shot the other airplane down, but when he got home, they found he had actually warped his own fuselage. They had to junk his airplane.

Wendell Pruitt of the 302nd and his wingman, Lee Archer, were inseparable friends and rivals. Archer scored his first victory to tie Pruitt, who already had one.

Others in the 302nd who counted victories were Roger Romine, Wendel Groves, and Hugh Warner. However, none of them ever gave an account of how or where he did it.

Memmingen could be called either a resounding success or a humiliating disaster.

According to *The Luftwaffe Over Germany* by Donald Caldwell and Richard Muller, the American bombers destroyed 50 aircraft on the ground, killed 170 personnel, injured 140, and destroyed three hangars.

In the air the American fighters claimed to have shot down 41 German fighters (which is corrected below to 38):

	victories	losses
1st	14	0
332nd	12	3
31st	9*	3
52nd	3	1
	38	7

* plus 3 strafing

American bombers claimed to have destroyed 28 more, but this is surely a gross exaggeration—if one loses 14 bomber planes, one had better have a damn good story.

The Germans say they lost 28 planes. If we split the difference, it would make 33 German fighters lost in the air.

The Yankee fighters shot down the Germans at a ratio of better than 5-to-1. One reason is that the Germans were concentrating on the bombers, not on their own self-defense.

The Americans lost 147 bomber crewman and fighter pilots. The Germans lost an estimated 38 pilots plus 170 personnel on the ground, for a total of 208.

Using these numbers, the Americans claimed victory. But the numbers—five enemy downed for every U.S. fighter lost—indicate that destroying enemy fighters was not that impressive an accomplishment. Of much more importance, they didn't need to lose any bombers at all. If the second wave had been on time, it might have gone over the target as safely as the first wave did, dropped more bombs, and caused more damage. And there would have been 140 less gold stars, denoting sons or husbands killed, in windows across America.

Yet none of the official histories and none of the surviving pilots ever mentioned the fiasco.

The operation had been badly conceived from the outset. Sending 37 fighter planes against 200 of the enemy was criminally stupid. The plan carried the seeds of disaster. There are several unanswered questions.

Why did 15th Air Force planners divide their force and try to hit two major targets at once? A secondary or diversionary feint is as old as Sun-Tzu. But not two major objectives at the same time.

Who signed off on the plan?

Any slim hope that it could have succeeded was ruined by the heavy weather. Why wasn't the operation called off at that point? Certainly, as soon as the bombers either were delayed or turned back, that should have set red flags waving before everyone on the staff.

Why didn't the bombers inform headquarters and their escorts that they were arriving late, or returning early? If they did tell headquarters, why wasn't the information relayed to the fighters?

Did the 332nd report that 21 planes were returning early after Udine?

If everyone did keep the 15th Air Force fully informed, why didn't General Twining order the 325th, the 52nd, the 31st, and the 1st to go to the target immediately and be ready to help?

The biggest question of all is: Why didn't Eaker or Twining call everyone in as soon as they returned and royally chew ass? As far as we know, neither one did. Nor was there a court of inquiry, as there was, for example, after George Custer's disaster at Little Big Horn.

An inquiry would have helped understand the causes and perhaps prevented more of the same in the future. Within the next six weeks, several more multiple-bomber loss missions would be flown. Could the sacrifices at Memmingen have prevented some or all of them?

The 15th Air Force never even tabulated its bomber losses by fighter Group, which would have helped the commanders learn where the problems lay and take corrective action. Protecting bombers was the reason the 15th Air Force had been created in the first place. Instead, they were more obsessed with counting enemy fighters destroyed—right back to the Eddie Rickenbacker mentality. The obvious command tool of counting which fighter Groups were losing the most (or least) bombers and why never even occurred to the generals.

Perhaps the generals on the ground did not conduct an inquiry because they may have realized that an investigation would have pointed a finger directly at themselves. Both commanders and the G-3 were criminally negligent in planning, executing, and approving the Memmingen operation. At the very least they could have been given a medal and promotion and sent back to the Pentagon, where they couldn't do any more damage.

The biggest single culprit, responsible for all the heavy losses, was Colonel Barton of the 483rd bomber Group. With no authorization, he arbitrarily took a different flight path without telling anyone. He knew he was going to be late and didn't tell anyone. He sacrificed his men's lives. He lost millions of dollars worth of planes that never dropped a bomb on the target that day and would never hit another target again. Yet he and his unit were given a Distinguished Unit Citation!

Barton stood at attention before his command, surrounded by press and photographers as the adjutant read the citation. It said: The 483rd, *without any fighter escorts*, fought alone through deadly fire from German fighter planes to successfully drop its bombs! The colonel who received it, and the adjutant who read it (and probably wrote it), both knew it was a lie, a direct contradiction of Barton's own report dictated hours after the battle, in which he said the Red Tails "were very effective" despite being outnumbered.

Why didn't Eaker or Twining step in to edit the citation? It is safe to say that it was never shown to Colonel Davis before it was forwarded to the Pentagon for the Chief of Staff, General George C. Marshall, to sign in the middle of a pile of other routine papers on his desk.

It was the old story: Blame the blacks. It would be repeated many times again, especially in Korea. "It's a good thing we weren't with General Custer," one black GI in Korea told me. "They'd have blamed the whole thing on us."

13

Summer Heat

IN the ten days, July 19–28, six tragedies even worse than Memmingen, would hit the 15th, which lost between 16 and 20 planes on single days. Could they have been avoided if Eaker and Twining had applied the lessons learned at Memmingen? Yet, as far as is known they never wondered. Their pilots—and the war effort—paid the price.

July 19. The next day 18 more bombers were lost, two more than at Memmingen, although none were charged against the 332nd.

July 20. The Red Tails were assigned "the monumental task" of escorting three B-24 bomber Wings Groups, or about 94 bombers—which were "too many to cover adequately," the 332nd wrote in its mission report. It lost two bombers while shooting down five enemy, plus two unconfirmed.

The 99th's hottest pilot, Ed Toppins, shot down his third plane.

Joe Elsberry of the 301st registered one, making a total of four for him. He was pursuing a fifth when his windshield frosted up. Squinting through the ice, he raced after his foe until he found a mountain looming before him and had to pull up. It was the last shot Elsberry would get at an enemy fighter.

Armour McDaniel, also of the 301st, caught a German plane trying to evade Elsberry. McDaniel went into a 17,000-foot dive, firing as he closed in, until the enemy sliced through a cloud and into the side of the mountain. McDaniel barely missed it himself.

Langdon Johnson of the 100th scored his first victory.

Bussey of the 301st claimed two victories that were not confirmed:

> Bomber Groups stretched out for miles and miles and miles. We would fly by one Group to cover another group in front of them. Passing them, I saw a flight of about five or six German fighters about one or two miles away in a continuous vertical loop. Every time one got his nose pointed up, a bomber blew up right in front of him. I'd never heard of this maneuver before; it wasn't in our training. But that's where the bombers were most vulnerable, up through the belly. They had a belly gunner, but he's standing on his head.

So we joined the loop; we just nuzzled right into their flight, and every time one of them got his nose up, we blew him out of the sky. I got one of them. It was damned dangerous business. We'd see a propeller come flying by, or we'd see a tail section come flying by, all kinds of crud.

Of course my squadron didn't stop for this but went on ahead to our bombers, and I was left alone. A single airplane in that killing sky was in a hazardous position, so I headed for home.

On the way back, somewhere in the Swiss Alps, I saw a German ship and got on him and put a couple of bursts into him. He started to dive, and I followed him, firing every time I was in range until he finally hit the field and blew.

I wish I'd gotten pictures, but gun cameras are like other cameras, sometimes they're good and sometimes they're not. I got pictures of firing at him, but I didn't get pictures of the final kill.

There was another victory claim, the most controversial in the record of the 332nd. After the war, Lee Archer claimed that he was chasing an enemy ship with Freddie Hutchins close behind. Archer reportedly fired and hit the plane, but Hutchins also fired a burst before their prey crashed into a mountainside.

This would have been Archer's second victory. He later scored three more, which would make a total of five if this claim is included, and that would make him the only black ace of the war. Archer said he and Hutchins were each given credit for half a victory. However, the victory has never been confirmed—the 332nd records do not credit anyone with it.

Red Jackson, the 302nd commander:

The dispute arose after we came back from Europe. I didn't even hear about it before that. No pilot had claimed five until we came home. Not until the 1980s did Lee claim one victory that was supposed to be shared by him and someone else.

Did Archer get five?
Bussey:

Hell, no. Lee flew with a guy who would never have given him a chance. Pruitt was a real hawk and wouldn't allow any room to anyone. Lee was lucky to have a shot at anything.

July 21. The 15th Air Force mounted a bombing raid over the heavily defended oil refineries at Ploesti, Romania. Oil was essential to the Nazis' fast-dwindling fuel supplies, and they always mounted murderous fire from air and ground against the attackers. The 15th lost eight bombers, none of them by the 332nd.

Jimmy Walker, a veteran of 80 missions, was returning from the battle:

I was leading the Yellow flight of four planes, and on the way home my commander told us to cover a crippled B-24, stay close to him, and keep enemy fighters away. He was losing altitude all the time, and he went over an area we hadn't been briefed on. When flak came up, three of our four airplanes got hit, including mine.

My oil line got shot up, and I could see the gauges going down like you'd punched a hole at the bottom; oil was all over the cockpit and windshield. My engine caught fire, so I shut off all the switches and slipped and slid the airplane and dived to get the fire out, which fortunately I did. But when I tried to start the engine again, it was frozen.

Intelligence told us that the Germans would shoot you in your 'chute, so I glided down to minimum altitude, between 1,000 end 500 feet, rolled it over and dropped out. I was about to land on a house, but I reached up and pulled on the lines of my 'chute and slipped the air out and landed on the cottage next to the house.

The Germans were aware there was an American in the area. They knew they had shot me down. They had my airplane, but they didn't have me.

Aleksandr Zivkovic was a 17-year-old anti-communist guerrilla in charge of gathering intelligence in a huge area of eastern Serbia. He was driving a two-wheel cart when:

I saw an American plane coming back from Romania. I saw it bank on its side, and I saw a 'chute, so I turned back about two miles, looking for where he could be. The country was flat, and I could see for miles and miles around. I saw approximately where he had jumped, and I looked in a big forest with big trees and small bushes between the trees. For five minutes I called, "Hey! Hello!" the only English word I knew. No one answered.

Then I heard something. I turned and behind a bush I saw a black man stand up, wearing a khaki military cap. He was the first black man I'd ever seen. My father had told me about them; he had been in World War I, and he had seen French colonial soldiers from Africa. So I had no hesitation. I said, "America? America?" In sign language I told him, "Hey, come," and in Serbo-Croatian I said, "I'm not Communist, I'm not German, I'm in the Serbian Nationalist army."

He spoke French, not perfectly, and I had learned some French in school. I said, "Where's your baggage?" and he went back and picked up his 'chute and his baggage, an inflatable raft.

Alex put Jimmy into his cart, covered him with straw, and drove about three miles to his headquarters. "I told my commandant, "Hey, I found an American!"

Walker:

I didn't have time to get nervous until that night. About two o'clock in the morning, all of a sudden I started shaking, thinking about what could have happened.

I was moved to Alex's family, who were part of the underground. One day they took me with a guard to a barbershop with a German soldier in the next chair while my protection sat over in the corner with his automatic rifle in his tap.

Walker was wearing his Air Force uniform so he wouldn't be shot as a spy and still doesn't know why the German didn't report him.

After 39 days, he and several other downed fliers were picked up by the U.S. Air Force in a daring nighttime flight.

The Yugoslavs set fire to bushes to form a runway, and the plane blinked its lights in code and lined up and landed with the fires on its right wingtip. We jumped in the airplane, and as soon as we were in, they lit another fire, the pilot pointed the nose of the plane at it, and we took off as the German guns shot at us.

Back in Italy, Jimmy's tent mates had just sent his gear home, and Hungry Peirson had moved into his bunk when Walker walked in with a beautiful white silk shirt. He explained that the Partisans had kept his parachute— silk was scarce for them—and had made him a shirt in return.

He thought he'd be going home.

They usually did that for pilots who had been shot down. But they were short of pilots, so I was told I would be flying again, which I didn't like at all. I objected until they scheduled a court martial. The next day I was on another mission. I flew 102 while I was over there.

Roberts told of another pilot who went down in Yugoslavia.

Emile Clifton was a hell of a good fighter. He had been a professional magician on the West Coast, and when the Partisans picked him up, he started picking lighted cigarettes out of the air for them, or some such sleight of hand, and eventually got back to us.

Many others also reported harrowing escape and evasion tales.

July 22. Meantime, what had happened to Ed Gleed, who had been exiled to North Africa as a test pilot in April?

After we test-piloted the planes, some of our guys from the 332nd came down and ferried them back. Like an idiot, I was taking them out every night, and when word got back to the Old Man that Gleed was living in high cotton in Casablanca, he demanded that the 15th Air Force send me back to Italy.

I came on back and got instructions from the Old Man to be on the mission the following day. I was off to the 301st Squadron, flying Tail End Charlie.

July 23–5. Jack Holsclaw of the 100th scored his third victory and Harold Sawyer his second.

July 26. Charlie McGee saw his first Messerschmitts over Markendorf Airdrome near Vienna.

Leon Jackson:

Captain Toppins was leading my flight when we saw three 190s ten minutes before reaching the target. Toppins turned into them and damaged one in the tail of the formation. Batting it was too far away to be effective, so we reassembled in battle formation.

Just then we sighted three ME-109s above us making vapor trails. We were at 28,000 feet, so we climbed as the ME-109s started a gradual climbing turn. I knew Captain Toppins wasn't going to let them get away, so I prepared for a good fight."

The Red Tails added four more victories. Toppins got his fourth to tie Elsberry, and Jackson, downed his third.

Four pilots of the 302nd counted victories. Roger Romine claimed his second, Luther Smith his first, and Chubby Green and Weldon Groves claimed one between them.

July 27. This was another big day with eight enemy down, all confirmed. Two were by Alfred Gorham. Leonard Jackson of the 99th got one—his third altogether.

Felix Kirkpatrick of the 302nd also scored one:

I was the flight leader of four fellows, and when the enemy aircraft made an approach to our bombers, we went over to intercept them. This one aircraft made a quick pass through our bombers and made a dive for the deck, heading for his base as fast as he could get there, and we followed him down.

There was no problem in catching him; you dropped the nose, and the plane would drop out of the sky. The problem was not to over-run him, and we caught up with him and shot him down.

But we were so intent on getting the airplane that we didn't realize where we were. We were so close to his base, the next thing we knew, we were in the middle of a lot of flak, so we climbed back up and headed for our own base.

Just five days after returning from exile, Gleed showed what the Group had been missing. He had been banished back in the P-39 days and had missed all the glory the Group had been winning with the P-51s.

We had just arrived at our rendezvous point with the bombers and had been S-ing over them 15 to 20 minutes with some 72 aircraft, when someone called, "Bandits high!" They'd sit up there and come into you out of the sun. I was leading the Group, so I said, "Stand by and watch them."

Then somebody called, "Here they come!" Most of the time the Focke-Wulf 190s flew like a gaggle, no real formation, just a bunch; the Messerschmitt 109s were in formation when they came in. It was the 109s that hopped us first.

I told my squadron to break left, drop fuel tanks, and pull up into them. They busted through us, and we lost two guys on that initial pass, but I think the bombers got a couple of the 109s. After the 109s had made their pass, the 190s came in behind them. They had a mess of them, just like a flock. Must have been about 30 of them.

I got some holes that day. They were firing 20-millimeter cannon; we had 50-mm machine guns, three in each wing. Two of my guns were shot out, probably on that initial pass.

When you get in those scrambles, your blood pressure goes up a little bit. Most of us were pretty split up. You break down into basic elements of two, and your wingman tries to help you out. You're yo-yoing back and forth, very easy to get mixed up, and the P-51 didn't look a whole lot different from a 109 in battle. It's hell for breakfast.

I was busy trying to keep from getting knocked out, and at the same time I was on the tail of a 109. I hit him, and he exploded—I must have gotten his ammunition. He just trailed smoke and went down. Meanwhile, my wing-man knocked another one off my tail.

When we attempted to get back to the bombers, we saw some more 190s, so we struck out after them and got into another running battle. I got one. I had to follow him right on down to the deck [the ground] to get him knocked down. Before it was over, two of my remaining four guns ran out of ammunition.

I'd gotten separated. My wingman went peeling off, facing a guy, and the battle proceeded on. I had two of them on my tail, one guy was peppering me, and part of one wing was gone.

I got down on the deck, where there were hills and valleys. They chased me down the stream and up the stream and around church steeples—I went past one steeple by five feet. Every time I would try to come up, they were sitting up there waiting for me. I was heading in their direction, away from home.

I finally maneuvered around into a valley and just flat-out flew on the deck and outran them. I had the throttle to the firewall as far as it would go. I was just going to go as long as I could, then pancake it in or jump out. Fortunately I got there.

At the end of the runway, the engine quit. Not a drop of fuel left.

Gleed was awarded a Distinguished Flying Cross. He had shown what the Group had been missing since he had been banished. Davis' show of temper back in April may have deprived his unit of a valuable pilot and leader just when he was needed the most. B.O. had not punished Gleed— he had punished the whole 332nd fighter Group.

Meanwhile, combat was taking its toll on Howard Baugh:

I had flown more combat than normal, 125 missions in the P-40, then ten in the P-51—all the way over to southern France, across Italy, across the Mediterranean Sea, strafing radar just before the invasion. But it never made the papers; the only invasion that made the papers was Normandy. Then we made a few runs over to Ploesti and southern Germany.

It worked on your mind. You know you've got to get up at five o'clock and fly a single-engine plane over water six or seven hours, encountering enemy aircraft. The mind can only take so much of that, so I went to see the flight surgeon and told him I was tired. He called it combat fatigue.

This one mission turned out to be my last one. We had been on a long flight, and everyone was anxious to get on the ground. We were supposed to stagger, one on the left side of the runway, the next one behind it on the right, alternating right and left. Spanky Roberts told me an airplane behind me almost landed on top of me, just barely missed me, and I didn't even know it. When I parked the airplane, he was there in his jeep and told me to turn in my gear: "You're not going to fly any more."

"Who's going to tell Colonel Davis?"

"I am. Right now. As long as I'm commander of the 99th, you're not flying any more combat."

Baugh called Roberts his favorite commander, even ahead of B.O. Davis. "He had a compassion for his people, and he looked out for me."

In all, in the 13-day period, July 16–28, the Red Tails scored 37 victories, plus two unconfirmed. They lost one pilot of their own. In that same period, the 15th lost 167 bombers, an average of 13 per day. (The 461st Bomb Group lost 11 B-24s one day and 11 more the next day—that's 22 of their 28 planes.) But none of the losses was charged to the 332nd.

July 30. Carl Johnson of the 100th closed the month with a victory.

August

THE 15th Air Force, which had lost 277 bombers in July, lost 158 more in August. But only one was destroyed by enemy fighters on the Red Tails' watch.

For the first 12 days of August, the 332nd flew seven escort missions, but the German air force came up to challenge them only once. Carl Johnson and George Rhodes scored the Group's only two victories.

August 2. One week after Gleed's close encounter, B.O. Davis created a new slot, Deputy Group Commander, and appointed Alfonza Davis to fill it. Who would replace him as operations officer?

Gleed:

> The Old Man told me to come to headquarters. "What do you think about taking over the Group Operations job? Do you think you could handle it?"
>
> He said, "I want you to go down right now" So I had the Group Operations job, as well as flying, and started getting compliments on the exactness of the planning. So now I'm back in the good graces of the Old Man; I'm not in the outhouse any more.
>
> My effectiveness actually improved.

That day the Group covered for bombers over France. It should be noted that the bombers were spread out over 50 miles, an area impossible to give adequae protection. Luckily, no bombers were lost.

August 4–5. Italy was struck by a furious rain storm.

Gleed:

> It was raining like holy be-jesus. You could hardly see the other end of the runway, and clouds were thick overhead—we didn't have any way of knowing how thick. The fighters would have to break out over the clouds and then join up with their leaders.
>
> The Old Man was flying the mission; I was in Group operations. It was near the time of take-off, and I called back to General [Dean] Strother's 14th Fighter Wing headquarters to find out if the bombers had taken off. I got some jug-head major down there who wouldn't give me the information. I said, "I want to talk to your boss. Is General Strother around?"
>
> "Yeah, he's here."
>
> "We'd like very much to know whether the bomber Group has actually taken off on time, because the weather is stinking here, and I don't want to jeopardize our men any more than we have to."
>
> Strother said, "You get that outfit off on time!"

I sent a jeep down to the other end of the runway to tell Colonel Davis. He said, "You call him back and ask him directly if the bomber outfit has taken off."

So I did: "I've got Colonel Davis at the end of the runway. He wants to know positively, because he can't see the operations office from there."

"You tell Ben Davis to get those airplanes off the ground and make that rendezvous!"

So I sent the jeep back down with the message. We initiated take-off three minutes late, but we got them off. He didn't know how deep the crud was, but they took off on blind faith and got up there. Ben Davis swung away and attempted to calculate mentally how to get to the rendezvous with the bombers. The join-up was at fifteen thousand feet. It would have been completely in the clouds to do it, but somehow our planes got up and joined up and started out. I don't think even I could have flown it, and I was pretty good.

The bombers never did take off. We were informed three minutes after we lost radio contact with our planes. Strother also called back and wanted to know did we get those airplanes off. I said, "General, I haven't seen any flashes [of colliding planes]." I banged the phone down.

We lost one man trying to get back home through that stuff.

A few days later Strother came down to our base and proceeded to give us a third-grade lecture about how to respond to authority: "The most vitally important thing is to make rendezvous." He particularly jumped on my tail for challenging his operations people and demanding to know whether the bombers got off. He never has apologized for the fact that the bombers didn't take off that day. That remained a bad taste in my mouth forever.

It was shortly afterwards that we had a visit from a reporter from the black New York *Amsterdam News*. They had been raising hell editorially about why the 332nd hadn't been put in for a Presidential Unit Citation, compared to what some of the other units had done.

This guy had gone to 15th Headquarters, and General Strother told him to his face: "Ben Davis is OK, but those other guys he's got flying for him are nothing," and he wasn't about to recommend us. The reporter came back and spread the word. You can imagine what a blow that was. That was a big dip in our morale there.

As it turned out, the request for the Citation was made by 15th Air Force Headquarters, General Twining's office, not Strother's Fighter Wing.

A month later Twining split the fighter wing into two wings and promoted Strother to command both. A new general, Yanis Taylor, replaced him as Davis's immediate superior, and there was no further report of friction between the 306th and the 332nd. Taylor probably deserves a share of the credit for the continued success of the Red Tails.

The Red Tails welcomed a famous visitor, heavyweight champ Joe Louis. They also got a hotshot rookie.

Roscoe Brown

I'M from Washington DC. My father was a member of Roosevelt's "black cabinet," in charge of health for blacks all over the country. It made me want to work harder to be better than my old man. As a child, on Sundays we'd frequently go to the Washington airport to watch the planes take off and land. My father had a little clout, so finally I said to him, "I want to ride in one of those planes."

He said, "Well, you know, they don't allow blacks in planes down here." But I kept after him and kept after him until one day he decided to try a gambit. He was light-skinned, so he told us to keep our mouths closed and told one of the officers, "I work for the government, and these are children of French West African diplomats, and they'd like to ride in an airplane." That was my first ride in a plane. After that, that's all I wanted to do.

I went to the Smithsonian with my parents after it had just hung Lindbergh's plane, the "Spirit of St. Louis." I could visualize myself flying it and imagine what this man did in this small airplane. He wrote a book called We, and I got that book and read every page of it about three times. By the time I finished, I almost knew how to fly.

In 1943 I graduated from Springfield College in Massachusetts, I was valedictorian of my class and had earned a lieutenant's commission in the infantry through the civilian military training corps. But the black press had so elevated the Tuskegee experience that every black man wanted to be a Tuskegee Airman. I resigned my infantry commission and started out as an aviation cadet.

We went to Keesler Field MS for pre-flight training. The base had a black side and a white side, but many of us from the North weren't accustomed to segregation, and we wandered into the white PX and got cussed out. We raised a little hell about it—we were smart asses and gave them a little mouth about being American citizens.

From Keesler we went to Tuskegee. We started with about 40 or 50 cadets, and when we graduated, I think our class was down to 24 or 25.

I had just graduated with my wings in March 1944, and was on a bus going from Montgomery to Tuskegee. We drove along about ten miles before the driver stopped the bus and said, "Lieutenant, the colored must sit in the back."

I said," Now, in a few weeks I'm going to fight a war for democracy and freedom, and I'm going to sit right here."

He said, "I'm going to have to call the state troopers and take you off."

I said, "You can do what you want to do. I'm sitting here. I really can't fight a war sitting in jail." So I sat there another ten minutes, and finally he just drove the bus away.

When Brown arrived he received a total of three hours transition training in the P-51, then he was off. He soon got a name as a hot shot. As he said years later:

The transition from being just a good pilot to being a combat pilot occurs in about four or five missions. If you don't get the feel of it, you'll be scared all the time. And if you're scared, you can't fly.

"We were all good pilots," Bert Wilson declared, "but Bruno was especially hot."

Chris Newman was Brown's tent mate and friend:

> Brown was aggressive. When he got an opportunity, he jumped on it.
>
> Some bombers next to us were being attacked, and we were going down to give them a little assistance. The leader said, "We're breaking left now," I didn't know what to expect. We pulled around 180 degrees and saw an enemy 109 on the tail of a B-17, just riddling away. It zipped by.
>
> There were four fighters coming through this bomber formation. We dove down behind them, my canopy popped open, and dust started flying in my face and eyes. We dove from 25,000 feet to 15,000. The enemy kept on going down, but we pulled back up with the bombers and continued our escorting. With luck, I would have had a victory, but I never got the opportunity again.
>
> If Brown had been in my shoes, he would have continued down.

August 9. Alfonso Simmons was shot down over Yugolsavia.

August 12. In one of the most dangerous and costly missions of the war, the Red Tails strafed ground targets in southern France in preparation for the Allied invasion there. Five pilots were shot down, the largest number in one day of the entire war. One was killed and four captured. Their stories are told in the next chapter.

August 17–19. For three straight days the Red Tails hit one of the most dreaded targets in Europe, the Ploesti oil refineries in Romania. Oil was vital to keep the Nazi war machine going, and they ringed Ploesti with deadly *ack-ack* fire. In a single day nine B-24s were hit. "At Ploesti I almost bought it," Moe Downs said. He banked his plane onto its side, and "as I looked down the wing, I looked right into a German gun." Luckily, "I clobbered it" before it clobbered him.

August 23. Luke Weathers and William Hill shared a victory, though for years the Air Force refused to credit them. But, Weathers insisted, the plane did go down.

August 24. On a mission to Vienna, three pilots—William Thomas and Charlie McGee of the 302nd and Johnny Briggs of the 100th—each scored victories, and this time there was no dispute.

McGee:

The bombers were hitting an airfield, with a lot of fires around and buildings burning. The Germans' tactics were to fly through the bomber stream and keep on going. We were over the target when we spotted an FW, and I got the order, "Go get him!"

The combat lasted about as long as snapping your fingers—you see him, he sees you, and you get mixed up. He took some evasive actions, diving for the ground. I stayed on his tail all the way down and was able to get a burst in on him; it may have hit something in his controls, because he took a couple of turns, then went straight into the ground.

I stayed low getting out, to stay out of the enemy ground fire. I saw a train pulling into a station, so I dropped my nose and made a firing pass at the engine.

Briggs:

We were coming back from the mission at about 16,000 feet, and a 109 pounced on us from above. My wingman, George Taylor, said, "Bogey, six o'clock." The 109 had pulled up in a climb, and when I saw the swastika under his wing, I dropped my tanks. After you drop your external fuel, you have to select an internal fuel source, turn on your guns, your gunsight, throttle, and proper controls.

The 109 didn't stop climbing until 23,000 feet. I was down behind him, and I don't think he could see me at first. Then he leveled off and made a turn to see if anyone was back there, a slow turn to the left. I said, "No, you don't," and I shot—ant. He started a slow turn to the right. Brrrt—I let him have it again. Bullets bounced off him. He slowed up, and I thought he was deliberately pulling power so I'd zoom by him and he'd be on my tail.

I said, "Oh, no you don't." I pulled up beside him and above him, and he went into a spiral, and I saw his 'chute open. He was probably saying, "Well, you got me today, but I'll be back tomorrow."

August 27–30. The Red Tails wiped out 22 enemy planes on the ground.

Three days later the 99th strafed a German airfield in Romania. Led by Alfonso Davis, they spotted German planes hidden under hay stacks on the ground. The number destroyed couldn't be confirmed because of the smoke. Not a single enemy plane rose to challenge them.

Roberts:

On another mission we shot up an estimated 150 German aircraft. Because of problems we had in proving the things we had done, after the second pass, I backed off, and as the other crews were going in, I took a long-range shot so you could see the aircraft burning.

They sent out a recon pilot to assess the damage and made the mistake of not telling him not to find anything. The poor fellow did what he was told and reported the damage.

After the war an officer in the Pentagon found my films to prove it.

But there was no tomorrow. For almost six months German planes almost deserted the skies over southern Europe to defend the homeland. Bussey believed they were also running out of gas as the bombers had blasted their refineries at Ploesti. The Red Tails didn't score another victory for more than a month.

Meanwhile, R&R was a problem.

Ed Gleed:

> Our guys got along well with the Italians, especially the girls. This made the white GIs pretty unhappy. They reportedly told the Italian girls to stay away from Negroes, that they all had tails. There were any number of incidents.
>
> Our guys needed R&R as badly as anyone else. We could have gone to Capri, they had the facilities, but instead, we had to scrounge around and find a place just for us. We were finally given a *villa* right on the Bay of Naples, and this became the rest camp for "the Black Air Force" pilots.

Actually, they were happy with it. "It was on a precipice," Sheppard said. "You could overlook the sea and could see Pompei and Vesuvius." But it took too long to reach the camp by truck across the mountains, so the 332nd found a twin-engine plane to take them there. Gleed was chosen to fly it:

> First time I'd ever touched a twin-engine. I got one of the finest crew chiefs we had, Sergeant Bobby Dansby of the 99th. He didn't have a flight manual, but he took this airplane and checked it out. In two days he said, "It's ready to fly."
>
> I said, "You going with me?" He got in that darn thing on his stomach behind me where the radio used to be, his forehead right behind my head. I said, "Well, if he's going to ride with me, he must believe it's flyable, and he must believe I can fly it." The engines sounded good to me, so I said, "Let's go." I poured the coal to it and we were flying.
>
> We contrived a way to fit people in the bomb bay. Later they gave us a B-25 with enough space to carry 15 guys, just jammed in.

The enlisted rest camp was a hotel run by the Red Cross. The men reported that the food was great, with a roaring fireplace and many games. Sergeant Buddy Huntley:

> Our main problem was, when we went into town in Italy, didn't no one respect us. The Service men would get nasty, because everything had to be segregated. We had our own theaters. Even over there!

We said, "This can't be!"

"It is."

I told them, "Please keep an open mind. Before we leave here, you'll respect us."

Meanwhile, the Red Tails had been in combat with the 15th Air Force for three months, and a statistical record had been building. The following data were supplied by Ron Bronstein for the four P-51 squadrons June through August 1944, the period of the most intense aerial combat for the 332nd. It was also the period when the Red Tails were breaking in as rookies of strategic bombing.

Combat Statistics June-July-August

	31st	52nd	325th	332nd	Totals
Missions	77	71	67	67	276
Enemy encountered	899	972	593	357	2821
Victories	194	185	157	49	598
victories/encounter	22%	19%	27%	14%	21%
Planes lost to fighters	12	9	10	3	34
Victories-to-losses	94%	95%	94%	94%	95%
Planes destroyed strafing	10	89	38	42	179

Notes:

The 332nd had four squadrons, compared to the normal three.

In June the 332nd flew P-47s while the others flew superior P-51s

The 31st apparently was given few strafing missions.

These numbers call into question the Air Force's obsession with aerial victories. Imagine a baseball team that wins 598 games and loses only 34. The words "ace" and "kills" become meaningless. Murder" was the more correct word.

At that stage the war, most of the best German pilots had either been killed on the Russian front or were being withdrawn from southern Europe to protect the homeland. The pilots who flew up to attack the American bombers were mostly teen-agers. They were given a few hours of training, pusehd into their cockpits, and sent up to face veterans five years their seniors, often with hundreds of hours of combat experience. The odds were 20-to-one against them—they were virtually *kamikazes*. Yet, for the most part, they didn't even try to protect themselves but dove into the bombers without taking defensive measures. Despite one's personal feeling about

Naziism, the real heroes of the air wars were not the men who shot them down, but the boys who went bravely to their deaths.

The original 99th pilots had faced superior German planes and better trained pilots. But even they racked up a victory ratio of 18-1.

The real question is: How many bombers were lost to enemy fighters by each Group? How many were saved? There are no statistics. The Air Force wasn't even interested.

However, the Air Force did keep stats on bomber losses by the 15th Air Force as a whole, as well as by the England-based 8th Air Force. It seemed to show a clear trade-off: The more enemy fighters killed, the more bombers lost and vice-versa.

Dr. Daniel Haulmann of the Air Force Historical Office, who discovered the bombers lost by the 332nd, subtracted their losses from the total and averaged the rest among the other six fighter Groups (including P-38s) for the period June 1944 to the end of the war.

(There is disagreement over the 18 bombers which the Red Tails lost over Memmingen. The Air Force includes them in the totals of the Red Tails. I ascribe them to bad planning and execution by the headquarters staff and the bomber force itself. Total Red Tail losses were 27 if one includes Memmingen, and nine without it. The reader may choose whichever number he or she prefers.)

In all, the 15th Air Force lost 285 bombers to enemy fighters during the period, or 276 without Memmingen and the 332nd. That's an average of 46 for each of the six Groups, compared to nine for the Red Tails. The other fighter Groups lost five times more bombers, on average, than did the 332nd. If every Group had cut its bomber losses to nine, that would have been a saving of 37 bombers per fighter Group and 222 for the 15th Air Force as a whole. That's 2,220 bomber crewmen who might have been saved.

There are two possible explanations. Either the Red Tails were superior pilots to the white Groups, or the whites did not stick as close to the bombers, looking for kills because that's where the glory, the medals, and the promotions lay. How "close" is "close air support?" One hundred yards away? One mile? Five miles? Ten? The 332nd stuck so close that its pilots could almost throw snowballs at the bomber crews. The Red Tail pilots bitched at the restrictions, but I have not read any account that pilots of the other fighter Groups chafed. One may draw his own conclusions.

One gets the impression that the U.S. Air Force considered the war as one between our air force and theirs, not our country against theirs.

In England there was some suggestion that the 8th Air Force used the bombers as bait to lure German fighters up to accept combat. (Goering had employed similar tactics over London earlier.) General Jimmy Doolittle, who replaced Eaker, reversed his "close support" policy in February in favor of sending the fighters to sweep the skies in front of the bombers. That pleased the fighter pilots, who could get more victories. Doolittle boasted that it also reduced bomber losses. However, this appears to be disingenuous. Statistics show that 8th Air Force bomber losses actually went up in February and remained up for the rest of the war.

The experience of both the 8th and 15th Air Forces strongly imply that the policy enunciated by Eaker and carried out by the Red Tails, was the right one.

A post-war study concluded that the three most dangerous assignments in the military were:

Submarine crews

Bomber crews

Infantry squads

If all fighter units had been as diligent as the 332nd, thousands of bomber crewmen would have survived to return home, and hundreds of bombers would have been saved, perhaps to hasten the end of the fighting.

But with the close of summer, the air war abruptly changed. Germany called its fighters home to defend the fatherland. More and more the emphasis switched from fighter escort missions to the less glamorous—but more deadly—job of strafing targets on the ground.

14

Ground Wars

August

GENERAL Eaker had another, more dangerous job for the Red Tails—
strafing ground targets, beginning with the invasion of southern France.
Lee Archer:

> I never thought that air-to-air combat was a big problem. I looked for it.
> I hoped we'd get some enemy aircraft. I thought it was a duel—one-on-one.
> Fine.
>
> What I worried about was air-to-ground combat, chasing railroad trains,
> hitting troops on the ground. It's a gory kind of business. You're seeing hun-
> dreds of people firing at you. You see these little, little things coming at you;
> you have no way to control that.
>
> Tactical pilots never get the credit they're due.

As the invasion forces gathered off Marseilles, the Red Tails flew
in to "soften the beach up." Bill Melton recalled: "We'd hit German
coast-watching stations, then go after rail traffic, vehicles—anything moving, we'd shoot."

August 12. Three days before the Allies' invasion, the Red Tails made
a low-level strafing run to knock out radar stations in the big harbor at
Marseilles.
Lucky Lester:

> We went in under the enemy gunfire, and all three of the other planes
> either got shot up or shot down, and there I was in the harbor all by myself.
> I decided the best way to get out was to get as low to the water as possible
> and try to get below the gunfire. They were shooting down at me from the
> hills, but I never did get a hit.

Six others did. Joseph Gordon and Langdon Johnson failed to return.
Robert O'Neal crashed on the coast and was picked up by the Free French
Resistance.

Bob Daniels' smoking ship pancaked into the water as Alexander Jefferson hollered, "Not the water, man, don't ditch it!"

Jefferson was "tail-end Charlie," the last to go over the target. Ack-ack was exploding all around him. His plane was bucking and shaking, and all his instruments were "in the red," or almost red. He was 50 feet over the target when a thump put a hole in the canopy "just in front of my head." Now all the instruments were red as smoke filled the cockpit and flames came up between his feet.

"Oops, Jeffie, boy, you're on fire."

He popped the canopy, went into a loop, punched his safety belt buckle, and dropped out. As the tail whizzed past his head, he pulled the D-ring of his parachute, and nothing happened. "They've sold the silk!" [on the black market], he thought. He later pictured the moment.

But it popped open just before he hit the ground, "which shows how low I was."

> When I got to my to my feet, I was looking into the shooting end of a German rifle—I had landed on top of the same gun-crew who had shot me down. He said, *"Ja, Ja, Herr Leutnant, fur sie der Krieg ist vorbei"* (for you the war is over).
>
> I said, "OK, OK, just get that damn thing out of my face."
>
> I was escorted to this magnificent home, and this resplendent German officer was having tea on the veranda. He smiled pleasantly and in perfect American English told me to have a seat. I was flabbergasted as I dropped into a chair. He offered me a cigarette (my own) and asked me if I knew anything about New York, Chicago, Detroit.
>
> When I answered yes, I lived in Detroit, he proceeded to tell me about his days at the University of Michigan and about the Forest Club and the Oakland bus line to the Cozy Corner cabaret. I was being royally entertained with the details of the ghetto areas of my hometown. He said he had lived in Detroit and he actually knew the names of some of the bartenders and the "good lovin'" he had received from the girls across the street in the "hotel." ("I was truly thankful for their efforts on behalf of the war," Jefferson wrote.)

In his book, *Red Tail Capture, Red Tail Free* (New York, Fordham University Press, 2005) Jeff added:

> He finally said, "Some of the best times of my life were spent in Paradise Valley. Let's hope this war ends soon so we can get back to the things that really matter." With that, he offered me one of my cigarettes, shook my hand, then stood on the porch in a typical Nazi stance, watching silently and forlornly as they loaded me aboard a truck.

At the town square he met another armed guard coming toward him with Daniels, "looking like a wet rat."

After three days of solitary confinement on bread and water, the interrogation began. An officer pulled out a book, flipped a page, and said, "Lieutenant, that's you." It was the photo of his Tuskegee graduating class. The officer then told him his birth date and birth place, his parents' names, and even his sister's latest marks in school. Alex himself had not had any news from home, but after the war he found out the officer was right.

Jeff wrote:

> He told me about our mission over southern France, and, even more amazingly, he had my crew chief's ten-hour inspection of the plane I flew, which was completed the day before I was shot down.
>
> The Germans had to have somebody at Ramitelli or higher up, who was giving them information.

The big question that has never been asked, and probably will never be answered, is: Who? Suspicion points to someone on the staff—possibly a washout from flight school, with access both to personnel records and operational plans, as well as to a secret radio. But how could he transmit without being discovered? It was a clear question of treason, but it was never pursued after the war.

Next morning Jefferson and the others were put on the flatbed of a train. "Do you know what it was carrying?" he asked. "Those goddamn German 88s [anti-aircraft guns], going west to be set up for another go at us." While Jefferson cursed, not a single Allied airplane tried to hit the train—luckily for the Americans on it.

Several miles away Dick Macon had also crashed while flying Ed Toppin's plane—"We new guys didn't have our own airplanes yet."

> I was strafing at 400 miles an hour. The plane crashed into a building and caught fire. Apparently it killed some people, because the building was completely demolished. So was my plane. I don't know how I got out. My 'chute must have opened just about the time I hit the ground.
>
> I "redded out." When you black out, the blood rushes to your feet. But if you're upside down, the blood rushes to your head, and you "red out." A negative G force popped the blood vessels in my eyes, so I bled out of my eyes instead of my brain.
>
> My plane was demolished, so they reported me dead, but some Power much greater was responsible for my escape.
>
> When I regained consciousness, I didn't know where I was or what I was doing. I tried to get up and hide the parachute and get to someone who was friendly. But my third, fourth, fifth, and sixth vertebrae were broken in my neck; I was paralyzed from the waist down. And my shoulder was broken with a compound fracture so the bone stuck out, and that's what started the pain. I lost consciousness again, and when I regained it, the pain was excruciating.

I saw three Germans standing over me with machine pistols, and 15 to 20 Frenchmen standing at a distance in a circle. The Germans said, "*Raus mitt ihnen!!* I didn't know what that meant, but I figured it meant "Get the hell up."

Of course I couldn't. They helped me up very roughly, put my arms around their shoulders, and took me to a waiting vehicle, which looked something like a VW Beetle. I saw charcoal burning on the back bumper in a big tank like a water tank. Throughout the whole ride it went *pop-pop-pop*.

They took me to a schoolhouse, which was a field hospital. Intelligence said the Nazis had some of the same fetishes as the Ku Klux Klan and that they would remove the genitals of an African-American and push them into his mouth before they killed him. I knew this was going to happen to me, so I tried to fight them off with my left hand. It wasn't much of a fight. They put ether over my face, and I was soon out.

When I came to, my first interest was to see if I was all still there. I'm happy to report I was.

The next day more trouble. The Germans learned that a plane the day before had killed a lot of Germans and the pilot had been captured. And that was me. "Let's go get the son-of-a-bitch and bring him over here and kill him in front of our troops."

There was quite a scene when they came and tried to get me. A French boy of about 15 was in the room to try to help me. He tried to tell them I wasn't capable of getting up, but they didn't pay him any attention. One of the guys kicked him, and the little fellow bounced across the room like a basketball. I passed out.

Next thing I knew I was in a vehicle, blindfolded; they were taking me to a place with walls around it, and I could hear a whole bunch of troops talking. By this time I could tell that they were going to kill me.

It wasn't a nightmare for me, it was a welcomed event, because I anticipated much more excruciating pain, and this would put an end to it. I didn't get frightened until months later when I was much better off.

They tried to prop me up against the wall, but my legs kept going limp. I even helped them; I wanted them to hurry up and get it over so I could get out of my pain. Once they got me on my legs, I could hold up my body, and when they leaned me a certain way, I saw I could stay upright leaning against the fence.

I heard an order by a guy, and some soldiers marched in. They were ordered to halt, and another order was given. I could hear the clack when they put a round in the chamber. Another order—it must have been "Aim!"

Then the gate opened—an old gate that needed oiling; it was creaking like the gate on the old "Inner Sanctum" radio program. "*Achtung!*" I could hear heels clicking, and shouting. One guy was talking loudly, like talking to underlings, and they said, "*Ja! Ja! Ja!* Like they would wipe the saliva off after he left.

He took my blindfold off and took me down to a *hauptmann*, a captain, to interrogate me. He spoke perfect English and had been in the States for ten years—New York and Los Angeles. Sitting in the room were two *Gestapo* storm troopers, over in the corner, just listening. The captain was very cordial, he even occasionally said, "Sir."

He showed me how much he knew already. He had my cadet graduation picture, with a circle around my head and Joe Gordon's head, who was also shot down, and the grades I made.

I asked him about William Griffin of the 99th. He found Griffin, a POW: "He has a tennis court and golf course. He's there because he's cooperating. You can have the same things."

When we took off on the mission, they gave us a second ID in case we were captured. One was mine, and the other one was a Moroccan airport worker who was deaf and dumb—how 'bout that? The Germans had searched me and found my two IDs. They didn't know whether I was me or the Moroccan.

"Why are you strafing there, when the fight is going on in the north?" he asked. I was thinking name-rank-serial number. "What field did you take off from?" The only thing I could remember was Walterboro. I didn't know how the hell I got here in France. He was really teed off. "Look, I've got a way to get the information if I have to." I looked at the two *Gestapo*.

"OK, here's the last chance you have: What was your code name in combat?" These were top secret, because lives were at stake. My code was "Subsoil 6." "If I give you the first half, will you give me the second?"

No use fighting; I told him yes.

He said, "Sub."

I said, "Soil."

He said, "That's right." I don't know how the hell he knew that, but he knew it.

They locked me in a stable. By this time I could walk a little, but very gingerly, because if my head shook, I would pass out. I had to walk with two people on each side. They helped get me into a trough, where they fed the animals, with straw to lay on. When I sat up, someone had to help me raise my head. When I laid down, they had to hold their hands cupped against my neck until I was in a supine position

That night I heard the lock unlock: Clank, clank, clank. I thought, "Hell, here we go again." A guy with a flashlight was speaking German. Then I heard other voices. They found me in the trough. When the light shone on me, I heard, "It's a spook!"

It was Jefferson and Daniels, but they didn't recognize me—that's how terrible I looked.

The prisoners went to sleep, with Macon shaking uncontrollably. He recalled:

The trip to the POW camp, *Stalag Luft-3*, took several days. We had three guards, and they'd commandeer any transportation that passed and make them take us as far as they were going—wagons, pickup trucks, even a train for a short distance. Then we'd start walking again.

We passed through a little country town in France. There was a German enlisted men's club by the side of the road and Germans going in and out with beer in their hands. Our guards wanted to go in and get a beer, so they told us to sit on the curb, and the three of us sat down while German troops passed by, talking.

Along comes a Frenchman, his lady, and a little girl, riding on bicycles. The man stopped and came back. He had taken out some francs and stuck them in Daniels shirt—the guy was giving us money in case we escaped.

Just then some Germans came and snatched it out of his hand, and there was a big commotion. Germans were running from everywhere. They grabbed the man, his daughter, and his wife, and along came a truck, bringing a cloud of dust with it. It came to a halt and they just threw those three people in there.

The last time we saw them, they were yelling and screaming, and the truck disappeared in another cloud of dust. We knew they must have been executed for helping the enemy.

Further up the road, there was a club with some women, and our guards made some passes at them. They commandeered a house to spend the night and said, "We want to chain you to the bed so we can go out and have a party."

I said, "No, no, no—Geneva convention—officers." They looked so sad, I said to the others, "Look, this may be the best deal we can make. If we give them a break here, they may give us one later."

The others said, "Oh, hell, OK, they can tie us up." The guards had their party, and after that every time they went to a farmhouse, they came back with six bottles of wine, three for them and three for us. They even came to attention when they talked to us. We got along very well with the enemy.

Once they went to a farmhouse about 500 yards away and left us on top of a wagon filled with hay. We saw some B-25s fly over and bomb the next city. One of the planes got hit, and we saw five 'chutes, so we knew they all got out. The Germans put a cordon around where they had bailed out.

Some soldiers with guns, thinking we were from the B-25, told us to get down from the wagon. They were about to shoot us when our guards came running across the field yelling, "They're our prisoners!" and they finally stopped aiming their guns at us.

To Jefferson,

The most frightening part of the war was when I saw the Hitler Youth at a railroad station. They were singing a marching song, and when they saw us, they started their tirade—"Ja!...Ja!...Ja!"—saluting and heel clicking and yelling obscenities. It reminded me of the Ku Klux Klan—running up and down the platform, screaming and yelling at the top of their lungs. Some of the adults also got aroused, and we expected to be dragged off the train and killed. Our guards even had to threaten to shoot the mob.

Scared? You're damn right I was scared! That's the only time I really became frightened. Flying combat, flying through flak? No big deal. Being shot down? No big deal. Bailing out? No big deal.

It was the terror of seeing how children's minds can be so warped.

September

SEPTEMBER 1. Roberts returned from the States and resumed command of the 99th.

The Red Tails continued to fly escort missions, usually without incident, but more and more of their missions involved ground targets.

September 8. In a strafing mission over Yugoslavia, the 332nd claimed to have destroyed 36 planes on the ground, but it cost them one pilot, James Calhoun, who was killed.

September 22. Chris Newman was returning from Munich over the Adriatic Sea when he had another close call in his plane, "Goodwiggle."

I got hit by flak up around 20,000 feet, and my engine started sputtering. I started smoking and burning, and my escort screamed, "You better get out of there, it's going to blow!"

To go down in the sea was the last thing I wanted to do. We had lost nine men in the Adriatic, and none of them were recovered, so I was trying to make it back to Italy. I could see the coast, and if I could just make the beach, I could bellyland easily, no problem. I was doing everything I could to keep the airplane going, but I didn't have any power and was coming down pretty fast.

All I could see was fire, and I radioed, "I've got to leave."

Yep, no doubt.

I pulled my oxygen mask and radio headset loose from where they snap into the airplane, because you don't want anything loose entangling you. Then I pulled the lever to jettison the canopy, roiled the plane over on its side, popped the stick forward, and the airplane ducked down and left me in the air, it just dropped out from under me. That was the system the Germans used. I tried it, and it worked fine.

I was tumbling out of control. Then I remembered in training we were taught to snap to attention, and when I straightened out, the tumbling stopped. I said, "It worked!"

Next I pulled the ripcord and waited for the 'chute to open, thinking, "How long does it take?" until I saw the oxygen mask in my hand and realized that I had pulled the oxygen tube instead, so I grabbed the ripcord and pulled again. The 'chute opened with a bang. It was quite a jolt. Luckily, I had altitude, so I could freefall for a while and recover from mistakes.

The 'chute has a survival kit with a one-man dinghy, dye, and other survival items. It's attached to your belt when you get in the plane, so that in the water you won't lose it. It had ripped open, so the dinghy was hanging beneath my feet by an umbilical cord, you might call it.

That meant there was more room in the harness than normal. The chest strap normally goes across your chest to hold you in, but it was above my head. If I had been thrown forward, I would have tumbled out. I had seen a movie where a guy fell out of his 'chute, and I was thinking about that, so I grabbed the strap and pulled myself back in.

Before I hit the water, I unfastened my leg straps and just hung by the chest buckle. As soon as my feet hit the water, I turned loose the 'chute harness. The wind pulled the harness over my shoulder and pulled me back to the surface. I pulled the CO2 tube and inflated my dinghy. I felt completely exhausted, just worn out. I guess I was just tense and thankful.

It took a minute or so to get my dinghy inflated, and my escort was circling where the plane went down, and was getting farther and farther away from where I was. It's easy to lose a man in the water, from the air he looks like the head of a pin. I started to wave my scarf at him, and it was bloody. I was bleeding from a gash on my neck, and I didn't even know it. A big fishing boat, splashing water, just chugged right on by me. I think I threw up once or twice, rocking around in that little dinghy.

Then a P-38 came along and saw the dye I had put in the water. He came down, buzzed me, and put in a May Day [call for emergency help]. He circled until a Spitfire came out and it circled for about an hour. I was in the sea about six hours when a twin-engine British bomber dropped a great big eight-man life raft. I got into it and an Air/Sea rescue boat, like a PT boat, picked me up.

When I got back, it was possible I could have been rotated back to the States. They must have thought I was losing my nerve, because they didn't put me back on the schedule for missions.

Alfonso Simmons, had gone down in Yugoslavia, and the guerrillas picked him up and brought him out, so the two of us walked around for two weeks, then we told them we'd get back on flying status.

He was subsequently lost in combat. I continued flying for the rest of the war.

October

THE 99th received some new graduates from Tuskegee:
Earl Lane from Cleveland, nicknamed Squirrel, was happy, fun-loving, popular, "and he was willing to take chances," a future cadet, George Iles, said.

Henry Peoples, on the other hand, was a "bad" guy. Spann Watson recalled:

> A terrible person. He was a strange guy. The first cadets in Tuskegee were clean-cut and eager; later on others came in. No matter what you tried to do, playing basketball or anything, Henry Peoples would hurt you.

Hannibal Cox was a 19 year-old Chicagoan, whose parents wanted him to be a doctor, but all he wanted to do was fly. He was nick-named "White Folks" because of his fair skin.

Spann Watson:

> He was one of those white/black people, but he was fervently "black." "Look, I'm not trying to pass as a white person, I'm a black. Don't tread on me." He was another one who had one of the most beautiful wives.

Cox was "flamboyant and fun-loving," Iles said. On leave in Atlanta, Cox hailed a cab and climbed in, followed by White and Iles. The driver balked. "Aw, let 'em in," Hannibal said with a grand wave of his hand. The others piled in, and the driver obediently drove away.

Hugh White "was as dark as I was light," Cox said:

> He was my best friend. He was the pepper of our pepper-and-salt team. We were inseparable.
>
> During the advanced program, some of us took a bus from Tuskegee to Eglin Air Force Base, Florida. After four hours on the road, we were hungry as heck, so we stopped the bus and said, "Let's get some sandwiches."
>
> I said, "Man, you know we can't go in there."
>
> Hugh said, "Well, White Folks, you're going to get our sandwiches for us. You go in there and play your role: Tell them you've got some niggers out here that you've got to feed."
>
> I said, "OK, fellows." I went in and said, "Ma'am, I got some niggers out here, and they're hungry as heck."
>
> The lady said, "Son, I understand the trouble you've got with these boys, and I'll fix them up." So she fixed up 19 fabulous bags.
>
> I said, "Lady, I thank you, and the niggers out there thank you."
>
> When I got to the door of the bus, Hugh was waiting for me and hauled off and hit me upside the head and knocked me down the steps. As I got up, I said, "Hugh, why'd you hit me?"
>
> He said, "Hannibal, you played the role just right. But you said 'nigger' one time too many."

Soon they received their orders to Europe:

> Sixteen of us arrived by bus in a small town in South Carolina, where we were to board a train to our port of embarkation. We were in uniform,

outfitted with field packs and armed with .45 automatics, and walked into a sandwich shop to buy sandwiches and soft drinks. As we walked in, the woman behind the counter screamed, "My God! The niggers are attacking our restaurant." We were dumbfounded.

A sailor jumped up from a booth and marched toward us screaming, "You niggers get the hell out of here!" One of our lieutenants, Henry Peoples, told him to "watch his mouth," that he was talking to officers of the U.S. Army. The sailor responded that we were a bunch of impostors; he had never seen nigger officers. He knew niggers were not pilots, and any nigger that carried a gun in that town was strung up. He said that was going to happen to us that night.

We decided to get to the train station and regroup. We had to pass the sheriff's office and saw lights coming on and people running in and out—we found out later the sheriff was giving out guns. It was after 9:30 at night, the train station was closed, so we decided to seek the safety of the darkness at the station and wait to see what would happen. More people arrived, a hell of a lot more, and they stood among the parked cars and screamed epithets at us; the worst of the screamers were women.

Cars pulled up, about 30 in all; they circled the station and played their lights on it. They were armed with everything from pitchforks to blunderbusses, to high-powered rifles with telescopic sights.

Cox was the designated negotiator, playing his role as the white man in charge.

The tobacco chewing, pot-gutted sheriff said, "Tell them niggers to come on out. We have to take them in."

Fortunately, a white lieutenant who was apparently on leave approached to talk with us. He said the people were ugly, but he'd contain them if we remained hidden.

When the train finally came, as luck would have it, the sleeping car stopped right in front of us and the door opened. As we filed out to board the train, the people formed a line and spit on us and hit us with their gun butts.

As they stepped off the train at Hampton Roads, Peoples said:

We were greeted by several men in Ivy League suits. To make a long story short, I have on my file in the Pentagon and at the FBI that I started a race riot in South Carolina!

They did the fastest processing job on record on us. We were checked in and out in eight hours and were on a ship heading overseas. They placed us in two stinking compartments, nine men in each one. We were locked in, practically standing on each other's backs, and given no food or water. When we were out at sea, about 32 hours later, they let us out.

"That," said Cox, "was our send-off to fight for democracy."

October 4. As the British were preparing to invade Greece, the 99th was sent in on a low-level attack against Nazi airfields in Athens. Cox remembered the day well; it was his first day in combat.

> It was a real hotbed. The fields were circled by ground fire. Guys were going down—we lost four out of my squadron that day. That's where I picked up my nickname, "Killer."
>
> We were supposed to make one sweep across, hit as much as we could, and get out of there. But there were a lot of aircraft left on the ground, so I pulled up and went in again in spite of the fire and shot up some more. I was the only one. I picked up a few hits, but by the grace of God, nothing vital.
>
> Later, when the gun films were shown at our base, my film showed pass, pass, and pass, aircraft after aircraft blowing up. The guys said, "That man is a killer!"

The out-going commanding officer, Erwin Lawrence, the last of the original 99th, was flying his last mission before going home; one report said he volunteered when another pilot was scratched.

"We came in right over the trees," Shelby Westbrook recalled. "The Germans had strung cables in certain areas and I believe Lawrence ran into a cable." He crashed and died.

"It was an unneeded mission," said Bill Campbell, who commanded the flight. "When we got down low enough to see them, most of the planes were already damaged. We lost two or three on that mission, and it really was a mission that intelligence screwed up on."

Most of the planes destroyed were on the ground, but Westbrook, flying his seventh mission, recalled: "Thomas and caught two Junker-52s in a landing pattern. They were slow, lumbering aircraft, and an easy target."

Charles Francis wrote that three more planes were shot down in the air, by George Gray and George Rhodes, plus one shared by Milton Hayes and Henry Perry. However, none of the victories was recognized by the Air Force. Campbell did not recall anyone claiming a victory in the post-flight briefing. The Germans had removed most of their fighters to protect Germany itself, he said.

All the pilots, except Westbrook, died before they could be interviewed for this book. Westbrook just shrugged: "The Air Force hasn't recognized a lot of the aircraft that we destroyed."

October 6. The 332nd strafed three Greek airfields. Carroll Woods and Joe Lewis were both shot down by anti-aircraft fire. Freddie Hutchins's plane was also raked by flak. He told Charles Francis:

> We were just approaching the target and I was flying with Jimmie Wilson on his first mission. I told Wilson to start his run, but he was slow opening up his plane. This retarded my run and cut down my speed. As I pulled up off the target, I was hit by a volley of flak. My right wing tip was torn off completely, and my tail was practically shot apart. I scooted down into my seat to get protection of the armored plates, but a volley burst through the floor and struck my leg.
>
> By some miracle I continued to gain altitude and headed for friendly territory—or at least a clear spot. I cleared a mountain peak by a few inches and then my plane began to lose altitude and was headed for some trees in a valley. I had very little control, but I managed to miss the trees and crash-landed into a small opening.

Roger Romine saw smoke and flew over to investigate:

> He crashed nose up, disappearing into a cloud of dust about two miles on very rocky, hilly ground along the edge of a river gulley. On my second pass the dust had settled, and I could see the fuselage, sitting upright, motorless, wingless and tailless....The canopy was missing. About 50 peasants were gathering around the plane, waving at me, trying to give me a message. With flaps lowered and moving at 150 mph, I could see that the plane people were very jubilant; I figured Hutchins was unconscious but alive.

Hutchins:

> When I came to, I found myself sitting at my controls with the engine of my plane lying several hundred feet away. My goggles were smashed on my forehead. My head was aching and my legs felt like they were broken. However, I found that they were all right except a deep flak wound on my left leg.
>
> I was pulled out by some Greeks and walked a few steps, then passed out. Some men raised me up and began to walk me around. Then they put me on a donkey and walked it around in a circle to restore my breathing. But my back hurt so bad I begged them to stop. They carried me to a doctor, who rubbed my back with some homemade olive oil, strapped me up, and put me to bed.
>
> The fleas had a wonderful time off me that night. I decided I couldn't live through another night like that, so though I was still in pain. I was taken into the city and got transportation back to the base.

October 11. The 332nd strafed railroads and shipping on the Danube, as well as an airdrome.

Cox:

> I was leading one Flight up to Lake Balaton, Hungary, and we destroyed everything in the airdrome, pass after pass, ripping everything to pieces. It was impossible for the enemy planes to get off the ground. One plane was taxiing to a takeoff position, and my number-three man clobbered him before he got into position.
>
> I hit a revetment that had aircraft in it and pilots attempting to get in the aircraft. The .50-caliber shells just lit up when they hit the enemy. We bored in on one aircraft, destroyed it, and came in on another.
>
> The 15th Air Force just refused to believe that four ships could do that much damage.

It finally acknowledged that 17 planes were destroyed.

October 12. The 302nd was strafing railroads in Hungary when, for the first time in almost three months, the *Luftwaffe* scrambled to repel them. Suddenly enemy fighters were buzzing as thick as they had been back in July.

The squadron had just crossed Lake Balaton, Hungary, Lee Archer told Charles Francis, when Lee spied a group of enemy aircraft at two o'clock on the tree tops, just taking off. He called out, "Bandits," and Pruitt immediately rolled his plane, "Alice," over and dived at a Heinkel bomber with Archer close behind. The Heinkel began pouring smoke, and Archer finished him off—"he disintegrated in the air"—though Lee refused to claim credit for Pruitt's kill (which was more of a strafing kill than an aerial victory).

Twelve enemy fighters then took to the air, and Chubby Green knocked out one of them.

At that point Pruitt saw a flight of enemy planes heading toward them. He flew directly at them, guns blazing. Then, Archer said, "we made a tight turn and fell in behind three enemy aircraft." Archer gave one of them a short burst and tore off its wings.

Pruitt sent a second one down in flames.

He was pursuing the third, when a 109 came from the side and slid in behind him. "I pulled up behind him," said Archer, "and gave a few short bursts, and the plane exploded, throwing the pilot out."

Meanwhile, Pruitt's guns had jammed, and Archer saw him furiously trying to unlock them. "Move over," Lee said, "and let a man shoot." Pruitt pulled away, and Archer eased into his position and fired two long bursts. The enemy appeared to be trying to land.

> I opened up at ground level with a long volley, and he crashed onto the runway. Then the German ground crew opened up with all their guns. Lights were blinking at me from all directions. For a few seconds I had to dodge flak and small arms fire that burst all around my ship. But I was lucky and managed to wiggle out.

Not entirely. Archer's propeller had been hit, and Pruitt pulled in beside his friend and stayed with him over the Alps to the emergency field on the Yugoslav island of Vis.

Luther Smith, Milton Brooks, and Roger Romine also received credit for one victory each.

The score for the day: Nine more enemy planes. But they lost one man, Walter McCreary, who was shot down by anti-aircraft fire.

For the next five months, the Red Tails would score only two more victories.

October 13. On an escort mission to a German oil refinery, Luther Smith was shot down. He parachuted safely but was captured.

On the way home Walter Westmoreland lagged behind, losing altitude. He tried a crash landing but slammed into a tree and was killed.

On a separate strafing mission that day, Chubby Green was forced to bail out over Yugoslavia. The Germans searched for him, but Communist guerrillas found him first. He stayed with them several days and helped them airdrop supplies to other partisans before some Russian pilots flew him back to friendly lines.

Strafing made the war personal.

Melton:

> The durnedest thing that ever happened to me was when I hit a haystack that caught fire. Two Germans came running out and disintegrated in front of these .50-caliber machine guns of mine. I never will forget it.

Purnell had a similar experience:

> We spotted a lot of German lorries filled with troops. We peeled off and came down, strafing them, thinking only of those swastikas on top of the trucks. The guys inside jumped out, headed into ditches, set up their machine guns, and started firing at us. We flew right into the fire with our guns going.
>
> When I got back to the airfield, as after every strafing mission, I checked the plane for bullet holes, Hanging over the edge of the scoop on the intake

under the P-51 was a strange object. On a closer inspection, it looked like a black-brownish glob, wet in some places. I took a stick and poked at it, and it fell off the scoop. It was fleshy, and then it came to me:

It was part of a man. I must have gotten a portion of his chest or his behind. It also hit me that his family had raised him, just as my family had raised me. You begin to think of the futility of war, that wars have been going on for ages and ages, and they never settle anything. And you wonder why we do it. You wonder why we do it.

15

Winter

FROM October 13, through March 23 Europe was hit by the worst storms in a century. The Red Tails scored only two victories in five months.

Another class of graduates arrived.

George Iles had started out a month behind the others but was promoted into their class because he had already had CPT. "He was a brain man," Watson said. "A gentleman's gentleman," Sheppard called him. Quiet and studious, Iles was elected class captain.

Bobby Williams, Iles' roomate, came from a well-to-do family from Ottumwa Iowa. Bob, his father, and brother all had pilots' licenses and flew their own family plane.

Williams volunteered for the Air Corps right after Pearl Harbor but was told, "The Air Corps don't take niggers." So he and his brother hopped in their convertible and drove to California to work as electric arc welders building Liberty ships until Bob finally got the call to Tuskegee. He drove up in his convertible to the envious stares of the other cadets—he was the only cadet in camp with his own car.

He was "very sincere, studious, and really wanted to be a soldier," Iles said. "Everything he did, he attacked with the desire to be the best."

Bert Wilson was a New York pre-med student and "a very quiet guy," according to Iles, "but recognized by all as an excellent flier."

Wilson's grade school teacher recalled the 12-year-old attending an assembly to hear President Franklin Roosevelt, but Bert ignored the famous guest. Instead, he spread his arms like a plane and "flew" out of the auditorium.

At Tuskegee, Wilson shrugged at the army's racial restrictions. "We knew what we were up against. You had to conform, so you conformed. It pisses you off, but it doesn't make you bitter—it doesn't make me bitter, anyway." Laughing at some of the "stupid" rules helped get him through.

Bert said he had never flown anything more than a broomstick before. Yet he soloed before Williams and liked to rib Bobby about it.

Charles Brantley was Wilson's roommate:

> He was always a happy go-lucky guy, crazy as hell. Everything was funny to him. I remember he had athletes' foot, and the doctor gave him some

medicine. I had jock itch. He said, "If this stuff works for my feet, it should work for you too." Like a damn fool, I tried it on!

One time he loaned me his parachute, because mine was wet. I was flying a Stearman and doing something over the school that I shouldn't have been doing. My engine started messing up, and I thought I was going to bail out. I got out on the wing and thought, "Hell, this isn't my parachute." I got back in and nursed the thing back to base.

Williams, Iles, and Wilson landed in Oran, Algeria after 29 days on a Liberty Ship that left everyone sick and vomiting.

Like ants, long lines of trucks took supplies from the ships. As soon as the ship docked, white troops poured off, but a second lieutenant stopped the blacks, because they didn't want "any trouble."

Williams "gave him a contemptuous look and just walked off," followed by the others.

They ended up in an Officers' Club, but none of the Arab women would dance with them. Commented Iles dryly: "We were told we weren't welcome. Gee, we had come back to Africa and were told we weren't welcome!"

The next day, on a ship to Naples, a British officer began assigning lifeboat commanders. "Are there any generals aboard?" No answer. "Any colonels? Any lieutenant colonels?" A black chaplain stepped forward. The officer just looked at him: "Are there any majors?"

Trucked across the mountains to Ramitelli on the eastern side of the Boot, they found P-51s lined up waiting for them. None had ever flown one. "You had to learn it on your own from the tech order, sort of an 'owners' manual,'" Wilson said.

November

NOVEMBER 3. Roberts took over as Group Commander as Davis returned to the States for R&R.

November 16. The weather grew worse. "One cold, cold morning it had snowed," Gleed said. "On a cold morning the darned engine on the p-51 was subject to detonate, that is, pre-spark." Crockett, "an old auto mechanic out of Fort Sill," speculated that after a few days layoff, water got into the engine and made it "spit and sputter on takeoff." For that reason pilots liked to warm their planes up 30 minutes before takeoff.

Gleed:

The only other way to correct it is to ease up on the throttle so you aren't going full-bore. That's a hard thing to tell a guy trying to get a P-51 off with loaded wing tanks. We had a single runway of interlocking pierced plank, and we had so many airplanes, with four squadrons instead of the usual three, that in order to get off in a minimum of time and to save fuel, we'd take off at five-second intervals. That's what we shot for. We came close.

Just as we started to take off, an Italian proceeded to drive a herd of sheep across the far end of the runway. The first two aircraft got off, but we could definitely hear the detonations. Roger Romine in my former 302nd, was the third man to take off. He barreled on down the runway, realized he wasn't going to get off the ground, and there was nothing else he could do—he plowed into the sheep and went off the end of the runway into the mud.

By this time the next man was already rolling down the runway behind him. He saw the mess, chopped throttle, and rolled off on the side, where Romine was mired down in the mud and slush and snow.

Romine never got out of his aircraft; why, I don't know. I started to stop the takeoffs then gritted my teeth and decided to keep going; I figured they could clear the two planes and the rest of the sheep.

About the 16th aircraft after that we had another guy cut his throttle, and he went straight into Romine's plane down there. Immediately on impact Roger's airplane blew.

Crockett was at the other end of the runway, having just sent off the last plane of his 100th squadron:

I had fired the flare gun to let them know my last airplane was off, and the other squadrons started taking off in the opposite direction. That's when William Hill's plane smashed into Romaine's. There were two airplanes, and everyone was fully combat-ready, all guns armed and full of .50-caliber ammunition, and each carried a full load of fuel, two 75-gallon tanks under the wing. That made a pretty good fire. There was a big ball of fire, ammunition was exploding, and I threw my flare gun away and ran out there wearing my British combat boots.

William Hill was trying to get out of the second airplane onto the wing. He didn't have his goggles down and got burned around the eyes, but I pulled him to safety.

Woody was awarded the Soldier's Medal for non-combat heroism. Gleed:

Now I'm looking at these two balls of flame, and I've still got 12 aircraft left to take off. Damn it, I sent them up. When I think of it, that may have been one of my worst mistakes, although I don't know what else I could have done. It was a matter of timing and making rendezvous when you're supposed to, and war was war.

Fortunately the rest of them got off, they didn't miss the rendezvous, and they also got in a scrap. But I had one damn good pilot gone and two severely injured. Those are hard ones to forget.

Bert Wilson, on his first mission, watched the tragedy from the flightline:

I was the third or fourth guy to take off, and I had to fly into all the smoke. I flipped my oxygen tank to 100% so I wouldn't breathe the smoke in my cockpit, but you get nervous trying to remember to do everything, and I forgot to turn it off, so I was using it even when I didn't need it. Over 20,000 feet, that's when you need it, and that's when I didn't have any.

Over the target, at 25,000 feet, I looked down and I didn't have any oxygen left, so I had to come down to where I could breathe. We were on radio silence over the target, but I broke silence and told my leader I was going down.

On the way home, Luke Weathers of Romine's 302nd told Charles Francis, he was escorting a crippled bomber when two bogeys were sighted at two o'clock high. Weathers flew into them. After a short burst from his guns, one fell into a dive.

At the same time Luke saw little red balls flying past his canopy—the whole German "wolf pack" was closing in. "It looked like they had me," so he dived and shook off all but one. "I chopped my throttle and cut my flaps. The fellow overshot me and left me on his tail. . . . A long burst and a few short bursts sent him tumbling to the ground."

It would be four months before the Red Tails scored another one.

Back on the ground, all the pilots assembled for a de-briefing. Davis looked them over. "Who was the asshole who broke radio silence and said he didn't have any oxygen?" he barked.

"Everybody looked around," Wilson said sheepishly. "I looked around too. I certainly wasn't going to say it was me."

On Bert's next mission:

My engine started acting up, and Crockett had to follow me down. I got my name in the paper, but Woody was the hero of the story.

However, it didn't take long to get to be a veteran. After ten or 12 missions you were made a flight leader because of the attrition. Older guys were going home, and you had to be the leader for the younger ones.

The 92nd Infantry

MEANWHILE, another dramatic experiment was going on, on the west coast of Italy. The all-black 92nd "Buffalo" Division had arrived in August and was about to receive its test by combat.

The Division was assigned the extreme left flank of the Allied line, facing a rugged mountain barrier, and went on the offensive in October. Replacement troops also began arriving.

The 92nd was soon the center of controversy. General Mark Clark would brand it the worst division in Europe. The 92nd and 332nd faced similar tests, but the differences between them were huge. For one thing, the top officers of the 92nd were all white. For another, its enlisted men were a far cut below the elite college men of the 332nd. Their commanding general, Ned Almond, was particularly controversial, and training at Fort Huachuca, on the blazing Arizona desert, had been beset by morale problems. Herb Sheppard, the kid brother of the Red Tails' Harry, served in the 92nd:

> I can't say anything great about Almond, and our assistant division commander was worse—he was a mean guy. The field grade officers were white, and many of the company-grade officers were white. Finally they began to move blacks up into captain's positions.
>
> A lot of the NCOs had come from the Army Specialized Training program and had pretty high IQs. But usually seasoned troops show the new guys all the things to watch out for; we didn't have any.
>
> For most of the enlisted men, we had a pretty high illiteracy rate; that was one of the major problems. Most of these fellows were from the deep South and had no schooling. The guys who had trained on mortars weren't mathematicians, but when they were trained, they were accurate.
>
> Also, we didn't have many trained infantry replacements. A lot of them came from the stockades; the Army threw them right overseas as replacements. They said they needed more bodies, but you needed someone who was trained. They used antiaircraft troops, quartermaster troops, truck drivers. That was another morale buster.
>
> When I think of all the guys who didn't have that basic infantry, I appreciated that I did. You can show a guy how to field strip an M-1 rifle, but squad tactics, or coordinating with other units, you need a team that's been trained together. To get an anti-aircraft outfit and throw them into the line immediately, it was pretty rough.

The Division went into combat on the left flank of the Allied line, on the west coast of Italy. They faced a wall of rugged mountains where the Germans were dug in on the Gothic Line and quickly got a reputation for "bugging out" and failing to take their objectives.

> We did take an awful lot of criticism, and we never got credit for doing things that were positive. Many good guys were wiped out and never got any credit.
>
> You'll find one or two in any division that might, after an artillery barrage, get nervous and fade out. But the way they tell it, whole units would just

take off. Although it's true that some people didn't hold up their end of it, it wasn't an overall truth.

We weren't the only ones who lost ground when the Germans were looking down your throat from the high observation posts. Every division takes ground one day, loses it, and goes back the next day. But in our case they made a special issue of it.

It looked at times that they were trying to get us wiped out. Most commanders would send a company to take an objective; we'd send a squad or a platoon. They were whittling down our squads.

The Germans would send a whole mass of people on an attack. If we hit them, you can bet that within an hour they would always counterattack. But instead of catching the enemy with their heads down and sending another patrol, our commanders would just whittle us down. They were trying to do us in instead of using us the way everyone else was using their troops.

We lost a lot of good guys.

Colonel Phelan, our regimental CO, got killed.

Captain Bundy, heavy weapons company, was up on a little cliff. He told his men to stand by, and he just went in there and attacked it himself. They really blew him away.

John Fox called for artillery fire on his own position, saying there were more Germans than there were of us. He turned the tide but didn't get much recognition for it.

When the Americans counter-attacked, they found Fox's body surrounded by about 100 German soldiers.

Vernon Baker was orphaned at four and grew up in Father Flanagan's Boys Town. He tried to enlist before Pearl Harbor but was told, "We don't have any quotas for you people." But he persisted and was finally accepted.

In Italy in 1945 he led his platoon in an attack on three machine gun nests, which they wiped out, along with 26 of the enemy.

Baker would spend 13 more years in the Army without a promotion. In 1997 he and Fox were among seven black veterans to receive the Medal of Honor more than half a century later. Baker was the only one alive to accept it.

But despite such valor, criticism of the 92nd remained vicious.

Sheppard:

> Morale sank to nothing. When they made all the remarks about the division, I was ashamed to say I was a part of it, until after I saw other divisions lose ground too.
>
> Mark Clark sent the 34th and the Texas 36th divisions across the Rapido River, and they were drowned—they caught hell. It wasn't until years later that the Army acknowledged those mistakes.

One of the 92nd regimental commanders, Colonel Howard Donovan Queen, charged that Clark himself, from South Carolina, had made the division a scapegoat for his own frustration because the Italian campaign was not winning him the glory that other generals were reaping in France.

Sheppard:

> Clark placed all the blame on the junior officers and enlisted personnel. The statement is unfair and untrue. Whatever shortcomings the 92nd had rested entirely on the shoulders of Major General Almond. His entire staff was incompetent, excepting Brigadier General Coburn, the artillery commander.

Toward the end of the war, the best men in the 92nd were formed into one regiment and augmented by the famous Nisei "Go for Broke" 442nd Regimental Combat Team. Sheppard called that one of the best divisions in Europe.

But the 92nd is remembered for its unfairly bad image, not its real accomplishments.

Almond would go on to serve under General MacArthur in the Korean War. He won praise for his brilliant planning of the Inchon landing that effectively liberated South Korea, but he received much of the blame for the headlong retreat after the Chinese invasion across the Yalu.

The 92nd went on the offensive in October. Harry Sheppard decided to "drop in" on their bivouac. "It cost me $100 and a three-month restriction," he said ruefully:

> E.J. Williams had just had an engine change, and I had to put four hours of slow time on it to break it in gently. I started out early in the morning and had put in a couple hours when this P-38 came down and "bounced me," trying to get a rat race or a dogfight started. When I didn't respond, because I didn't want to over-tax the engine, he pulled up on my wing and we just flew formation.
>
> We just took off and went along a dry riverbed through the Apennine Mountains, through the spine of Italy, and ended up at Caserta on the western side of Italy. As we dropped down the slopes, here was the Fifth Army Replacement Depot and hundreds of tents.
>
> My brother had just landed. They were all sitting on boxes in an open area, evidently having a lecture; the old-timers were breaking the newcomers in, and these two crazy airplanes came over at head-level and buzzed that cantonment area up and down the company street, just raked them back and forth. As we pulled up after the first pass, those guys were heading for the weeds!

Herb:

> I was very afraid for him. The tents were only 15 feet high at the ridge pole, and he was 15 feet off the ground. He cut our communication wire,

and it looked like he was going to clobber the town, with the mountain right ahead of him. I tried to wave him off, but he came back four or five times. Scared the daylights out of me. I was no good for weeks after that.

I saw the commanding officer writing his number on a pad, so I went AWOL and went to the 332nd rest camp and told them to tell my brother he's in trouble.

Harry:

The booms on a P-38 are rather narrow, so the other plane's numbers were not as conspicuous as the numbers on my big flat-sided P-51. So they sent a report: "Find this man." It went all the way up to the 15th Air Force and came back down to the squadron. I was worried sick.

When the report came in to Spanky Roberts, he said, "That's E.J. Williams' plane."

So I went to Roberts: "It was me."

He said, "Well, were you lost?"

I said, "Nah."

He said, "Well, was it cloudy or anything?"

"No. Clear day. Could see forever."

He said, "You're not making this any easier."

I said, "What I want you to do is give me company punishment [in lieu of a court martial]." The Old Man was back in the States, and if he saw this report, with the signatures that were on it, I could see myself down there, stomping around attacking on foot.

So he said, "OK, a $100 fine and three month restriction to the base."

I said, "Hey, wait a minute, don't overdo this damn thing." I wasn't making too much, and I was sending my money home. I just had a new son.

He said, "No, that's it."

So nothing ever happened to me except I lost the money that I would have sent home for Christmas.

The parallels with the green and untested 99th in Africa are apparent. Colonel Momyer had also wanted to scuttle the 99th. Without the leadership of B.O. Davis and the determination of his officers and men, the 99th might be remembered as is the Black Buffalo Division. The comparison makes the accomplishments of the Tuskegee Airmen that much more impressive.

December

SPANKY Roberts:

I remember one seek-and-destroy mission when all Europe was covered with clouds. After we got airborne, the order came down canceling the mis sion, but we were already gone. A Major Gray had come down from head-quarters to fly with us, and I let him fly number-two spot on my wing.

I found a hole, went down, penetrated, found the target, brought the group down, and proceeded to wreak havoc on German trucks on an open plain just south of the Alps. They weren't expecting us, with the cloud cover what it was, and it was great hunting—I hate that term, but that's what it was.

To get back home with that cloud situation, we had to form up in a formation which we did quite well, a squadron of planes in a line abreast going down the east coast of Italy. I went down on the deck, not more than 50 to 75 feet off the water. I had to get down that low to find out where we were. The only way was by sight. The major on my right was a few feet lower than me and so on, so the 16th man was just skimming the water.

Everybody had to fly perfectly and stay in position for the whole hour or two it took to get home. I think that major went back and advised all the people in headquarters that he knew where the best fliers in the theater were.

Roberts also almost faced a court martial:

I was called in by a colonel who talked to me for hours about a night cover mission for parachute drops in Italy on the darkest night of the month. I told him as nicely as I could that the plan stank. We wouldn't have been able to see. The 99th would be wiped out.

"What if I order you to fly this mission?"

"If you do, I would refuse it."

"Well, I'm going to order you."

"Well, I'm going to refuse."

I went back and told my operations officer to be ready to take over; I would either be shot or sent to prison. Neither of those happened, however.

December 9. Bill Campbell and four other Red Tails got a close look at the new German jets, the twin-engine Messerschmitt 262, which flew 100 miles faster than the P-51. They seemed to be merely checking out the Americans and made no attempt to attack. The Americans fired some shots but scored no hits.

As Christmas approached, the weather grew worse.

December 23. Lawrence Dixon, the guitarist, went down in the Alps. His engine quit, Woody Crockett said, and he started down, then tried to return to the formation to complete the mission but went down again. This time he didn't return. "He must have walked away from his plane and then went back to it for warmth. We heard he was found frozen to death in the cockpit."

When the Germans launched their big counter-attack at the Bulge, most black ground troops were employed driving supply trucks on the "Red Ball Express" or in other rear-echelon tasks. But as the Germans smashed forward, Eisenhower, over the protests of his chief of staff and Third Army commander George S. Patton, called for rear area volunteers "of all races" to fight "shoulder to shoulder" with whites.

Some 45,000 responded. One black quartermaster battalion picked up infantry weapons and captured 49 German prisoners. African-American artillerymen fought beside the beleaguered 101st Airborne at Bastogne. Segregation was dropped until the German drive was stopped.

Back in Italy, according to Gleed:

> We ran into snow so bad that half the bombers aborted before they got to the target because the targets were also closed in. So we, in turn, turned around and came back, and I think we got all our guys but two or three back to the field.
>
> One bomber outfit, not one of the ones we had gone out to meet, did get to their target but got the holy be-jesus shot out of them. They found their way back through the crud somehow and came in to our field—four B-24s, a couple shot up too much to take off again, one guy pretty badly hurt. In all, they had some 35 white crewmen.
>
> We got extra cots and spread them out among the enlisted men and put several more bunks in the officers' tents. The mess hall started cranking out extra chow.
>
> This one captain wouldn't allow his men to leave the aircraft. He himself came out to our operations office, which was an old farmhouse where we had phone contact with 15th Air Force Headquarters, and for over an hour he tried to convince them that they didn't know what they were talking about, that he could get back to his home base.
>
> When they finally told him he would not take off, he went back and told his guys they would stay in the aircraft overnight and eat C-rations [army canned food].
>
> One of his sergeants went up to our enlisted mess and found everyone else sitting in tents with pot stoves in oil drums and actually comfortable. The sergeant flat-out defied his commander and stayed there.
>
> I went out and tried to convince the guy that he and the rest of his men were going to freeze to death and to at least come into our operations building, where we had stoves upstairs and down.
>
> At last, about three a.m., he reluctantly said OK, his men could come in. He himself accepted one of our cots, but he didn't sleep in our office, where we were sitting, waiting for possible orders for the next day's mission. And he brought his own C-rations from the plane.

Lou Purnell:

> When we weren't flying, we had "other duties as assigned." My duty was to censor the mail of the enlisted men. I came across a V-mail letter, and I couldn't believe it. It said:

"Dearest: The most sentimental time of the year is approaching. It makes my heart bleed to know I'll not be with you at Christmas. May God speed the end of this war. It's bad enough I'm not on my home base. I'm stranded at a nigger base, eating nigger food, and sleeping in a nigger bed."

I said, "My God! They're the very guys we're protecting!"

It was from a Sergeant Schwartz. My mother was part German, and I knew a few words of German. Translated into English, the man's name was 'Sergeant Black.' I decided to find out who Sergeant Schwartz was. So I got an orderly and a guest book and went to different tents and asked all the visitors to sign the book until I found Sergeant Schwartz.

At their own base, the visitors shivered trying to sleep in their overcoats under piles of blankets. At Ramitelli, burning oil cans kept them toasty. They relaxed at music and comedy shows in the evening. At home they ate standard army chow; here they ate fresh meat and eggs bartered from farmers.

Gleed:

> We never got another mission off for six days. About the third day this captain finally came around and found out that the color wasn't going to rub off. We weren't monsters. I'll be damned if before he left there, he wasn't converted!

Davis, who returned the day before Christmas and reported that by New Year's "our bomber friends were still weathered in with us and took communion with us at the Sunday service."

At last the weather cleared.

Purnell:

> They all jumped in trucks and were driven to their ships. When they were assembled in front of their planes, I rode up to Sergeant Schwartz and said, "Why, Sergeant Schwartz, you're not leaving anything behind, are you?"
>
> He looked surprised that I knew his name. He said, "No."
>
> I said, "The word is 'No, Sir.'"
>
> That just boiled him. I said, "After all, it wasn't so bad sleeping in nigger beds and eating nigger food, especially when we protect you in flight. I'll see you up there."
>
> I walked away. I knew he wouldn't shake hands. I never turned to see the expression on the guy's face.

Colonel Davis told his command:

> Your achievements have been recognized. You are known by an untold number of bomber crews as those whose appearance means certain protection. The bomber crews have told others, and your good reputation has preceded you in many parts where you might think you are unknown.

Sergeant Melvin McGuire, a bomber crewman, in his book, *Bloody Skies* (Yucca Tree Press, 1993) told of another mission, when his crew was limping home, carrying 75 bullet holes, with one engine out and their fuel almost gone. They were about to bail out and had radioed one last distress call when a strange voice came over their frequency:

"This is Gallant. We're right off your starboard wing, the landing strip that's right under you. You're welcome to come in here. I can see you."

The pilot didn't wait but went straight in and sputtered to a stop on his last drop of fuel at the end of the runway bordered by red-tailed P-51s.

Trucks raced up with fire extinguishers, and the crew was driven to head-quarters, where they finally yielded to hysterical laughter. There were not enough chairs for everyone, so McGuire sat on the desk, laughing, when "suddenly this black major walked in, looked at me, and said, "Get your ass off my desk, will you?" (The major is not identified, but it sounds like something Spanky Roberts would have said.)

He turned out to be "a fine man," however, and asked when they had last eaten. They told him 0230 that morning, more than 12 hours earlier. He said, "I figured that, so I stopped by the kitchen, and the cooks are going to fix up a snack for you."

McGuire wrote:

> That day I ate the finest meal I had in Europe. They didn't serve us standard fare. They had dipped into their goodie bag for treats they were saving for special occasions and served us pork chops, all we could eat. They wanted to make sure we didn't leave hungry.
>
> While we were eating, the terrible screeching and banging and hollering and noises of props beating on the landing strip assaulted our ears. A P-38 was crash landing, a solid mass of bullet holes.... It came skidding in, stood on its nose, and plopped back down.
>
> Ten minutes later the pilot arrived, his head swathed with bloody bandages, saying, "They told me we're having meat!" and helped himself to a plate of pork chops too.
>
> Most squadrons stockpiled some good things or materials for special occasions, but these guys were sharing them with us.... We knew we were eating somebody else's pork chops, and we ate enough for 15 to 20 men....
>
> That meal was just another example of the excellent outfit they were. The relationship between the Tuskegee Airmen and the bombers in the 15th Air Force couldn't have been closer. They were one of the premier groups in Europe. I can't say enough good about the Tuskegee Airmen....
>
> When you were 600 miles from home, those red tails looked mighty nice. I never heard any racial slurs from bomber crews directed towards the Red Tails. Lord, we loved them.

16

The New Year

MEANWHILE, as weather permitted, flights resumed.
The first German jet, the ME-262, had been blitzing American bombers in northern Europe for months. General Adolf Galland, chief of the German fighter command, wrote:

> Again and again they broke through the American fighter screen with ease and shot down one bomber after the other from the tightly closed formations despite an inferiority of 100-to-one.

In August 1943 two P-47s from the 8th Air Force out of England had shot the first one down.

In December the 15th Air Force also spotted some jets.

Roscoe Brown:

> I had seen them three or four times, when we were escorting P-38s on photo reconnaissance missions. The jets had been maybe 5,000 feet above us, sometimes as close as 1500, trying to scare us; they flew around but never made a pass.

George Iles said he "got into a few frays" with them:

> It was a mismatch in some ways, but not in others. They were extremely fast, but to engage in a fight, they had to slow down, and we were more maneuverable. The dogfights didn't last very long, we were moving so fast.
> The ME-262 pilots would play with us. They could come from behind, then zoom up right in front of you. All of a sudden, for a brief second you had his full silhouette right in your gun sight. If I'd been fast enough and had the reflexes, I might have had a hit.

On December 22 two pilots from the 31st Group had sent two of the jets spiraling to earth.

December 29. One of the Red Tails' hottest pilots, Frederick Funderberg, was lost in a storm over Germany and never found. Andrew Marshall, Robert Frind, and Lewis Craig also went down.

In the month of December the entire 15th Air Force scored only 26 victories, while the Eighth downed 1,000 planes. Not until March did the 332nd once more meet enemy fighter planes in strength.

The POWs

A LEXANDER Jefferson and Dick Macon wound up in *Stalag Luft-3*, mid-way between Berlin and Warsaw. That's the same camp that became famous in the Steve McQueen movie, *The Great Escape*, though the breakout and executions had taken place before they arrived.

Back home Macon's family received notice that he was dead:

> My sister-in-law had a *ouija* board and got the vibes, and it said, yes, I was dead and buried in France. My Mother gave up. But my wife knew I wasn't dead, that I had miraculously survived. It was her strong will not to accept that I was dead.

As soon as they arrived, a B-17 officer spotted Jeff and ran over to hug him: "You're a Red Tail! You goddamn Red Tails—if you'd been with us, we'd have made it back home. You guys saved our asses many times."

The old-timers got to pick their roommates. One "cracker with the deepest southern drawl," pointed to Jefferson: "Ah thank ah'll take this 'un." Jeff's new roommates represented every state of the Confederacy. They had chosen him because they knew he couldn't be a German spy.

> They could trust a black man, but they were afraid of a strange white face. Ain't that a bitch?"
> They treated me as one of them. Each man performed a duty, we combined our rations, cooked our meals together, and shared equally.

For the first few weeks, Saturday nights were tough, wondering if some draft dodger was making out with your girl back home. Sometimes the mailbag contained a "Dear John" letter—Jeff himself got one from Margo, the girl on the nose of his P-51.

All the new captives thought about was wine, women, and song. "After the first week we forgot about wine; next we forgot about song; after four weeks we forgot about women. But we never forgot about food."

> The camp commander was named Galadowich, from Budapest. He was dressed immaculately in jacket and leather boots and said, "Men, you are prisoners. For you, the war, she is over."

I think he had in the back of his head that when the war was over, he wanted to live in America, because he kept asking us about things in the U.S.

All the prisoners got to be good friends with him. But he couldn't understand a joke. All the things they did in the TV show, "Hogan's Heroes," we did as prisoners.

January 27. Near midnight the prisoners were suddenly told to be ready to move out in 30 minutes. With the Russian army pushing closer, the Germans had decided to move their prisoners several hundred miles southeast to Moosburg near Munich.

They hastily threw on all the clothes they could wear, stuffed as much food as they could into their pockets, and trudged out single-file into temperatures 10–15 degrees below zero with six inches of new snow.

Their guards were "Peoples Guards" in their 60s and 70s, who suffered worse than the prisoners. Some POWs took pity on them and carried their rifles for them. Still, they often stumbled and fell and were left behind to freeze to death. No one wanted to stop to rest, because they'd freeze, so they slogged on all night with only the food in their pockets. Then they reached some hills "and it really got tough."

One Red Tail survivor, Kenneth Williams of Los Angeles, had been shot down in Greece. He told reporters after the war that they marched 60 miles in snow at a temperature 15 degrees below zero. It took six days, two of them without food—his hands were so numb he couldn't open the Red Cross food can he was carrying. At one point, Williams said, some trigger-happy Peoples' Guard troops (militia) mistook them for American infantry and opened fire, killing several of the regular army guards and wounding four prisoners.

Macon:

On the "Atrocity March" we were going through the mountains, it was freezing rain. I was completely exhausted when we got to a little town with a wall around it; they had closed the gates and wouldn't let us in. The guards couldn't find any place for us to sleep, so we slept out on the highway in that rain. I almost froze that night.

I don't know what happened to my jacket, and I was freezing, so Jeff took his jacket off and let me wear it. If he hadn't done that, I don't know whether I would have survived or not.

Just about dawn two guys got me up and started walking me around, and we started walking toward a light. One guy, his parents were born in Germany, knocked on a door. A lady came to the door, and he told her I was his comrade and I was freezing. At first she was a little hesitant—I guess we'd have been the same way—but she let us in.

She told us about her son on the western front, in the Battle of the Bulge.

She said they had been overrun and she hadn't heard from him in two or three weeks. She didn't know whether he was well or not. She hoped wherever her son was, if someone saw him, they would be kind to him, too.

They covered 40 miles in 27 hours before they got their first warm rest, dry socks, and some black bread. Then they walked from morning to night, when they were assigned a barn and slept, "crowded on top of each other for warmth."

Next they were herded onto cattle cars designed for 40 men. "We packed in 80 men to a car," Jefferson wrote. Williams said fights broke out among the prisoners when one tried to move an arm. "It was human nature at its worst." While half the men rested, the other half had to stand. Those who slept laid on manure. There were no toilets—sanitation consisted of tin cups—so at every station they were allowed to throw open the doors and "moon" the startled people on the platform.

There was only one guard per car. Why didn't they escape? Williams:

> Where would you go? If you got out, you didn't know anything about the country, you'd stand out like a sore thumb in that snow. If you got very far, you'd probably ran into some of those crazy SD troops. Some of the men tried it, but they always came back. No food, no way taken where you were going. It wasn't any use.

February 3. They finally arrived at a new camp, Moosburg, near Munich, where they were given a delousing—stripped, stood against a wall, and soaked with a hose. But their clothes weren't washed, and the camp was so infested with bedbugs, many took their blankets back outside to sleep.

Williams said guards attempted to "weed out" any Jews, but the POW commander told them, "Everybody is a Jew. If you kill one, you've got to kill all of us."

For cooking and warmth, they burned their bed boards, floors, "and anything else we could find." According to Williams, Red Cross food packets stopped coming, because there were no trains to bring them. Prisoners picked potato peelings from garbage cans, scraped them with tooth brushes, and fried them.

Pit toilets overflowed into the living quarters. "To make matters worse, the majority of us were suffering from diarrhea." Jefferson designed a coat of arms reading *"In Excretia."*

For others in the camp, conditions were even worse.

> A lot of Russians and Poles were across the wire—the Germans treated them horribly. Conditions weren't too much better for us either. Lavatories were open pits, the place was full of lice, and we didn't have enough food, so it's a damn good thing the war ended when it did.

Meantime the war went on. The 332nd continued strafing missions, with railroads a favorite target. "The pilots had overlays on their maps and divided them into sectors, Bob Williams said. "If it was moving, we'd blast it."

February 17. On a mission to Munich:

On the far side of the tracks there was a wooded area, where they had anti-aircraft guns—intelligence hadn't told us that. Suddenly that forest looked like a New York Christmas tree. It was like flying through raindrops all around me, great round circles with orange in the center. How I got through without being hit, I'll never know.

Bert Wilson led a four-man flight:

I was the only one who got back, because when I pushed the button to drop my tip tanks [on the wings], one just hung. The other three planes went across the field to strafe. I don't think any of them made it. It's "target fixation." You get so intent on the target, you get lower and closer until you hit it yourself.

Roscoe Brown:

We used to have film sessions Tuesday nights. They'd have your trailer on the screen, and if you made claims that you couldn't substantiate, you got a big boo, and it sort of pushed you to do more than you really needed to do. So when I was flying ground support, on each mission I fell lower and lower and lower, because I wanted to get good pictures.

Williams:

Brown was flamboyant, he really took chances, When we'd come in off a mission, everyone tried to make the tightest turns and real steep approaches and buzz the field—it was show-off time. Brown would always get down lower than anybody else, just barely touching the ground. One day he didn't quite make it.

He flipped the plane over and ended up with 100-octane gasoline pouring all over him. Richard Caesar, our engineering officer in the 100th, dug him out from under that plane. He had to dig in the ground from below so Brown could get out of the hole he'd dug.

Caesar:

Gasoline was flowing everywhere. Brown was inside with his seatbelt on in this little cockpit. I had to go under the plane and maneuver his legs up to unhook his seatbelt and finally got his head coming out and dragged him out. Just about the time I got him out, the sucker [the plane] blew up.

February 25. Brown hadn't let a little accident change his style. With a new plane, on a strafing mission to Austria:

> I was doing about 350 miles an hour. There was a lot of *ack-ack*, so I dropped even lower than I normally dropped until I was below the level of the train. In fact, I got so low that just as I went over it—*boom!* I must have hit it with my left wing just as the train exploded.
>
> The plane almost went into the ground, but fortunately, I was able to grab the stick with two hands and wrench it to the right and added a right rudder. That's one of those split second things—if you don't do it, at that speed you're dead. I pulled it up and looked over. One wing was half off and was turning upside down.
>
> Gradually I pulled it up to 10–12,000 feet and flew it on home. At the base there was a question whether I was going to bail out. I called in to the tower and said I was coming in to land, get the emergency equipment ready. When I got close to the ground, I cut the engine and pulled back on the stick, held it hard right, and it settled right in, a three-point landing.

Wendell Hockaday's wing also clipped his train. He managed to fly to the Alps, before he was forced to bail out. He was never seen again.

George Iles was shot down returning from the same mission.

> I got hit by the "flak train," as we called it. Flames were licking past the cockpit and got sucked in, and I started to bail out. I even turned the plane upside down so I'd fall out, but then I turned it back upright and decided to ride it down myself. I did everything according to the book, except I forgot about the air scoop on the underside of the P-51; it acted like a shovel and dug into the dirt and plowed a big line across the field. I would have slid in much better without it.
>
> We had classified gun sights, so I shot mine up so it wouldn't fall into the hands of the Germans. I don't know to this day whether the plane burned completely or not—I got away from it as fast as I could.
>
> At first no one was around, so I started to hike toward the Swiss Alps, which I could see in the distance. I stopped a fellow on a bicycle coming down the road, trying to find out where I was, but he didn't speak English, and I could only speak a few words of German.
>
> In half an hour I became a guest of the Germans. Two trucks converged from two directions, and an element of the Home Guard picked me up. They treated my injuries, and I was taken to a jail in a little town near Munich.
>
> I was fortunate to be grabbed by the military. One of our pilots in the 332nd, Lincoln Hudson, was beaten severely by civilians before the German

military got to him. The civilians had been bombed and shot, their homes had been burned, and they were more angry than the military, who thought of war as a job.

The next day I was put in a boxcar with a couple of guards for the long ride to the interrogation center at Frankfurt. The guards treated me very well and shared their food with me.

At Frankfurt we went out of the station to catch a streetcar to go across town to the prison camp. As we stood there, a mob gathered around. I was roughed up by the civilians, and if it hadn't been for the guards, I would have been beaten, I'm sure.

(Incidentally, the streetcar conductor refused to let us on until the guards paid three fares, one for me. It tells something about the German mentality.)

The Germans tried all the old tricks to get information out of us, such as planting English-speaking Germans in the group to try to elicit information. They didn't have any English-speaking blacks they could fly in, but they had obviously made a study of our Group.

We were required to tell only our name, rank, and serial number. So the interrogator said, "OK, then I'll tell you a few things," and took out a book with "332nd" on the cover. He opened the book and began to read. He had a list of all the classes that had graduated from Tuskegee, with names of all the pilots and a lot of personal data, the radio call signs of the units, and even the code for the day of the flight I went down on.

Obviously someone was feeding them information from our camp.

If you talk to other black prisoners of war, we all mention the same thing: We had been segregated all along in the Air Force. Prison camp was our first experience in the military of being non-segregated. The Germans treated us just like any other American pilot. It was ironic: You had to get shot down to be treated as an equal.

One German spoke excellent English and had lived many years in Chicago before the war. He told me, "I know how they treat you people, especially in the South." He wondered "why you fellows choose to fly and fight, and perhaps die, for a country that treats our German prisoners better than it treats you."

That was sort of thought provoking.

I was the only black at the interrogation center at that time, and the other Americans were kind of stand-offish to me. There were no overtures of friendliness. My best friends were not Americans, but British. Everywhere it was the American soldier who carried prejudice with him. Not until you got in life and death situations was all of that torn away.

Prison camp was not like *Hogan's Heroes* on TV or the movie *Stalag 17*. There was no time for escape schemes—survival was uppermost in our minds. No food was coming in, and the Germans had even begun to take the prisoners' Red Cross parcels. In all fairness, though, the Germans themselves didn't have enough food. So our whole day was centered around eating, getting ready to eat, or trying to find scraps of wood to make a fire if you did get something to eat.

Black bread and soup was a staple. We'd get barley soup, but the barley had weevils in it. The weevils would float to the top, but you drank it anyway—well, some drank it. Some didn't have the stomach, but if they didn't, some of the oldtimers would take it until the newcomers got to the point where they'd eat anything.

Some people, who were supposed to be officers and leaders, sank to a very low level, while some of the enlisted men emerged as real leaders. That kind of experience brings out the real person.

Iles' camp was also forced to move to Moosburg:

I guess it was 70–80 miles, and it took us 16 days walking. The clothes we wore were the ones we had arrived with. Some men who bailed out lost their shoes; with the shock of the parachute opening, the shoes just flew off—so they had to wear makeshift shoes.

On one occasion, our column was strafed by four American P-47s. Everybody just ran—blindly ran—guards included, and seven or eight prisoners got killed. But as the planes came down low, they recognized that they'd made a mistake, and the fourth one didn't fire or drop his bombs.

After that, every day a couple of P-51s hovered over our line of march to prevent it from happening again.

Once you're down to the bare bones of survival, prejudice seems to fade away. One guy from Macon, Georgia and I just hit it off during the march. In Moosburg, he was in the bunk on top of mine, and we would talk far into the night. He asked me if I was going back to the States. He said that, just seeing how I was treated overseas, he thought it was better to stay there than go back.

We were pretty good friends by then, and he said, "Weil, I'd like you to come visit me when you get back. I know things aren't very good in Georgia, but if you ever come that way, I want you to come to my house, you're welcome, and we'll talk about old times." He was sincere, but I didn't take him up on it, I didn't want to impose on him, because it would have put him under pressure from his fellow Georgians. I don't remember his name, and I never saw him again, but it took quite a bit for him to make that offer.

In the spring good flying weather returned, the air war intensified, and Hitler's once-vaunted *Luftwaffe* became increasingly powerless to defend its homeland.

March 6. With prospects of victory growing, the 302nd was deactivated. They had written a unique record: In aerial combat they shot down 27 enemy craft, twice as many as any other squadron:

302nd	27
99th	14
100th	10
301st	9

(The 99th had scored 22 victories before joining the 332nd.)

The 302nd had not lost a single pilot to the enemy. Two—Chubby Taylor and Roger Romine—perished in accidents: two others—Walter Westmoreland and Emory Robbins—were presumed downed by ground fire.

For the rest of the war, the totals were:

301st	11
100th	10
99th	6

March 10. In the States, *Liberty* magazine published an article claiming that the 332nd had not lost a member in its last 100 missions. The claim was demonstrably false. Nevertheless, it grew into a myth that the 332nd had *never* lost a bomber! It would take half a century to track down that myth and destroy it.

March 16. On a strafing mission against railroad targets, some ME-109s come up to challenge them, and William Price of the 301st shot one of them down. It was the Group's first victory in four months. But Jimmy Wheeler of the 99th was killed when his plane hit a tree, illustrating once again that the fliers faced more danger down near the ground than up in the sky.

17

Rockets Over Berlin

MARCH 23. Buddy Huntly recalled:

> I never will forget. All the airplanes had returned back home. We'd
> put them down for the evening, and they made an announcement: "All per-
> sons will fall out in the company street." We knew there was something big.

The Red Tails were going on their biggest mission of the war—a
1600-mile round trip to Berlin. The German capital was in the sphere of the
England-based 8th Air Force; this would be the first time the Italy-based
15th would attempt it.

To do it, the P-51s would need large fuel tanks. Finding 110-gallon tanks
on a day's notice seemed impossible, but "we just had to get them immediately," said Elmer Jones, CO of the Service Squadron.

The tanks were on a slow-moving train that would arrive too late, so
Omar Blair, the tech supply officer, grabbed some men and trucks and
raced along the tracks until they reached the train. He waved a sheet of
paper and in a voice of authority demanded the tanks. His men quickly
off-loaded them and sped back to Ramitelli before anyone realized the
paper was meaningless. Blair called it "The Great Train Robbery."

But when the crews started to install them, the fittings didn't fit. The box
said, "For P-47s."

Crew chief Ellsworth Jackson informed Davis, who barked, "Well, those
planes have to fly in the morning!"

"So," said Jackson, "everyone went around the field and picked up spare
parts and fitted those tanks with the scraps. And they flew the next day."

Huntley:

> We all went back down to the field, got the new 110-gallon wing tanks,
> replaced the old 75-gallon ones, refueled them with gas, made sure every-
> thing was all right. We just rejuvenated the whole doggone operation.
>
> The next morning we found out, this was it—they're going to Berlin! It
> was a seven-hour flight, round-trip. The fighters had to go all the way. And
> try to get back home.
>
> That made us all skip and holler!

Reid Thompson Downs a Comet

MARCH 24. What made the pilots' hearts skip a beat was the prospect that the enemy force included 40 of the new ME-262 jets with speed 100 mph faster than the P-51s. Every man who took off that morning was itching to bag one.

Also across the Alps lay an even greater surprise—and a place in the history books.

Why was the 15th Air Force given this job and not the 8th Air Force, which was much closer to the target? The answer is that the 8th was sending every plane it had—up to 12,000—to the Rhine, where Patton, Bernard Montgomery, and their armies were about to smash across the river on a broad front and begin a race across Germany.

Having learned its lesson at Memmingen, this time the 15th Air Force divided the B-17 wing into two waves of three Groups each and assigned separate fighter wings to each one.

And, instead of one undermanned Group—the 332nd with 37 planes against 200 or more enemy fighters at Memmingen—this time they would send five Groups—about 250 planes. A German force of about 40 fighters lay waiting. This was going to be a turkey shoot.

The 332nd would escort both waves to the target. Then it would turn responsibility over to the 325th, while the Red Tails conducted a futile fighter sweep. Next, as if they weren't exhausted enough, they were to strafe ground targets on the way home.

The 31st would escort the second bomber wave.

The 52nd would take both waves over the target.

The P-38s of the 82nd would take the armada home.

The 332nd would rendezvous with the Fortresses at 11:45.

To their surprise, the 31st and the 82nd also appeared. Why the latter two showed up early is not clear. Perhaps they were anxious to get in as much combat time as they could against the jets. One can assume that their commander had argued long and loud to be allowed to be first. Why the Red Tails got the assignment is not clear. But the 31st just got there early anyway. Since they had no responsibilities, they were free to go hunting for almost half an hour before taking up their assigned duties beside the bombers. Would the extra dogfights burn up fuel, leaving them short when their own bomber wave arrived? Clearly, they were willing to take that chance. They weren't about to let anyone else steal any glory before they got there.

After his earlier accident, Brown was flying his new P-51-D, with Lucky Lester's old #7 on the side, and "Bunnie" painted on the nose in honor of his infant daughter. The ship had a bubbletop canopy, which gave the pilot a wider view of the sky around him. It also had a new electronic gun sight. Brown explained:

> With the old sights, you had to count your "rings of lead," like a quarterback leading a pass receiver. But with the new sight, you put the sight around the wings of the enemy plane as they do now, and that automatically gave you your lead.
>
> The B-17s were about 25,000 feet, and we were a couple of thousand feet above them. We flew in flights of four planes, two flights on one side, two flights on the other side. We would sort of weave across them, spread out all over the sky.
>
> I was the 100th squadron leader, but I decided, since I thought it was going to be an easy mission, to break in a new leader and let one of my flight leaders lead the squadron, while I flew "Tail End Charlie" to watch him.

Then suddenly at about 12:05, the German jets appeared. The 325th had just joined the other three Groups, so the sky was filled with about 150 American fighters, plus the Germans.

The action became furious as several Red Tails spotted the enemy at about the same time. In the next few minutes the 332nd would shoot down at least three, and possibly six, of the speedy enemy, and damage two more.

Brown:

> The jets could reach a top speed of 450, compared to 380 max for the P-51 in a dive.
>
> I've tried to think how we were able to get the jets. For one thing, in spite of their great speed, they had to throttle back somewhat to hit the '17s, and before they could accelerate, we were able to get them.

The Mustangs could also out-turn the 262s, who made slow, easy turns in order to maintain speed.

There was much competition to be the first to bag a jet, and some controversy over who should be given the honor. Three men actually got credit, and eight others may have deserved it as well. However, all came within two or three minutes of each other, and who had time to check his watch at a moment like that? Anyway, the 8th Air Force and the 31st Group had already scored victories over the jets, so the question was academic. All three victories were scored by the 100th.

Brown saw M-262s coming in at 11 o'clock low and called, "Drop tanks and peel right!" He fired at one from a range of almost half a mile, the extreme range of his gun sight. The jet went into a dive, Brown in pursuit, but he had to break off because the enemy was just too fast.

Climbing back:

> I sighted a formation of four ME-262s under the bombers, below me going north—I was going south. I peeled down on them toward their rear, but almost immediately I saw a lone ME-262, climbing at 90 degrees to me and 2,500 feet from me. I pulled up in a climb and fired three long bursts from 2,000 feet at eight o'clock.
>
> I went *brrrt, brrrt, brrrt* and got him right in the middle. Almost immediately I saw flames burst from his jets and the pilot bailed out from 24,500 feet. I got a beautiful picture with his parachute and everything. Great show.

Earl Lane, meanwhile, was 3,000 feet above the bombers. He had just finished flying Ss and was turning back when he saw a 262 diving across the formation.

> I came in for a 30-degree deflection shot from 2,000 feet. I fired three short bursts and saw the plane emitting smoke. A piece of the plane, either the canopy or one of the jets, flew off. I pulled up and circled over the spot where he went down and saw a crash and a puff of black smoke.

Charles Brantley and his flight leader saw two dark-colored ME-262s coming at the bombers from behind and below, seemingly "coasting" without using their power boosters. The two Red Tails picked out one of the jets. "I dropped my nose, being very well within range, and made several bursts from dead astern." Each jet turned in opposite directions. "I followed my target in a dive, observing hits in the fuselage." His flight leader saw the ship go down in flames.

As Brantley rejoined his leader, another jet crossed his path, from right to left. He fired but couldn't turn fast enough, because, he discovered, he still had one wing tank stuck on his wing!

Two Iowa Hawkeyes from the 100th earned probables.

Bob Williams of Ottumwa saw the jets in a line abreast as soon as Brown called, "Drop tanks!" Williams and his wing man, Sam Watts, were attacked by two of them at five o'clock high.

> They came in in a closed formation and fired at Watts. I was about 500 feet above them, so I rolled over into a steep wing-over and developed a high-speed stall, from which I recovered, but I immediately developed another.
>
> When I pulled out, I dropped down almost in trail of the jets. I noticed a simultaneous trail of propulsion from both aircraft, still in very close formation, and they started a shallow left turn.
>
> I picked up a lead on the jet on the right and fired a long burst. I fired another and held it for two seconds. I noticed hits on the aircraft and saw

him fall out of formation, and I believe he went down, but I had to break off the attack, because Watts called to me for help.

Joe Chineworth of Bloomfield saw three 262's break toward him at ten o'clock:

> I broke right and down on them, pursuing them through a series of turns. When I got within 1500 feet, I started fighting on the rear-most aircraft. I fired three bursts, and my guns stopped. Pieces come off him and black smoke began to pour from the plane.
>
> I last saw him going into a dive. He appeared to be out of control, and it made a couple of turns while diving.

The 99th damaged two other jets.

Richard Harder spotted four jets with blue-gray bellies attacking in a string at five o'clock high, firing at the lead bombers from about half a mile away. Harder pursued two of them and closed to 900 feet. He hit one jet's fuselage before black smoke from one of its jets indicated the German had applied his speed booster and pulled away.

Harder saw three more jets at five o'clock and chased them off before they reached the bombers. He and Mitchell turned inside number-two and hit the wing and fuselage before it hit its booster and zoomed away.

He was credited with one damage, though it would seem to be two.

The first four enemy had been very aggressive, Harder said; the last three seemed less experienced.

Ed Thomas and Vince Mitchell, pursued two jets and turned inside them. They fired at one from 450 yards, hitting it in the tail. It did a half-roll and dived away. Each shared a damage claim.

Most of the jets came in behind the bombers and from below, the pilots said; since the P-51s were above the formation, it was hard to pick the attackers up immediately. The Germans didn't seem to use their jet boosters in the attack but employed them to zoom away from pursuers. Their other defensive maneuver was to dive when attacked.

Meantime, history was being made.

Reid Thompson, a New Yorker with the 100th, saw a strange sight almost a mile away at two o'clock. It was short, had swept wings, and was ultra-fast. No one in the 15th Air Force had ever seen anything like it:

It was the Messerschmitt 163 Komet, the world's first rocket plane, capable of speeds up of 700 mph—250 mph faster than the jets and twice as fast as the P-51s. It was Hitler's secret weapon to save the Third Reich.

Thompson:

> He went into a dive, almost vertical, and I dived behind him, still out of range and looking for him to pull up and allow me a shot at him. We began

the dive at 26,000 feet, and on the way down he did three barrel rolls to the left, and I rolled with him. I pulled out of the dive and leveled off at about 6,000 feet.

When I last saw him, he was still going down. I circled the area and located a puff of smoke and wreckage.

Even Thompson didn't realize that he had just defeated the fastest plane ever built until then. The 8th Air Force had tangled with the Komet since July, when they shot the first one down. But this was the first time anyone in the 15th had even seen one and the only time anyone had shot one down.

The official 332nd verdict: Thompson "probably" destroyed it. But it's not clear why he wasn't given a victory. Would he have received one with another Group? He didn't even get a DFC.

Roberts:

The kills and damages we scored are probably many more than we have records for. If a plane wasn't clearly seen crashing or burning, or the pilot wasn't clearly seen jumping out, we didn't even try to claim it, because we knew we weren't going to get credit for it.

So Thompson's feat went unnoticed for 65 years, buried away in the dusty, unread pages of the archives.

The next day all the front pages in America were filled with the Rhine crossing, plus the invasion of Iwo Jima. If the papers mentioned Berlin at all, it was buried. Apparently neither Davis nor the 15th Public Information Officer understood the public relations value that Thompson had handed them. With one headline he could have wiped away much of the negative publicity "the black air force" had borne for almost two years.

If the 31st, or another white unit, had blasted a Rocket out of the sky, it is hard to believe that it would have been modestly ignored.

The 31st, the only other fighter Group that engaged the enemy that day, bagged five jets.

	332nd	31st
victories	3	5
probables	3	0
damaged	2	4
total	8	9

The 332nd was in combat for 40 minutes; the 31st, about an hour and a half.

Although the German planes were out-numbered 6-1, they knocked down three Fortresses. Since there were five American Groups in the sky at the time, it is impossible to tell which ones should be charged with the losses.

Twenty-three other bombers were downed by *ack-ack*.

The jets also shot down two U.S. fighters, both from the 301st. Leon Spears was downed and presumed dead. Squadron leader Armour McDaniel was captured and sent to POW camp. (He would be replaced by Moe Downs.)

Meanwhile, Brown said:

> When I looked around for somebody else, they were all gone. Next I looked around for any other planes to shoot down, and I saw one 1,000 feet above me with a German cross. I said, "Oh boy, there's another one. This must be a Messerschmitt. Let me go get him."
>
> Then I said, "Damn, that's a P-51." It was a captured P-51, and I was dying to shoot him down over Berlin! I could shoot him down, I knew that, because I had a better plane, a newer plane. But I'd burn up my damn gas. So I just broke off and let him go and flew back home by myself about 3–400 miles.

Lane also spied the enemy Mustang and quickly broke into it, but it sped away.

Three Red Tails went missing: Ronald Reeves, Robert Robinson, and James Michell ran out of fuel on the way home.

Hannibal Cox of the 99th had half his wing shot off but made it back safely, completing his 65th mission.

Most of the other weary pilots finally set down at Ramitelli almost 12 hours after they took off.

Brown:

> When I landed, I must have had two drops of gas left. It pooped out on the runway.
>
> Someone had seen me get the jet, so the crew chiefs were out there jumping up and down.
>
> They refueled me, and I went back up and had a great time "tearing up the field," doing victory rolls. The tents were in squadron areas, and I found my own area, dropped down to about the level of the tents, and came down one company street, pulled back up, turned upside down, did a roll, and came back down going the other way. I did that for about ten minutes.
>
> At the farmhouse we used for headquarters, they had these telephone lines, and I came in under the wires and pulled up and did another roll and landed.

18

Victory

MARCH 31. The Red Tails downed 13 more enemy planes. Brown and Lane each got one, to go with their jets of the week before.

Lane's flight of four was just below the clouds at 4,000 feet, when he called, "Bogeys, 11 o'clock." There were 10–12 German fighters below them, and Lane dropped his tanks and dove.

Bobby Williams:

> The ideal tactic was to yo-yo—hit and take off—because we were outnumbered.
>
> But my wing tanks wouldn't fall at first. The element of surprise was lost for me, but I was going down, no matter what. I got on the tail of one plane and gave him a few short bursts. He fell off and tumbled to the ground.
>
> As I was pulling out, a German fighter was on my tail, so I made a steep turn, and just as I turned, another enemy plane shot across my nose. I fired and fired and fired until he went into a steep dive and crashed.
>
> A steady stream of tracers was coming out of my guns, which indicated I was practically out of ammunition. I poured the coal to my engine, but it started to cough and buffet, because it was too much power. Oil from my cowling was running across my windshield, and I thought I'd been hit.
>
> I told the guys, "Fellows, it looks like I'm going to have to walk home."
>
> Lane asked, "Did you push your prop pitch forward [to absorb the extra power]?" So I did, and the power surge was just immense. That beautiful little P-51 took off like a banshee, and I accelerated out of the area.
>
> I looked back and saw another German plane with his wings lit up with fire coming out of his guns, but I disappeared into the clouds and joined up with our other two planes and came on home.

Rual Bell was another 100th pilot. "He was a short fellow," Williams remembered. "Every morning he'd walk into the mess hall and announce himself: "One heaven, one hell, one rule—Rual Bell." That day Bell also scored one victory.

Hugh White of the 99th and Carl Carey of the 301st were also victorious. Bert Wilson found himself in a low-level dogfight.

I got on the ME-109, and we were in a very steep bank, so steep that when I started shooting, the centrifugal force wouldn't permit my guns to feed. When you're really sucking it in, it pulls the ammunition belts out of the magazines in the wings. Only one of my guns was shooting. It sounded like a BB gun—*pop, pop, pop, pop.*

I got him anyway.

Eventually Wilson's other guns resumed firing, and he got a second enemy, plus a "half-victory."

> Somebody else claimed it too; I don't know who. It all happened in about three minutes. It's pretty hard to recall it accurately. It was all a blur, and after 50 years you're going to embellish it.

Other victories went to Daniel Rich, Thomas Brasswell, John Davis, and James Hall. But the caliber of the German pilots, in the waning days of the war, was questionable. There seemed to be nothing for Hitler to gain by sending these boys up to certain death. Even so, the youths shot down three Americans—Arnett Starks, Clarence Driver, and Frank Wright.

Bill Campbell, now commanding the 99th, described his victory in his usual soft-spoken way:

> We had released the bombers to another Group, and coming back we had permission to shoot anything moving north of the Alps, so we dropped down, hunting something to shoot at. We attacked, and actually, we out-numbered them. They weren't looking for a fight, we had to chase them and catch them. I got behind one, fired, and hit him, and he crashed.

April

THE Red Tails flew 54 missions, their best record for one month.

The war was almost over. Germany had lost it more than a year earlier, when it failed to conquer Russia and lost the bloody battle of Stalingrad. It was clear when the Allies seized a beach head on Normandy, or when Hitler's desperate Battle of the Bulge was stopped, or when the Americans crossed the Rhine and leveled Berlin, Dresden, and other cities.

To go on was madness or murder. Yet Hitler went on. It's not clear why he didn't stop fighting on the western front and let Eisenhower march into Berlin before the Russians, whom he greatly feared. Instead, the Reich's borders steadily shrank to a small perimeter around Berlin.

The *Luftwaffe,* its veteran pilots almost all gone, was reduced to rushing boys through training, pushing them into cockpits, and sending them into the skies. It was pointless murder to send them up—and murder to shoot them down.

A new class of Red Tail rookies reported.

Jimmy Fischer, a tall, skinny youngster from Massachusetts, had been waiting since Pearl Harbor to get into the war.

> I was kind of naive about segregation. There were only four or five black kids in my high school, so we really didn't catch any hell. My father disappeared when I was a baby, and I have no recollection of him. My grandfather had a big farm, but he got wiped out in the Depression. When I was about four years old, I got TB and was in a hospital for four or five years; by the time I got out, I was in the third grade, and the farm was gone.
>
> I was 17 on December 7, 1941. As soon as I graduated that June, I went right off, all starry-eyed, to join the Army Air Force. That's when I first ran into segregation. Twenty guys went over to the local Army field for an interview, and they called us in alphabetical order, but when they got to me, they skipped over me. The guy told me, "I can't recruit you. There aren't any Negroes in the Air Corps."
>
> When the new 99th squadron was being formed, I sent over my application to Washington and waited and waited but never heard anything. Finally the draft board sent me over to Fort Devens, where a colonel, a doctor, typed on my record: "Qualified, aviation cadet."
>
> The other officer looked right at it and stamped "Infantry" on it. And that's where they sent me. I did a lot of bitching, and eight months later I finally got into the Air Corps.
>
> You had to have two years of college to go in, but if you could pass an exam, they'd send you to Tuskegee Institute for a six-month university program and flight training.

April 1. The day before Easter, with Germany's surrender just a month away, the Red Tails scored 12 more victories. Harry Stewart, only 19 years old himself, out of Queens, New York, scored three, using the new gun sight:

> We were on a fighter sweep. After we brought the bombers out of danger, we were permitted to go out and look for enemy aircraft—"looking for trouble."
>
> We were spread out quite a bit, and I saw two or three planes about 1000 or 1500 feet below us. I called, "Bogeys at ten o'clock low." They definitely looked like 109s. My flight leader, Captain Charles White out of St Louis, couldn't see them, so he said, "You take the lead, we'll follow you."
>
> Now, I know they were acting as decoys, because about 500 feet above us were about eight other German aircraft, which I didn't see.
>
> I peeled off and picked up quite a bit of speed, closing in on the ones below. They just sat there. They didn't see me, I don't know why. I closed in, diving full throttle.

When I was about level with one of the aircraft, I pulled back on the throttle to slow down and gave him a burst and hit him right away.

When I saw his wingman turn away to the left, I was in a slight dive, and I pulled inside of him. You had to get behind the enemy on his tail, and of course he doesn't want you to. He was starting into a Lufberry circle. You're both making very steep turns, going round and round. One of the fighters out-maneuvers the other and gets inside to get an advantage, and I got enough deflection, and I hit him.

Just about that time I heard someone scream, "It's on your tail! It's on your tail!" I looked around. My wingman was gone, and I saw this fighter close in on me.

It's hard to remember all the details 60 years ago. I saw the Louis-Schmeling fight and watched it over and over. But if someone asked me, "Did Louis put Schmeling down with a right cross or a left jab?" I'm not too sure which one. It's the same way remembering my fight in 1945. Very little detail is fresh in my mind.

I took my plane into a very steep dive toward the ground. I pulled in very, very tight. Both planes were going round and round trying to get inside to get an advantage "right at the edge of the envelope." He was in a very steep spiral, trying to get a deflection shot at me, above my left wing. He was trying to turn inside, but he was in a steeper dive than me. We were very close to the ground, and when I pulled around, I couldn't see him any more.

Carl Carey was taking the place of a wing man for me. Carl said the guy on my tail probably went into a spin, lost control, and hit a high-speed stall and was unable to recover.

Carey himself scored two enemy planes, as did John Edwards. Walter Manning and Harold Morris each claimed one.

But three American planes were lost. One was Jimmy Fisher's:

We got into a little scrap up in Germany. On our way home, we were free to hunt for trouble, so the 301st broke away from the rest of the Group and flew straight down the Danube river. When we got to Linz, we ran into a lot of flak, and the only thing to do was break away from it. We were looking for enemy barges. Instead:

The Jerries attacked us from the rear, and I tried to release my wing tanks, but they were stuck, and by the time I finally released them, the fight had started. I wheeled around and plowed through the enemy, and by luck, I didn't get hit.

I picked out one of them, and the fight was on. Then, just when it got hot and heavy, we were bounced by another formation of 109s, who had come up to join the fight.

It seemed as if every Mustang up there had three enemy aircraft on him.

I could see an enemy smoking, and looking down, I saw one of our planes crash into the ground.

I fired and hit two Jerries, but they just wouldn't go down, and I was pouring it onto a third when I spotted one of our P-51s above me with smoke streaming out and an FW-190 right behind him, firing with all his guns.

I broke off my attack and pulled up behind the Focke-Wulf and gave him several bursts and succeeded in driving him off. He made a dive for the ground, and I was right on his tail, but he went down to the deck and lit out across the airdrome, where they threw up everything but the kitchen sink at me. I could feel the hits on my aircraft.

I finally caught up with the Jerry, and I didn't intend to turn him loose until I had knocked him down. I could see my bullets going into his aircraft until he finally hit the ground and exploded.

The ground fire cut my rudder cable and just missed hitting my heel. If you know anything about flying, that's the end, so I got up a little speed and got the hell out of there. I ducked over a hillside and was checking my gasoline when I happened to look up to see tracer bullets sailing past my canopy.

I finally out-distanced the Jerries and looked around at my tail, and the darn thing was almost in shreds. I was about fifteen miles from Vienna, so I called my leader and said I was going to head for Russian territory and turned south to try to get to Yugoslavia.

Both my rudder cables were gone, but my trim tabs were still working, so, making very gentle turns and climbing very slowly, I began to start back toward friendly territory, begging my aircraft to please make it just a little longer.

I flew over a small freight yard and a little factory town, and the enemy opened up with their 88 gun. Suddenly the plane lurched, and I looked out at my left wing, and there was a huge hole right through my wing tank. Losing all that precious gasoline, I almost felt like crying.

Well, I still had about 60 gallons left, so I decided to try it just a little longer. I flew over the lowest part of the Alps that I could find and shortly broke out over the coast. I can't tell you how happy I was. I began calling for help on all the channels, but nobody answered.

Finally I got a response. A British emergency station picked me up and steered me to an emergency field on an island off the coast of Yugoslavia. They gave me a heading, which I flew for a few minutes, and finally the best-looking friendly field I have ever seen came into sight. I don't know to this day what I did to deserve such luck.

But just as the field was in sight, my ship ran completely out of gas, so I knew it was time to give up the ghost. I unbuckled my safety belt and tried to jump.

They told us to roll the plane over and drop out, but I can tell you it isn't an easy deal. I crawled over the side and fell out, but when I came out, I hit the tail surface, and it banged up my leg pretty good and threw me into a somersault.

I pulled my 'chute cord, and when I opened my eyes, there I was hanging upside down, with my leg tangled up in the shroud lines, floating down to earth with silk over my head. I began kicking until I finally shook myself free.

Then I whacked into some heavy branches in a wooded area.

I had landed in an orchard of some kind and was immediately surrounded by a large crowd of unfriendly-looking Yugoslavians. They must have thought I was a German or something, because they had big sticks and clubs. After I finally convinced them that I was an American, they all hugged and kissed me.

Soon a Cub plane flew overhead, and evidently it was directing some motor transport to the place, because a jeep soon rolled into sight. My luck had finally changed. I was taken back to the airdrome and arrived just in time to catch a C-47, which happened to be going my way, and I got home in time for dinner.

I still don't know how it all happened. It was the worst April Fool's day and the best Easter Sunday I ever experienced.

Meanwhile, Hugh White was shot down in Italy's Po Valley near Florence. His friend, Hannibal Cox, recalled:

A couple of us wanted to go back up there, find some way to land on the beach, and get him out. There was room for two to ride in a P-51, and we thought we could make a break for it, but Bill Campbell, our squadron commander, got mad at us and ordered us back. In retrospect, I realize the idea was foolish as hell and never would have worked.

Hugh got out OK without us. As he told the story later, the Germans captured him, uncaptured him, and finally they became his prisoner.

Back in Moosburg, General Patton's American army was closing in. Dick Macon recalled:

We saw American planes strafing some marshalling yards. One came close enough so we could see his red tail, and we knew it was one of our boys. We saw one get hit, saw the smoke coming out of the exhaust, and pretty soon the smoke got so thick the pilot bailed out. We saw his 'chute open and the plane crash.

About an hour and a half later we saw them bring Clarence Driver into the camp. He was from Los Angeles, and we called him Red, because his skin was red, and he had a few pimples. He wasn't hurt, but his clothes were almost burned off him.

In ordinary circumstances, Red cursed like a sailor. Under these circumstances, he had all kinds of epithets about getting himself shot down.

April 12. Back home President Roosevelt died suddenly. Four days later the Boston Red Sox give a tryout to an infielder named Jackie Robinson. They said they'd call him if they ever needed him.

Meanwhile, the dashing Pruitt had gone back to the States, where his hometown, St. Louis, welcomed him as a hero. The city named a housing development after him, Pruitt-Igoe, in a big ceremony attended by Senator Stuart Symington. Pruitt told him, "Give my people a chance." It turned out to be one of the best things he could have done for racial equality.

Then Pruitt returned to Tuskegee to train new students, but he chafed with boredom and begged to go back to the 332nd.

April 20. Pruitt was about to return to Europe when Bernard Knighten's wife drove him to the airfield on a Sunday afternoon. He was flying with a student doing a low-altitude slow roll, and the plane smashed into the ground, killing both men.

One theory is that the student froze on controls. Another is that the AT-6 trainer did not feed gasoline while upside down and that Pruitt tried the maneuver too close to the ground.

"He was showing off," Knighten says.

April 26. The ground war would slog on for 12 more days. But the killing in the air war finally ended. The Allies shot down the last enemy planes in Europe. The Red Tails of the 301st destroyed four of them over Prague.

Richard Simmons, a New Yorker, got one.

Jimmy Lanham, a Temple University grad and a shipfitter at the Philadelphia navy yard, got one. He fell in behind one plane and chased it, roaring over a village 50 feet below that threw up flak as the German plane rolled over on is back and fell off sharply. He said it must have hit the ground, but he claimed a probable.

His wingman, Tom Jefferson, 21, a dental assistant from Chicago, got two. He jumped a "tail-end Charlie" pumped bursts into it until orange-black smoke poured out of it, and the pilot bailed out. He spied another and gave it several short bursts until it also trailed smoke and crashed.

It may have been the last one of the war.

The results of the Red Tails' ground wars:

Planes destroyed or damaged in the air	136
On the ground	273
Barges and boats destroyed	40
Locomotives	126
Rolling stock	619
Trucks, cars	87

An Interview With General Strother

As the war ground down, a reporter for the *Afro-American* newspaper interviewed General Strother, who still didn't grasp what the war had been all about. He said it hurt the morale of his white pilots to see the 332nd getting so much publicity for knocking down half as many planes as they had. What accounted for this, he was asked.

The other Groups "just seemed to have the knack of finding enemy planes in the air." It still hadn't dawned on him that his white Groups didn't seem to have "the knack" of protecting their bombers and lost almost six times as many as the 332nd.

The general damned with faint praise, saying that at first the Red Tails had lacked leadership, but added that Colonel Davis "had done wonders" in shaping them up.

He said they had a poor maintenance record, which he attributed to lack of experience by their mechanics. Actually, the records of the 15th Air Force don't support his statement. On a per-squadron basis, the four squadrons of the 332nd were virtually tied with the 31st Group for the lowest number of early returns due to poor maintenance.

The newsman asked why the 332nd was the only Group in the 15th Air force that did not receive a Distinguished Unit Citation. The general replied that his Fighter Command had given much consideration to the question, but "Nowhere could we find a mission outstanding enough to merit such an award."

If there was anything to be learned from the experience of the past 12 months, General Strother apparently hadn't learned it.

May 8—VE Day

LLOYD Hathcock of Dayton, who had been shot down a year earlier with the 99th, was on his bunk, above the newly arrived Daniels:

> I heard the [homemade] radio say the Third Army was 20 miles north of Munich. I told him, "That's right here," and went out and looked at a map. It wasn't long before we saw a Cub [light plane], then some P-51s.

George Iles:

> To our great astonishment, an American jeep pulled into the POW camp under a white flag, and that night U.S. tanks threw shells over the camp into the town all night.

The next morning we saw in the distance an American flag going up. It was an indescribable feeling that few other people have experienced.

The duel between the big guns had ceased," Macon said. "We were hiding in slit trenches so as not to be hit by a bullet at this late date, and we saw two American Sherman tanks in the distance. Presently some half-tracks arrived, carrying black GI's.

Hathcock:

It's one of the more inspiring sights of my whole life. We didn't get to talk to them. They went right on chasing "goons," but they sure were mixed right in with the whites. It was a surprise, but it helped make just about everything pretty that day. I had lived in a room with 23 whites, and I was proud some colored soldiers helped free us.

Before long, General George S. Patton, wearing his ivory-handled pistols, strode into the camp in the center of a swarm of MPs.

Iles:

The American soldiers grabbed Galadowich, three on either side, marching in cadence. One of the prisoners called, "Hey, Galadowich! Where the hell are you going?"

Galadowich stopped and did an about-face, and said, "For me, the war, she is over." He did another about-face, and they marched him out of the camp.

The most exciting thing that happened was to see the GIs go over to the flagpole and lower the Swastika and smash it into the ground and step on it. Then they pulled out Old Glory and hooked it onto the same pole and raised it to the top.

I looked around at all the tattered prisoners in all their tattered clothes, looking like they're not worthy of a salute, all standing at attention, saluting that flag as it went up, in complete silence.

We got a bath and uniforms with rank insignia. Once they got back in uniform, some of the officers who had withered under pressure looked down on the enlisted men, who had done such a yeoman job, and treated them as their inferiors. That came across as a lesson learned for me: Blacks always say you don't judge a person by the trappings of authority, but by what he is inside.

Jefferson took a jeep to Dachau concentration camp. "Bodies were everywhere," he recalled. The odor was nauseating, and he got sick to his stomach.

Macon and Iles flew back to France in "some old Gooney Bird" with the cargo doors open, Macon recalled.

It made more noise than it made speed and was the only time I ever got sick to my stomach in a plane.

I had just married my college sweetheart before I left the States, so I opted to go home.

Jefferson opted to stay in France, so he went to Paris and had fun.

Jeff said he didn't remember too much about Paris, except that "the girls in Pigalle treated us very well."

Ed Gleed was a major when the fighting stopped.

I'd finally gotten over to our rest camp myself. The second day I was there, I was loaded just about to the gunwales and was getting ready to have the next blast when a phone call came. It said a captain from the 15th Air Force headquarters with a piggyback [two-seater] P-51 was sitting at the airport with instructions that I report to my unit with him.

As drunk as I was, I said, "You got to be kidding, the war's over; I've waited so long, I'm flat not going." And I proceeded to get drunk again.

Early the next morning, about eight, somebody was shaking me, saying, "By orders of General Twining, 15th Air Force, you will proceed back with me to your unit!" He said if they had to bring me orders, they would, along with a few MPs.

When I walked into the Old Man's tent, surprisingly, he wasn't mad. He said, "Gleed, how'd you like to be in New York Sunday?"

"How do I get there?"

He said, "We've got a C-47 plane due tomorrow."

Beautiful. I didn't ask any further questions. Later I found out he wanted me to go back with him to form a cadre of the 477th Bomber Group and take them to the Pacific, but he didn't tell me this. I got pissed off. But then I said, "OK, anything to get back to the States."

Jefferson remembered sailing past the Statue of Liberty, with the ship's horns blasting and everyone shouting at the top of his lungs. When they filed down the gangplank, "a short, smug, white buck private shouted, "Whites to the right, niggers to the left."

"I knew I was back home."

19

Mutiny

THE 477th was in virtual mutiny, its morale shot, its training at a standstill. Once more the issue was whether blacks and whites could use the same Officers' Club.

Commented Gleed: "Based on the good record of the 99th and 332nd, I think the fracas was absolutely asinine."

The 477th and its commander, the 332nd's old nemesis, Colonel Robert Selway, had been sent from Selfridge Field to Godman Field, Kentucky.

James Wiley:

> Selway was a terrible leader. He was my commanding offcer, and I never did see him, just like I never saw Kimble, and I saw Momyer only one time, when I flew his wing. Selway never even assembled us to give us a welcome or anything. He didn't demand attention and respect, and his staff didn't demand respect. We could take off and fly whenever we wanted to. We never did march as a unit.
>
> Under B.O. Davis we had parades every Saturday. You got all dolled up, it made you feel good. That's the way to keep an organization together, make them work.

In April, the 477th was to be moved again. It included Chappie James, who had been considered too big for fighters but became bomber pilot instead. Bill Terry, who like James, was a former instructor, was also now flying bombers:

> They were going to move us to Freeman Field, Indiana. We sent a cadre up there, and they found out we couldn't go to the Officers' Club, the tennis court, the swimming pool, the theater. All blacks were called "trainees," even those with 120 combat missions. They took the enlisted men's club and made it Officers' Club #2, like an Uncle Tom's Cabin.
>
> The president had issued an executive order that there would be no segregation at any recreational facility on any military air base. We knew that. I guess they thought we couldn't read or write.
>
> The very day we arrived, we said we're going to test Army Regulation 210, paragraphs A and B. Were we going to be declared first-class citizens and officers and gentlemen in the United States Air Force?

Clarence Jamison, an instructor in the 477th, recalled the events that led to the "mutiny."

Some of the white officers had never been in combat, but they were designated "instructors," and we black instructors were designated "students."

Selway called a formation and said, "I want everyone to sign this statement," saying we had read and understood his order. It was a setup for a court martial for disobeying an order. You understand that this was wartime and you're talking mutiny, where the penalty is death, so they had a terrible sword hanging over our heads:

By rank I was the first one in line. I said, "I've read it, but I don't understand it," so I deleted that part and signed it. Some of the other fellows behind me did the same thing.

The lieutenants were more rebellious—some were very rambunctious—and said, "Hell, I'm not signing a damn thing." I think Coleman Young [later mayor of Detroit] was a second lieutenant. He was kind of wild anyway, a real young rebel. Young was a good soldier, he just didn't take any stuff.

They decided to integrate the Club.
Jamison:

I was sitting at a table, screening the guys to be sure they had first-class uniforms, that their uniforms were on straight, so there would be no objection to them, except that they were colored.

You know the old Army saying, "Eyes bright, assholes tight, fingernails clean." And we sent them down to the Club two at a time. If you see forty scrappy young Negroes together, people think it's either a riot or a football game.

Someone had snitched to the Man—we called him an Uncle Tom. By the time the guys got there he had the MPs outside, a couple of lieutenants and a major. They took the names and said, "You're under arrest, go back to quarters."

We had sent about 60 when it was my turn. The guy at the Club told me, "You can't come in here." A major there told me I was under arrest. They say I pushed him out of the way and forced my way in.

Spann Watson had just arrived:

I rented an apartment, and my pretty new wife had me putting up curtains when someone knocked on the door. They said, "Spann, we're going to the Officers' Club tonight. I know you're going with us."

Three or four people had already gotten arrested, but I had a pretty good reputation. I wouldn't take any bullshit from the white folks.

They were trying to make us sign a statement that we wouldn't go in certain buildings. I called Hook Jones, a captain, and said, "Don't sign that statement. Go to the club and go in there."

He gave me holy hell! "Who are you to tell me what to do?"

I said, "I thought we were all for the same cause, trying to change the situation. If you're not, I am, so forget it!"

Then I told Chappie James what they were doing. "Don't let them force you to sign any paper."

He said, "I got you, Spann. I'm with you. I'll get the order out." That's the difference between the two men. Some people try to knock Chappie James and say he didn't participate, but goddam, I know first-hand he did.

I said, "Let's go see if we can get some more of the guys." I went to see some of the brothers, knocked on their doors.

Some of them said, "Look, I'm making more money now than I ever made in my life, and you guys are fouling it up. No, I'm not going."

Bill Ellis and I went and were arrested.

In all, 101 were arrested. Jamison was not among them. James:

I had gotten a lot of publicity selling war bonds and so forth, so it would have been poor public relations to arrest me. But the "mutiny" shut down the whole operation. We played bridge or volleyball and wrote to our contacts in the civilian world.

Selway finally closed the Club altogether. Wiley:

There was anarchy on the base. There just wasn't any control. Colonel Selway would walk around, and nobody saluted. No black guys would salute white guys. They had the rank, but there was no respect for them. It was chaos. Selway was supposed to be the commander, but he didn't command.

I couldn't understand how a colonel could allow his command to deteriorate so badly. What colonel would have permitted the arrest of a hundred and one of his officers? He should have guarded against that, but he just wanted to settle a score.

Had he been our commander in Europe, I don't see how in the world we could have succeeded. Or suppose we had had a commander like Momyer. We wouldn't have made it, and that would have been the end of aviation for the American colored man

B.O. Davis was a good commander. We all looked up to him. Without Davis, we wouldn't have made the progress we made. If it hadn't been for his tenacity to get the best from his troops, we wouldn't have succeeded.

Good troops are well led.

Meantime, the 101 were unceremoniously lined up and taken to Godman Field by C-47s "with a whole bunch of MPs on board." They were put in a BOQ (Bachelor Officer Quarters), with big lights on outside the building, which was cordoned off with MPs walking around.

Watson:

For the next several weeks we helped direct "the Freeman Field Movement." We were organized and had more telephone calls going out than they had coming in. Coleman Young was running the show, and we were sending out news bulletins.

My wife would drive by in my beautiful convertible that I had gotten in the fight over. We'd throw notes and news releases to her, and she would drop them in the mail box.

One of the "Guardhouse lawyers" was Bump Coleman, who later became Secretary of Transportation under President Gerald Ford. Coleman contacted Thurgood Marshall. Watson contacted Judge William Hastie, who had been Secretary of War Stimson's assistant for civil rights.

He wanted a copy of the reprimand, so we agreed we'd meet in the Howard University library at nine P.M. that same day. I didn't arrive until ten, after the library was closed, but he was still sitting in the library lobby waiting for me.

He wrote the rebuttal, and the Air Force didn't have a leg to stand on.

When they saw we weren't going to give in, we were marched between rows of heavily armed soldiers and flown back to Godman.

As an added insult, Watson said:

There were some German prisoners of war sweeping up the service station at Fort Knox, and they'd go to the Brown Hotel in Louisville on passes. We couldn't even go *near* the Brown Hotel.

Terry:

They were going to give 101 guys reprimands but court martial three of us. I was one of the three lucky ones. I was charged with pushing an officer, mutiny, treason, and incitement to riot.

Lieutenant Bill Parker's mother was the chief housekeeper in the White House, a personal friend of Eleanor Roosevelt. He flew to the White House and talked to his momma, she would talk to Eleanor, Eleanor would talk to Franklin, and he would say, "Let my people be free."

But Eleanor was in Hyde Park, New York and Franklin was down in Warm Springs Georgia for rest and relaxation.

The joke at that time was Roosevelt said, "The Germans gave us hell in Europe, the Japanese are giving us hell in the Far East, and now the colored people are giving me hell at home."

I was put in jail on April 5. Roosevelt died April 12th. The new President was Harry Truman, whom we didn't know.

First, he was from the South.

Second, I knew he had been sponsored by Boss Pendergast, who was anti-us—everyone in the South was, and maybe half in the North too. We didn't know what Truman was going to do.

I spent three months by myself. Nobody could speak to me. I had to knock on the door and ask the corporal of the guard to get the officer of the guard to take me to the bathroom. On the hour, every hour, they asked who you were. It was a pain in the ass. After a month and a half, I said, Hell, I gotta get some exercise. Ten o'clock at night, three nights a week, they'd take me to the gym and I'd shoot baskets.

People like A. Phillip Randolph of the Brotherhood of Pullman Porters, Senator Robert LaFollette of Wisconsin, and Judge Hastie brought political pressure. So did the black newspapers. Congressman Vito Marcantonio [a Socialist from New York] sent legal help.

My mother was from Goldfield Nevada, and one of her classmates was the Senator from Nevada; he said, "Why didn't you call me earlier?" Senator Hiram Johnson of California was also in on the deal.

The one who helped most was Helen Gahagan Douglas, the Congress-woman from Los Angeles. [In 1946 she would would lose a bruising reelection campaign to Richard Nixon, who accused her of being a Communist.]

That was the situation when Davis arrived in June, accompanied by General Ira Eaker, now acting commanding general of the Air Force, replacing Hap Arnold.

Davis was wearing a brand new star of a brigadier general, the second black to wear one in U.S. history. The other, of course, was his father.

Watson:

Eaker got all the blacks on one side of the auditorium and all the whites on the other and said, "Here are your new officers [indicating Davis and his staff]. And these people"—the entire white complement at the base—"are fired."

Eaker added: "It was upon my recommendation and insistence that General Davis is to take command, because of the excellent work I saw him do overseas."

Davis was also named commander of Freeman Field. "And that," said Watson, "was how the first black officer became commander of a U.S. Air Force base."

Most of the white civilians walked off their jobs, so Davis sent for black WACs to replace them. When the civilians wanted their jobs back, they were told, "Too late."

"We got rid of all the white personnel," Gleed said. "I became base Operations Officer, and we started training in earnest."

With war raging in the Pacific, General MacArthur was desperately in need of trained pilots—he said he would take "anyone who will fight." But the training of the 477th had virtually come to a standstill for a year and they had never dropped a bomb in combat. Before it could leave the States, Japan had surrendered.

Hunter and Selway had taken an entire fighter-bomber Group out of the war more effectively than the combined German and Japanese military forces could have.

Four days later a court martial convened to try the "mutineers."

Terry:

> I didn't see my lawyer until the day I was court-martialled. A buddy of mine was Thurgood Marshall of the NAACP. My brother and mother got in touch with Thurgood, and he got in touch with Ted Berry, a fraternity brother of mine and a damn good lawyer. Ted was later the first black mayor of Cincinnati and number-two man in the Peace Corps under Sargent Schriver.
>
> We had four hours to prepare. That's all.
>
> Our defense was: The order given was illegal. All colored people can't be "trainees"—how the hell are you going to "train" a doctor? [Black officers in the medical corps were classified as trainees.]

Wiley, one of the members of the court, recalled:

> It was strictly a black board; I don't know why Hunter set it up that way, he should have made a mixed thing of it. But it turned out better in retrospect. There was no pressure at all, especially from the command that left with Selway. They all came in to testify and saluted the flag, and George Knox [the senior member of the court] reminded them they had to salute the court, which they reluctantly did.
>
> We found only one man guilty, Terry. He admitted he had pushed the major, and he was a second lieutenant, so we had to find him guilty. We fined him $50. At General Hunter's First Air Force headquarters, they raised it to $150.

And with that the Godman Field "Mutiny" was over.

The Baltimore *Afro-American* newspaper asked why Hunter and Selway had not been court martialed? They were the ones who had violated the law.

Howard Baugh had an experience that underscored how unnecessary the whole episode had been. When his tour in Europe was over:

> I went to Lubbock, Texas to an instrument instructor school with Charlie Hall, Ed Toppins, and Bill Melton. We drove up to the main gate, and the MP told us to get out and take our luggage out, without an explanation. We wondered what we were running into.
>
> A staff car came out and the driver took us right to base headquarters; the base commander, Colonel Estes, wanted to see us.

We reported to him, and he said, "I want to welcome you to the base. This base is open for your use." He said he was a classmate of Colonel Davis and gave us his office phone and home phone. "If you have any trouble at all, call me up, day or night."

Everyone had been briefed and warned that we were to be treated like everyone else, and we were. We didn't have a bit of trouble.

Bob Deiz had a similar experience:

They sent me to Louisiana, which was a fighter field, as a supervisor and I got along well. It was strange, this prejudice we ran into—some places it was awful and some places there wasn't any at all.

Meanwhile, when the rest of the Red Tails arrived home from Europe, they discovered that some things had not changed.

There were no victory parades for the 332nd down Broadway. Buddy Huntly added: "The city of Los Angeles never gave any recognition to us. No parade. Nothing. It happened in New York, too. That stayed with you quite a bit."

Bill Melton:

We came back to an ungrateful country, just like the Vietnam veterans did.

I was married to a very light-skinned young woman who appeared to be Caucasian. Charles Hall, Willie Fuller, myself, and our wives went to the bus station in Tuskegee to go to Montgomery to do some Christmas shopping, and when the bus driver used some nasty language, I saw red and went after him.

Willie grabbed me and knocked the hell out of me. He said, "Don't you know you can get killed?" But I just forgot where I was.

Another time when I went into the train station to buy a ticket for my wife, I was wearing the uniform of my country with my decorations and wings. There was no one at the colored ticket window, so I went over to the white side. A little 12 year-old kid was very insulting. A kid! This kind of treatment left scars. Those scars will never disappear.

Spann Watson couldn't get a motel room, even in Pennsylvania. The owner flipped off the "vacancy" sign when Spann arrived, and flipped it back on when he left. "That was so routine."

Happily, Walter Palmer had a better reception.

My wife and I spent ten wonderful days in Atlantic City on R&R. We immediately went to a black hotel. We knew we wouldn't be welcome in a white hotel. But we told the manager we were expecting a call from the US Army. Sure enough, we got this notification to report to the Ritz-Carleton on the boardwalk: There was a room for us.

The black hotel manager said, "If you can get a room in the Ritz-Carleton Hotel, I'm not even going to charge you for last night's rent." He was so proud to see one of our kind getting a room in one of the swankiest hotels.

While we were there, we met many of the bomber crews we had escorted. They were always asking, "Were you members of the Red Tails?" Naturally I answered in the affirmative. They'd say, "Oh, there was a time when my buddy was hit, and some Red Tails escorted him back to safety. Come on, have a drink on me."

A few of us black officers and our wives went out bowling one night with a bunch of white officers. We waited an unusually long time until finally the alleys were clearing up. "How come we can't bowl?" one of the white officers asked.

The manager said, "The pin boys won't set up the pins for a mixed group like you."

So the officer said, "Let's ask the pin boys then."

They said, "We don't care, we get paid for setting up pins; we don't care who knocks them down."

So we spent an enjoyable evening bowling. As I've written in my book, *Flying With Eagles*, the manager must have figured, "What's this world coming to when blacks can walk around with wings on and overseas ribbons and socialize with white officers and their wives?"

However, the civilian airlines gave the Red Tails a different reception.

Buddy Huntly: "I tried to get a job, but we weren't accepted—it was hard to get into these defense plants like Lockheed and Douglas."

Like many others, Brown applied as a civilian pilot, and arrived for an interview at Eastern Airlines, but a secretary kept him waiting all day until closing time. As Brown got up to go, he suddenly remembered something and turned back just in time to see the secretary toss his application in the waste basket.

Roscoe Brown went to work as a social welfare investigator at $1800 a year, "which was a cultural shock," before teaching physiology and anatomy at New York University, one of the first blacks to join the faculty there. He later became Dean of Bronx Community College.

Harry Sheppard:

The aviation industry wasn't ready to absorb us. It absorbed a lot of mechanics—they were unseen faces. But I think the airlines had to service all kinds of communities, and they were afraid that if people were to see a black face on a pilot up there, they would lose business.

Bernard Knighten:

I had only 300 hours of multi-engine flying time, all in twin-engine bombers. There were thousands of white pilots with thousands of hours in the same type of airplanes the airlines were using. Why would they hire me and train me?

I went back to the railroads as a waiter until the fall of 1946, when I used my GI Bill and entered law school. To make ends meet, I was editing and publishing a magazine and waiting tables at night in Brooklyn.

Charles Bussey bought two surplus training planes and went into business for himself, towing signs and dropping political leaflets. It took a year to pay for the planes, and he decided to go back into Service.

Jimmy Fischer:

It was harder getting into civilian aviation than getting into the military. I put in an application, but I was an old man when they finally hired blacks, in the 1970s, I believe.

A fellow who had five or six drive-in theaters in Brockton gave me a job towing a sign, advertising the theaters. Then I was crop dusting gypsy moths up in Maine, blueberries in New Hampshire, and spraying mosquitoes around Brockton. But the DDT killed everything else too, so they cut that out.

Dick Macon went back to Alabama and, against all advice, joined the Alabama National Guard until officials used his wartime injuries as an excuse to put him out.

So he and Chief Anderson bought a couple of planes and started a flying school. They dropped leaflets over black neighborhoods "to tell them the air belonged to all of us." They offered Sunday rides for five dollars, and business was so good they bought three more planes.

Traffic was bogged down with people. Bull Connor (who became notorious in the 1960s for using police dogs and fire hoses on Civil Rights demonstrators) was police chief at that time. He had to provide police for us, and he didn't like that too much.

I had one run-in with Bull Connor. We were on our base leg, about to land, and Bull Connor's twin-engine airplane was taxiing to take off. The landing airplane has priority, so the tower asked him to hold position, and we came in and landed.

The next day he made an announcement on the radio: "They held up my airplane so some nigger could land. If they ever do that again, I'll close the airport."

Macon became a mathematics professor and was called to Detroit to teach in a black high school—a professor teaching high school.

I've devoted a great deal of time to monitoring young people *pro bono*. I enjoy getting kids jobs, seeing that they get scholarships, and sending them to the Air Force Academy. When I talk to youngsters, I let them know that the tunnel is not as dark as it seems to be. Hope reigns eternal, so don't give up hope but make plans about how you're going to escape and be what you want to be.

Many Tuskegee Airmen decided to stay in the Air Force.

Palmer and Lee Archer drove from New York for Tuskegee in a snowstorm. Palmer was sleeping in the back seat when the car went off the road in Virginia. Archer suffered a broken leg.

Palmer had a fractured skull and lost a lot of blood while they lay in the rain for some time until a civilian ambulance arrived; then they lay on the roadside some more until a military ambulance was dispatched. The closest military hospital, McGuire Army General near Richmond, did not admit blacks, so the ambulance proceeded to an Air Force hospital.

However, on the way, the driver decided that Palmer was close to death and rushed him to Army General because "if I didn't survive, the record of my admittance could be expunged." Archer was taken to the Air Force hospital.

When Palmer came to three days later, he learned that the nerve in one eye had been severed and could never be repaired.

> I could never fly military aircraft again. I could stay in the Air Force, but without being able to fly again, my heart would break every time I heard a plane taking off. After five months in the hospital, I voluntarily retired on a lieutenant's pension.

Palmer tried stock car racing with his brother, but when his brother was killed, Walter decided to give it up and bought a service station in Indianapolis.

Ed Toppins married the widow of Sidney Brooks. Top himself was killed in a plane crash, leaving his wife a Tuskegee widow for the second time.

Harry Sheppard became a B-25 instructor at Tuskegee, then was assigned to Westover AFB in Massachusetts to support the Berlin Airlift.

Watson helped reorganize the 99th as a part of the composite 477th Fighter-Bomber Group. "We had some of the most experienced fighter pilots in the business, and I was one of them. When I got through, the squadron was second to no one."

Among its members was one of the martyrs in the fight for the right to fly combat—Yancey Williams, the man whose lawsuit had paved the way for all those who followed. Watson said:

> They had put him in the infantry and wouldn't let him out until the war was almost over. That's the price he had to pay for being the complainant

against Hap Arnold. Williams made his way through combat flight training and they were going to put him in B-25s. I got him into the 99th, so
he finally got where he wanted to go. He went to Germany as an engineer
officer and test pilot and was killed in 1953 in an F-86.

Would the post-war armed forces be segregated or integrated?

The Marines had already integrated, although, as the Washington
Afro-American headline noted:

18,000 BLACK MARINES,
NO BLACK OFFICERS

In February 1946 the War Department named a blue ribbon panel of
generals to study the question.

Generals Eaker, Touey Spaatz, and Ned Almond of the 92nd Division,
B.O. Davis, his father, Colonel Noel Parrish, and others testified.

Eaker believed that both whites and blacks would do their best work
when segregated.

Spaatz said he didn't think Negros "could stand the pace" when integrated alongside whites.

Parrish declared simply, "Whether we dislike or like the Negro," they
are citizens under the Constitution with the same rights as all citizens.

The panel concluded that segregation was still desirable and the same
segregation that existed before the war would continue after it.

Then, in 1948, history was made. President Harry S Truman faced a
seemingly impossible uphill fight in the election. The South had walked
out of the party, and he needed every vote he could get. That summer he
issued a fateful order:

> It is hereby declared to be the policy of the President that there shall be
> equality of treatment and opportunity for all persons in the armed services
> without regard to race, color, religion, or national origin. This policy shall be
> put into effect as rapidly as possible.

There was strong opposition, however, as B.O. Davis pointed out:

> The Army Chief of Staff, Omar Bradley, told Truman bluntly that the
> Army was not going to have anything to do with social reform. And it didn't
> do a thing about that Executive Order.

Gleed:

> In spite of themselves, the top brass of the Air Force were less
> bound and determined to keep the segregated ways. Everything didn't

flow rapidly; there were still diehard officers. Hap Arnold may have been one of them.

Roberts:

> There were still officers who insisted that "this is a hell of a mis-take.... They're no damn good.... They won't.... They can't...."
> I was told that only when Davis was flying as lead did [black] missions suc-ceed. So someone simply went down the missions when Davis wasn't there and recorded what happened in each one. Missions succeeded under every leadership. Everyone who led missions led them successfully.

Roberts said: "Stu Symington, Secretary of the Air Force, made the decision to go with integration. One of the reasons was his meeting with Wendell Pruitt."

"When the war ended," Bill Campbell said, "I think we were the equal of any squadron doing the same thing."

In May 1949, the Air Force conducted its first continental gunnery meet among every fighter Group in the United States, sort of the first "top gun" competition. The 332nd under Campbell sent three pilots: Alva Tem-ple, James Harvey, and Harry Stewart, formerly of the 301st and 302nd in Italy. The overall team winner for piston aircraft was the 332nd, with Temple second in the individual. The 332nd was disbanded about a month later.

Years later, about 1993, Stewart recalled, Campbell was looking at an issue of *Air Force* magazine and saw a list of winners, but the 1949 winners were marked "unknown." Bill sent a letter to the magazine, saying, "Heh, look at your own archives there," because it had been published correctly in the 1949 issue.

In 1996, the magazine made a change but still got it wrong. It mentioned only the individual top gun and again left out the winning Group. Presum-ably the record will be set straight eventually.

Meanwhile, Roberts said:

> During the war, white officers moved up by moving laterally, from one unit to another, wherever a higher vacancy existed. Black officers couldn't do that. When it came to flying, we had as much experience as anyone, but in staff work we were quite short. So when we were integrated, we were one step behind, maybe two.
> But the Tuskegee Airmen were the cream of the crop, and they didn't stay behind long. It took a lot of hard work, but we did catch up. But what if we had started out in an integrated setting?

The light-skinned Cox recalled his first integrated assignment.

> I reported to O'Hare Field, Chicago to Captain Sam Elias in a military fashion: "Sir, Captain Hannibal Cox reporting. Here are my orders, sir."
>
> He said, "Damn, we were expecting a nigger officer."
>
> I said, "Captain, if that's what you were expecting, I think that's what you got."
>
> He and I went on to become very good friends.

Bob Deiz was one of the first lieutenants to go to the Army Command and General Staff School at Fort Leavenworth, which is usually for captains being considered for major.

Watson graduated from the Air Force C&GS at Maxwell Field, Alabama:

> When I went to Maxwell Field, no damn black officer could go to the barbershop. It was many weeks before I broke that down, but it took a lot of courage to have a white woman shaving my neck with a razor.

Ironically, Spann said, integration actually made the future of black officers bleak.

> Here I was, a first lieutenant. There weren't many black captains and almost no majors; the white Air Force was full of them. No matter how much experience you had, if I went to a white unit, with my rank all I could qualify for was a wingman."
>
> Only about 35–40 black pilots stayed in the Service, and most of them were shunted into non-flying roles. "I went to communications, others to weather school, and Bill Campbell, the greatest flight leader we had, went to comptroller school.

The Air Force announced plans to cut 10,000 reservists, and most black officers were reservists. Watson warned that the combination of integration and force reduction would virtually mean the end of black officers in the Air Force.

He headed a study committee, along with Charlie Dryden and George Iles, which urged keeping the 332nd as a pool of experienced black veterans. White lieutenants would be brought to the 332nd for training, while black lieutenants went to white units. Spann was "argumentative, a take-charge guy, very outspoken," Iles smiled. "He told you what he thought all the time."

"Did they give us *hell*!" Watson whistled. Black leaders charged that he wanted to continue segregation, and the few black regular officers told him,

"Don't screw up my career. You're right, but, damn, don't get me mixed up in it."

Chauncey Spencer, by then personnel officer at Lockbourne Field, Ohio, the 332nd's new home, also urged blacks to request transfers to white units in order to spread their talent more broadly; however, he wrote, they balked, fearing competition in an integrated setting.

Watson saw his prediction come true. By 1949, no African Americans were being admitted to the new Air Force Academy, "and everyone I knew had been either grounded or separated. That just about destroyed us.

"The only thing that saved us was the Korean war."

20

Korea and Vietnam

WHEN the North Koreans invaded the South in June 1950, many of the Red Tails strapped themselves back into the cockpit and put in a second combat tour.

Charlie Bussey was the first ex-Red Tail into Korea, and he did it on the ground. When the Air Force became an independent service, Bussey was a reservist in the still segregated Army as a combat engineer. His unit was immediately rushed to Korea from Japan with the 24th Infantry regiment of the 25th Division, the direct descendent of the old Indian-fighting Buffalo Soldiers.

When he arrived, the news was desperate as the North Koreans bowled over the South Korean defenders. The 24th Division, the first to arrive, was almost annihilated and their commander, General William Dean, captured. That very same day Bussey, a company commander, jumped in a jeep for what he thought would be a routine trip to one of his platoons, which was supporting the infantry.

Just my driver and—I had no idea the country was as hostile as it was, or I wouldn't have been out there by myself.

When we arrived at a village called Yech'on, there was a big firefight going on. I climbed a hill, and below me was a series of rice paddies which ran the length of a small valley. I saw a column of about 2–300 men three-quarters of a mile away, coming out of a defilade arroyo, dressed in white like Korean farmers. I could have driven away, but if they cut the road, there would be no getting out for our troops.

I pressed into service three enlisted men. I put two men on a .30-caliber water-cooled machine gun. I had an air-cooled .50-caliber, and I got one man to feed me ammunition. I let the column move in close enough so they wouldn't be able to back out, and put a burst over their heads. They immediately took cover, someone blew a whistle, and things started happening! They started to move toward my hill.

I was scared shitless, absolutely shitless! I had no business facing that many people, whether out of stupidity, drunkenness, or for any other reason. I kept thinking, "God damn it! Why didn't you mind your own business!" I didn't think I was going to get out of that thing. But now that I was engaged,

I didn't have any alternative. There was no place to run to and nothing to do except fight. Air combat was sort of a game. Ground combat is not a game— it is dead serious action on the killing floor.

I had a tremendous advantage by virtue of being up on a hill, and I had fairly good cover, while they were down in a rice paddy with almost no protection. But they had a mortar behind them, and it put several bursts on us. I got hit early with a fragment in my wrist and another in my cheek. They bled a little, but a small wound was not important at that time.

The mortar also killed one of my kids on the .30 and wounded the other. My big gun got hot and stopped firing. That's when I was in real trouble. I didn't think the .30 could do the job, but there was no other way, so I went down and manned the .30 and kept the fire up.

It's very difficult to estimate time in a firefight. It must have been seven to ten minutes, but it seemed very prolonged, because things were happening so fast.

I shot them up pretty effectively and continued to fire until they were all still. I took troops down, and we found a few of the enemy still alive but badly maimed. Since we were probably 50 miles from the nearest doctor, we helped them on their way as an act of mercy. We made a body count—258 bodies. It was a grisly business.

"Thou shalt not kill." That troubled me at the time. It's still not a thing I have fully resolved.

The 25th Division commander, General Keane, came up to our bivouac and passed out some ribbons and told me the Division was going to recommend me for the Medal of Honor. He said as soon as the paperwork was in, he'd forward it.

That was the first U.S. victory of the war. MacArrthur's headquarters hailed it, and U.S. papers headlined it on page one, although Bussey's role was ignored.

The feat is a subject of controversy, and the Army still refuses to recognize it. There were few eyewitnesses, although several gave affidavits supporting Charlie's claim. However, three of them died before Army investigators could reach them.

The most compelling evidence is the photo of a mass grave, which a 24th Infantry sergeant, Alfonso Spencer, identified as the grave he dug out with a bulldozer and photographed two days later.

[In 1918, Sergeant Alvin York became America's most decorated soldier and received the Congressional Medal of Honor for single-handedly killing 25 German soldiers and capturing 131st. At Bastogne, in 1944, Jose Lopez was credited with killing 100 enemy with his machine gun and received a Medal of Honor. In 1945, Audie Murphy won a CMH for killing "about 50" enemy in one fight.]

Ten days later Bussey and his men were sleeping in a schoolhouse:

Right at midnight artillery began coming in. I started yelling and getting the troops out of the building, through the yard, and out the back gate. When the last man was out, just as I went through the gate, a round blew up the mines and threw a twelve-foot mud and rock wall over on top of me.

It was my tomb.

There was three or four feet of rubble on top of me. My head was under it, but I could breathe. I was in a sitting position, but my head was bent over, and rocks were pinching me.

I exhausted myself trying to get out, but the weight of rubble was too much. I had to sit there completely penned all day. It was the most devastating experience of my life.

I was cold. I was hungry. Never in my life have I been so thirsty. An insect crawled into my inner ear; it felt as big as a turtle, but I was powerless to scratch. My eyes and nose were filled with dust. I was hours overdue for urination. I ached in every fiber. I lost consciousness.

When I came to, my sphincter had failed. One thigh, hand, and arm were wet, and it felt as if ten thousand ants were crawling over them.

I recited the 91st psalm, and the 23rd: "The Lord is my shepherd." I had a lot of religious—and blasphemous—thoughts. "Why me, Lord?" And a towering voice chilled me: "*Why not you? Why NOT you?*"

At about 4:30 in the afternoon, the sun warmed the rubble, and I began to hear artillery in the distance and even small arms fire. Finally, I could hear very faint speech and felt that people were close by me. I yelled.

A voice said, "Hey! It sounds like one of the mothafuckas is under that stuff there"—that's when I knew they weren't North Koreans. "Take that rubble off, and I'll shoot him." They dug down to my helmet, and I heard someone yell, "Hey, this is a captain!"

They pulled me out and stretched me on the ground. Few men have ever come back from their tombs, but by five or six o'clock I was ready to go again. There was work to be done. My faith was restored, and I had a reunion with God.

But for 15 or 20 years, any time I was on my back, almost asleep, I felt millions of oriental soldiers double timing over my grave, until I'd wake up in the middle of the night screaming.

Corporal John French:

Lieutenant Bussey was our company commander, a hell of an officer. He knew what he wanted to adopt—a straightforward, cocky son of a bitch.

When we got into combat, we found out Bussey wasn't scared either. I wasn't at the firefight at Ye'chon, but Sergeant Fields said, "You should have been there and seen how Bussey was machine-gunning them down."

If you've got an officer who's scared, he spooks the whole unit. But an officer with a lot of courage, it flows down. We would follow Bussey into hell with gas-soaked clothes on.

Soon after Yech'on one of Bussey's squads was cut off 20 miles behind enemy lines. They were out of food and water, and several men were badly wounded. Bussey's CO ordered him not to go to the rescue, because it was in enemy territory and too dangerous. Charlie flat-out disobeyed. One of his men, LaVaughn Fields, told about it:

> Bussey called the company together: "I want volunteers to step forward." The whole company stepped forward, including the cooks.
> "Saddle up." The order was passed.
> As we passed through our lines, the checkpoint guards asked, "Where you guys going?"
> "To get our goddam wounded out, that's where."
> They gave us a thumbs-up and hollered, "Give 'em hell."
> We drove behind enemy lines, then hiked on back trails around low hills out of sight until we came into "Death Valley." It might have been five miles—no more than ten miles. We walked all day, and toward the evening, we hit the hill.

French:

> When we turned off the trail, we came upon three or four black GIs killed the week before. They had their hands tied behind them, their ears were cut off, their noses cut off, and there was puss coming out of them. You never saw so much puking in your life.

Fields:

> The CO told Sergeant Whitaker, "Take the third platoon up on the high ground. Lieutenant Wills' second platoon, you take the saddle [between the hills]. Sergeant Green, you take the left side." Bussey took the fourth Platoon, with Sergeant Knight, to go in and perform the rescue.
> "Tell the men to shoot to kill." And he said, "If you fuck this up, I'll have your ass when we return."
> Whitaker told me to take my squad up on the high point, "because you can command the area with the .50-calibre machine gun. Give a burst of three rounds when you're in position. That's the signal for Knight to move in."
> I got up on the hill and set the .50 up and hollered, "Test fire!" and kicked off some rounds.
> That was the signal for Knight and the CO to take off up the hill and down the other side to where the dead and wounded were.
> Minutes later a squad of North Korean soldiers appeared. I gave the command, "Cut loose," and my squad ate them up—we blew them away. The rest took off.

French:

> Bussey walked around, hunched over, calling: "Chet? Chet?"
>
> We heard Lieutenant Lenon's voice say, "I knew you were coming. What took you so long?"
>
> Getting out of there, we came under more fire. Burp guns basically—if you've ever heard one, you know what it sounds like. We wanted to get out before dark, and Bussey did the fastest memorial service you ever want to see.
>
> We were under fire until we got over the crest of the mountain.

Fields:

> As we moved through the checkpoint, the GIs cheered.
>
> Bussey and I were recommended for the Silver Star, but Division downgraded it to a Bronze Star. For a black person, this is nothing new. If a white boy had done it, it would have been different. Yes, it happened—it happened many times.

Bussey would make history later when two white lieutenants, both southerners, were assigned to his company, the first time in Army history a black had ever commanded whites.

Meantime, three different regimental commanders sat on Bussey's Medal of Honor.

> Months went by, and finally, the last commander, John Corley, a white man, told me, "Well, I thought I should downgrade this thing" to a Silver Star, the Army's third highest medal. He changed "258" enemy killed to "numerous" enemy. He was a drinking "friend" of mine, so I asked him why.
>
> He said, "I belong to a group who believe it's our responsibility to keep Negroes in their place, and the most effective way is to deny them leadership. Then there's never any threat to anyone. If the medal was posthumous, no problem. Or if you were an inarticulate enlisted man, I would have no objection. But being who you are, you'd be out encouraging Negroes to do the things you do." Without leadership, Negroes were harmless, he said, but with leaders they could be a threat of some kind. "Our country can't afford this, and that's my considered opinion."
>
> We were almost at the Yalu River on the Chinese border. That's when I found that whites can run as fast as blacks. Winter came on viciously, and I didn't have time to worry about medals.

Two African-American enlisted men did receive Medals of Honor, the first ones since the Spanish-American War. William Thompson slowed an enemy advance with machine gun fire. Though badly wounded, he refused orders to withdraw and was killed.

Twenty-one-year-old Cornelius Charlton led troops up a steep hill through a rain of grenades. Although wounded in the chest, he led three charges and was finally killed, still firing from the top of the hill.

However, not until Captain Wiley Pitts was honored posthumously in Vietnam did a black officer receive the highest award.

Meanwhile the Air Force put out an emergency order for P-51 pilots to report. Japan-based jet fighters had only enough fuel to stay over their Korean targets for a few minutes, but the workhorse P-51 could stay aloft for hours.

Bussey remembered stopping his jeep when someone called his name. He looked up to see George Gray. Charlie followed him to his hootch for a big reunion with eight or nine Tuskegee Airmen—Red Jackson, Peepsight Smith, Evil N. Smith and others. "We laughed and talked and had a good time. Every damn one of them got shot down. Most of them died—the Koreans were tremendous gunners."

Charles McGee was stationed in the Philippines when the war broke out:

> On the 19th of August 1950, I was riding a P-51 down the runway of Johnson Air Base, Japan. When we landed in Korea, the engineers were still laying a thousand feet of steel planking on our runway. That night I slept under the wing of my plane. The next day we were flying combat.
>
> On one mission supporting the 24th Division, I attacked gun emplacements on a hillside. I was on my dive, firing, with shells going by me just as fast as I was pouring the .50-caliber rounds out on them. About two-thirds of the way down, I took a hit in the left wing and had to break away. It was at least a 20-mm hole, much larger than a half dollar. I'm glad it was out there on the wing and not in the cockpit.

In all McGee flew 100 combat missions in Korea.

Bernard Knighten, an aircraft controller at La Guardia Airport, received orders on Friday night to report for active duty the next morning. Saturday night he was on a plane—"next stop, Tokyo."

He was sitting in a base movie theater when the lights went on, MPs took up posts at the doors, and a lieutenant colonel began barking out names: "Get your bags and be at the flight line. You have one hour to be there."

Knighten found himself flying co-pilot on a C-46 transport plane in an all-weather night takeoff with a full load of passengers. I had never been near a C-46 before in my life, and the pilot had never flown on instruments before. Providence was with us. We made it to Korea."

His job was to carry orders to the fighter bases, flying every other night, almost always under bad-weather instrument conditions. When he arrived back home, he was given "a hearty breakfast, a shot of Scotch, and a day off" before doing it again until the flight surgeon took him off the run for exhaustion. "Meanwhile," he said, "you really learned to fly."

One mission was to pick up wounded troops.

> The weather was rainy and miserable, and I was told by the Army captain, if we had any trouble, "Just throw those guys out the door." Of course I wouldn't do that.

They arrived at Pusan out of fuel and found the airfield closed. While they prepared to ditch at sea, they finally found Cheju-do Island in the nick of time. "We were glad to get down alive."

Red Jackson was also rushed into combat:

> I got home off leave on a Saturday morning "They've got your orders already cut, you leave tomorrow." The record for a ship going across was 11 days. We did it in eight. They sent us up on the east coast of Korea and told us to get a brushup training and sent us into combat.
>
> A Major Dean Hess was training South Korean pilots in the P-51 and wanted some volunteers. I should have known better. You know what they say in the Army: "Keep your head up, your other part down, and never volunteer." But I volunteered. I trained them until we started pushing the North Koreans back.
>
> Korea wasn't a very exhilarating war. In Europe there was more of a spirit to get the war done: We were going to fight that war and fight it to the end. But in Korea we weren't too sure what was going to happen.

Shortly after the Inchon landing, Knighten's unit moved up by land to be the first outfit in Pyongyang, the North Korean capital:

> We flew missions up to the Chinese border and down the roads, attacking everything we could.
>
> The North Korean troops pushed civilians ahead of them. We learned that to our great sorrow: Refugees would go behind our lines and hit us in the back. They shot one mechanic in the back out on the runway one morning.
>
> So we said, "Don't let any more refugees come down that road." They had women and children among them, but we had to turn them back. We used to see bodies floating in the river, didn't know who killed them. You didn't know who was who.
>
> I was given a mission with one of the Korean pilots of strafing the sampan boats coming across a river. I said, "Shoot a few bursts in front of them."
>
> "They're not turning back."
>
> "OK, destroy them."

My wingman didn't want to do that. When they got to the shore, we could see soldiers from the first boat dashing into the bull rushes as fast as they could go to get hidden and become guerrillas. We said, "We're not going to let any more go," and went back and shot up the other five boats. We knew there were women and children aboard. That bothered me very much. It was a vicious, cruel war.

Then, all hell broke loose: The Chinese started coming down.

That night Knighten was given another emergency mission. "The only cargo aboard was an ice cream machine for some general at the farthest northern air base our troops controlled." When they arrived, the retreat had begun. "The only people left were some firemen who had trucks loaded with napalm to burn everything so the Chinese couldn't take it"—planes, plus tents and warehouse filled with clothing and ammunition. The Chinese were virtually across the road.

All of us ran over and got all the fur-lined jackets and high-top boots we could carry. They loaded as many GI's as they could carry and we left in a hurry. I don't know what happened to the general's ice cream machine.

On "another awful trip," Knighten flew a load of ammunition to Marines trapped in a valley on the east coast. "When we arrived, there was no airfield," only a tiny, primitive airstrip, already littered with wrecked planes that had run off the end. The pilot, "an old crop duster," switched off his engine, stomped on the brakes and stopped just in time. "Dead marines were stacked like cordwood along the runway." The crew unloaded their cargo, turned around, gave the plane full throttle and barely cleared one of the wrecked planes. "Needless to say, operations to that field were discontinued almost immediately."

Returning from another fight to the North, Knighten "lived through another of the many crashes in my flying career." On landing, the plane suddenly veered to the right into an embankment, shearing off both engines. "I sat there, trying to figure out what happened." He learned later that the flight engineer, a fresh reservist, had raised the landing-gear handle before landing.

When I looked up, the general was outside, yelling at me, "Get out, get out!" I jumped out the window and sank ankle-deep into gasoline from a ruptured tank. My luck held out one more time, but one spark and it would have been the end of the whole crew.

Jackson was in the thick of the action:

The Korean pilots had stopped flying and Colonel Hess and I were going up to attack the Chinese facing the Second Division. The Americans were in full retreat, the Chinese were chasing them, and we were trying to kill as many of them as we could.

We were doing very close ground attack when I heard the plane get hit. Black smoke from the engine cowling covered my windshield with smoke and oil, and I couldn't see. The P-51 has portholes on each side, and fire was coming out of them. I cut the gas off to keep it from feeding the fire, turned around and tried to get back to where the Americans were—there were no "lines."

I got ready to bail out. The enemy were still very close, and Colonel Hess says, "Don't jump yet, you're almost there."

There were a lot of hills and valleys and I was losing altitude fast. Colonel Hess said, "You're there now, it's safe to jump." I yanked my cord, and the canopy flew off, but I could see trees beside me, and I knew I didn't have enough altitude to bail out, so I straightened my plane out. Unfortunately I had ripped my seatbelt open and had no time to fasten it again.

I said, "I'm going to land on this road." I looked out the side of the windshield, and there in front of me were cars, bikes, jeeps, everything, a stream of vehicles bumper-to-bumper, running as fast as they could. I was going to land on *that*?

So I peeled off to the first little hill I saw, and my wing hit one of the pines and jerked me around. I remember the shock from hitting, then blacked out. An ambulance crew came over and pulled me out before the plane burned me up.

Colonel Hess returned and told the people that Captain Jackson had been killed—burned up. They packed my belongings and sent the word home that I was dead.

A field artillery crew noticed my plane had Korean markings, so when one of my squadron mates' plane conked out, an ambulance rescued him, and said, "What kind of plane you got there? We just rescued a pilot with a marking like that."

Red Jackson wasn't dead!

Two days later I woke up in Japan.

The left side of his head was badly injured, and he almost lost his eyesight. He would never fly again. "I got out of the Air Force then, decided I'd had enough. I was tired of war, tired of killing people.

Hannibal Cox also flew P-51s in Korea and saw action with ground troops following the Chinese attack:

I was forward air controller, directing air strikes. We were encircled and fought our way back.

Color was insignificant.

Those of us with combat experience were relied upon. However, it was different in Japan during R&R; in a social situation we were back to the old ways. There were some in the unit who were hard core and some who were not.

Chappie James finally got into combat, flying 101 missions in jet fighters. Spanky Roberts commanded Suwon Air Base.

Charles Dryden also was rushed to Korea. He said George Gray of the old 99th had "a very distinctive voice. When he was speaking over radio, you knew exactly who was talking." "I yelled. "Is that you, George Gray?" "Yes! Is that you, Charlie Dryden?"

I was a "mosquito pilot" in a tactical air control Squadron flying 50 missions in 33 days in light T-6 trainers. We were the link between the ground controller and the tactical air control headquarters. We were the eyes of Tactical Control Center.

One day on patrol I was able to detect Korean caches of weapons and had fighters blast them to hell and gone. There was so much notoriety about it, a news reporter, Ben Price, came to my outfit and asked to let him ride in my back seat and see the hulks that were damaged.

We had some more action that afternoon. At one point troops on the ground reported getting fire from a hill, and what could I do about it? I started making diving passes at the hill. "What are you doing that for?" Price said.

"Trying to get them to shoot at me to see their muzzle flashes," I said.
"What! You're crazy!"
I said, "We do that every day."

Woody Crockett worked on the development of the F-86 fighter, the jet workhorse of Korea. In 1951, he was radiological safety officer for an atomic bomb test in the Pacific and visited "shot island" the day after the blast: In North Korea he flew an F-80 Shooting Star jet:

I reported in May 1952, to the 8th Fighter-Bomber Wing, about eight minutes due south of the Demilitarized Zone as the base flight safety officer. I wasn't supposed to fly combat, but since you had to give the pilots a briefing on safety every one or two weeks, I told my wing commander there was no way I could gain the respect of these young guys if I didn't fly myself. I flew 45 missions.

I think we ended up with the lowest accident rate of any flying tactical unit in Korea at that time.

I was hit twice in Europe, around Naples, and once in Korea over Pyongyang on a dive-bombing mission. It must have caught me going down in the dive, because it stuck in the topside of the wing.

Woody won a second Soldier's Medal.

I was in my jeep, midway on the 900-foot runway when I saw an F-86 taking off with full power and his nose wheels still on the ground. I knew he was going to crash if he didn't abort, because he couldn't pick up the nose up at that speed. So I just turned my jeep around and followed him to the end of the runway. He ran out of runway, ran three hundred more feet over a railroad track, and dropped off into a rice paddy 300 feet below.

I drove up to the railroad tracks and went down and tried to pull him out as the aircraft began to burn. I'd pull him up to the top of the cockpit, but he had on this heavy suit and boots, and he'd slump back.

I didn't want to stay there and get killed in an explosion, but I couldn't leave him in there to die either. I waved at the crash crew at the top of the hill and finally got someone to come down, and we pulled him away.

Crockett almost won a third:

A British pilot came to pick up his aircraft, which had had a wing replaced. He went up for a test hop and lost his engine on the final approach and crashed into a dump just off the runway. His left wing broke off, and he had a two-inch hole in the fuel line from the wing tanks. We could see the gas pouring out, and if it hit a hot surface, the whole plane could explode.

He was inside there, apparently injured, and couldn't get out. The canopy was closed, it was operated electronically, and we couldn't figure out how to open it. We were worried about creating a spark, trying to keep anybody from walking over there with a cigarette. We finally opened it and got him out, but it had been close to becoming a catastrophe.

On another occasion, Crockett received a famous visitor:

Ted Williams was returning from a mission flying Panther jets out of Pohang and we were the closest air base to the front line. He made a left turn overhead and came in for a landing when he heard an explosion over the field. A piece of the plane dropped off, and you could see the flames coming out of his airplane.

They tried to get him to bail out, but he crash-landed wheels up and skidded on his belly exactly 6,200 feet, heading for the kids in the ambulance. They had to roll up their windows, and he stopped just short of them.

When he got out, he looked at the bullet holes in his plane and said, "They were *shooting* at me!"

I said, "You're darn right they were."

I had to do a lot of paper work on that.

I had lunch with him. His birthday is one day different from mine. I was born August 31, 1918, and he was born August 30.

The next day he was on another mission and landed at our field again. I said, "Ted, are you back to give me more paper work?"

He said, "No, Major, I'm only short of fuel today."

In the election, Dwight Eisenhower made a pledge to go to Korea and end the war. Crockett recalled:

> They got everybody airborne again, just like when Roosevelt visited Italy. So I flew protection for President Roosevelt and for President-elect Eisenhower. Not too many guys get that chance.

Charles Hill was in the reserves and volunteered for active duty in Korea. Instead of orders, he got a special delivery letter from the War Department charging him with being a Communist! Hill's sister was a member of a leftist university student group. His father, a Detroit Baptist minister, was active in civil rights, and when Paul Robeson was denied a hall to sing in in Detroit, he sang in the Reverend Hill's church. ("Fifty percent of the people came to hear Paul," Hill said, "the other 50% were government people who wanted to see who the first 50% were.")

Hill's investigation reached the newspapers, and he began receiving hate letters and calls until he had to disconnect his phone. In the end he received an apology from the Secretary of the Air Force, and all charges were dropped. Still, "I was never called up for Korea, even though experienced fighter pilots were needed."

Chauncey Spencer was also accused of being a Communist. A month after receiving the Air Force's highest civilian award, the accusation arrived in the mail. Neighbors threw garbage on his lawn, he was suspended without pay for nine months, and he was not permitted to have a defense lawyer. Spencer believed it was because he refused to drag his feet on integration. In the end, Secretary of the Air Force William Talbot stood up for him, and he was exonerated. Talbot was later fired by President Eisenhower.

Lucky Lester was flying jets in Europe along the East-West border, playing "peek-a-boo" with Communist migrate jets.

> In 1951, when General Eisenhower decided to come home and run for President, they had a ceremony in Paris to honor the change in command, and our unit was to do a fly-by in F-84s. About fifteen minutes after takeoff, I heard this loud bang and saw my fire-warning light come on right away. I called to my wingman: "What's going on?"
>
> He said, "The Air Force star has burned up on the side of your plane."
>
> I said, "Well, I've got deep problems here. *Auf wiedersehen.*"
>
> They have an ejection seat with a shell, which blows you out of the airplane. I was doing about 450 miles per hour at about 800 feet altitude. In those days the thought was that you should slow the airplane up before you ejected, but obviously, if the star had burned off, the controls were going to go next, and I didn't have time to slow it up. So I pushed the ejection button and started looping through the air doing somersaults, still in my seat. The

minute the controls burned off, the airplane turned straight down to the ground, and I saw it hit with a big explosion.

Before I could open the parachute, I had to get rid of the seat. So I loosened the seat belts and kicked the seat away, and when I saw it clear, I pulled the rip cord, and the parachute opened. All this sounds like it took a long time, but it was probably the space of eight to ten seconds—fifteen at the very most. The funny thing: I wasn't losing much altitude, because of the speed I was traveling.

I landed in a soft, newly plowed field, didn't even sprain an ankle. The SOP [Standard Operating Procedure] was to get to the nearest telephone and let them know where and how you were. The nearest telephone was in a pub.

The other three pilots, who had been circling, came flying down the middle of main street, very low and very noisy, glad that I was OK. That was their salute.

They radioed back to headquarters that I was going into a beer hall to have a beer!

After that the Air Force decided that maybe it wasn't a good idea to slow up before ejecting. Before this, they had encountered a lot of trouble with pilots hitting the airplane. Pilots had been decapitated, had their legs cut off, and things like that. But when nothing happened to me, they decided to try some tests. The results were, you clear the airplane a lot better the faster you go because of the physics involved. I like to believe my ejection started them thinking that faster is better.

That was one of the luckiest things that ever happened to Lucky Lester.

After Korea, McGee returned to the Philippines as commanding officer of the 44th Fighter-bomber Squadron, flying jets. One of his second lieutenants was Frank Borman, who had ear problems and was about it be given a medical discharge. "I bootlegged some hours for him [gave him some unofficial flights], and the flight surgeon relented. Borman credited McGee with saving his flying career:

He was a good, tough squadron commander, as good as I've had in the Air Force, and an important model for me in my Air Force career. I was permanently grounded because of a broken eardrum, and the doctors kept insisting that if I flew again, I'd break the eardrum again.

Major McGee was kind enough to give me a ride unbeknownst to the doctors, and my ear's been fine ever since. He took a chance on me, and I'll always be grateful.

McGee:

I rated Borman as Outstanding. Fifth Air Force came back, saying, "Outstanding is reserved for officers who are ready to take higher level commands." I sent it back unchanged, and this time it didn't come back.

Borman went on to command the first space flight around the moon.

Vietnam

VIETNAM brought a third combat tour for three Red Tails—Cox, McGee, and Charles Cooper. In addition, Knighten was a ground-air controller north of Danang.

Chappie James flew in his second war and went on to make four-star general. "This is my country," he declared. "I will hold her hand, I will fight for her. I shall protect her. But I'll make her treat me the way she should."

Clarence "Red" Driver flew a transport plane out of Cambodia, though several Red Tails believe he was actually a CIA agent. His plane exploded in the air—perhaps sabotaged—killing all aboard.

Cox was a full colonel, a staff officer who flew some F-100 ground-support missions: "Race was not an issue, either operationally or socially. We had good people, and we had a good wing. We were completely integrated in every respect."

Wilson Eagleson had been so unhappy out of the Service after World War II, his wife told him, "You won't be happy until you get back in," so he did, as an enlisted man.

He was stationed in the Philippines airdropping supplies to the French at Dien Bien Phu, when the pilot had a heart attack. Eagleson slipped into the pilot's seat and brought the plane back. He was awarded the Distinguished Flying Cross.

McGee flew an RF-4 reconnaissance jet. They had to fly low and slow over their targets. He told *Aviation History Magazine*:

> The shooting got your adrenaline up. You'd put on more speed, which was about all you could do. You were too busy to dwell on the danger. Many times we had nothing to fire back at the enemy, and in that case, we used speed, at night particularly. You could see the enemy tracers, but they were usually behind you. You could look back and see them, so you knew there was a lot of other lead out there too, but as long as they were behind you, you were safe.
>
> I was on a daylight mission on the trail the Communists were using through Laos into Vietnam. Of course they claimed they weren't doing it, but they were.
>
> I was just dropping down to go to my target, when I took a high-caliber hit, fortunately again out in the left wing. But the loss of fuel meant I wasn't able to get back to my base. I was losing fluids, though I couldn't tell which ones, and I didn't know whether I had enough hydraulic fluid left to use the brakes.
>
> I was able to get to a friendly base at Da Nang on the coast and radioed them to have a tail-hook ready. That was my first tail-hook landing expe

rience. It was also the only time I had to make a front-end engagement landing, using my tail hook to make sure we wouldn't run off the runway. I resumed flying the next day.

When the Tet Offensive broke out, most of the squadron pilots were at our walled compound off base. There were only six of us on base, and for three days we flew all of the squadron's missions. The VC started mortaring the place; we had foxholes, but I'd just put my helmet over my head and stay in bed. Who knew where a round would land? Six or seven of our planes were hit on the ground.

I flew 143 combat missions in Europe, 100 in Korea, and 176 in Southeast Asia; that's 419 total missions and 1100 combat hours.

McGee was probably shot at more than any man in history. The Air Force recognizes him as America's all-time leader in combat missions, and it is doubtful if any other man in another country can touch his record.

21

Final Triumph

In later life many of the Tuskegee Airmen left large footprints. Some went into research.

James Wiley:

> After integration in 1949, I chose Wright Field, heading up a group of German scientists working on supersonic flight. We didn't know yet about going from trans-sonic to super-sonic and back, and we had to do a lot of experiments in the wind tunnel by looking at airflow over a model. I was able to get the contractors and put them all together, and it worked.
>
> Then I became assistant manager of a pilotless aircraft with an atom bomb on its nose, the predecessor of ballistic weapons, and a single-pilot orbiting aircraft, the X-20, the predecessor of the space shuttle.
>
> I had 55 people working for me in my division, the space division. We were assigned to Boeing in Seattle to develop a lunar orbiter to take pictures of the moon in preparation for the lunar landings.

Bob Deiz also went into research:

> I was more proud of what I did after I got out of fighters and into flying experimental planes and electronics. I was at Cambridge Research Center in electronic research. Then I worked at North American Aviation in their weapons analysis group.

Deiz indulged his old love, music. Harry Sheppard remembered when they went to school together at MIT:

> I used to sneak off and go down to a Boston nightclub, the "High Hat." One night I went down there and got a seat right down front, and who sneaks in wearing dark glasses with a bass fiddle but Bob Deiz, saying "Shhhh."

After retiring, Deiz played with the Columbus Ohio orchestra:

> My biggest problem was I was playing big instruments, the bass strings or the bass horn. I had to carry them up, set them up, go back, get something

else, carry them back down afterward. The damn piccolo player just put it in his pocket while I was still making my second trip. It just got to be too big a chore.

Bob served on the suicide hotline in Columbus for about a year and a half but had to quit.

> It gets you down after awhile. When you look at the average Negro pilot, you're looking at a guy who has his sanity. But he fought for it. If we let the things we went through bother us, we could be a bunch of nuts walking around.

Jefferson earned an advanced degree. He wrote:

> In graduate school I had a history professor who literally called me a liar when I wrote a term paper on my experiences as a World War II fighter pilot. He told me Negroes did not have the intelligence to enter the Air force. He also did not believe a Negro could earn an "A" in his class, because we were supposedly incapable of such high-quality work. I proved him wrong, but only after I went to the dean with my term paper along with the results of the tests I had taken in class.

Percy Sutton, an intelligence officer with the 332nd, attended law school, bought the Apollo Theater in Harlem, entered politics, and went on to become Manhattan borough president and a millionaire.

Bob Williams went into show business. He attended UCLA, studied business and theater arts, and got a role in the movie *Pork Chop Hill*, with Gregory Peck. He also appeared in films with Rock Hudson and Dick Van Dyke.

> I was in the Phil Silvers TV Show—not "Sergeant Bilko" but the one before that, set in a factory. Silvers was a kick in the head, a very funny guy, but he was hard to work with. He ad-libbed a lot, and you never knew what the cue was. If you jumped in on his line, he'd give you a bad time; if you didn't come in on time, he'd give you a bad time.

Williams had one of the first black radio talk shows, which premiered during the Los Angeles Watts Riots of 1967. It won an award from the NAACP.

For over 40 years, 1952–96, he tried to sell his script for a TV drama on the Red Tails. After years of rejections, he finally saw it produced on HBO-TV with Laurence Fishburne starring as Williams.

Bert Wilson agreed that "it's a hell of a story," but he laughed that "Williams got me killed off in his script."

A play about the Red Tails was produced in the 1980s, though Sheppard for one didn't like it. "They had us depicted as bubble-brained, hard-drinking, and foul-mouthed. That never happened. Why dilute the truth with a bunch of baloney?"

Bernard Knighten retired from the Air Force in 1967 and worked for the FAA for 20 years. By that time, he cracked, "I was too old for the rail lines, the airlines and even the sidelines." He moved to Las Vegas:

> I was trying to be a stand-up comedian. I was on stage every Friday and Saturday at Debbie Reynolds' Hotel, the Celebrity Room. When she takes a break, she puts me on: Mother-in-law jokes, ugly wife jokes. My wife sits in the audience and boos me. We have a party.

Ed Gleed spent several years in India as an advisor on strategic air defenses on the China border.

He retired in 1970 and went back to law school at the age of 57. "I didn't want to practice, I just wanted to see if I could do it. Those were three of the roughest years of my life." At graduation he was surprised to find that he was "married to a grandmother."

Jimmy Walker moved to California, where he was active in his church.

Aleksandr Zivkovic, the 17 year-old boy who found Walker in the Serbian woods, was imprisoned after the Communists took over Yugoslavia. He spent many weeks watching mass killings of civilians through his bars. He went to college and, in 1967, migrated to America, working in Syracuse and Chicago as an air conditioning maintenance expert.

Alex never stopped looking for Jim. At a big air show in Oshkosh, Wisconsin in 1993, he ran into Bill Campbell, who told him, "Walker? Sure, I know him. He lives near me." That Christmas Jimmy and Alex were reunited in Chicago and spent the whole day talking.

Galadowich, the POW camp commander, got his wish and also migrated to the United States. He often attended American veterans' reunions.

Charles Dryden earned a Master's in public law and government at Columbia. He retired in 1961 and worked for 13 years for Lockheed in Atlanta. He wrote his story in a book, *The A-Train*, an important historical source for the history of the Tuskegee Airmen.

Willie Fuller spent 28 years as a Boy Scout official in Miami.

Clarence Jamison traveled to Fuller's funeral from Connecticut, where he had been on kidney dialysis for three years.

Hannibal Cox became a vice-president of Eastern Air Lines.

Lee Archer was a vice-president of General Foods.

Bill Melton inherited a foundation his mother had set up to help elderly people:

> The state of California was discharging mentally retarded adults, and they asked me if I would take them. I still have a small 15-bed facility with very intensive health care and rehabilitation.
>
> I helped found one of the largest adult day centers in California. In fact, it was the first one, "Willing Workers." The people entrusted to us have been with their parents all their lives. Our whole purpose is normalizing society's attitude to them and their attitude to themselves through education, music, field trips, speakers' bureaus, and elected officers.
>
> I discovered myself when I got into this work; I discovered my real potential by helping these persons.

Melvin Jackson thought about going into the ministry:

> I wanted to do something to help people, so I enrolled in the University of Connecticut School of Social Work and got a job as director of social services for the Hartford Council of Churches. Then my school called me back to teach two years. Next I got a job at Howard as director of a research project.
>
> When Kennedy's anti-poverty program was started, that was very exciting. I worked in that program in Washington for four years before coming to Harrisburg, Pennsylvania to take charge of the anti-poverty program here. Then it was on to New York and Washington to counsel Vietnam vets.

Jackson also headed the Harrisburg Housing Authority until he retired and became a Meals on Wheels volunteer.

Spanky Roberts retired as a colonel and worked as a banker in Sacramento for 13 years.

> I'm a "peopler." I help senior citizens who have nobody to manage their finances and handle their estates. I'm on the board of directors of Meals a la Cart, delivering meals to those who need them, mostly senior citizens, but for everybody who needs good nutrition. Our organization is open to everybody, payment on a sliding scale.
>
> I'm on the board of the metropolitan education council, bringing school and industry together for high school grads. I'm with the Computer Learning Center, a system of continuation schools for everyone from ex-offenders to youngsters who are not making it in regular schools or need help in certain subjects.
>
> I've had two hips replaced, so I helped form "Hipsters," a support organization for people who need operations.

None of this is for pay. Oh I do get reimbursed. I get lots of love letters, often in shaky handwriting.

They call to say thank you and that they still remembered.

Bert Wilson:

When I came back from Vietnam, my doctor said they were starting a new program in Connecticut, called Perception House, for kids on drugs and wondered if I'd be part of it. It's expanded from five of us to at least 50 or 60 employees now. I'm a volunteer on the board of directors.

We have an Alternative Incarceration Program; instead of going to jail, they are in-patients in one of our facilities. We also treat battered women and sex abusers, so it's a pretty big program.

Jimmy Fisher suffered a stroke in 1983.

Blew hell out of my memory, and when I tried to go back to work too fast, I had a seizure. But I was able to get a little retirement from the Veterans' Administration. The Purple Heart opened the door for me.

Lucky Lester earned a degree from Stanford in international relations, then worked in President Kennedy's Pentagon in the office of Defense Secretary Robert McNamara and the "Whiz Kids."

They were a bunch of bright kids, all right, just out of Harvard Business School. I was the "Old Man." I guess they needed a wiser, experienced head around to keep them on the right track.

In 1975, our daughter Wanda went to the University of Pennsylvania and took a course in ethnic studies. The professor made the casual observation that there were no black officers in the Army at the time of World War II.

Wanda raised her hand and told him, "I beg to differ with you, but my father was in World War II, was a pilot, and was an officer: in fact, he was a captain."

The professor more or less told her, "This is very nice, and he meant well telling you this, but in effect, he lied to you"—not quite those words, but that's the gist of what he said.

She was humiliated, so she called me that night and said, "Send me some of the things from your scrap book." I sent her clippings and pictures, and she gave them to him.

He looked at them and said, "I didn't know this." But he never apologized or admitted that he was wrong and never saw fit to correct it to the class.

(In 2011 President Obama named Wanda to be assistant chairman of the U.S. Export/Import Bank.)

Charlie McGee became manager of the Kansas City airport and served as president of the Tuskegee Airmen Association.

Joseph Elsberry, who had downed four planes in a week, plus a probable, stayed in the Air Force with tragic results, according to Charlie Bussey:

> He had emotional trouble. He wasn't treated as well as he thought he should have been under integration. He became hostile against whites and was rather vociferous about it. He started to drink and drank himself to death.

Charlie Hall was another.

Spann Watson:

> He got out of the military and couldn't get a job anywhere. He tried insurance, but that didn't work out.
>
> He made several attempts to get back in the squadron. I was operations officer, but I guess he had real trouble with the command channel. The word came back that as a flight leader he didn't listen to management, so they said, no, let's not make that move.
>
> I was at the FAA office in Oklahoma City, and Hall had been working for the government in Tinker Field. The best they could do for him was a job on a forklift in a big warehouse.
>
> I was outraged. When I came back to Washington, I knew someone in FAA and said, "Will you do me a favor? This is one of our great heroes."
>
> He said he'd work on it. It took one and a half or two years to get Hall a job in the Will Rogers Center. When I saw him, he was wearing a suit and as happy as he could be.

Hall died of leukemia in 1977. The Tuskegee Airmen led a move to erect a large-than-life statue of him at Tinker Field.

Chappie James went on to become the Air Force's first black four-star general.

Woody Crockett twice broke Mach 2, two times the speed of sound, and may be the only man with two Soldier's Medals and two Mach 2 cards. Even some of the astronauts were envious of that.

As a "cool" 78 year old, Crockett was a skier and tennis player (two-time senior doubles champion of Virginia).

He attended VE-Day ceremonies in Washington as guest of his fellow Arkansan, President Bill Clinton.

> In the hangar at Bolling Air Field, a gentlemen walked in with a World War II uniform, a first lieutenant, with his wings and a 15th Air Force patch—the 445th Bomber Group, B-24s. He said, "You escorted me, and I want to thank you. If it wasn't for you, I probably wouldn't be here." You get those compliments all the time.

Crockett spent 30 minutes in the Oval Office with Clinton, whose Secretary of the Treasury, Lloyd Bentsen, had also flown a B-24 alongside the
Red Tails. His photo with Clinton and British Prime Minister John Majors
appeared on page one of the *New York Times*.

Buddy Huntley:

> I've been working as a skycap since 1952. I was going to retire in 2001,
> but no use me hanging around the house, so I kept working—I'm still work-
> ing. Over 50 years. I love it. I love it!
> They found Turner's P-51, the original one I had in Italy, at a school in
> Montana and took it to Minneapolis. Today it's flying again as "the Tuskegee
> Airman."

Bill Campbell was a victim of Alzheimers. When Watson visited him, "it was
the shock of a lifetime. Sometimes he recognized me, sometimes he didn't."

Lou Purnell became a curator at the Smithsonian Air & Space Museum
in Washington and helped set up the 1982 "Black Wings" exhibit.

Tom Allen, the early cross-country pioneer, came up from Oklahoma
City for the opening.

Chief Anderson also came. "You know," he told Purnell, "I drove up this
time, 900 miles, because Gert, my wife, didn't want to fly with me." Purnell
shook his head and smiled: "I don't think he'll ever slow down." Anderson
succumbed to cancer in 1996.

Hubert Julian was invited, but "I understand he had died," Lou said. "He
would have run the whole show!"

Harry Sheppard served in the Tactical Air Command under, of all people, General Spike Momyer. He didn't show any racial prejudice, but he
was "a miserable man personally, he abused everybody." Sheppard once
watched while Momyer chewed out his second in command, a three-star
general, in front of everyone.

Shep retired as a colonel and served on the board of the Arlington
Virginia Coalition for the Homeless, played the piano, listened to good
music—jazz, classical, and sacred—and was one of the leading living history resources of the 332nd.

"I wouldn't take a million dollars to do it all over again," he said, "but I
wouldn't take a million dollars to have missed it."

Swampy Eagleson retired to raise show dogs and thoroughbred horses.

Gwynne Pierson spent 20 years as a detective in Marin County California.

Walter Palmer became a racecar driver.

The Tuskegee Airmen agree there have been big changes since they first
flew.

Lucky Lester:

When I left, there were no black generals, just a handful of black colonels. I knew almost every black officer in the military. In the last ten or 20 years, progress has been fantastic as compared to the first 27 years. You started to get normal progression, people getting their talents recognized.

Spanky Roberts went on ROTC duty at Tuskegee "and was privileged to have taught, graduated, and commissioned two men who became the first black Air Force major generals—Titus Hall and Rufus Phillips."

As my wife says, about every five years the media discovers the Red Tails. I'm on radio, TV, in newspapers. I was on a radio talk show in Sacramento, and I don't know how many calls there were, saying, "Hey, you saved my tail," or, "My father told me about you Red Tail guys; he was a gunner"—or pilot or bombardier—"on a B-17 or B-24."

They call to say thank you and that they still remembered.

Despite the problems, Spann Watson fondly looked back on his military career.

I don't say all black people are good and all white people are bad. I spent 24 years in the military and served all over the world, and I had some of the best leaders, black and white, I'd ever want to serve with.

I joined the Federal Aviation Administration. They didn't want me under any circumstances—I had to shoot my way in. It was a tremendous battle of double crosses, but finally, with the help of Bobby Kennedy, they were forced into it.

I became the power in civil rights at the FAA, a prime mover for changing the complexion throughout the industry.

There were only three or four black air traffic people in the United States then; I'm the man who started the ball rolling and got more in. I knew all the black pilots who were qualified to work in the airline industry, and I did more for civil rights in the FAA than all the civil rights officers since.

C.C. Robinson shook his head admiringly:

When Spann makes up his mind something is right, he goes at it all the way. There's no holding back with Spann. If he's for you, he'll do anything for you. You always want Spann on your side.

There was a meeting of the heads of the airlines at the FAA, and Spann complained about not being able to get black hostesses on planes. They said, "We'd hire them if we could find any."

So he held classes, taught them how to talk, how to walk, how to do their hair, how to be interviewed, and they hired every one he presented to them, a total of 708—the first black hostesses. And he got 25 of the first black pilots, all recommended by Spann. He was a crusader.

Of course he made enemies. But that didn't bother him. Once he made up his mind that he was right, nothing would stop him.

Watson:

I had the biggest retirement party they'd ever seen in Washington, over 550 people; they came from far and wide.

The National Aeronautic Association recognizes all records and extraordinary accomplishments and elects big-time aviators like Admiral Byrd and Jimmy Doolittle. In 1990, they elected me as the first black, and I was instrumental in getting Chief Anderson, Ben Davis, and several other blacks elected.

Robinson opened a chain of pharmacies in Washington DC.

B.O. Davis retired as a three-star general and spent several years as an official of the Federal Aviation Authority. He was still referred to by Tuskegee veteran as "Percy-One," his radio code name as Group Leader. Despite arthritis, he made daily walks across the bridge from Arlington to Washington and back, into his eighties. He died in 1977 at the age of 93.

Davis:

The Tuskegee Airmen are one of the major reasons why President Truman was able to sign an executive order ending segregation in the Armed Forces. Major problems still exist, and everything is not perfect—the Armed Forces are an example of improvement, not of perfection.

But for all their warts, they are superior, without any question, to the situation in our civilian society. I can remember when my wife was escorting a young lady from Haiti to a clothing store in Washington's Georgetown; the lady was surprised to learn that she could not try on clothes in the store.

People talk about the good old days. The good old days are today. We hope for better old days to come.

Babies are not racists. Parents and teachers and others make racists out of them, and they perpetuate these indignities.

I believe victory in the Persian Gulf War can be attributed in some degree to the fact that integrated units fought with a cohesiveness never before attained.

The Tuskegee Airmen made a difference.

Bert Wilson:

It's hard for young people to understand what the Red Tails had faced. The country was as bad as South Africa.

But you can't get mad. When you get mad, you get bitter, and if you get bitter, you lose it all. So you've got to keep your cool.

Things have changed for the better, yes, but not as much as I would have liked. You have changed some people's personal views. But you haven't changed them all.

Still, when I see a black airline pilot, I say, "If it hadn't been for our Group, he wouldn't be in that cockpit."

At the Smithsonian, Purnell said:

Sometimes I like to play visitor, slip a camera on my neck, and go downstairs to the exhibit on black aviation and the Red Tails and listen to the remarks of the visitors. You hear such things as, "I can't believe it...," "I never heard of them...," "I didn't know this before...," "It's hard to believe." That's because most of the publicity about us was swept under the rug and after 50 years is just becoming known.

The Smithsonian received more newspaper space on that exhibit than any other it's put up. At last we're coming out from under the stones and being recognized.

It's good for the morale of the black race, because many are still unaware that there was a black squadron. It's good for history books and for the role image for kids coming up. That's the main thing. I don't care about adults— give the kids something to aspire to.

In the Air Force I think you're subconsciously reaching for higher things, both figuratively and literally. To look back at the accomplishments of the guys who were Tuskegee Airmen, a lot rose to heights—judges, doctors, millionaires, civic leaders—you name it, we've got it, enough to gag a maggot:

James T. Wiley was vice-president of Boeing; Jack Rogers was a judge in Chicago; Ace Lawson a city councilman in San Diego; Willie Ashley a PhD with the Environmental Protection Agency; Bill Campbell was a professor in California.

Those fellows didn't turn out so bad. All from a little group of guys called the 99th.

I'm not a sentimental person, but by God, just to see the old guys, you get choked up and can't talk. Your memory goes back to little things that happened in combat. When we get together, we laugh about some things, and other things are really touching.

Had it not been for the war, we would never have been able to fly. I think we proved one thing: After the war black fliers became commercial pilots. In Korea and Vietnam the Air Force was integrated. B.O. Davis and Chappie James became generals. We have black astronauts.

I think they were all accepted a little more readily than they would have been had we not gone through the Tuskegee experience. It's just another rung on the ladder we were trying to climb. We hope we've done something anyway.

Lee Archer: "One hundred percent to a man, those of us who went through that look back now, and, compared to what is possible today, would say it was all worthwhile."

Will there ever be another outfit like the Red Tails?

Roscoe Brown shakes his head.

This effort was unique and will never be repeated. Hopefully there will never be, and there should never be, a time when one group of African Americans has to be so superior.

The real meaning of the Tuskegee Airmen goes beyond what I call the "combat B.S." The story on the ground is what it was all about. The stories in the skies are exciting, sure, but they're not unlike those of a lot of white pilots. The thing that makes them important is that we did exactly what the white pilots did and sometimes did it better.

This is the story of some very serious, committed people attacking the most serious social problem of American history. We fought two wars, one against Fascism, one against segregation, and sometimes you couldn't tell which one you were fighting. It goes back to the ethos of the times. Every black person put up with a lot of crap that they wouldn't think about putting up with today.

The key to the civil rights movement was the Tuskegee Airmen. Our aim was to convince white people that if we could do the job as well as, or better than they, they wouldn't be prejudiced. You and I know that's not really true. The only way people learn not to be prejudiced is if they have a whole range of social experiences. But we neutralized an excuse for excluding us.

It's like baseball. If you're the first black player and you hit .200, nobody remembers you; if you hit .300, everyone remembers you. If we had lost a lot of bombers and screwed up, we'd have been remembered, but not well. But because of our outstanding record, we showed that black people could do technical and courageous things and could do them as well as, or better than, white folks. Branch Rickey and Jackie Robinson built on that.

We've made progress. Now when you see a black in a high position in a company, it's a function of what we did. So I feel we made a difference.

Bill Melton:

No question about it: The integration of the Armed Forces was a key, and we were catalysts.

I love this country just as much as you do—this is my turf. Philosophically I guess I've accepted it with its faults. But I don't have any hatred. Ill beat them at their own game. Just plain orneriness has kept me going.

I know this country pretty well. I've been to damn near every corner of it. I have one hell of a faith in the common sense and compassion of the American people. They're a good people. Hell, no one's perfect. I've been around other parts of the world, and there's no place I'd rather live. It's a good country. It has a lot of faults. But that sense of commitment to positive social change seems to be our dedication.

Americans are good people, man, very good people. It will be all right.

Dick Mason became a mathematics professor and was called to Detroit to teach in a black high school—a PhD teaching high school:

I've devoted a great deal of time to mentoring young people *pro bono*. I enjoy getting kids jobs, seeing that they get scholarships, and sending them to the Air Force Academy. When I talk to youngsters, I talk about life with light at the end of the tunnel, letting them know that the tunnel is not as dark as it seems to be. Hope reigns eternal, so don't give up hope and commit suicide but make plans of how you're going to escape and be what you want to be.

Roberts was active in the Tuskegee Airmen.

It's an educational organization which grew out of meeting and doing the war-story bit. Out of this has grown a national organization of 22 chapters, now including everyone who is interested in supporting our ideals—people of all ages, all services, all races and backgrounds.

We're dedicated to the proposition that there will never be another time when Americans are denied the right to serve their country by virtue of such arbitrary things as race or creed. We believe the best method of accomplishing this is education.

Our scholarships totaled about $75,000 and have gone to every racial group—Caucasians, Asians, Blacks, Hispanics. I doubt that 50% of the people so assisted have been black. And they've gone predominantly to women, because they have been most qualified and need the help. Our position is, we are against segregation in any form.

Obviously there are people who grit their teeth at the thought of assisting people whose fathers or grandfathers have been diametrically opposed to what we stand for, but we think there's a bigger battle to be won. If you want to be a Tuskegee Airman, you can join up.

Ed Gleed:

Fourteen of us went into our own pockets and contributed money. Our goal was one million dollars as a memorial to Chappie James. It was his idea to start the fund. There are three criteria:

Scholarship—at least a B average,

Need—at or near the poverty level,

Desire for further education in aerospace fields.

I tell youngsters: You're able to learn and, given the opportunity—and this is important—you can do just about anything anyone else can do. You are not necessarily going to face the same type of barriers out there. But it can be done. You can overcome them. Do one and a half times more than the average white person, that's all right. Push yourselves and do it. This is one of the goals of the Tuskegee Airmen.

Roberts:

Why did it take so long? Or how did we move so fast? It depends on how you look at it.

Americans have always had in their hearts a response that I call "good-guy violence." Our heroes have been those who fought our wars, or the Daniel Boones. You couldn't permit blacks to become heroes, because then they would become a part of our political system on an electable basis.

I am amazed at what happened after World War II, when for the first time we were allowed to be heroes. The 92nd Army Division, the Tuskegee Airmen, the Red Ball Express logistics units in Europe, the Japanese-Americans who fought in Italy—look who came out of all that.

Most Americans, I firmly believe, are solid at heart and will do the right thing under most conditions, given a fair chance to do so.

Charles Bussey waited for more than 40 years while friends tried to get the Army to reopen his case for a Medal of Honor. Investigators looked up witnesses to find that many had died, including one man who passed away only days before the interviewers arrived. In 1999 President Clinton took a personal interest, and two members of Congress formally called for a review, but nothing came of it. Bussey was philosophical:

It would be nice to have the Medal of Honor. The only practical advantage would have been a free West Point education for my children, but they're way past college age now. I'm not bitter, but I would have more respect for the American system if there were equity for those who fought and were willing to die for our country.

Still I deeply love the U.S. Army, and I am proud to be an American. When I hear our national anthem, I can feel the hair rise on my spine, and goose pimples cover my arms.

Charles Dryden was chairman of the 1995 Tuskegee Airmen convention in Atlanta, with astronaut Brigadier General Charles Bolton as featured speaker. The theme of the convention: "We've made history, now let's make a better world."

The president of the Airmen, Bill Terry, sat on the dais next to the Air Force Chief of Staff, General Ronald Fogelman, and the Assistant Secretary of the Air Force, Rodney Coleman, Dryden's protégé in ROTC.

Bill Terry:

> Coleman rose and said that by the provisions of section so-and-so, the reprimands of the 101 "mutineers" would be removed from the record.
>
> My name wasn't there. The guys all came up and got their papers from the Assistant Secretary, and he still didn't call me. You know know what's going through my mind: Goddamn, they passed me over again, the !@#$%&°'s!
>
> But after they all had their pictures taken, Coleman started again and said that under the provisions of section so-and-so, the conviction of Roger "Bill" Terry is also set aside!
>
> I jumped up, spilling water all over the Chief of Staff, looking for my wife. For the first time in my life I was speechless. I didn't have a damn thing to say.

Epilogue

When the war ended, the 332nd and the 99th had flown 1578 missions and more than 15,000 sorties. They had sent 450 pilots into combat. Sixty-six, or more than one out of seven, had given their lives.

It is easy to fall into the trap of emphasizing aerial victories, which were not the main objects of their job. Their mission was not a game in which both sides kept score. There was much more at stake.

How many bombers and their crews were saved because the Red Tails were weaving protectively above them, warding off enemy fighters? The cost of the bombers and the training of their crews alone was incalculable. How many wives, parents, and children welcomed home men who had been spared death thanks to their red-tailed escorts?

And without the brave fighter Groups, black and white, the entire daylight bombing strategy, with its increased accuracy, could not have been carried out. How can one measure the damage wrought against the Axis war industries or how much it may have shortened the war?

Roberts:

> I remember the day in Italy when I stood in parade formation alone in front of my squadron to get the Presidential Unit Citation, surrounded by newspapermen and photographers. The general leaned forward to pin the medal on and in a low voice called me every unprintable name he could imagine: "Baboons can't fly.... Baboons can't fight." He said the gun photos on our planes had been faked.
>
> I stood and looked him in the eye and said absolutely nothing. For my money, I proved myself to be a better American than he was.

There were many whites who were for us and helped us every step of the way. I am thanking all those who helped and forgiving all those who didn't.

—Spanky Roberts

Per Aspera Ad Astra
(Through Difficulties to the Stars)

Sources

Bussey, Charles M., *Firefight at Yechon*, Washington, DC, Brasseys (US), Inc., 1991.

Caver, Joseph; Ennels, Jerome; Haulman, Daniel, *The Tuskegee Airmen, an Illustrated History*, Montgomery AL, New South Books, Montgomery, 2011.

Davis, Benjamin O. Jr., *Benjamin O. Davis, Jr., American*, Washington, D.C. Smithsonian Institution Press, 1991.

Davis, Burke, *Black Heroes of the American Revolution*, San Diego: Harcourt Brace & Company, 1976.

Carisella, P.J., and James W. Ryan, *Black Swallow of Death*, Boston: Marlborough House, 1972.

Francis, Charles E., *The Tuskegee Airmen*, Boston: Branden Publishing Co., 1988.

Freydberg, Elizabeth, *Bessie Coleman*, New York: Garland Publishers, 1993.

Greene, Robert Ewell, *Black Defenders of America*, Chicago: Johnson Publishing Co., 1974.

Gropman, Alan, *The Air Force Integrates*, Washington, D.C.: Office of Air Force History, 1985.

Hammell, Eric, *Aces Against Germany*, Novato, CA: Presidio Publishers, 1993.

Hardesty, Von, and Dominick Pisano, *Black Wings*, Washington, D.C.: Smithsonian Institution Press, 1983.

Jefferson, Alexander, *Red Tail, Captured, Red Tail Free,* Fordham University Press, 2005.

Leckie, William H., *The Buffalo Soldiers*, Norman, OK: Univ. of Oklahoma Press, 1967.

Lee, Ulysses, *The Employment of Negro Troops*, Washington, D.C.: U.S. Army Center of Military History, 1994.

McGuire, Melvin W., and Robert Hadley, *Bloody Skies: A B-17 Bomb Crew, How They Lived and Died*, Las Cruces, NM: Yucca Tree Press, 1993.

Palmer, *Flying With Eagles*, Indianapolis, Nova Graphics, 1993.

Pyle, Ernie, *Brave Men*, New York, Holt & Co., 1944.

Rich, Doris, *Queen Bessie*, Washington D.C., Smithsonian Institution Press, 1991.

Rose, Robert, *Lonely Eagles*, Los Angeles, Tuskegee Airmen Inc., 1976.

Spencer, Chauncey, *Who Is Chauncey Spencer?* Detroit, Broadside Press, 1975.

Photographic Sources

1. National Archives and Records Administration
2. U.S. Air Force Historical Research Agency
3. U.S. Air Force Historical Research Agency
4. U.S. Air Force Historical Research Agency
5. U.S. Air Force Historical Research Agency
6. National Archives and Records Administration
7. National Archives and Records Administration
8. National Archives and Records Administration
9. National Archives and Records Administration
10. National Archives and Records Administration
11. Library of Congress Prints and Photographs Division
12. National Archives and Records Administration
13. Library of Congress Prints and Photographs Division
14. Library of Congress Prints and Photographs Division
15. Library of Congress Prints and Photographs Division
16. National Air and Space Museum

Index

About the Author

John B. Holway has written extensively about U.S. history. A graduate of the University of Iowa, he served in the infantry in Korea where he was wounded. After studying Chinese at Georgetown University, Holway joined the U.S. Information Agency. In addition to the books listed below, his articles have appeared in the *New York Times, Washington Post, USA Today,* and *American Heritage.*

The Pitcher
Voices From the Great Black Baseball Leagues
Blackball Stars (Casey Award for the best baseball book of 1988)
Black Diamonds
Josh and Satch
Josh Gibson
The Last .400 Hitter
Baseball Astrologer
Complete History of the Negro Leagues
Japan Is Big League in Thrills
Sumo